The
L

The Humanism of *Doctor Who*

A Critical Study in Science Fiction and Philosophy

DAVID LAYTON

McFarland & Company, Inc., Publishers
Jefferson, North Carolina, and London

LIBRARY OF CONGRESS CATALOGUING-IN-PUBLICATION DATA

Layton, David.
    The humanism of Doctor Who : a critical study in science
fiction and philosophy / David Layton.
        p.   cm.
    Includes bibliographical references and index.

    ISBN 978-0-7864-6673-3
    softcover : acid free paper ∞

    1. Doctor Who (Television program : 1963–1989)
    2. Science fiction television programs — Moral and ethical
    aspects.   I. Title.
    PN1992.77.D6273L39 2012
    791.45'615 — dc23   2012006723

BRITISH LIBRARY CATALOGUING DATA ARE AVAILABLE

On the cover: Billie Piper and Christopher Eccleston in the
2005 series revival of *Doctor Who* (BBC/Photofest)

Manufactured in the United States of America

*McFarland & Company, Inc., Publishers
  Box 611, Jefferson, North Carolina 28640
  www.mcfarlandpub.com*

To Denise, First Always

"A straight line may be the shortest distance between two points, but it is by no means the most interesting."
— The Doctor, *The Time Warrior*

"Courage isn't just a matter of not being frightened, you know. It's being afraid and doing what you have to do anyway."
— The Doctor, *Planet of the Daleks*

Table of Contents

Preface

As I write this preface, the revived *Doctor Who* is in the middle of its sixth season. Since it came back to television in 2005, *Doctor Who* has become a popular cultural phenomenon, surpassing its "classic" period popularity and reaching a larger and more diverse audience in the English-speaking world. Although created as a family program for the widest possible audience, the series has dramatized serious themes in philosophy, science, religion, and politics.

I have been a devoted fan of *Doctor Who* ever since I first saw Tom Baker wrap his oversized scarf around his neck in "Robot." It was 1984, I was in college, and *Doctor Who* was being broadcast on PBS in Los Angeles. I had been a fan of science fiction for as long as I could remember, and the prospect of seeing a British take on the genre intrigued me. I have stayed with the program ever since. Eventually, I discovered that I had actually seen *Doctor Who*, probably "The Time Monster," in 1975 on UHF when Time-Life broadcast a few episodes of the Jon Pertwee series. I remembered the car, Bessie, traveling at impossible speed.

I also discovered that as a *Doctor Who* fan I risked bemusement and ridicule from many of those around me. Compared to American science fiction on television, *Doctor Who* was low-budget, talky, quirky, and just a bit unusual. It often did not look or sound like science fiction was supposed to look or sound. Science fiction in American television and film was big, grandiose, militaristic, and loud. On the surface, *Doctor Who* was a "Play of the Week" in science fiction dressing. This strongly suggests that what one ought to seek in science fiction is *Captain Blood* or *The Green Berets* set in space. That, at least, is what so many others thought science fiction ought to be. In *Doctor Who*, the sets creaked and the costumes often looked like costumes. It just seemed that one ought not to take it at all seriously.

I knew otherwise. As I said, I had been a longtime reader of science fiction, real science fiction. I knew there was no requirement for science fiction to be all about who has the biggest laser gun or the fastest spaceship. I knew that the best science fiction was about *ideas*, about confronting the standard definitions of "humanity" and the commonly accepted opinions of what was socially "right." Where too much American media science fiction failed to deliver in these areas, *Doctor Who* filled in. At its best, and sometimes even at its worst, the program dramatized ideas. The writers and makers of the program had to be inventive because they could not make the surface shiny. While so much American science fiction, especially after *Star Wars*, was about the *look*, *Doctor Who* had to provide stimulation in other areas. For this reason, the talk that so many in the States found too long actually served a purpose other than to transition from one special effect to another. There were ideas here, like the ideas I had found in science fiction in print.

About five years ago, I started thinking about those ideas in *Doctor Who*. There was a continuity in the show that went beyond its format. Certain ideas kept coming back, getting reworked and restated. These ideas had many similarities to the ideas in the philosophical reading I had been consulting since the late 1980s. It seemed logical to pursue these connections. I had already written an essay on the theme of media and political power as portrayed in two *Doctor Who* stories. This essay, published in *Extrapolation* in 1994, gave me a start on thinking about the political dimension of *Doctor Who*. By 2005, I was ready to start looking at the whole field in earnest, to see what were the central ideas and values, if any, of *Doctor Who*. The successful relaunch of the program made it seem that the time had come for a more complete and detailed survey.

No book-length work on *Doctor Who* has yet delved into the philosophical and thematic content of the program. Most books about *Doctor Who* have been "insider" books discussing productions, actors, and so on. Two academic books exist about *Doctor Who*, but these are in the media studies field. There are also a couple of books in England about the science of *Doctor Who*. The primary difference of my book is that it focuses on philosophical themes in the series from both the classic and revived periods of the show. Another difference is that it is more in-depth and focused than the recently published *Philosophy of Doctor Who* book (Open Court, 2010), which only skims the subject for a general readership.

The present work discusses both the classic series running from 1963 to 1989 and the revived series begun in 2005 and broadcast to this day. My contention is that *Doctor Who* presents audiences a secular humanist view of the universe and humanity's place in it. The chapters are built upon philosophical themes, each chapter taking up one theme. Beginning from "Existence" and working through to "Justice," each chapter builds upon the discussion from previous chapters. The book explicates both individual *Doctor Who* episodes and the overall program while explaining fundamental concepts in secular humanist philosophy in clear, nontechnical language.

Portions of this book were first published elsewhere, and appear here in significantly revised form. Parts of Chapter 5 were used in "Male and Female Archetypes in *Doctor Who*," published in August 2010, in the online journal *Consciousness, Literature, and the Arts* (University of Lincoln, UK). Additionally, parts of Chapter 10 were excerpted and revised for "*Doctor Who* and the Critique of Capitalism" for the J. Lloyd Eaton Conference on Science Fiction in February 2011.

Acknowledgments go out to the following people for helping me with this project. Wilfrid Koponen, a longtime friend from my graduate school days, provided valuable input for Chapter 6. Gregory Benford planted some ideas for revision and rethinking of Chapter 10 in a breakfast conversation at the Eaton Conference. Finally, thanks to Howard Hendrix for his encouragement and pointing me to a good publisher.

CHAPTER 1

Why *Doctor Who?*

Anybody remotely interesting is mad, in some way or another.
— The Doctor, "The Greatest Show in the Galaxy"

Doctor Who

As the longest running science fiction program in television history, even with a 16-year production gap, *Doctor Who* is a phenomenon unto itself, worth considering on that basis alone. There are many reasons for the worldwide success of the program, for its wide audience appeal, and for its longevity. One reason for its continued appeal is the philosophy, or worldview, to use a popular term, that the program consistently portrays.

Many factors flow into and help shape the philosophy of the program. Though made by the drama department of the BBC, *Doctor Who* was originally conceived as a children's or family program. Even so, it has fans from all age groups and has had from its beginning (Tulloch and Alvarado 13). The program has been broadcast to over 40 countries. The revived series of 2005 all by itself raised the Friday night viewing ratings for America's Sci-Fi cable channel. The first book-length academic study of *Doctor Who* provides several convincing reasons for the program's longevity and popularity. One reason for this is that the program does not "patronize or insult the intelligence of children" (Tulloch and Alvarado 5). The program never becomes a stilted "how to," rarely breaks the narrative flow for obtrusive lecturing, rarely waters down its moral perspective, and never soft peddles death.

Another reason is that the program ranges freely over multiple genres: traditional science fiction, "space opera," historical drama, social satire, Gothic horror, action/adventure, quest Romance, even philosophical allegory (Tulloch and Alvarado 5). The idea that the Doctor and his companions can go to any time and any place provides a plausible reason for the generic variety, while other programs often seem "wrong" when they break from their more limited generic conventions. As one critic has noted, *Doctor Who* "has thrived most when it has resisted indulging the science fiction impulse too much" (Butler 9). In other words, generic variety prevents the program from going stale.

Another reason has to do with the program's more fantastic elements, usually involving the transformation of ordinary objects into extraordinary objects. The effect of such narrative transformations is to tap into the fundamentals of storytelling, to reinvigorate the universal human storytelling impulse. J.R.R. Tolkien noted that "when [making a secondary world is] attempted and in any degree accomplished then we have a rare achievement of Art: indeed narrative art, story-making in its primary and most potent mode" (49). By imbuing ordinary objects with fantastical properties, *Doctor Who* blurs the boundary between ordinary and extraordinary (Butler 8). A police telephone box becomes a high-tech cabinet of tricks; a telephone cord becomes an assassin; a television literally sucks the life out of people. The transformation of ordinary objects plays in the imaginative world that many people visit during their "off" time.

On a more formal level, we may say that *Doctor Who* operates in the narrative genres of the fantastic and the uncanny as literary critic Tzvetan Todorov defines them. When a police telephone box appears to house the interior of an entire building inside of it, the viewer is faced with the fantastic, a moment of hesitation when the viewer cannot determine whether the event is natural or supernatural, "that hesitation experienced by a person who knows only the laws of nature, confronting an apparently supernatural event" (Todorov 25). It is important that the fantastic event cannot be interpreted either as poetry (i.e., as a metaphor) or as allegory (i.e., as a symbol) (Todorov 32–3). In such a circumstance, the viewer hesitates between two choices. If the events prove to be natural after all, then they may be said to be *uncanny*; if the events prove to be inexplicable by naturalistic means and the reader must accept a supernatural explanation, then they may be said to be *marvelous* (Todorov 41–2). Since, as we shall see, *Doctor Who* always opts for the natural explanation, the fantastic resolves itself into the uncanny.[1]

Beyond the labeling, what does such an analysis signify? Despite the expanding explanatory powers of science, the marvelous remains a distinct possibility in many people's minds. The extensive knowledge is too vast for one person to hold. People regularly experience the fantastic, the hesitation in interpreting an event as either natural or supernatural. Thus, *Doctor Who* replicates common experience. As science extends its reach into everything that was once "mysterious" (i.e., fantastic), people ever more commonly opt for the natural explanation, for seeing surprising events as uncanny rather than marvelous, real rather than magical. *Doctor Who* replicates this common experience, as well.

Finally, despite budgetary constraints, disdain for science fiction in certain sectors of the viewing audience and among BBC executives, and the constraints imposed upon any "family" show (no sex in the TARDIS), for the most part those involved in making *Doctor Who* have taken the program seriously.[2] Many actors have turned in some of their best performances in *Doctor Who*. There are many memorable, genre-breaking scripts. Production designers, costumers, make-up artists, and directors have devised creative solutions to problems created by tight schedules and low budgets. The drive to get it right has kept *Doctor Who* from being merely an interesting curio in the history of TV.

Science Fiction

Doctor Who is a science fiction series. Thus, the discussion about science fiction that follows applies to *Doctor Who*. Science fiction is the literature of our times. As literary critic Mark Rose puts it, "Science fiction is in large part a response to the cultural shock created by the discovery of humanity's marginal position in the cosmos" (37). As scientific discovery pushed aside humanity's privileged position, philosophy needed to think through the issue. More than any other form of literature, science fiction struggles with and fuses the two most influential philosophical strains of our times — Enlightenment and Romanticism.

Novelist Italo Calvino noted in the 1970s that "the term 'Enlightenment' is rather unpopular." The situation is little different today. As Calvino stated, "The Enlightenment is accused of being at the root of the technocratic ideology that wields power in the industrialized nations" (35). One need only review the great mass of New Age books (as well as a large amount of what passes for literary criticism in the last half century) to see just how almost every social problem in existence is attributed to supposed "Enlightenment values."

In reality, most of these considerations are caricatures of the intellectual movement called Enlightenment. As is often the case, going to the source solves many problems and clarifies many misconceptions. The Enlightenment philosopher Immanuel Kant is the most influential of Enlightenment philosophers. In answer to the question What is Enlightenment? Kant in 1784 wrote a letter outlining the fundamental ideals of the philosophical movement already a century old when he described it. Kant states that Enlightenment "is man's emergence from his self-imposed nonage." It is the stage at which humanity grows up. Independent thinkers, given freedom, "will spread about them the spirit of a reasonable appreciation of man's value and of his duty to think for himself." "Freedom" is the key term in Kant's explanation of Enlightenment. He defines this freedom as "freedom to make public use of one's reason in all matters." There is also no doubt that Kant's "freedom" refers to scholars. However, by "scholar," Kant means any person who investigates, analyzes, and evaluates a topic and publishes the result. "Freedom" is thus public discourse and debate of ideas using the tools of reason and investigation.

Enlightenment also involves a materialist and realist understanding of the universe. Materialist realism for Enlightenment philosophers is labeled Nature. In the Enlightenment, philosophy conjoined with the emerging discipline of modern science. Enlightenment philosophers viewed Nature as a purely material realm, largely without spiritual or supernatural properties. They believed in the regularity of Nature, characterized in the word Law, and sought to apply the Laws discovered in material Nature by use of Reason to human society. One historian of religious ideas characterizes Enlightenment thus: "Reason, Law, Nature. These are the pivotal concepts for any understanding of the Enlightenment" (Thrower 97).

Probably no philosophical movement has had such tremendous success as the Enlightenment has had in nearly every part of Western culture. Modern representative democracy is a wholly Enlightenment creation. Enlightenment philosophers made it legitimate to question absolute authority, religion, and all the vestiges of ancient cultures. At the same time, it replaced faith and tradition with reason and education as the necessary tools for creation of a good life for both individuals and nations.

The Enlightenment strains in science fiction include, of course, science. Many have noted that the supposed "science" in much science fiction, including *Doctor Who*, is not scientific at all. Pseudo-scientific gobbledygook runs wild. One may take a famous example from *Doctor Who* itself: "reverse the neutron flow." Among the many tools the Doctor owns is a "Ganymede driver." Some of this technobabble is on a par with Marvin the Martian's Eludium PU-36 Explosive Space Modulator. The point is not that the science be accurate, but that the discourse sounds convincingly scientific. That this discourse makes no sense simply reflects the position in which most people find themselves. Not many of us know even the first principles of how our computers work. And we are fully aware that the jargon readily used by the "geeks" who fix our computers when they "crash" add not a spot of illumination to our understanding of how these machines work. Yet, the geeks' command of the terminology is in a way reassuring, letting us know that the principles are within the realm of human understanding. Similarly, when the Doctor casually unrolls sentence after sentence of scientific-sounding nonsense, the viewer is suitably reassured that the situation is not beyond understanding.

That all phenomena, no matter how strange, can be explained through the use of knowledge and reason is the pinnacle of an Enlightenment perspective. Nothing is inexplicable, only not yet explained. Many of the direct precursors to modern science fiction "began as an integral part of the French Enlightenment's confidence in cognitive and social progress" (Suvin *Metamorphoses* 118). This Enlightenment perspective controls the plots of much science fiction and determines to a great degree what the stories are "about."[3]

For instance, much science fiction takes the form of a kind of "future realism," in which existing technology and scientific theory are "extrapolated," to borrow a term from science fiction writer Robert Heinlein. The future possibilities of these existing technologies and theories are worked through rigorously and logically, to show how they might really affect humanity. More often, however, future possibilities are worked through metaphorically as a test of ordinary concepts of "human." When we look at machines that think and trees that feel, we no longer have the comforting assumption that humanity is the pinnacle of divine or natural creation. In science fiction of all kinds, the one concept under study is "human." This, too, is an Enlightenment legacy, for it is during the Enlightenment that "human" is placed as a concept within the natural world and made capable of being an object of rigorous thought and study.

While no one *Doctor Who* story fully exemplifies the purely materialistic and realistic kind of science fiction, nevertheless many ideas in *Doctor Who* begin from these sorts of extrapolated explanations. In "The Face of Evil" (1977), for instance, the basic premise that drives the whole story is that a computer can literally go mad. The speculative trail is easy to follow. Given the high probability of the development of artificial intelligence, what becomes of the intelligent machine? Given enough intelligence, could it not develop a personality? And could it not be possible that such an artificial personality can become unstable? Such a speculative chain typifies Enlightenment attitudes — that the challenges of the future are primarily materialistic ones, a direct result of cause and effect beginning and ending with humans' ability to solve problems, even those created by human ingenuity.

Another typically Enlightenment way of thinking is the location of moral and ethical standards in nature, and not in supernatural or metaphysical ideals. For Enlightenment philosophers, ethics did not derive from pre-existing eternal morals, but from experience of cause and effect. Likewise, *Doctor Who* shows ethics as deriving from choices made in the material world. Ethics involves *thinking* about a situation, and making determinations based upon the best available evidence, not upon recourse to ready-made, high-sounding ideals.

In political outlook, too, much of science fiction is very Enlightenment.

These attitudes include significant skepticism toward governments of any sort, grudging acceptance of democracy as the least offensive form of government, distrust of joining religion and government, belief that the moral basis for law derives from nature, affirmation of inherent and inalienable rights, and belief that debate and dissent are the engines that constantly preserve, refine, and improve government.

However, science fiction may seem to have a fractured personality. As much as its intellectual framework is Enlightenment, much of its drive and spirit comes from Romanticism.[4] This philosophical set of ideas and attitudes arose as a direct response to the Enlightenment attitude of placing reason above all other human characteristics. One may easily intuit from this the fact that there are not many "Romantic" philosophers as such. Instead, most "Romantic" philosophy is extrapolated from the writings of theologians, poets, and novelists, who saw "philosophy" as a project of those whose ideas they reject. As a consequence, Romantic thinkers and artists stressed the role of feeling, especially spontaneity, sensitivity, aestheticism, and creativity. "It was also a movement of the individual over against the mass" (Thrower 118). The Enlightenment hero was the common person given intellectual and political freedom. The Romantic hero was a figure of talent and vision beyond what the ordinary person could hope to achieve, even when that extraordinary person had a "common" origin.

Romanticism is still the predominant perspective in artistic and literary matters in the West. For instance, one consistently finds romantic characters of sensitivity, imagination, and advanced intelligence as protagonists of science fiction stories. Indeed, the Doctor himself is just such a figure. Typically, even when such characters are not artists, they have an "artistic temperament." In science fiction, one often finds protagonists who are "artists" of science or technology. Thus, science itself is romanticized in much science fiction. The Doctor is a highly Romantic figure of "artistic temperament," and both espouses and displays a romanticized view of science.

Romanticism has had an uneasy relationship with science. On the one hand, Romantics approve of science that demonstrates the relationships between humans and nature. On the other, they deplore science that gets applied to "dehumanization" through rigid control and unchecked mechanization. This contrast is apparent in much science fiction. Typical is *Brave New World*, in which the mechanized state, using scientific principles of mass psychology, dehumanizes by turning adult people into overaged children. However, an equal amount of science fiction proposes science and technology as saviors of humanity. In Clifford D. Simak's *City*, robots preserve humanity and more importantly keep peace, eliminating war and senseless death.

A constant focus of Romantic thinking, as in Enlightenment thinking, is nature. Romantics especially focus on the fact of life as an inspirational source. The Romantic poet Percy Bysshe Shelley writes, "What are changes of empires, the wreck of dynasties, with the opinions which supported them; what is the birth and the extinction of religious and of political systems, to life?" (45). As with Enlightenment philosophers, Romantic philosophers think of nature as the key to understanding. Shelley remarks, "Nothing exists but as it is perceived" (47). From this premise, Shelley concludes that there is no difference between a natural object and the mind that perceives it. Both the thing and the idea *are* Nature, which is always unified. Nature is the One Mind, and each person but a part of that Unity (49–50). If Shelley's words typify Romantic thought, then Romantics find their inspiration in the appreciation of nature, not in the study of its particulars. In a sense, Romantics "romanticize" nature, elevating it to the status of divinity.

Romantic philosophers agree with Enlightenment philosophers that moral and ethical standards begin in nature, but argue that morals and ethics come from *human* nature, not a uniform external nature. Arthur Schopenhauer states the point as a maxim: "*From what we do we know what we are*" (98).[5] The belief in Romantic philosophy is that human *will* is the determining agency of ethics and even, to some degree, of reality itself. Schopenhauer states, "All acts of man are of his own making, no matter how necessarily they proceed from the empirical character when it encounters the motives" (97), which means that the *will* transcends empirical reality, or what Enlightenment philosophers tend to call "nature."

Romanticism takes the idea of will to its extreme. Romantic literature plays out struggles on the cosmic scale: man (and they did mean man, mostly) against nature, man against science, man against industry, man against himself. Where Enlightenment writers such as Voltaire see only cosmic indifference to human affairs, Romantics see the contention of great, sometimes even supernatural forces. The cosmos treats Voltaire's Candide by not treating him at all. Candide gets blown about and battered by nature on the cosmic scale, nature which kills thousands in minutes and leaves Candide no time to weep. Mary Shelley's Victor Frankenstein, on the other hand, fights against nature, tries to wrest control from it and finds himself as part of an all-consuming battle between himself and his creation, scientific man vs. natural man.

Politically, Romanticism is primarily an "anti" philosophy. Romantics stand opposed to rapid industrialization, destruction of nature, urban development, economic egoism, and utilitarianism. One can see this Romantic streak repeatedly in the plethora of dystopic science fiction stories. Take any of the political or economic strains that the Romantics opposed, and one can find hundreds of stories that show it as a creation of a nightmare society. In *Doctor Who*, one finds such themes throughout the series. "The Green Death"

(1973) exhibits opposition to the destruction of nature. "The Sunmakers" (1977) exhibits opposition to economic egoism.

Yet, these apparent opponents, Enlightenment and Romanticism, come together in science fiction. Literary critic Mark Rose, though he calls the Enlightenment component "materialism," has proposed that science fiction's "paradigmatic concern" is the confrontation between the human and the non-human (34). The Enlightenment strain in science fiction pulls toward study and application as the method for resolving the confrontation. "Nonhuman" is a problem that can be solved. The Romantic strain in science fiction pulls toward a contest of wills that is also a contest between cosmic forces, what Rose calls "good" and "bad" magic (9).

An example of this human/nonhuman confrontation in *Doctor Who* comes from "The Mind of Evil" (1971). Here, the nonhuman is the mind parasite the Doctor's arch enemy, the Master, uses. The "problem" in the story is how this mind parasite may be controlled or destroyed. Repeatedly in the story, the difficulty is posed as a technical problem. However, the Romantic strain exists in the conflict of wills between the Doctor and the Master. Since both these characters are in a way nonhuman and superhuman, the problem is not just technical, but also involves cosmic forces of which the human characters have little understanding, in this case the mind parasite's ability to "eat" emotions and intelligence.

The resolution of the Enlightenment — Romanticism opposition in science fiction comes in the nature of the "magic" in question. The first form of magic is superior technology. A famous maxim stated by space engineer and science fiction writer Arthur C. Clarke applies to this case: "Any sufficiently advanced technology is indistinguishable from magic." The readers of these stories, and most of the characters in them, *know* that what appears to be magic is not. It might have magical properties, but that simply accords with Clarke's law. In "The Mind of Evil," the mind parasite is a living creature from another world. Its natural origin requires a natural solution to the problem its existence poses.

The second form of "magic" is known cosmic phenomena, such as black holes, whose abilities outperform human endeavor and whose properties outpace human understanding. These are treated sometimes as faux supernatural phenomena, sometimes as the source of supernatural phenomena. The result in most cases is that the "supernatural" explanation is thrown out. The "magic" is just another part of the grand universe. In several *Doctor Who* stories, seemingly supernatural, almost godlike beings put in appearances: Chronos from "The Time Monster" (1972), the White Guardian from "The Ribos Operation" (1978), the Black Guardian from "The Armageddon Factor" (1979), Fenric from "The Curse of Fenric" (1989), and "the Devil" from "The Satan

Pit" (2006). However, these entities are not treated as "super" natural, not as above and beyond nature. Rather, they are explained as being created at the same instant as the universe, and are described as gaining their powers from the mysterious forces of this first event. They are products of known cosmic phenomena.

Furthermore, science fiction tells of the "romance" of science. Science may be an Enlightenment product in that it presumes the materialism and scrutability of nature and the ability of human intellect to understand nature. Science is also thrilling. Scientists often speak of the "romance" of science, of a "beautiful" theory, of the wonder and joy of their work. The Romantics were wrong about science, and about Enlightenment arguments regarding reason in general. In science, intellect is not divorced from sentiment. And science, too, has its romantic heroes: Galileo, Johannes Kepler, Albert Einstein, even Sherlock Holmes. The Doctor has this scientific wonder, a Romantic appreciation for the "art" of nature. Thus, in "The Green Death" the Doctor, having killed a giant insect to save his own life, pauses to state, "What a beautiful creature." When dissecting a different giant insect in "The Ark in Space" (1975), the Doctor marvels at its "superb adaptation." Such moments reflect the Romantic spirit that motivates many scientists.

Finally, too often critics mistake the "romance" structure of science fiction stories as coequal with a "romantic" philosophical outlook. Yet, romance as a structure goes back to the beginnings of storytelling, as we shall see in Chapter 4 of this book. The Romance structure is capable of harboring many sorts of philosophical outlooks, even diametrically opposed ones. And there is not so much a Romantic philosophy as there is Romantic literature that espouses a certain set of beliefs. In general, science fiction and *Doctor Who* take from this Romanticism mostly a belief in the value of aestheticism and imagination, and a habit for taking the concepts normally ascribed to divinity and reassigning them to nature. Science fiction, when it is successful, replaces superstition with wonder, belief with inquiry, certainty with doubt, ideal with material. However, it structures the replacement in terms of Romantic idealism, using the Gothic and mythic features of Romantic literature to give humanity a prominent place in an apparently hostile, powerful, dangerous, and thoroughly natural universe.

The Science Fiction of *Doctor Who*

Science fiction has propagandistic effects. Readers and viewers take from it a consistent set of values and ideas. It is "a literature of persuasion and debate" (Bainbridge 197). As we have seen, the ideas under debate derive from those two apparently contending worldviews that dominate modern intellectual life, Enlightenment and Romanticism. We have seen that the very form of science fiction unites these contenders. What are the results, intellectually?

First, science fiction propagates the idea that technological humanity *is* humanity. Technological advancement has never gone backwards on the large scale. There may be certain areas of the world that have historically degenerated, but since the discovery of how to use fire technology has always advanced *somewhere* in the world, and eventually the technology has spread. So, science fiction always begins from this equation: technological human = human.

Doctor Who teaches that humanity is changing, and tells us something about the nature of that change, specifically how technology drives the changes. Science fiction "challenges our sense of the stability of reality by insisting upon the contingency of the present order of things" (Rose 21). A case in point are the conjoined stories "Rise of the Cybermen" and "The Age of Steel" (2006). Taking place on an alternate Earth, the story has all of technological society tuned into the internet through earphones that download information directly into their brains. The technology has been extrapolated from current mobile phone technology, especially the use of "hands free" technology.

The Cybermen themselves, like the Doctor's most feared enemy, the Daleks, are products of the replacement of organic body parts, the soft machine, with mechanical body parts, the hard machine, to the point that the people become more mechanical than organic. And being more mechanical than organic changes the way they think and behave, changes their outlook so that they no longer see themselves as human. Could humanity technologize itself into an entirely new species? Would it be worth it to do so? The *Doctor Who* stories suggest that the process of mechanical augmentation of humans can and ought to be controlled to prevent a nightmare future. This perspective is in tune with Enlightenment values rather than with Romantic values, which would regard human/mechanical amalgamation as inherently abhorrent.

An idea of integrated technology similar to the earphone technology described above is the computer access technology in "The Long Game" (2005). In this story of the future, people have brain implants that allow them direct streaming access to all the information available in the computer network. The most advanced of these implants actually opens the brain up to access so that the brain becomes a passive conduit for concentrated streams of pure information. Will we reach the point where people are a means for machines to do their work, rather than machines being the means for people to do their work?

Such ideas are not new in *Doctor Who*. In "The Krotons" (1968–9), teaching machines respond directly to the learner's ability and plant the idea that the machines are "pleased" by correct answers. In "The Keys of Marinus" (1964), the leaders of the city of Morphoton have lost their bodies, being merely brains acting as overseers. In "The Green Death," the chairman of Global Chemicals Corporation is not the actual head of the company, but is mentally linked to a computer that truly runs the operations, acronymically named BOSS.

By now, an astute reader will have noticed that most of these visions of technology/human integrations are cast in the form of warnings and nightmares. This does not diminish the basic premise that *Doctor Who* assumes the persistence of technological humanity. That humanity is technological is a simple statement of fact. The purpose of imagining the possibilities that technological advancement might take is simply to note that change has unintended consequences, and that it is best to pay close attention to just what technological changes come along.

Second, science fiction advocates for certain technologies over others. The notable example is space flight. Many space scientists and engineers were directly inspired by reading science fiction. Few readers and viewers of science fiction would argue against the idea that space flight is a good in itself. Some other technological favorites in science fiction include robots, computers, clones, light weapons (from laser guns to light sabers) and teleportation. Virtually all the characteristic devices of science fiction have appeared in *Doctor Who*. Readers and viewers of science fiction assume both the inevitable progress of or toward these technologies and the intrinsic value in that progress.

Advocating some technologies over others often takes the form of warnings about minding our technology. In science fiction, there are good technologies and bad technologies. For instance, as in most science fiction, *Doctor Who* assumes the intrinsic value of space flight. Probably the story most openly affirmative of space flight is "The Seeds of Death" (1969). The Doctor and his companions, Jamie and Zoe, arrive at a private museum dedicated to space flight. The Doctor, whose values and opinions are strongly asserted as right throughout the history of the program, deeply admires the rockets modeled in the museum. However, rocket travel, and with it space exploration in general, has ceased because of the new technology of instant matter transmission, T-Mat, which has made people generally lazy and content with a cozy life as it is. However, when the T-Mat system fails because of some invading Martian Ice Warriors, rockets suddenly regain their value. The story promotes the exploratory spirit of rocketry and warns against technologies that are too convenient.

Of course, the technology most admired and admirable in *Doctor Who* is the time-space capsule known as the TARDIS. What a magnificent invention it is. Being "dimensionally transcendental," it is bigger on the inside than on the outside. This idea alone has a myriad of possibilities. However, the real treat is that the TARDIS can go anywhere in space and time. The TARDIS symbolizes the exploratory spirit, the spirit of adventure. It symbolizes imagination, being capable of what only imagination can currently do.

Third, science fiction provides thought experiments for all sorts of "crank" theories. Sociologist William Sims Bainbridge claims that "SF is a storehouse of deviant ideas of a nontechnical sort and thus ... has become a fertile breeding ground of new social movements." Bainbridge notes that the abundance of "unusual concepts" in science fiction "allows the reader to consider alien perspectives and unexpected options" (151–2). A case in point is the commonality of extraordinary mental abilities in science fiction, *Doctor Who* included. Much science fiction takes for granted telepathy, telekinesis, pyrokinesis, mind reading, precognition, and other parascientific mental phenomena. Mind control, for instance, is so common in *Doctor Who* that it would take a whole page just to list its appearances. Similarly, transportable essences, or the idea that a personality can transfer from body to body, is too common in *Doctor Who* to make listing worthwhile, though "New Earth" (2006) does deserve special mention because the movement of personality from body to body gets humorously out of control. Telepathy, the ability to communicate mind to mind, features prominently in "The Sensorites" (1964), "The Three Doctors" (1972–3), "Snakedance" (1983), "The Five Doctors" (1983), and "The Twin Dilemma" (1984). Invisibility of living beings finds its way into "The Daleks' Masterplan" (1965–6), "The Ark" (1966), "Planet of the Daleks" (1973), and "Planet of Evil" (1975). There are many similarly pseudo-scientific ideas throughout *Doctor Who*. These paranormal abilities are in part a legacy from the Romantic idea of the unity of Nature and Mind.

That science and logic have demonstrated the improbability for the existence of any of these mental feats means nothing in "science" fiction. What would otherwise be magic becomes scientific in science fiction when it receives a scientific-sounding explanation. In a typical science-fiction explanation, parapsychological abilities could be the next step in human evolution, or a latent ability brought forth by new technology. Any concept, even the apparently impossible or supernatural, is valid for consideration and debate in science fiction. As I noted earlier, the important concept is not that an explanation be scientific, but that it sound scientific. Thus, one finds in *Doctor Who,* and in science fiction in general, that writers assume the extraordinary is both true and natural, and then run with it.

While there is little place for such things in real science, science fiction is an open field, wide as the universe. If the only thing science fiction did were to turn scientific practice into narrative, it would never have gained the cultural prominence it has today. There would be no point if *Doctor Who* were only about an eccentric scientist who likes calling himself "the" Doctor, and tinkers with various ideas on science's fringes. History would do a much better job of rendering the story of scientific endeavor than imaginative narrative ever could.

Fourth, and most important for the rest of the discussion in this book, science fiction promotes free thought. The relationship between science fiction and the real world is always a critical one (Suvin "Poetics" 64). In his sociological study of science fiction fans, Bainbridge found that a higher percentage than in the general population was dissatisfied with the future facing them and their families. Science fiction fans tend to be better educated and more affluent than the general population. A higher percentage of fans are irreligious than in the general population.[6] A higher percentage of fans are more liberal/left politically than in the general population. Additionally, a larger minority of fans are radical libertarian than in the general population. While fans are not the only consumers of science fiction, they are the principal ones and the ones that writers have in mind. In sum, "SF is a subculture of free-thinkers rather than of believers" (Bainbridge 151–71). The preceding analysis is a two-way system. On the one hand, the literature provides the intellectual impetus toward free thought. On the other hand, the fans seek out the literature that best reflects their opinions and values. Those values involve questioning orthodoxy, even scientific orthodoxy, and presupposing a universe that operates solely on natural principles.

Being science fiction, *Doctor Who* demonstrates the four characteristics outlined above. Like all true science fiction, *Doctor Who* is not about actual science, but about the imaginative possibilities that science and technology open up. Bainbridge notes that in science fiction, while a particular idea may not conform to known science, it is treated in a scientific manner. He says, "SF of all kinds proposes the widest range of conceivable solutions and provokes us to see problems we have not even considered" (204). This is the "what if" factor that has led many authors to rename science fiction as speculative fiction. What if in the time between the demise of the dinosaurs and the development of the first apes, there were on the Earth a species of intelligent reptile that had developed a full civilization and a technology somewhat advanced beyond current human abilities? And what if some of them emerged today? The basic idea is, of course, scientifically preposterous; none of the expected evidence for it exists. Yet, if one were to suppose it for a while, would it not immediately come to one's mind that these civilized reptiles would believe that the Earth belonged to them and that mankind was nothing other than a squatter and a pest? Thus is born "Doctor Who and the Silurians" (1970).

The point of such an imaginative exercise is to provide a kind of model for debate. By presenting ideas as debates between contending worldviews, science fiction has its four characteristics dialectically interact. One can readily relate the contest over who has right to the Earth, humans or silurians, to real political hotspots and wars. Who has a right to Palestine, the Jews who were there, left, then recolonized, or the Arabs who took over when the Jews left? To whom does Kosovo belong, the ethnic Albanians or ethnic Serbs? Does being there "first" give the greater right? Or is possession and use, as Adam Smith argues, the determination of the right to a piece of property? The value of considering crank theories and pseudo-science is that it allows free play of the mind, to step outside the immediate matter of a debate and consider at length the ideas and assumptions involved.

Thus, the presence of crank science in *Doctor Who* actually folds into the fourth and most important characteristic, promotion of free thought. One of the main ways that *Doctor Who* takes up the theme of free thought is through its potential educational value. When science fiction is about science, it can teach science. When it is about history, as *Doctor Who* often is, it can teach history. Indeed, the program's creator, Sydney Newman, viewed the program as principally a way to teach history and science (Haining 13). In the early days, stories tended to alternate historical/futuristic. The historicals were often reasonably accurate, especially those John Lucarotti wrote ("Marco Polo," "The Aztecs," and "The Massacre").

The problem with this assessment is that science fiction has never done a particularly good job of educating about specific science, technology, or history. It tends to be out of date, and very often grossly inaccurate. A good example of this in *Doctor Who* is the explanation given for the moon in "Doctor Who and the Silurians." The story uses the theory that the moon is a planetoid captured by the Earth's gravity. However, even at the time of writing, that theory was mostly discredited in favor of the "coaccretion" theory that the moon and Earth were created at the same time. The story also gets wrong the time at which this moon capture supposedly occurred. Currently, the favored theory is the "Big Whack," which suggests that a planetoid did strike the Earth early in its development and that large parts of that planetoid along with Earth stuff blown off by the impact formed into the current moon. As "education," "Doctor Who and the Silurians" was not particularly good in 1970 and is even worse now.

While a science fiction story may teach particular scientific ideas, it more commonly teaches about the concept of science itself, the scientific method, and the use of reason rather than tradition to solve problems. Later in this book, there will be more to say about the scientific method and critical thinking in *Doctor Who*. For now, I will merely note that often in *Doctor Who*, as in much science fiction, the primary conflict of a plot is presented as a technical problem amenable to a rational solution. The Doctor is the most romantic figure in a story, but also the most scientific, through whom viewers see the scientific method and critical thinking at work.

Free thought also involves considering "the proposals and critiques of obscure intellectual movements" (Bainbridge 204). In the story "Earthshock" (1982), for instance, the Doctor accepts as given the theory that the dinosaurs were wiped out as a result of the Earth's collision with a massive object. This particular theory was relatively new at the time and not widely accepted in the scientific community. In the story, the causal event turns out to be an anti-matter explosion (another bit of highly speculative science) from the drive of a spaceship that collides with Earth.

Bainbridge further notes that science fiction reminds us of "intellectual, political, or religious issues that our culture has repressed from consciousness" (205). One example involves pest control. Insects cause immense capital damage to crops and livestock every year. Powerful insecticides have greatly reduced the economic damage that pests cause; however, for decades few thought about the unintended consequences of loading the earth with poison. Criticizing overuse of pesticides ran counter to political and social will, which saw increased crop production as a necessity in counteracting the "population explosion." Rachel Carson's famous 1962 book *Silent Spring* brought attention to this problem, as did the *Doctor Who* story "Planet of Giants" (1964). In the story, an insecticide manufacturer has created a pesticide, DN6, that is too effective, killing all insects including those useful to agriculture, such as bees and earthworms. Furthermore, DN6 does not break down in the soil, but remains indefinitely toxic. Eventually, by drawing attention to the real problem involved in over-reliance upon pesticides, Carson's book, and the many articles and stories that took up its cause, such as "Planet of Giants," brought much needed reforms to agriculture beyond the "more and more" ideas that were the acceptable norms of the time.

Finally, as an exercise in free thought, science fiction prepares readers and viewers to think about the future (Bainbridge 213). The *Doctor Who* story "The End of the World" (2005) takes place on the last day of Earth's existence. "Vengeance on Varos" (1985) explores the ways that television may be used as a tool of government oppression. "The Robots of Death" (1977) has us imagine what a society would be like if it becomes overly dependent upon robots. *Doctor Who* repeatedly has the viewer take the long view of human history, not just what could happen in the next few decades, but what can happen in the next several centuries, and further out than that. What sort of humanity will exist in the distant future?

Doctor Who and Philosophy

As a family show watched in the home by families, *Doctor Who* functions to encode and engage its audience, especially its adolescent and pre-adolescent audience, in fundamental concepts of identity formation (Bignell 48). Children learn about social roles, right and wrong, the value of knowledge, and other abstract concepts. Adults have their own ideas about these matters tested as they explain and discuss the Doctor's adventures with their children. Furthermore, starting in the early 1980s and even more so now, the makers of *Doctor Who* were people who grew up watching *Doctor Who*, who absorbed its ethos and worldview.

More will be said in the next chapter about the specific relationship between *Doctor Who* and philosophy. We have already seen that as science fiction, *Doctor Who* pushes its audience into contemplating unusual ideas and in perceiving a worldview at work. The Doctor models critical thinking and ethical behavior. *Doctor Who* operates in a naturalistic worldview that does not steal "wonder" from the universe. All these components are philosophical. The narrative components of *Doctor Who* are also suitable for philosophical analysis.

The Doctor

The center of *Doctor Who* is the Doctor. Rarely has a long-lasting television program had so much focus on just one character, even when that character's name is in the show's title. Though the personality of the Doctor's character has altered with each actor who plays him, some things about the character remain consistent. Chief among these consistencies is the Doctor's worldview, which includes a consistent understanding of how the universe works, a consistent ethical system, and a consistent view of what makes a good society. Through the Doctor's character and values, the audience sees a distinct set of ideas.

As a man without a name, the Doctor is as much an absence as a presence. To the human mind, absences are just waiting to be filled. Thus, the Doctor holds the viewer in fascination. The program continuously draws attention to this absence. From the beginning, there is this question: "Who is he?" The question gets repeatedly reworded every time a new Doctor takes over. Doctor 4 in his inaugural episode "Robot" (1974–5) says to Surgeon-Lieutenant Harry Sullivan, "You may be a doctor, but I am *the* Doctor. The definite article, so to speak." The statement draws our attention to the question of just what is definite about the Doctor. In "The Christmas Invasion" (2005), the newly regenerated Doctor 10 repeatedly questions what kind of person he is.

The very first program, "An Unearthly Child" (1963), continuously draws attention to the presence of this absence.[7] At first, the mystery is displaced onto the Doctor's granddaughter, Susan, who perplexes her teachers because she knows more science than her science teacher but does not know that in 1963 England's currency had not been decimalized. The constant confrontation of the familiar with the unfamiliar, first seen with Susan, sets the program's major thematic motif in motion. Along with Susan, there is the familiar/unfamiliar TARDIS, a comforting police box on the outside and an otherworldly box of tricks on the inside. And there is the Doctor himself, a curious mixture of arrogance and sophistication, petulance and reason, a grandfatherly absent-minded professor with just a hint of the vast, cool, and unsympathetic temperament of H.G. Wells's Martians.

Over the years, certain features of the Doctor's character have become fixed. His temperament has mellowed somewhat, beginning with the third story, "The Edge of Destruction" (1964). In this adventure, an accident in the TARDIS causes the suspicions and antagonisms between the four principal characters to come out fully revealed. By the end, the characters have survived only by working together. The Doctor comes to understand his two human passengers much better, and realizes the terrible plight he has put them into by forcibly removing them from their home. This softening of the Doctor's character could be a reason for the program's longevity. It does help the viewer come to trust the Doctor and accept him as the moral center of the program. Even so, there is something of a back and forth swing regarding the Doctor's general temperament. Doctors 2, 4, 5, 8, 10, and 11 are all comforting, vulnerable, and familiar. Doctor 9 starts out very similarly to Doctor 1, being rather cool and distant, then gradually mellowing. On the other hand, Doctor 3 often remains an imposing and authoritative figure. Doctor 6 regains much of the original irascibility of the original. Curiously, only Doctor 7 makes a reverse transition from being friendly and familiar to being cool and manipulative. Nevertheless, these are all matters more of shading than of stark contrast. No matter the portrayal, there is always a touch of the inhuman (though not inhumane) about the Doctor.

The surprise of the success of *Doctor Who* derives from the fact that it is quite probably the longest running television program never to reveal the "secret" of its protagonist. While little tidbits of information have come along, the name of a home planet for example, most of these factoids leave the viewer not much wiser. Throughout the '70s and early '80s, the program was able to set aside the question of the Doctor's origin and identity almost completely. In "The Time Warrior" (1974), the new companion-to-be, Sarah Jane Smith, spends some time convinced that the Doctor is actually the villain, a mad scientist of some sort. Of course, she does come around, and normally this change would provide opportunity for inquiry into and revelation of the Doctor's character, but it does not. The only new information the reader gets is the name of the Doctor's home planet.

With Doctor 7, Sylvester McCoy, there was a conscious effort to return to the question of the Doctor's origin, not to reveal anything about it, but to *enhance* the mystery. In "Silver Nemesis" (1988), the villainous Lady Peinforte claims to have special knowledge about "who" the Doctor really is, but never gets the chance to reveal it. The program ends with the Doctor's companion Ace asking, "Who *are* you?" The Doctor's reply is simply to put his finger to his lips. "Doctor Who" (1996) returns to this question with a newly regenerated Doctor suffering temporary amnesia. However, this plot device serves more to reveal old information to potential new viewers rather than give new information. The exception is the revelation that the Doctor is half human on his mother's side, a blatant attempt to link the Doctor to America's favorite science fiction brainiac, *Star Trek*'s Mr. Spock. *Doctor Who* fans in general hated this touch and the revived series of 2005 dropped it. The new series has once more shone a light on the question of "Doctor Who?" again more to highlight a mystery than to provide an answer. In "The Girl in the Fireplace" (2006), Madame du Pompadour hints that the use of the title "Doctor" for a name hides not just the facts of his life, but also the emotional and psychological center. This great hole in the center of the program's "world" is quite remarkable, propelling the program through decades. In all likelihood, filling this hole would kill the program and take out of it one of its most valuable elements in both symbolic and philosophical terms.

There are other constant traits to the Doctor's character. In almost all cases, the Doctor is the most intelligent person on the show. He is not just more knowledgeable than the other characters, but he is also mentally quicker, more insightful, more thoughtful, and more intuitive. Indeed, *Doctor Who* is one of the few television programs that promotes intelligence as a good in itself, as something valuable and desirable.[8] As such, *Doctor Who* is a very unusual product of television, or of mass-consumption entertainment in general.

Gradually through the twentieth century and into the twenty-first, the American heroic model has come to dominate media presentations. Partly, this is so because an increasingly large proportion of media output has been directed toward adolescents and their perceived values and tastes. "Adolescent media have virtually no heroes who achieve their heroic status because of rational use of their mind and knowledge" (Paul and Elder 153). The heroes of such programming, whether in television, film, radio, comic book, or fiction, are "successful," and their habits and attitudes are touted as models of virtue. Such heroes are usually of the mind to "shoot first." They react with their "guts" rather than think through a problem. They live in a good guys vs. bad guys world without moral complication. "Love" for such heroes is instantaneous and overwhelmingly "passionate," a product of "destiny" and not in any way a response to a person's character.

The Doctor is in many ways the antithesis of this dominant American strain of hero manufactured for adolescent tastes. He is a scientific polymath, often shown working on a scientific problem or experiment. He conscientiously avoids violence and strives for cooperation. He relies on a vast field of knowledge to think his way out of problems. Finally, he is famously unsexual, and though recent seasons of the program have flirted around a little with a slightly sexualized Doctor, he remains free of unthinking and unrealistic "love" so often a part of media's heroic tales.

The Doctor is in some ways that icon of English upper class society — the man of leisure. Having no "job" and all the universe to play with, the Doctor dabbles and explores. However, he does not do nothing. Indeed, he takes his leisure quite seriously because leisure has a value equally as important as work. Duties accompany leisure. These duties, according to the English novelist John Fowles, are to enjoy leisure and to share it, "to give some of it to those who still have insufficient leisure" (134). Thus, the Doctor has his companions, sometimes willing companions and sometimes not. No matter what the attitude of the companion, the Doctor always shares his leisure. He is perpetually trying to take companions to various interesting places — the Eye of Orion (supposedly the most tranquil place in the universe), Brighton Beach, Paris, the leisure planet of Argolis, a Victorian theater, a space platform for viewing the Earth's final hour. Sometimes they get there, sometimes not. It is typical of the Doctor to seek intellectual stimulation and to share it with his companions, and thus share it with the audience through the companions.

The Doctor practices those virtues that Nietzsche calls "The Good Four": "*honest* with ourselves and with whatever is friend to us; *courageous* toward the enemy; *generous* toward the vanquished; *polite* — always" (91). In the original brief for the Doctor's character created by producer Verity Lambert and script editor David Whitaker, the Doctor was described as "a citizen of the universe, and a gentleman to boot" (qtd. Tulloch and Alvarado 100). The Doctor's persona can be encapsulated in the many connotations of those two labels: citizen and gentleman. Honesty is absolutely required to maintain social order. Courage helps one face down the forces of disorder. As a citizen of the universe, one does not think in terms of accidental associations such as race or nation; instead, one thinks that a thinking and sentient life is equal in rights and dignity with oneself, and thus worth one's generosity. Being polite spreads peace. Politeness is a matter of consideration for the other and thus adds to general well-being.

The most paradigmatic Doctor in terms of Nietzsche's Good Four is Doctor 3, Jon Pertwee. His persona played up the gentleman image to the hilt. Generally cool in manner, he dressed in style, a cross between Victorian man of leisure and late sixties hip, appreciated life's finer things, and relied as much on character as on brains to carry him through a tough situation.

In contrast is the most unparadigmatic of the Doctors, Doctor 9 Christopher Eccleston. This was a working class Doctor where all the others have been leisure class. Only the second Doctor not to use Received Pronunciation (what Americans know as BBC English), his northern accent, leather jackets, and facility with popular slang sets him apart in many ways from the other Doctors. Even the Scots-accented Doctor 7 of Sylvester McCoy maintained the essentially leisure class "gentleman" attributes of the other Doctors. Of the Good Four, what gets lost in this working class portrayal mostly is politeness. Doctor 9 is brash and "in your face," though never pointlessly violent. Perhaps this was needed to establish the show on a 21st century footing, where there is more distrust of upper class mannerisms than in the past.

Interestingly, his replacement, David Tennant, another Scotsman, reverted to Received Pronunciation and a combination of Tom Baker's bohemian student with Peter Davison's youthful energy, a kind of typical Oxford/Cambridge student let loose upon the universe. With this return to form, politeness also returned as one of the Doctor's attributes.

Humanism

As we have seen, *Doctor Who* fuses the two poles of modern thought, Enlightenment and Romanticism. This fusion is a philosophical framework one can call "humanism." The rest of this book will demonstrate the parameters of this philosophy and how *Doctor Who* exemplifies a modern humanistic outlook.[9] That is not to say that most or all of the people making *Doctor Who* would identify themselves as secular humanists, or existentialists, or some such. Most have probably not thought much about the philosophical foundations of *Doctor Who*. However, the makers of *Doctor Who* live in a society made from specific strands in the tapestry of Western culture. They have been brought up and educated in the principles of the Western tradition. Most of them were college educated, and had some direct exposure to the ideas and authors discussed in this book. They are formed by the drama of Shakespeare, Shaw, and Pinter. They know the novelistic heritage of Austen, Dickens, and Eliot. Even if they had no direct contact with the philosophies hereinafter discussed, they had indirect contact through drama and literature. This is not to say that their minds were wholly formed and controlled by Western culture, but that all their choices are made within it and in reference to it. Even expressly Buddhist makers of *Doctor Who*, such as writer/director/producer Barry Letts and writer Christopher Bailey, have a form of Buddhism attenuated by the influences of Western culture. The modern culmination of these influences has been secular humanism. *Doctor Who* demonstrates most of the principal ideas of secular humanism, and this book will show what these ideas are, when they occur, and why they are there.

As a preview, we can look at one story from the series. The story "Ark in Space" encodes this humanistic perspective. Communications scholar Peter B. Gregg notes several moments in the story that draw attention to this humanistic perspective. The Doctor makes several remarks about human ingenuity, creativity, and indomitability. The story involves a race of insects, the Wirrrn, that propagate by absorbing human bodies, taking in their thoughts and memories as well. When the human leader, Noah, is gradually being taken over by fusion with an insect alien, the Doctor appeals to Noah's memories of Earth and his sense of humanity to gain some control over his transforming mind. Noah, even though apparently completely taken over by the insect species in body and mind, nevertheless manages to use the last vestige of his humanity to mislead the Wirrrn, destroying both them and himself.

This story also contains a speech of the Doctor's that is almost a panegyric to the human spirit:

> Homo sapiens. What an inventive, invincible species. It's only a few million years since they crawled up out of the mud and learned to walk. Puny, defenceless bipeds. They've survived flood, famine and plague. They've survived cosmic wars and holocausts. And now, here they are, out among the stars, waiting to begin a new life. Ready to outsit eternity. They're indomitable.

There is much in *Doctor Who* that would seem to go against such encomium. A multitude of characters are petty, greedy, stupid, arrogant, narrow-minded, oafish, bullying, power-mad, and downright evil. Fundamentally, however, the program operates from the Dickensian idea that despite rotten individuals, most people are basically good. Furthermore, even some bad characters can reform. For every Uriah Heep, there is a Sydney Carton or Ebenezer Scrooge capable of overcoming his misanthropy. This is the humanist creed: To discover the ways of ennobling the human character and increasing general happiness. This creed gives us access to the philosophic currents of the show and gain an understanding of humanism in action.

CHAPTER 2

What Is Humanism?

Doctor: You're improving!
Harry: Am I really?
Doctor: Yes! Your mind is beginning to work. It's entirely due to my influence, of course, you must not take any credit.
— "The Ark in Space"

Philosophy

Philosophy is the field of thought that attempts to answer fundamental questions of what, how, and why. Typically, such questions are applied to abstract concepts, such as knowledge. What is knowledge? How does knowledge occur? Why does knowledge exist? While the questions themselves are simple, their answers are immensely complex.

Philosophy is not merely "ivory tower" or "pie in the sky" thinking void of concrete application or social value. In fact, the great philosophers are "great" because their works have had a lasting effect not only in the field of philosophy, but also in the field of life as it is lived. Artists, writers, musicians, politicians, generals, all have been tremendously influenced by ideas stated and explained in the great works of philosophy. Yet, philosophy is not just for the social elite. From union workers inspired by the writings of Karl Marx to the person at home reading pop psychology and self-help books to the ordinary citizen curious about the nature of human existence, readers of philosophy are everywhere in society.

The German philosopher Ludwig Wittgenstein says that "the goal of philosophy is the logical clarification of thought," which means that "a philosophical work consists essentially of clarifications." Thus, according to Wittgenstein, "philosophy is not a theory but an activity." Because philosophy's purpose is to clarify thought, "it must limit the thinkable and thereby the unthinkable" (15).

Those who philosophize have, broadly speaking, a distinct way of viewing the universe. This point of view simply stated is that *concepts matter.* This is what it means to say that someone is thinking "philosophically." The contemporary humanist philosopher Kai Nielsen says that "philosophers engage in careful, somewhat systematized reflection on fundamental conceptual matters" (*Naturalism* 70). The focal point of philosophical thinking about any subject is always primarily going to be the concepts involved, roughly speaking the "what it means."

As a mode of thinking, philosophy is a tool for answering particular kinds of questions. As already mentioned, broadly these are what, why, and how. However, another way to look at it is to say that a philosophical question occurs when the substance of the question is abstract. For instance, if one asks the question "Did the Doctor act ethically in this case?" one is substantially considering the abstraction "ethical," which must be clarified before one can give a proper answer to the question.

To give any proper answer to a philosophical question, one must first analyze the context, determine what concepts apply, consider what others have said about the concept, and gather data regarding relevant cases. Any one philosopher may not do any of these aforementioned activities, but any philosopher is guaranteed to perform at least one of them to be doing philosophy at all. Some philosophers may argue that empirical data are irrelevant and confusing, and that only by pure reason or logic can one arrive at philosophical truth. Even these philosophers, though, will still be determining what concepts apply.

Philosophy continues to maintain a presence in societies around the world. There are still working philosophers whose arguments and ideas affect both government and the general populace. One may consider the case of Peter Singer, whose work on ethics, especially with regard toward domesticated animals and the environment, provides standard reading for those in the relevant political movements and affects public policy in several countries.

However, most people encounter philosophy through the arts and the mass media. Many writers, from high literature to popular entertainment, have read some philosophy and see in their work a way to engage philosophical ideas. Much of fictional literature and entertainment puts ideas into action. Even at the most naïve level, where good is good simply because it receives the label "good" and evil is evil because it receives the label "evil," audiences still encounter the concepts "good" and "evil" and can still reflect upon the validity of these concepts as presented in the story.

Doctor Who ranges from something like the naïve presentation of fundamental philosophical concepts to sophisticated reflections upon existence, knowledge, religion, science, ethics, and politics. Though often referred to

in its native England as a children's show, the program has always been produced for *family* viewing, which has meant a significantly more highly developed consideration of ideas than in standard children's television. While it is
difficult to get a breakdown of audience figures by demographic, the revived
series has regularly produced viewing figures of around seven million in Great
Britain. Certainly, it is not seven million children who are watching *Doctor
Who*. If one were to judge by the conventions, fan clubs, and DVD purchase
figures, the largest share of the audience is roughly the same demographic as
for science fiction in general, ages ranging from 15 to 35 years old, more than
60 percent of whom are male. More importantly, *Doctor Who* has been on television so long that a large portion of the British public, and a smaller portion
in the Anglophone world in general, have grown up with the program, with
repeated exposure to its general ethos and particular philosophical concerns.

Philosophical terms can be matters of some concern. Philosophers work
with terms such as teleology, ontology, metaphysics, and the like, terms that
many people simply do not fully comprehend even when given a definition.
However, I am going to focus on the philosophical terms that exist as part of
the general language, and thus have a firmer hold in the general audience's
mind.

The German Enlightenment philosopher Immanuel Kant provides a
brief overview of philosophy for the general reader in the Preface to his *Foundations of the Metaphysics of Morals* (1785). As Kant characterizes it, there are
three sciences of philosophy, based upon ancient Greek practice: physics,
ethics, and logic. These three divisions themselves divide into two types:
material and formal. Physics and ethics are material, which means that they
have to do with "definite objects and the laws to which they are subject" (Kant
3). Physics refers to material philosophy regarding the laws of nature. These
are the laws of what happens. Ethics refers to material philosophy regarding
the laws of freedom. These are the laws of what ought to happen. Logic is
formal, which means that it has to do with "the form of understanding and
reason itself and with the universal rules of thinking" (Kant 3).

In this book, we will venture into all three divisions of philosophy, but
mostly Logic and Ethics. *Doctor Who* is amenable to such musings because of
its subjects. Typical *Doctor Who* stories involve much problem solving, and
allow a viewer to consider various modes of thinking and applications of logic.
By comparing the way the Doctor solves problems with the ways other characters solve problems, we can see how knowledge is acquired and applied. We
can see the rules of logic and critical thinking in operation. *Doctor Who* is also
a show very much concerned with "values." Honesty, fair play, human rights,
and justice are core subjects of the *Doctor Who* ethos. Characters repeatedly
face ethical dilemmas that test their values and various ethical orientations.

Philosophy professor Frederick Patka called philosophy "the road to wisdom" (Introduction 5). This is not an easy or safe road. Unfortunately, the human mind is not the perfect organ for sensing, interpreting, and understanding every thing or event encountered on that road. Many impediments cause the faculties to stumble, to miss important details, to misinterpret the import of events and things. It is a very long road, with philosophy as a kind of relay — one philosopher passing on the burden to the next until the goal is reached. Typically, a philosopher can interpret some things correctly, and get others entirely wrong.

However, the situation is not totally hopeless. Through experience, comparison, and knowledge gained in other fields of study, we can see what is valuable in a given work, and what is not. We can accept Aristotle's system of logic, and relegate his support of slavery and his fallacious theories of physics to the realm of intellectual history, useful mostly in seeing how we came to our present position of understanding. We can throw out Nietzsche's statements regarding national character as a product of their time, no longer useful if they ever were. We can, however, keep his theories about the nature of being since they build the foundation for much of Western philosophy in the twentieth century. As with science, there is much in philosophy that is cumulative, and there is much that is self-correcting over time.

The Thomist philosopher Bernard Lonergan states, "In philosophy a single all-inclusive goal is sought by as many different methods as arise from different orientations of the historically developing by polymorphic consciousness of man" (428). Because the goal of philosophy has always been the same, Patka calls philosophy "perennial," meaning that no matter what the various movements and labels applied to it, it remains itself. Just as the Doctor changes his outward appearance and nearly every other thing that we may identify as personality (such as body type, voice, habits, reactive patterns) and yet remain essentially "the" Doctor, so too does philosophy undergo seemingly dramatic changes and yet remain philosophy. Patka calls the perennial essence of philosophy "the law of organic continuity of ideas" ("Five" 13).

By analogy, one can devise a *law of organic continuity of Doctors* to demonstrate the application in philosophy. On the surface, the 11 official incarnations of the Doctor are remarkably different. The face and body can be the vigorously youthful Doctor 11, played by Matt Smith, who took over the role at age 28, or Doctor 5, played by Peter Davison, who took over the role at age 29; or the face and body can be the somewhat frail and elderly Doctor 1, played by William Hartnell, who began the role at age 55, though he played the part more as if he were 75. In general, however, the Doctor's incarnations have appeared as middle-aged men, roughly in their forties. Then again, these men are remarkably different. Doctors 3, 4, 5, and 9 were all tall by human standards, while Doctors 2 and 7 were short by human standards. Doctors 3 and 6 were physically imposing, and Doctor 3 was especially authoritative. Doctors 2, 4, and 7, in contrast, could come off as buffoonish, preferring to disarm threateners through humor or to fool them by appearing less competent and dangerous than they really were. Doctors 4, 5, 8, 9 and 10 have a romantic bohemianism in their behaviors, often appearing emotionally vulnerable. This contrasts quite sharply with the remote, know-it-all aura of Doctors 1 and 3. Doctors 1, 3, and 6 could often be petty and petulant, temperamental, to use a more modest word. Most of the Doctors speak in what is sometimes called "R.P.," or "Received Pronunciation," the parlance of the educated and generally well-off in British society. However, Doctor 7 had a Scots accent and Doctor 9 a Northern English accent.

How, then, could all these disparate characters be somehow the *same* person? Later in this book, I will discuss how this question relates to questions of existence. For now, though, I will focus on the basic question as it relates to the *law of organic continuity of Doctors*. The law is deduced from the behaviors and statements of all the Doctors, which demonstrate that no matter what differences there may be in appearance and disposition, certain fundamental personality strains remain constant. First among these strains is intelligence. In almost all situations the Doctor is more knowledgeable than just about everyone around him. This knowledge covers nearly every area of human concern: physics, chemistry, medicine[1], literature[2], philosophy[3], biology, mysticism[4], history, etc. There are also permanent character traits. As the writers' brief written by *Doctor Who* script editor Terrance Dicks has it, "The Doctor believes in good and fights evil. Though often caught up in violent situations, he is a man of peace. He is never cruel or cowardly. To put it simply, the Doctor is a hero."[5] All these attributes exist no matter other transformations in the Doctor's character.

Similarly, philosophy is a seemingly chaotic discord of movements, schools, and theories, many of which directly contradict each other. Both a thoroughgoing atheist such as Jean-Paul Sartre and completely devoted religionist such as Boethius are philosophers. Some philosophers specialize. Martin Heidegger concentrated mainly on deriving the ultimate definition and meaning of being. Others, such as David Hume, range over the large areas of the spectrum of thought called philosophy. Some important works of philosophy were written by experts in non-philosophic fields. Sigmund Freud's *Civilization And Its Discontents*, C.G. Jung's *The Undiscovered Self*, and John Fowles's *The Aristos* all exemplify worthy philosophic thinking from non-philosophers. The spectrum of thought covered by the term "philosophy" is perhaps larger than in any other intellectual field, as the chapters of this book demonstrate.

Yet, for all this disparity and diversity, there is a core set of principles, values, and methods which make it all one. First, there is the commitment to truth. Though it is impossible that all philosophical statements arrive at truth, all philosophers seek the goal of truth. Second, there is the reliance upon the right and necessity to question any value, idea, or opinion. This process of testing ideas is the fundamental intellectual process of philosophy. Third, there is the reliance upon logic as the principal tool for making and analyzing truth claims.

Furthermore, philosophers seek to answer questions. Only certain questions are "philosophical." Immanuel Kant, one of the central philosophers in the history of philosophy, simplified the field to four basic questions: 1. What can I know? 2. What shall I do? 3. What may I hope? 4. What is human? Indeed, these are all questions examined in this book.

Philosophy and Literature

"Philosophy and literature are embattled enemies," states the novelist Italo Calvino (39). Calvino argues that in order to understand the relationship between philosophy and literature in modern times, since the Enlightenment, one must add a third term — science. Like literature and philosophy, science "makes patterns of the world that are immediately called in question ... swings between the inductive and deductive methods ... and must always be on its guard lest it mistake its own linguistic conventions for objective laws" (45). Science fiction, therefore, seems best placed to negotiate these three fields of knowledge, though it might have competition from popular science nonfiction. For this reason, most modern philosophical fiction writers, such as Jorge Luis Borges and Calvino, tread very close to science fiction and often cross over into it. *Doctor Who*, as one of the most popular science fiction productions, draws out the conjunctions between these fields.

At the heart of this book, there is an idea about the nature of literature. I borrow the idea from Calvino, who says, "Literature is not composed simply of books but of Libraries" (60). If we look at *Doctor Who* as literature, it is, in a way, gathered from a selection of other works, which are then given particular significance for being part of the *Doctor Who* library. Using the term "books" loosely to include media outlets beyond print, one can see in the library of *Doctor Who* such works as the *Quatermass* serials on English TV, the science fiction of H.G. Wells, Gothic Romances, Buddhist works, the *Tao Te Ching*, and other sources discussed in later chapters.

Drama, such as *Doctor Who*, belongs to the broad category of Literature, and does what literature does. In 1960, English literary critic Laurence Lerner answered the question of Literature's identity in three parts: Literature is Knowledge, Literature is Expression, Literature is Rhetoric. By "knowledge," Lerner means knowledge of humans' emotional lives. By "expression," Lerner means expression of emotion. By "rhetoric," Lerner means arousal of readers' emotions (2). Lerner limits his understanding of Literature somewhat by focusing too much on emotion. His terms help us to see something more, though, for when we combine Knowledge with Rhetoric, we get philosophy. Here, I use "Rhetoric" in the Classical sense of speech and writing designed to persuade using the techniques of reason, demonstration, and logic.

Lerner contends that "if literature is a kind of knowledge, then poems all make statements, and these statements are, or ought to be, true" (4). This knowledge is not a set of empirical truths and factual events, but instead, "knowledge of the workings of the mind" (5). Lerner concerns himself with the "cognitive" dimension of these statements, with Literature as a study of "how we live." This cognitive dimension is certainly ubiquitous in Literature, even fanciful Literature such as *Doctor Who*. It is also similar to many popular ideas about Literature and its experiential truth. However, again Lerner limits his understanding a little. In what other domain are people concerned about making true statements and understanding the workings of the mind? In philosophy[6]. The method of expression in Literature is different from philosophy's, yet the intended broadening of understanding is the same. Literature makes philosophical statements.

In treating *Doctor Who* as Literature, I am looking for the statements about the workings of the mind that are outside of the experiential dimension. Literature is not just about emotion; it is also about ideas, and these ideas may be explained and tested using the methods of philosophy. We can also, in this way, come to a preliminary understanding of the Literary dimension of *Doctor Who* and its nature as science fiction. As Lerner indicates, the literary expression of emotion is the Romantic aspect of literature (34). The conjunction of potentially true statements designed to persuade is the Enlightenment aspect. As such, *Doctor Who* has both emotional and intellectual effects. Our concern in the rest of the book will be primarily its intellectual effects, which I am broadly calling *philosophy*.

Humanism Explained

Humanism as a term is first assigned to a branch of European philosophy developed in the Renaissance. Hence, historians of philosophy will talk of "Renaissance Humanism." During the Renaissance, among the educated in society, bodies of knowledge were not as clearly separated as they are now.

Virtually any inquiry into nature and reality was called "philosophy." Thus, Renaissance humanism co-developed with Renaissance art and shares many of the same assumptions and forms of logic. In particular, Renaissance art shifted focus away from types and toward a finely detailed study of the human subject. Anatomy was rendered accurately and the subtleties of human life were brought into focus. Renaissance philosophy likewise shifted from restatements and glosses on received ideas to finely detailed study of the human subject, with a focus on the subtleties of human life.

An example of Renaissance humanism is the "Oration on the Dignity of Man" by Pico della Mirandola, written in 1486 C.E. Pico makes two bold moves away from the standard philosophical thinking that had dominated Europe from the 1100s. Medieval philosophy saw mainly a few sources of wisdom, such as the Bible, approved theologians such as Augustine, and Aristotle. Philosophy in this conception was mainly the means of devising the arguments that would prove these sources true, a method called scholasticism. Pico instead argues against Aristotle, and especially against the notion of a "Great Chain of Being" that placed all creatures in an exact hierarchical relationship. Pico offers this alternative: that people are varied and multiform, not fixed. The special place of humanity, according to Pico, is the ability to choose whether to be like the beasts or like the divines. According to Pico, man "fashions and transforms himself into any fleshly form and assumes the character of any creature whatsoever." He further states that "we are born with this condition, that is, that we can become whatever we choose to become." The key concept here is *choice*, that human destiny is formed by human will. The second bold step Pico takes is to find the sources for his arguments from places other than Aristotle, in particular in Persia and pre–Socratic Greece. Thus, by implication Pico argues that philosophy should turn away from scholasticism and focus on the effect that choice has on defining what *human* is.

Other Renaissance humanist philosophers, like Pico, sought to revise Medieval Christian philosophy, especially scholasticism, by arguing that its focus was wrong. Desiderius Erasmus argued that too much of theology was focused on trivia. Michel de Montaigne argued that true philosophy was not contained in a rigid set of rules and ideas, but in the application of critical judgment to the problems of nature and humanity. Both of these writers looked to classical sources for inspiration. Montaigne in particular did much to revive the spirit of Greek skepticism. For the Renaissance humanists, there was more to classical philosophy than Aristotle. They found the principles of open-mindedness and critical inquiry advocated by classical philosophers to be a better kind of wisdom.

The change in philosophical orientation in Renaissance humanism coincided with another development of the time, what is broadly called the

Scientific Revolution. While humanist writers revolutionized matters of theology, a new group of thinkers revolutionized what was then known as "natural philosophy." These thinkers had the famous names of Copernicus, Galileo, Kepler, Newton, and so on. They brought several changes to the orientation of philosophy. First, they demonstrated that, contrary to the Medieval view, not all the answers to the puzzles of nature had been solved. Indeed, they went further in demonstrating that the Medieval answers were mostly wrong. Second, they proposed that the universe was made principally, if not entirely, of material substances. Third, because they saw the universe as made of material substances, they argued that anyone with sufficient reasoning power could contribute to an understanding of the true nature of the universe. Fourth, they argued for a new way to study and explain phenomena in the universe through precise observation, inductive logic, and applied mathematics, the system that would later become known as the scientific method.

The new philosophers of the Renaissance founded their ideas on certain key ideas from classical antiquity. For centuries in Europe, the majority of Greek and Roman scholarship and learning languished forgotten, abused, or destroyed. The Renaissance philosophers brought these ancient writings back to light, and so made them part of the story of humanism. Two of the rediscoveries more important to the history of humanism were Skepticism and Epicureanism.

Skepticism is thought to have begun in the thinking of the Greek philosopher Pyrrho of Elis, who lived in the 300s B.C.E. The Greek derivation of the word "skeptic" means something like "seeker" or "inquirer." Little is actually known of what Pyrrho thought or said. The most thorough working out of Pyrrho's ideas comes from Sextus Empiricus, who lived more than a century after Pyrrho. According to Sextus, the ideas of skepticism are as follows. First, there is a recognition that because so many philosophers disagree about so many things, it is logical not to accept any philosophical system without careful study. Second, therefore, a true philosopher avoids dogmatism, favoring instead a constant seeking for the truth. Third, one should suspend judgment on controversial matters, and instead seek to compare oppositional ideas. Fourth, the most basic rule of skepticism is doubt. Philosophers should not trust the senses, nor should they trust pre-conceived moral rules.

Epicureanism was founded by another Greek philosopher living in the 300s B.C.E., Epicurus. As with Pyrrho, little today survives of what Epicurus actually said and thought. And as with Pyrrho, most of what is known about Epicurus's ideas comes from a follower of his ideas. That follower was the Roman poet Lucretius (98–55 B.C.E.). In his work *On the Nature of Things*, Lucretius lays out the principle ideas of Epicurus. The most important of these ideas for humanism is that the "world" was purely material. Epicureans believed that the world was composed of tiny particles called atoms, an idea first proposed by Democritus. There is, then, for the Epicureans no spiritual or ideal counterpart to nature. Nature simply *is*. Change in nature is simply the process of recombining atoms. Because Epicurus rules out the supernatural, he also rules out divine laws that people mistakenly believe govern their behavior. Instead, Epicurus argues that morality derives from the proper study of nature, and that this study leads to the conclusion that the ideal state for people is *repose*, by which he means enhancing pleasures that produce calmness of mind while reducing pain.

Having reintroduced the classical philosophies of Skepticism and Epicureanism, as well as others, to Western philosophy, and having reoriented Medieval theology and natural philosophy, the Renaissance philosophers began the process that would lead to modern humanism. There would be further radical transformations along the way.

Toward Enlightenment

From the late 1500s to the mid–1700s, European philosophy developed further away from Medieval views. The most important new thinking for the history of Humanism would receive the names Rationalism and Empiricism. Both schools of thought proposed fundamental challenges to traditional theology while also shifting the focus of philosophy onto the rational thinker.

The most significant figure in Rationalism is René Descartes. Like Erasmus and Pyrrho, Descartes was impatient with what he saw as the "error" of philosophy. There were too many theories, many out of discord with plain fact, and all full of more opinion than sense as far as Descartes was concerned. In the mid 1600s, Descartes set about to find the source of intellectual certainty. The answer he arrived at would become the foundation of modern philosophy. Descartes determined that the system of true knowledge could be founded only upon human reason. He insisted that knowledge must be based on a rational scheme, and that this made method necessary. The method would be systematic, orderly, logical thinking. In his *Rules For the Direction of the Mind*, Descartes' Rule 3 states, "Concerning the objects presented to us we should investigate, not what others have thought nor what we ourselves conjecture, but what we can intuit clearly and evidently or deduce with certainty, since scientific knowledge is acquired by no other means" (5). As with Montaigne, the most important critical faculty to Descartes was doubt. In *Discourse on Method*, published in 1637, Descartes set on a course of radical doubt so he could find the one certain truth. Famously, the one certainty he found was "I think; therefore, I am." Thus, Descartes contributes to modern humanism two important methods: (1) the study of what can be investigated and thought about logically, and (2) the rational, thinking person as the center of knowledge.

Another important figure in the move toward Enlightenment was Baruch (Benedict) Spinoza. Like Descartes, Spinoza believed that philosophy needed to be formulated rationally, and that the philosopher's job was to set out the rules and axioms for proper thought. In the mid–1600s, Spinoza proposed a major break with theology. For Spinoza, God was not outside the universe, God *was* the universe. God was not pure spirit, but a substance with particular attributes. Thus, for Spinoza "God" is interchangeable with "Nature." Though Spinoza's philosophy is not truly naturalist, Spinoza does turn toward naturalism. The idea's implication for modern humanism is more significant in the field of ethics, for Spinoza argues that human nature is not apart from Nature and Nature is not apart from God, so there is no division. Thus, morality must conform to the rules of nature. For Spinoza, morality is not a set of rules proposed and enforced from outside, but instead is a set of perceptible directives deriving from the laws of nature, in particular from cause and effect. Spinoza's separation of ethics from metaphysics becomes an important contribution to what modern humanism would become.

The second school of thought leading to the Enlightenment was Empiricism. Its two most notable figures are John Locke and David Hume. Both would write on a wide range of subjects. Both would challenge orthodoxy by attempting to clear out what Locke called the "rubbish" lying in the way of true knowledge. Both proposed theories of knowledge based upon doubt as a principal method. Their theories are far too complex to go into here, but certain key ideas carry forward into modern humanism. The first of these is the emphasis on experience as the basis for knowledge. Another is that the laws of morality and ethics are found in nature and can be understood through study and rational inquiry. The third is that society creates government, not the other way around as had been commonly thought, and that government's duty was to protect the rights of the citizens.

The Enlightenment

The Renaissance humanists, the rationalists, and the empiricists had created the environment ready for a thorough overhaul of Western philosophy. This overhaul would become one of those rare entities, a philosophical movement that received its name while it was happening. The Enlightenment covers a broad range of ideas and all areas of philosophy. It begins in the mid–1600s and ends at the end of the 1700s with Immanuel Kant.

The various Enlightenment philosophers would not agree on many matters. However, there are particular directions and strains of thought that are clearly Enlightenment. The four areas that had most lasting effect are knowledge, religion, politics, and ethics. While all their theories in these matters have seeds in the prior philosophical theories already discussed, the Enlightenment philosophers would make bolder and clearer statements of these matters. In particular, the Enlightenment philosophers would complete the turn of philosophy away from being principally concerned with divinity to being principally concerned with humanity.

In the area of knowledge, Enlightenment philosophers were clearly followers first of Locke and Hume, and by similarity of Epicurus and Lucretius. Basically, the Enlightenment philosophers asserted the deep link between knowledge and experience. In 1780, Denis Diderot boldly stated that reasoning people do not seek rules in authorities and approved texts, but in nature. Furthermore, knowledge was not to be horded, but to be shared. Anyone who had a reasoning intelligence should be allowed access to any form of knowledge he or she saw fit. For the Enlightenment philosopher, *reason* was the most reliable means for acquiring knowledge.

In the area of religion, the Enlightenment philosophers would go beyond what had been only implied in the works of Locke and Hume and had not even been dared by the Renaissance humanists, and that was a clean break with all standard forms of religious understanding. Kant favored a vague and non-dogmatic form of Christianity. Voltaire, Thomas Paine, Thomas Jefferson, and others proposed the belief in a creator god that otherwise had no part in human affairs, a concept called deism first proposed by Edward Herbert of Cherbury. Still others went further in stating a complete rejection of all religion and the concept of God itself. Baron D'Holbach was especially forthright in stating the fully atheist view. Whatever the position of the particular philosopher, the effect of Enlightenment thinking was in accord with social forces of the time in significantly reducing the influence of religion in all spheres of life.

In the area of politics, Enlightenment philosophers made two significant contributions. One was to establish the concept of rights as central to political organization. The second is the concept that government exists in a specific relationship to the governed. The relationship is often called the social contract. The phrase comes from the French philosopher Jean-Jacques Rousseau in 1762, but the central ideas had been variously proposed by other philosophers. The fundamental idea is that society is a collection of individuals who *agree* to live together for the common good. The people are sovereign, i.e., hold the power, and not the government. The government receives its authority from the governed, who in turn willingly give up some individualistic freedoms for the sake of the common good. The purpose of government is to protect the remaining freedoms in the name of the people and for the good of the people. This means that a government that fails to fulfill its side of the contract may be legitimately replaced.

In the area of ethics, most Enlightenment philosophers were opposed to traditional metaphysics. That is, they argued against the notion that ideas are independent entities existing in their own realm. Therefore, morality came not from divine, eternal rules, but from direct experience given rational interpretation and formulation. The most important Enlightenment philosopher in the realm of ethics was Immanuel Kant, who proposed that people have a "practical reason" able to determine moral "laws" of behavior because such laws are both universal and necessary. Such laws do not exist independently of material reality, but arise in the mind from experience in the form of maxims of duty that one realizes as an obligation to obey. Thus, such rules are *categorical* because universally applicable to all rational beings, and *imperative* because one is obligated to obey them. This is the central idea of what Kant called the "categorical imperative."

Utilitarianism

The next great contributing philosophy to modern humanism is Utilitarianism. The two philosophers most closely associated with this theory are Jeremy Bentham and John Stuart Mill. Formed in the early nineteenth century, Utilitarianism is concerned mainly with two fields of philosophy: politics and ethics. The principal concept guiding Utilitarian theories in both fields is the principle of utility, which measures the rightness of an act by how much happiness it produces and how much pain it reduces. The justification of an act is the amount of "good" it produces, and it is best when it produces "the greatest good for the greatest number."

Therefore, matters of politics were principally about determining how to maximize general happiness. So, by a different route, the utilitarians come to a conclusion similar to Rousseau's: government's function is principally in providing for the sake of the governed. According to utilitarians, the only sanction that government has in revoking a person's rights is that the person's act has demonstrably harmed others, either through crimes against property or crimes against persons. Utilitarians, therefore, believed in a government of limited, clearly defined powers.

In ethics, the utilitarian view is that as with governments, individuals have an obligation of increasing happiness and reducing pain. Bentham believed that all pleasures, those things that produce happiness, are equal.

However, Mill argued that some pleasures are qualitatively better than others, so that an act's goodness is measured by whether it produces a qualitatively better good than an alternative act produces. Mill's theory requires more subtlety in judging an act than does Bentham's theory, which simply measures pleasure against pain. Utilitarian ethics is, like Enlightenment ethics, principally materialist, determined by action and consequence.

Pragmatism

Primarily thought of as an American school of philosophy, pragmatism is a direct precursor to modern humanism. Its three main proponents are Charles Sanders Pierce, William James, and John Dewey. Pierce coined the word "pragmatism" "in order to emphasize ... that words derive their meaning from actions of some sort" (Stumpf and Fieser 373). The general principle of pragmatism is the uniting of materialist philosophies, the rapidly developing sciences, and the idealist philosophies of the nineteenth century.

In the field of knowledge, Pierce and Dewey argued that scientific method was by far the best for creating justified beliefs. Science provided a realistic basis for knowledge located in experience. Science was also the best means for eliminating personal prejudice. James argued that pragmatism was only a method and was concerned with understanding the concrete aspects of life based upon facts and actions. Dewey specifically argued that knowledge needed to be understood in relationship to environment, which meant that one must recognize the biological origin of human existence and the struggle for survival.

The pragmatic view of ethics was likewise located in the facts of human existence. Pragmatists argued against the notion that ideas and moral rules are eternal entities. Dewey placed the theory of ethics into concerns of value. He believed that values could be discovered in the same way as facts, and that ethical choices needed to be evaluated partly on the intended end of the choice.

Existentialism

The last direct contributor to modern humanism in this rough history of humanist philosophy is Existentialism. Like Pragmatism, Existentialism reaches back into the mid-nineteenth century and extends into the mid-twentieth century. The term itself is primarily associated with Jean-Paul Sartre. The concern of existentialism is the question of what it means to exist. Though there are some religious and some atheistic answers to this concern, the concept shared by all existentialist answers is formulated by Sartre as the phrase "being is becoming." There will be a much more thorough account of existentialist ideas in Chapter 3 of this book. For now, the important considerations are those relevant to the development of Modern Humanism. In Existentialism, these are that people "make" themselves, that they are primarily responsible for whatever definitions they have of themselves, and, therefore, people are burdened with the responsibility that comes with this freedom, which is to define oneself well and to live authentically.

Eastern Philosophy

Before we come to Modern Humanism itself, we should take a slight detour into Eastern philosophy, and especially Buddhism and Taoism. One reason for this detour is that some *Doctor Who* episodes specifically address Buddhist and Taoist ideas. The other is that in the twentieth century these ideas made their way into Western thought and have had some effect on modern humanist thought.

Buddhism is founded upon ideas attributed to Gautama Siddhartha, called the Buddha, meaning awakened or enlightened one. He is said to have been born in northern India near Nepal around 566 B.C.E. as a prince who renounced his heritage and lived an ascetic life in pursuit of truth. He is said to have attained enlightenment, a full understanding of the universe, and to have passed on his wisdom through sayings and teachings. The principle idea of Buddhism is "a systematic analysis of the nature and causes of suffering" that provides "a manifold of means for the overcoming of suffering" (Koller 133).

The system of Buddhism consists of two parts: the Four Noble Truths and the Noble Eightfold Path. The four truths are: "(1) There is suffering; (2) Suffering is caused; (3) Suffering can be extinguished by eliminating the causes of suffering; (4) The way to extinguish the causes of suffering is to follow the Middle Way constituted by the Noble Eightfold Path" (Koller 136–7). The eightfold path consists of right views, right intent, right speech, right conduct, right means of livelihood, right endeavor, right mindfulness, and right meditation (Koller 137). In Buddhism, "the craving of a self ... gives rise to suffering" (Koller 140). Thus, suffering may be eliminated when one reaches *Nirvana*, the state of being "blown out" like a candle. What is blown out is the craving self. The Noble Eightfold Path is a total life discipline for achieving nirvana.

Buddhism touches upon humanist ideas in a few areas. Foremost of these is that responsibility for the quality of one's life rests in large part upon oneself.

In Buddhism, there is no hope for supernatural guidance or intervention. Instead, the way people conduct their lives determines what their lives mean.

Taoism, like Buddhism, has a misty, legendary origin. It is supposedly founded in the fourth century B.C.E. in China by a man called Lao Tzu, which means "old master." The old master's teachings were collected after his death into a book called *Tao Te Ching*, the Book of Change and the Way, or The Way to Virtue, or The Path of Power. The central idea of Taoism is that the principles for life may be found in nature, and that these principles constitute a "way" or path for living virtuously.

Taoism is an almost entirely materialist philosophy. Its precepts are that the answers to life are in nature and that these answers can be read. Chief among these precepts is the recognition of change as a rule of nature. The wise person recognizes change, accepts it, and lives by its principles. The unwise person fights against natural change, tries to control nature and make it suit his or her own desires. This fight against nature is the source of unhappiness and suffering. Interestingly, Lao Tzu argues that these precepts are not merely matters of personal conduct, but are also matters of political conduct. "Bad" rulers are those who do not recognize the way of changing nature, and so try to impose their will upon the people, causing unhappiness for all. "Good" rulers follow the way, ruling with a light hand and generally allowing the State to run itself.

Taoism's contact with modern humanism is readily apparent. It is a materialist philosophy focused on nature as the source of moral guidance. Its concern is with how to reduce suffering in the world. Its answer has both personal and political ramifications. Finally, it argues for limited government responsive to the will of the governed.

Modern Humanism

The new humanism has had its fullest development after World War II. It has several varieties, among them Christian Humanism, Spiritual Humanism, and Ayn Rand's Objectivism. However, the most fully developed and widely influential form of modern humanism is secular humanism as formulated by Anthony Flew, Paul Kurtz, Kai Nielsen, and others. The ideas of secular humanism are widespread in Western Europe and North America, and widely diffused among their populations. The humanism of *Doctor Who* is primarily in the form of secular humanism, and this book will develop a description of these ideas and how they manifest in *Doctor Who*.

Corliss Lamont, one-time director of the American Civil Liberties Union, in his book on humanism defines it as "a philosophy of joyous service for the greater good of all humanity in this natural world and advocating the methods of reason, science, and democracy" (12). Lamont identifies ten "central propositions" of humanism:

1. Naturalistic metaphysics, considering "all forms of the supernatural as myth" and regarding "Nature as the totality of being."
2. Acceptance that people are evolutionary products of nature, that mind is "indivisibly conjoined with the functioning of [the] brain," and that the personality has no conscious survival after death.
3. Belief that "human beings possess the power or potentiality of solving their own problems, through reliance primarily upon reason and scientific method."
4. Belief that humans are "masters of their own destiny" within "certain objective limits," and are not subject to fate or predestination.
5. Belief that the grounds for human values are in earthly experience, and that the highest goal of ethics is "happiness, freedom, and progress" in this world.
6. Recognition that an individual attains the good life by "harmoniously combining" personal satisfactions, continuous self-development, significant work, and activities contributing to the welfare of the community.
7. Belief that the widely dispersed development of art and aesthetic awareness is a high good.
8. Social good based upon democracy, peace, and high living standards ought to be spread throughout the world.
9. The complete implementation in the social sphere of reason, scientific method, democratic procedures, parliamentary government, freedom of expression, and civil liberties.
10. The "unending questioning of basic assumptions and convictions, including its own," and thus the avoidance of dogma [Lamont 13–4].

Lamont gives to this new form of humanism described above the label *naturalistic* Humanism (22). The word "naturalistic" indicates its rejection of recourses to the supernatural.

As a leading American humanist philosopher, Paul Kurtz affirms the values Lamont identifies as central to secular humanism, but emphasizes a few areas differently. In particular, Kurtz pinpoints free inquiry as the central tenet of secular humanism. As Kurtz argues it, the dedication to free inquiry necessarily entails other propositions. These include "tolerance of diverse life styles," separation of church and state, a naturalistic and scientific worldview, skepticism regarding ideologies, defense of civil liberties, use of "reason and critical intelligence in testing claims to truth or morality," and a positive moral outlook emphasizing "creative fulfillment" (*In Defense* 27–8).

To French humanist philosopher Luc Ferry, humanism is intimately tied to the question of meaning. Ferry contends that only an intentional subject (a thinking mind capable of transmitting and interpreting information) can respond to the question of meaning and thus assign a meaning to human life. Meaning for a human life, then, cannot come from a source external to the thinking person (Ferry 16–7). Ferry notes that most of the humanist values are not new or even modern. He says that what is new "is that they are thought through starting from human beings" and rest on what he calls "the principle of principles constituting modern humanism," which is the rejection of arguments from authority (22).

To summarize, modern secular humanism is a naturalist and materialist philosophy. Its core propositions are that meaning derives from the natural existence of humans; that people make their own fates within the confines of nature and society; that society and government should be organized to maximize the happiness and personal freedom of citizens; that no proposition is sacred or beyond scrutiny; and that reason and science are the best tools for understanding the universe. These propositions will be discussed in greater detail in the remaining chapters of this book.

Humanism in *Doctor Who*

There are several reasons for *Doctor Who* to present a primarily secular humanist view of the human condition. One reason has already been discussed, and that is that *Doctor Who* is in the science fiction genre, which more often than not presents a secular humanist view. Another reason is that *Doctor Who* is a very British program, and so draws from a British literary and philosophical heritage that has been progressing toward a secular humanist view. Another is that the makers of *Doctor Who* (the writers, producers, actors, and directors) mostly come from educational and experiential backgrounds that make them sympathetic to the secular humanist view. This last reason is beyond the scope of this book, but some positive evidence for it does get mentioned herein.

Though the term "secular humanism" never appears in *Doctor Who*, the show provides multiple case studies for defining, revealing, and testing secular humanist ideas. Many episodes expressly raise philosophical and ethical principles related to secular humanism, and usually the show will promote the secular humanist interpretations of the ideas. In some instances, stories are nearly allegorical regarding some of these ideas.

The rest of this book is devoted to showing how *Doctor Who* works as secular humanist science fiction. I will isolate specific themes important to the secular humanist outlook. I will define and clarify these ideas, often by using the words of philosophers studying and theorizing in these areas. Scenes, dialogues, and sometimes plots from whole episodes of *Doctor Who* will provide the test cases for demonstrating the ideas and for demonstrating that *Doctor Who* considers the ideas mainly from a secular humanist perspective. Finally, the book will show that despite decades of production through a transforming British society, and even through a long production break, the philosophical outlook in *Doctor Who* has been remarkably consistent.

CHAPTER 3

Existence

There is no indignity in being afraid to die, but there is a terrible shame in being afraid to live.
—Alydon, "The Daleks"

A "There" to Be In

Philosophers have for thousands of years contended over the nature of "reality." We will see in more detail the relevant speculations for understanding reality as *Doctor Who* presents it when we discuss mythology, religion, and science. For now, it is best just to focus on the basics. That means that whatever this reality is, and one can call it a space-time continuum or a multiverse or something else, it provides room for possibility. This fact has been recognized from very early on. The Milesian Greek philosopher Anaximander, living in the 600s B.C.E., thought that Earth was not alone, that there were many worlds and many universes coexisting in a constant cycle of creation and destruction because of conflicts between opposing forces in nature (Stumpf and Fieser 7). The Roman philosopher Lucretius argued that multiple other worlds exist, with other forms of people, animals, sky, moon, and sun, because nothing in nature is a unique type (Lucretius 63–4). Being means existing in an expanding universe, expanding in time, space, information, and knowledge. A being with a perceptive mind is either a passenger or a traveler.

Existentialism Explained

Philosophers who ponder the question of being, especially its origin, come to one of two conclusions: either *Logos*, the Idea, came first, or *Bios*, Existence, came first (Patka Introduction 9). Among ancient philosophers, the Epicureans argued that there were no absolute or divine forms that existed before and apart from the material world. Those modern philosophers who argue that

45

life as it exists is the only life, that there are no ideal or heavenly forms that real objects merely shadow or imitate,[1] and that philosophical systems must start from the understanding of the previous two principles, have been broadly called the existentialists. The term "existentialism"[2] used to define their philosophical writings, covers a very broad range of opinion and value. There is however, a consistency of assumptions that runs through existentialist thought, and these assumptions accord very closely with those found in *Doctor Who*. This is especially true regarding agnostic and atheist existentialists. For that reason, and for ease of reading, in the discussion that follows I will be using the term "existentialist" and its cognates to refer to nonreligious existentialism only.

Sartre in *Existentialism and Human Emotions* defines existentialism as "a doctrine which makes human life possible, and, in addition, declares that every truth and every action implies a human setting and a human subjectivity" (10). In this way, existentialism is a *humanist* philosophy, concerned with ideas of human being and human potential. According to existentialists, the life of any person is a "concrete duration" without a prior or subsequent different kind of existence. There is no prior life, so no reincarnation, and no afterlife, so no eternal soul. There is only the continuous now of duration, the time that one spends living. Sartre characterizes the situation this way: "Man exists, turns up, appears on the scene, and, only afterwards, defines himself" (15). Clearly, therefore, it follows from these premises that there is no such thing as fate or destiny, which implies a pre-arranged plan of existence (what Christian philosophers call Providence). Whereas living life according to a pre-arranged destiny obviously restricts the amount of control one has over one's own life to make it fit with the plan, life as concrete duration opens up a person to total freedom. Nietzsche states this position clearly:

> What alone can be *our* doctrine? That no one *gives* man his qualities — neither God, nor society, nor his parents and ancestors, nor he himself. (The nonsense of the last idea was taught as "intelligible freedom" by Kant — perhaps by Plato already.) No one is responsible for man's being there at all, for his being such-and-such, or for his being in these circumstances or in this environment. The fatality of his essence is not to be disentangled from the fatality of all that has been and will be. Man is not the effect of some special purpose, of a will, and end; nor is he the object of an attempt to attain an "ideal of humanity" or an "ideal of happiness" or an "ideal of morality." It is absurd to wish to devolve one's essence on some end or other. We have invented the concept of "end": in reality there is no end [*Portable* 500].

By "end," Nietzsche means "purpose" or "goal," not "finality." He argues, and other existentialists will follow from his lead, that there is no specific reason for any person to exist, thus that person's being (essence) simply is, free from judgments, first causes, or determinations of value, which cannot accurately refer to being.

It is important to recognize the effect of context in this matter being and self definition. In *Doctor Who* the story "Blink" (2007) demonstrates the relationship between being and context. The alien "menace" of the story is a group of living statues that appear to be "weeping angels." These statues feed off the time energy of other beings by removing them from time and placing them somewhere else, thus creating a paradox that releases energy. The removal of a person from his or her native time and into a different time equates to removing a person from context. All that the person *is* derives from the context, in this case early twenty-first century England. In such a time, a young black man can be a police officer. However, removed from his time and dropped into the 1960s, he must become a different person, a video producer in this case. A feisty young woman from the same time gets transported to the north country in the 1920s, where she finds comfort in a standard domestic role. Each person must create a new self in the new context.

The Doctor is in many ways an existentialist hero, an embodiment of existentialist theories of existence. In one *Doctor Who* story, the Doctor comes squarely down on the side of the existentialists. In "Time-Flight" (1982), the Doctor realizes that the Heathrow Airport he is viewing is not real. At that moment, he quotes from an obscure parody of Bishop George Berkeley's argument that existence is determined by outside perception.[3] That is, something exists because some person perceives it. When one of the other characters does not recognize the Doctor's allusion, he quotes Berkeley's most famous dictum: "To be is to be perceived." Berkeley had used this axiom to demonstrate the existence of God, for if we exist though no one is around to perceive us, then we must be perceived by God, the universal perceiver. The Doctor calls Berkeley's perceptual theory, "a naïve eighteenth-century philosophy." The existence of the hallucination, which is clearly perceived, yet does not exist in the sense that Berkeley means it, refutes Berkeley's theory. It also, by implication, refutes Berkeley's "proof" of God's existence, since if a person perceives the illusion and that means that it exists, then God too perceives it, which leads to the conclusion that God could be fooled or is not in total control of existence. This moment is perhaps the closest that both the Doctor and *Doctor Who* have come to denying openly the existence of God and fully embracing existential humanism.

Freedom

As stated above, the existentialist position is that in the absence of a pre-existing reason to be, a person is totally "free." However, existentialists define "freedom" narrowly. The nature of existential freedom is that people make their own lives, they "become" all the time, and through becoming transcend their previous modes of existence (Patka "Five" 34). "Being is becoming" is the oft-used catch phrase to summarize the existential definition. Even religious philosophers, otherwise wholly opposed to existentialist thought, agree on this one point. The Catholic philosopher Bernard Lonergan states, "The concrete being of man ... is being in process," and further declares, "His existing lies in developing" (625). Erich Fromm, a disciple of Freud and developer of "humanistic psychoanalysis," argues that the individual is constantly in the process of being born, of making real the potential called "human" (26). The concept of being as becoming means that a person's life is always on the edge, so to speak. The realization of being as becoming causes a fear, what Sartre characterizes as "nausea," the dread of annihilation. To live an "authentic" life is to realize, in the sense of "make real," one's freedom. To turn from the edge, give in to the fear, and embrace safe, explanatory modes of existence, to give up one's freedom and live according to rules of organized religion or nationalism or some other system of comforting regulation, is to live an "inauthentic" existence. A man is "not the being he was yesterday, and tomorrow he is not going to be the being which he represents today" (Patka "Five" 37). Becoming, therefore, is the process of constant self-transcendence.

One may notice that there is a great emphasis among the existentialists on what one *does* rather than what one *is*. Indeed, most existentialists will argue that the two are really the same thing. For instance, as individuals we think of other people exclusively in terms of what they do because the only way we can know what they are is through what they do. We cannot get inside the heads of others to find the "real" person. Heidegger says, "In that with which we concern ourselves environmentally the Others are encountered as what they are; they *are* what they do" (163). And since it is clear that I am an Other to all other people, my sense of an essential self apart from what I do is a misperception. Either all people are special cases in possessing an essential self, or, through following more logical reasoning, all people *are* what they *do*. Watching characters (in other words, imitation people) act on television confirms this idea, since the audience experiences the characters by what they do, just as people experience each other. Thus, every person is in that state of becoming known as free will.

One can easily see that the existentialist and humanist position is that free will exists in a meaningful, if limited, sense. This corresponds with a growing scientific and philosophical literature that rejects a purely mechanistic, deterministic view of human behavior, which was popular in the first half of the twentieth century. The existentialist, humanist, and scientific positions also clearly reject supernatural predestination, fate, or "providence."

The idea of free will is not new to the existentialists. Arthur Koestler, a commentator on science and politics, points out clearly that the concept of free will is fully entwined in language. In English, we say that people "ought to" do things and need to "control themselves," for instance. The language reflects the subjective experience of free will, "the feeling of making a not enforced, not inevitable, choice." Systems and game theory in particular provide some objective proof of free will. A very limited system, such as a game of noughts and crosses (what Americans call tic-tac-toe) contains a small set of possible actions, and so very few degrees of freedom. As one moves up the levels of complexity, through checkers (what the English call draughts) and on through chess, the complexity provides significantly more possibilities of choice, more degrees of freedom. Free will is thus just the experience of the complexity of personal and social interaction, which makes decisions far less predictable given higher degrees of freedom (Koestler *Ghost* 214–7).

The experience of freedom opens future possibilities; one literally makes one's own destiny. As Sartre states, "Man first of all is the being who hurls himself toward a future and is conscious of imagining himself as being in the future" (*Existentialism* 16). One is not thrown into being so much as one throws oneself into being. "Authentic" existence means meeting the future with "courageous exercise of choice, preference, and decision." One eschews systematic and abstract doctrines, and instead constantly strives for "true identity as a free, spiritual existent" (Patka "Five" 34–5).

In *Doctor Who*, many of these existentialist arguments operate as assumptions. The Doctor may be mistaken for a certain kind of character in popular fiction, particularly American Western and detective fiction, that of the lone seeker. This character wanders from place to place searching for the "secret" that will reveal his or her "true identity." A typical example is the American TV series *Kung Fu*, in which the half–Chinese Kwai Chang Caine roams the American West of the late nineteenth century searching for his brother, who symbolizes the family, or original being, that he has lost. Such characters search for a pre-existing reason for their being, hoping that having been disjoined from it they can rejoin it. The Doctor is a lone wanderer, but not this kind of lone wanderer. In the original series, he actively flees from his past. In the revived series, his past and home are obliterated by war, giving him nothing to return to. Both series provide grounds for the Doctor's modern existentialist life, which is to create his own reasons for being. Few scenes show this better than early in "The Unquiet Dead" (2005), when the Doctor, disappointed at having arrived in boring Cardiff in 1869 instead of thrilling Naples in 1860, hears a scream, grins like a boy, flings his newspaper, and says, "That's more like it!" The Doctor almost literally hurls himself into whatever situation he happens to be in. Such is the life of the existentialist hero.

However, this very freedom places burdens on the individual. Without the care provided by social systems, most especially religion, one is in one's own care. According to Heidegger, only through this realization can one become one's authentic self. One of the many professors who have summarized and clarified Heidegger's theories, argues it this way[4]: Care starts from knowledge that one's existence is temporary. A person's primary concern is for one's self; however, this expands because everyone else is precisely in the same temporal position. One's care is not just for oneself, but for helping others to relieve their burdens, their care, as well. Such care for others requires communication. Indeed, one becomes fully conscious, and hence gains a conscience, only through disclosing the burden of oneself to others, a process of "being together."

Looked at from this existential perspective, two common aspects of *Doctor Who* "make sense." One is the Doctor's constant need for at least one "companion." The times the Doctor travels alone are rare, and in those episodes in which he does travel alone, he quickly picks up a temporary companion. If being is what one does instead of what one is, then being becomes meaningful only in the presence of others. The companions are there as part of the requisite disclosing process. The point has been increasingly stressed over the years as the companions' personalities play a more integral part in the stories. Companions such as Ace, Rose, Martha, and Donna gain their consciences through their time with the Doctor, while they act to keep the Doctor in contact with his conscience. The other aspect of *Doctor Who* that Heidegger's theory of care explains is the Doctor's hurling himself into a situation to prevent a wrong. Wrongs are rarely righted, but they can be prevented or mitigated. The Doctor's awareness of the fragility of life and permanence of death makes him care to disburden others.

Because of its burdens, freedom is neither easily recognized nor easily accepted. Koestler identifies two "enemies" of freedom in the human psyche. One is habit, which replaces free will with machine-like repetition. Habit becomes self-transcendence when ideology replaces conscience, and people act according to dictates not of their own. The other enemy is passion, "the self-assertive, hunger-rage-fear-rape class of emotions" (*Ghost* 217).[5] One can see in legal concepts of "diminished capacity" and in common phrases such as "losing control" or "losing one's head" that such passions reduce freedom. However, habit and passion are enemies of freedom only when they become dominant behaviors. In the ordinary course of behavior, self-assertion is necessary both for the survival of the individual and the species. It becomes dangerous when a person places his or her own freedom above that of others.

However, according to Koestler, the more dangerous human behavior is the self-transcendent, what are all too often identified as the "better" qualities.

Self-transcendence is the tendency to allow oneself to be absorbed into causes, to identify with abstractions, to give up one's free will to the will of powerful leaders or to the mob. On the one hand, self-transcendence has produced great works of art, science, and philosophy. On the other hand, it leads to nationalism, jingoism, racism, and other dangerous kinds of oversimplifications. Koestler comes by means of natural philosophy (i.e., science-based) to very similar conclusions drawn philosophically by the existentialists. More death, violence, and atrocity have been perpetrated in the name of a cause or a religion or a leader than ever was perpetrated by all the self-assertive individual criminals combined. Followers perpetrate these horrors fully convinced that what they are doing is right, that they are saving souls, expunging evil, executing the will of the state, restoring the social order, propitiating the gods, or performing some other "higher service" that justifies doing without thinking and obeying without questioning (Koestler *Ghost* 233–8, 243–6).

The Doctor is an existentialist hero in his rejecting the two enemies of freedom. While he has primarily the same emotions as ordinary people have, he rarely lets his passion run away with his reason. Plus, the Doctor entirely avoids self-transcendent ideologies. He has no loyalty to a corps, cause, or leader. Instead, he acts from a sense of *duty* to others as beings with rights. Thus, he values such concepts as life, truth, and justice, which affirm the standing of others as beings with equal rights, and devalues such concepts as nation, business, and race, which place the idea above the person. In existentialist terms, the Doctor leads an authentic life.

Authenticity

To existentialists, authenticity is the awareness that one's life is temporary, contingent, and bound to the equally temporary and contingent lives of others. All this comes about because one faces the inevitability of death. Only by facing death, and not running away from it into comforting lies, does one become an authentic self. However, one never has a choice as to the circumstances into which one is thrown into being. Thus, not all the possible authentic selves will be realized. When one projects oneself into some possibilities, one rejects others, and thus incurs a debt to the authentic self, the debt being the gap between what one is and what one's authentic self can be. This debt is manifested as Guilt, apart from theological or moralistic definitions. Just as the authentic self is the one who faces death's inevitability, it is also the self that faces the guilt of indebtedness to one's possibilities. Thus, "authenticity requires *honesty* and *courage*" (Moenkemeyer 106–9).

The Doctor embodies an authentic existence along the lines that existentialists lay down. Few characters have faced their own deaths, or the fact of its inevitability, more than the Doctor. Though his ability to regenerate may seem a way to cheat death, the program never presents the matter that way. Instead, it is quite possible for the Doctor to die without regenerating, and "The Impossible Astronaut" (2011) demonstrates the exact means of accomplishing this permanent death. Given how the Doctor faces the inevitable, and what he does about it, one can see what it means to be authentic. One example comes in "The Caves of Androzani" (1984). The Doctor and his companion, Peri, have been caught up in war, and both have been poisoned by a substance called spectrox. The Doctor has been badly beaten up and the two companions separated. Late in the program, the Doctor has seized control of a spaceship so that he can return to rescue Peri because, as he says, he "got her into" her trouble. Threatened with death by the ship's owners, the Doctor states that the threat is not persuasive because he is dying. The relevant point comes as the ship goes hurtling into the planet of Androzani Minor. Staring at the view screen showing the enlargening planet, the Doctor briefly sees a kind of shimmering void. This void appears to him again at the end of the story when he thinks he actually is dying before he regenerates into a new body. Shaking off the vision of the void in the spaceship is the act of authentic being. At this moment, the Doctor sees what might be his death, but through an act of will puts it off until he completes his ethical duty to his friend.

Sartre defines authenticity based upon a set of realizations. The first is anguish, which he also calls anxiety, by which he means the realization that every decision one makes involves all humanity, not merely oneself (20). Looking at the example of "Caves of Androzani," we can see how the Doctor does not indulge in the selfish act of giving in to oncoming death, nor of trying to run away from it. His decision for action rests upon his realization of the involvement of others, even of their fates, in his decisions. According to Sartre, the next realization for authenticity is forlornness, the realization that in a godless world all things are possible. So, a person is stuck with nothing to cling to for an absolute set of values. Morals emerge from the situation, and not from any pre-existing good. Forlornness is the product of absolute responsibility and absolute freedom (22–3). Again, the example of the "Caves of Androzani" demonstrates this process of realizing both freedom of choice and the need for responsibility. The final realization is despair, by which Sartre means reckoning with what is possible in a given circumstance. A person is not constrained by pre-existing values, but only by the possibilities (29). The Doctor's decision in "Caves of Androzani" comes from his assessment of the choices for action available to him. He can try to hijack the ship entirely; he can accept death as it arrives; or he can try to escape his captors and save his friend. Saving his friend means risking death by his captors or by crashing the ship. Meaningful decision comes from recognizing the constraints of that decision's circumstances.

The Social Being

Because of the fear of the unknown future, and because nature works to preserve the species, manifested at the social level among human beings, there are social rules, obligations, and institutions. According to existentialists, these rules, obligations, and institutions have the purely pragmatic purpose of preservation of society. For this reason, such systems tend always toward control and domination, rigidly enforced by the threat of death for transgressing the laws, customs, taboos, and procedures of the social control systems. The English novelist and existentialist John Fowles makes the point more bluntly: "All states and societies are incipiently fascist" (123). The legal system, morality, and religion are not, according to existentialists, derived from transcendent and supernatural sources, always sacred and always right, but from temporary (even when lasting centuries) needs to maintain social equilibrium (Patka "Five" 42–3). Such social control systems define each person in a given society according to specified roles, and require that people always maintain those roles, always be one thing, and act within one socially predetermined set of behaviors. The authentic person stands apart from social control systems, often actively fighting against them, because they impede the process of each person's self-transcendence.

However, existentialism is not a selfish set of credos. It is humanistic not merely because it places human existence first, but also because it takes into account the concept of humanity. When one is responsible for oneself, one is also responsible for one's humanity, and thus, by extension, for all humanity (Sartre 16). A person's choice of what he or she would like to be affirms the value of what that person chooses. And since such a choice can never transcend one's humanity, the choice involves all humans, too (Sartre 17). At an individual level, when one chooses an action, it is chosen based on a self-conception. If one chooses to be a wandering expatriate, that is based on how one defines oneself. However, more is involved in the decision because the self-conception is based upon an idea of what humanity itself is. Thus, a person's choice to be a wandering expatriate is also based on the notion that this is an ideal mode of action for people in general. In choosing to be a wandering expatriate, or to be anything else, one sets an example for the rest of humanity (Sartre 15–18).

In his actions relative to the societies he finds himself in, the Doctor lives a life of good conscience as Nietzsche describes it. Basically, Nietzsche says that most people are "timorous," rather than lazy, and "hide behind customs and opinions." Such hiding runs contrary to the true nature of human being. Nietzsche says, "At bottom, every human being knows very well that he is in this world just once, as something unique, and that no accident, however strange, will throw together a second time into a unity such a curious and diffuse plurality" ("Live" 101).

The series repeatedly contrasts the Doctor's Niezschean understanding of life as creative experience and the timorous actions of those who live by received ideas. Sometimes, the contrast is obvious. In "The Pirate Planet" (1978), Balaton, a citizen of the planet Zanak, watches his son Pralix be taken away by the Mentiads, whom Balaton believes to be evil. When Pralix's sister Mula, with the help of K-9, goes after them to rescue Pralix, and the Doctor convinces their friend Kimus to help him track down Romana, Balaton refuses to join in. He calls these activities "madness" and longs for the good days when everyone just did as they were told. While Balaton is something of an exaggeration, his reaction makes a key point central to the *Doctor Who* ethos.

The larger context of this story makes that ethos clear. Zanak was once ruled by the rapacious Queen Xanxia, but is now, at least to all appearance, run by the Captain, whose ship had crashed on Zanak several years earlier. As far as the people of Zanak are concerned, the Captain is tremendously benevolent, providing them with numerous mineral riches (precious stones, mostly) each time he announces a "golden age." Such is the nature of most of the people of Zanak that they are willing to put up with the stifling of free expression and the constant presence of police as long as they have their "golden age." Thus, as Romana finds out, there are forbidden questions, and forbidden investigative objects such as telescopes.

In keeping with the usual process of science fiction, careful viewers should not view the society of Zanak as something "other," but rather as a distillation of trends in their own society. Thus, Balaton's timorousness (to use Nietzsche's vocabulary) should not be seen as the exception, even in modern Western culture, but rather as the rule. Given enough entertainment and comfort, people are likely to accept limitations of personal freedom as a price for the comfort. Those who question from within, such as Mula and Kimus, are the exceptions. When Mula asks "why" in relation to how the people of Zanak live in general, Balaton rebukes her, speaking with the voice of the whole society. But for all his comfort, Balaton is frustrated, tired, and unhappy. One can contrast this to Kimus's exhilaration when he is flying in aircar with the Doctor, his excitement at being "free to think."

When entertainment or comfort is not a distraction from accepting one's true individuality or from desiring free thought, then industry becomes the distraction. People feel that they must work all the time, "relentless industry from early till late," as Nietzsche describes it ("Live" 104). The problem with busy work is that it uses up the energy that might be applied to true thought and reason. It sets a continuous series of small goals as one's principal satisfactions and thus provides "security."

The Doctor presents a winning contrast to the timorous lives of most members of society. He lives the life of *purposeful* action, as opposed to mere busy work. He shows that what people do matters. Additionally, he shows that the "security" of timorousness is both illusory and deadening. One can live in society, but not necessarily by its rules.

The Existentialism of *Doctor Who*

The Doctor's life in many ways exemplifies the ideals of existentialist philosophers. Consider the matter of life as "concrete duration." The Doctor began on television with almost no past at all. We learn that he comes from "another time, another world" as Susan, his granddaughter, states it. He summarizes his past this way: "Have you ever wondered what it is like to be wanderers in the fourth dimension...? To be exiles! Susan and I are cut off from our own civilization, without friends or protection...." In "An Unearthly Child" (1963), Barbara mistakenly calls the Doctor "Doctor Foreman." Ian's correction to her is instructive: "That's not his name. Who is he? Doctor Who? Perhaps if we knew his name, we might have a clue to all this."

Throughout the years, little bits of the Doctor's past come out, but none that have the effect of defining the character. We learn first that he is not the only wanderer from his own world in "The Time Meddler" (1965). We finally get a glimpse of the Doctor's home world in "The War Games" (1969). The society of this world seems to be hierarchical, elitist, aloof, and austere. While these characteristics can certainly apply to the Doctor, he also has strong compassionate and humane qualities that set him quite apart from this society, and supply us with some sense of why he may have left it. This planet gets named as Gallifrey by the third Doctor in "The Time Warrior" (1974), who calls his people "galactic ticket inspectors," a dismissive remark that again suggests something of his relationship to his past. Eventually, we learn a bit more, that the Doctor was a member of the elite rulership of this society, the Time Lords, but that he "renounced" his association with them.[6] He becomes "Lord President" of Gallifrey by accident or by force three times,[7] and each time finally rejects the office. We learn that before he left home with Susan, he had probably held some very high position within Gallifreyan society.[8] In the revived version of the program, this Gallifreyan past is completely wiped out when Gallifrey and the Time Lords were first reported as utterly destroyed in the last great time war[9] and later revealed as being taken out of time.[10] These are mere tantalizing details more than anything else, and reveal very little about the forces and influences that shaped the character. Without any distinctive past, the Doctor simply *is* the Doctor, and nothing more.

Mysterious pasts are nothing new for heroic figures. It is often part of the pattern of the hero's life to have this mystery of identity. What makes the Doctor an existentialist hero and not a mythological hero, though, is that there is no compulsion to reveal this past. The Doctor does not seek his past, does not desire to know his origins, actively avoids going "home," and rebuffs all attempts to unlock the vault of his past. Because he is a hero without a past, he is also a hero without a destiny. As a hero without a destiny, the Doctor to a great degree typifies a modern human: "unhistorical, estranged from himself and from his past, opposed to traditional values, and disloyal to his cultural heritage" (Patka "Five" 44).

This absence of a past or a destiny, in existential terms, is perhaps the most important. Mythological heroes all have a sort of predetermined existence, a plan laid out for them by the supernatural forces to which they partially belong. When they discover their pasts, their futures are revealed, and they must bravely go off to face it. In their youths, they often display signs of this link to the supernatural, hints at their destinies. Thus, the mythological hero is always apart from human existence, always something other and beyond. The supernatural forces take great interest in them in the way that they do not for the rest of humanity. This interest means that the heroes' lives, their fortunes, their destinies are never their own nor of their own making. In existentialist terms, the mythological hero demonstrates the folly of belief in divine forces that watch after people. Under those circumstances, a person cannot be held responsible for his or her own life or actions, since they are merely the inevitable unfolding of some cosmic plot.

The Doctor, in contrast, is constantly plunging headlong into the future, without predestination, without divine guidance, a maker of his own plots. For this reason, the Doctor continually insists that he is nothing special, just a traveler. Also, for this reason *Doctor Who* is almost always better when the Doctor is a kind of cosmic tourist stumbling upon trouble, as in "The Aztecs" (1965), rather than actively seeking out trouble like a cosmic crusader, as in "The Happiness Patrol" (1988).

As a traveler with no particular past and no particular direction, the Doctor is repeatedly placed in situations equivalent to what many existentialist philosophers argue is the reality of existence. Joseph Mihalich describes Sartre's views of human reality this way: "The individual human being acts, not in some kind of socio-personal vacuum, but rather within the context of a concrete situation in which he finds himself involved or *engaged*" (129). Many times, the Doctor begins a new adventure by finding himself in a concrete situation — a looming space war, a planet trying to enter the Galactic Federation, Marco Polo trying to escape the Khan's power — and almost immediately becomes involved, or engaged in the situation. Throughout the series, a common observation made by the Doctor and others is that he gets "involved." Because each situation in these circumstances is new, the Doctor finds himself constantly inventing his place and identity within it. It is only through such engagement that he can become the Doctor in story after story.

Indeed, the Doctor is constantly before the viewer and the other characters, most especially his various companions, as an example. Time after time, he *sets* the example, and thus embodies another important concept of existentialism: that when one chooses, one chooses for humanity. Each time a person chooses a course, that person revisits the question, "What if everyone did so?" As Sartre argues, to shrug off the question with the answer, "Not everyone does," is merely to deny the fact that one is always an example to others (18–19). The Doctor consistently sets the example by acting both explicitly and implicitly from the question, "What if everyone did so?" More than anything else, this awareness of responsibility for all humanity (defined in the show as intelligent life of all kinds), the consistent pattern of choosing humanity, makes the Doctor a moral character and gives him his tremendous moral authority.

Additionally, the Doctor, as a true existential hero, remains constantly aware of the inevitability and finality of death, and consistently faces it honestly and courageously, to use Heidegger's conception. Indeed, the Doctor's privileged position as a Time Lord with extended life (over 900 years so far) and capacity to travel throughout history heightens his awareness that all things pass inevitably and irrevocably. A moment in "Tooth and Claw" (2006) reflects on this existential understanding of the finality of death. Queen Victoria, contemplating the death of her husband and his love of ghost stories, says:

> That's the charm of a ghost story, isn't it? Not the scares and chills, that's just for children, but the ... hope of some contact with the great Beyond. We all want some message from that place. It's the Creator's greatest mystery that we're allowed no such consolation. The dead stay silent. And we must wait.

In *Doctor Who*, the viewer often sees what at first appears to be a ghost story, but, like Queen Victoria, is denied the consolation that such a story would imply. All supernatural phenomena are naturalized, and nature's harsh reality is death.

In the attitude taken toward death, *Doctor Who* sometimes leans toward an Epicurean interpretation. Such interpretation anticipates the arguments of the existentialists, and so is worth looking at. To the Epicureans, there is no afterlife, nowhere to go after death. Death is the end of the individual, what Lucretius calls "mind" (*anima*, or "major spirit" in Latin), and since whatever it is that creates the "person" is mortal, death is "nothing to us and no concern of ours" (Lucretius 87). By this, Lucretius means that there is no "thing" that is death that one has to fear. When the end comes, we will not "know" it in the strict sense, and it will bring peace by ending personal discomfort and misery. While *Doctor Who* does not go quite so far in considering the nature of death, the program does take the assumption that death means cessation of the individual person.

Lucretius goes further, arguing against various means of preserving and preparing bodies. Because death is simply part of the natural process and because there is no afterlife to prepare for, there is no reason for elaborate ceremony. Furthermore, one's life may have been lived enjoying the bounties of nature, in which case it is time to make room for others to enjoy the bounty; or, one's life has been mostly miserable, in which case death comes as a release from misery. The motive for such ceremonies is self-pity that comes from imagining what will happen to the body after it dies. Coupled with superstition, self-pity drives people to make a pretense that death has not really happened, either through imagining an afterlife or through trying to prevent the decay of the body (Lucretius 88–91). In *Doctor Who*, one can see hints of this Epicurean attitude. In "Remembrance of the Daleks" (1988), the program ends with the Doctor and Ace standing outside a church as others go into a funeral. It is clear that they have no place in such a ceremony. During the story, the Doctor uses the system of funerals, including funeral parlors and burial plots, to hide a powerful alien artifact that resembles a coffin. An earlier story, "Revelation of the Daleks" (1985), takes place almost entirely in a funeral parlor on the funeral planet of Necros. Apart from intricate funeral arrangements and a grotesquely grandiose cemetery, the facility contains a section for cryogenic suspension, where people have been frozen at the moment of death in the hope that some day their ailments will be cured. The idea is mocked when we find out that one person's disease has been cured, but that his wife is using the money from the fund for curing the disease for something other than his revival. The gently satirical attitude toward funeral arrangements shown in *Doctor Who* suggests at least some sympathy with the Epicurean position regarding death. It also coincides with the existentialist view that what matters is the life one has now rather than the imaginary afterlife one does not have.

One revealing incident in this regard occurs in "The Trial of a Timelord: The Mysterious Planet" (1986), when the Doctor's companion Peri realizes that the world they are on, apparently empty of animal or intelligent life, is

Earth in the far future. Though Peri had been traveling with the Doctor for a while, the concrete reality of her world totally devastated still upsets her. The thought that "none of this really matters" because she can return to her old Earth with the Doctor does not comfort her, though. The scene plays out a passage from Lucretius, who tells his reader that contrary to common Roman thought, the "whole substance" of the world will one day "crash" and break into fragments. Lucretius is well aware of the difficulty of persuading someone of this future, since it lies outside of people's experience, and seems when it is spoken to be "novel and strange" (Lucretius 131). The Doctor finds himself in such a position as Lucretius. Characteristically, the Doctor tries to convince Peri of the long view: "Planets come and go, stars perish, matter disperses, coalesces, forms into other patterns." Again, the *Doctor Who* view mirrors the Epicurean view: "To none is life given in freehold; to all on lease" (Lucretius 91). The Doctor's statement also closely parallels Enlightenment skepticism as Baron D'Holbach states it: "Suns encrust themselves, and are extinguished; planets perish and disperse themselves in the vast plains of air, other suns are kindled, and illumine their systems; new planets form themselves...." (58).

An even more poignant reminder of this reality occurs with Rose in "The End of the World" (2005). The Doctor has taken Rose five billion years into the future, when the Earth will be finally devoured by the expanding sun. While on an observation platform built for spectators to watch the event, the Doctor augments Rose's mobile phone so that she can talk to her mother five billion years in the past. The event reminds Rose that she is in her own future, and that everyone she knew is long dead. The sadness of death as obliteration of all experience and knowledge is heightened to near depression for Rose when she and everyone else on the observation platform miss witnessing Earth's destruction, while they were "all too busy trying to save themselves." Through an act of caring in this instance, the Doctor does take his companion back to her Earth in her time to demonstrate that though it is gone, it still exists. Time travel concretizes memory, which preserves the past so long as one is alive to remember it. Memory is part of the burden of existence, what, in existential terms, we owe to ourselves and to others.

The Doctor's enforced exile on Earth during the seventh through ninth seasons (1970–2) and subsequent several duties acting on behalf of the Time Lords, by force most often,[11] demonstrates quite well the constant tension that existentialists argue about regarding the struggle of the individual for self-determination against the social and political forces that would control him or her.[12] These social forces have the entire weight and power of popular opinion, a police apparatus, and invested authority to require others to work on their behalf, especially when opting out would result in punishment or death.

The series of related stories that made up the season-long "The Key to

Time" series (1978–9) demonstrates the ways in which the Doctor, as an existentialist hero, breaks the "plan" of apparent pre-determination. In this series, a cosmic force called the White Guardian has chosen the Doctor to assemble the six parts to the Key to Time, which will allow the Guardian to realign the balance of the Universe. The Guardian has chosen the Doctor's companion for him. The Guardian also warns the Doctor that there is a malevolent Black Guardian who would use the assembled key for his own ends. When the Doctor asks what will happen to him if he refuses, the Guardian replies, "Nothing. Ever." Thus, faced with taking the quest or annihilation, the Doctor accepts the quest.

It would seem, then, that this series places an external structure of cosmic destiny atop the existential humanist foundation of *Doctor Who*. However, within the structure of this quest, the Doctor actually has some free agency. He chooses to tell his companion Romana that she has been tricked into joining the quest, instead of keeping her in ignorance as the Guardian apparently wished. In "The Androids of Tara," the Doctor decides to take a break and go fishing. As is usual for the Doctor's life in general, he can never manage just to do the job of getting the segment, but becomes directly involved in the lives and politics of wherever he happens to be. Finally, the Doctor is able, without supernatural aid, to gather all the segments, assemble the key, and avoid mistaking the Black Guardian for the White. Furthermore, though the White and Black Guardians seem to have supernatural power, they are in fact limited, natural products of the formation of the universe. What powers they have are part of the universe, and thus they cannot be fully in control of the events, cannot act as the hands of destiny. The existentialist theme is maintained. Free will and personal identity exist, but always within the limited framework of material nature and the particular circumstances in which one happens to be.

The Doctor's situation within the universe of the program consistently conjures the questions of existence in a material universe. The emphasis by the show's producers on taking the title quite literally as a question has meant that the Doctor is always an unfixed existential duration. In less technical terms, having no past of any depth, the Doctor is literally thrown into being, and from here constantly forging out his own future, making it new and fresh with each adventure.

The character of the Doctor similarly mimics existential ideas of human character. If we recall Sartre's idea that the authentic person recognizes his or her anguish, forlornness, and despair, we find the Doctor fits the parameters. One sees the Doctor repeatedly anguished or anxious about his responsibilities over the lives of others. A key example occurs in "Genesis of the Daleks" (1975), when the Doctor has the opportunity to wipe out the Daleks and their menace, erase them from history and thus save countless lives in the future. Nevertheless, the Doctor hesitates to perform the act. "Do I have that right?" he asks. At the same time, the Doctor is forlorn because there are no absolute moral principles to guide his action. His companion Sarah argues that there are: "To wipe out the Daleks — you can't doubt it." However, the Doctor does doubt it, and he does so because his knowledge of the possibilities brings forth his despair. He notes that wars will be settled and alliances built purely as a response to the Dalek menace. The implication is that it is quite possible that equivalent evil will be accomplished by other hands, that there is no guarantee of peace just because a particularly nasty enemy is removed. Eventually, further along in the story, the Doctor does make the decision to destroy the incubating Daleks, but only when all other possibilities for effecting a positive change have been nullified.

Yet, every person has more than just his or her own person to worry about. The realization that one exists, formally stated by Descartes as "I think, therefore I am," automatically involves a condition in which one can exist. That condition necessarily includes other thinking beings, for, as Sartre points out, a person cannot be or become anything unless there is some thinking other to recognize it (Sartre 37). Jaspers describes the matter similarly: "The individual cannot become human by himself" (147). In practical terms, this means two things. First, since the nature of one's existence requires at least one other to verify it, similarly one must be some other person's "other" and recognize that person's existence. This mutual otherness plays a significant part in the existentialists' idea that in choosing one is also choosing for all of humanity. Second, since there is no universal human essence (nothing that is "essentially" human), but there is a universal human condition (set of boundaries as to what is humanly possible), every configuration of this condition has a "universal value." Thus, while a white American may not "know" from experience the particular configuration of the human condition of a black American, yet the white American can easily imagine what it is. A thinking person can imagine every configuration, and thus "understand" those configurations, "sympathize" in the true sense of the word (Sartre 39).

The Doctor, while a solitary figure in a sense, is still a social figure. Within the fictional universe of the series he is not "human," yet it is clear that he is a human character, a type representing some configurations of the human condition. More importantly, his status as outsider (stranger) in almost every situation gives viewers ample chance to see his understanding of other configurations. Whether those configurations are "alien" is irrelevant, since as with the Doctor, the configurations of aliens are merely typified human configurations. In less abstract terms, the Doctor's perspective toward other species (human configurations typified) is a kind of cultural relativism based upon his understanding of, his sympathy for, their perspectives. This is not an ethical relativism that argues all perspectives are equally valid. Instead, it is a recognition that all others have equal value as oneself because they are equally existing and self-aware realities.

Science and Existence

One aspect of existential philosophy that runs counter to *Doctor Who* to some extent is its opposition to "science." The opposition takes different form depending upon the philosopher in question. Thus, Jaspers believes that science produces only knowledge of humanity's external circumstances, but fails to grasp experience and so cannot by itself provide an understanding of Being. Nevertheless, science has become a leading factor of the historical condition of Being. Therefore, science cannot be ignored. Jaspers resolves the issue by subordinating science to philosophy. Science helps one to answer the first of Kant's basic questions of philosophy — what can I know? — but fails to provide answers to the other three. Thus, science is merely the first step of philosophizing, or as Jasper's puts it, "a tool of philosophy" (139–45). Heidegger, however, especially in his later writings, is quite disdainful of science in general.

Nietzsche, among the earliest of existentialists, is quite different in having a generally positive view of science. In particular, he thought the problem with both psychology and philosophy was that neither was scientific enough. He alone among existentialists saw that the scientific insistence on the particular, on strict observation, was really what knowledge, even self knowledge, should be based upon.

The opposition to science needs some explanation. First, the science that these philosophers have in mind is of the nineteenth century variety, which to a great degree was concerned with measuring and categorizing, much more than science as practiced after World War II. Second, most of the principal existential philosophers focus their animus against science principally on psychology (Kaufmann "Existentialism" 28). A probable reason for the animus against psychology (and psychoanalysis) is that it is the principal scientific rival in the field of knowledge about the human being. As existential philosophers see it, science attempts to explain the human from external and prior conditions. For existential philosophers, the scientific approach seeks explanation of being in the wrong place. Instead, existential philosophy locates being only in the being of the individual. Each person makes his or her own being only through choice, and these choices alone are what define one's being. For this reason, Jaspers and Heidegger both wrote scathing critiques of psychoanalysis, while Sartre proposed his own brand of "existential psychoanalysis."

By the 1980s or so, however, psychoanalysis had lost much of its potency among scientific psychologists. Most intellectuals had begun accepting the insights provided through scientific psychology. Finally, rejections of science became increasingly seen as antiquated and unrealistic. One could be an existentialist, accept the major principles of existentialist philosophy, and still appreciate and practice science. *Doctor Who* exists within this updated intellectual climate. The Doctor can be a premier scientist, a benign mad professor and symbol for science, and an existential hero, too.

However, the Doctor does share with existentialist philosophers a disdain for the purely academic. Much of what unites the disparate tempers and arguments of the existential philosophers is that they dislike what they see as "academic" philosophy. By "academic," they refer to those who simply paraphrase and comment upon other philosophers, and, more importantly, those who proceed in an almost mathematical fashion. Existentialist philosophers see true philosophy, and thus true knowledge, as originating in *self* knowledge. Philosophy is created each time a person philosophizes. "Academic" philosophy seeks truth in abstract prior existences (i.e., God, or the ideal realm, or the soul), or in minute transformations of logical units. For the existentialist, truth is experience — not discovered, but created. Furthermore, to have any meaning as a philosophy, existentialism must be a lived philosophy and not merely a written one (Kaufmann "Existentialism" 47).

The Doctor, too, rejects mere academic knowledge. He had renounced the Time Lords, academics elevated to be politicians as well. The Doctor repeatedly belittles the distant "hands off" attitude the Time Lords take toward whatever they are studying. For the Doctor, to study something means to live it, not merely to observe it or to read about it. It is not that the Doctor is opposed to books. He is very much a book person. However, he does oppose academic reliance upon the authority of books when it replaces direct experience. In this way, the Doctor can be an academic and a scientist as well as an existentialist hero.

Doctor Who and Death

A final consideration in this matter of the existential humanism of *Doctor Who* is the issue of death. As mentioned earlier, it may seem that the Doctor can cheat death because he can regenerate and because he has lived so long compared to the human lifespan. Nevertheless, the program clearly establishes that the Doctor is mortal and that his death is a real possibility. Even during one regeneration process, in "Caves of Androzani," the Doctor believes that he is really dying. In the resurrected series of 2005, we find that the Time

Lords and the planet Gallifrey have been destroyed, thus reinforcing the possibility of the Doctor's own death.

In *Doctor Who*, it is important to note that in nearly all cases, none of the main characters, and certainly not the Doctor, acts as if there is a certain afterlife.[13] In fact, the show repeatedly emphasizes the point that dead is dead. Thus, the Doctor and his companions stand outside the majority of public opinion, which is firmly convinced of basic religious notions. A symbolic moment in this regard is the already mentioned ending of "Remembrance of the Daleks," where the Doctor and Ace remain behind while a group of mourners enters a church. The church door closes firmly before them as the Doctor tells Ace that it is time to go. An implicit message of this is that for the dead, at least, there is nothing more that one can do for them.

In the existentialist perspective of *Doctor Who*, death is inevitable and final. Even a time-traveling scientific wizard cannot change that. When the companion Adric dies at the end of "Earthshock" (1982), in the immediately following story "Time-Flight" (1982) the remaining companions plead with the Doctor to go back in time to save Adric. However, the Doctor is adamant: "There are rules that cannot be broken." Something similar had happened in "The Massacre" (1966), in which the Doctor realizes that he and Steven had arrived just before the slaughter of the Huguenots on St. Bartholomew's Day in 1572. Rather than rescue a young serving woman who had befriended Steven, the Doctor sends the woman home warning her only to "stay inside." When Steven finds out why the Doctor did this and that he chose not to rescue her, Steven is furious. The Doctor's action, as Steven sees it, shows a callous disregard for human life. The Doctor insists, though, that he dare not change history, and that from this perspective some things must be. There is no certainty that the woman died[14] and she would have to take her chance just as everyone else must. The Doctor simply cannot go around plucking everyone out of time and saving them as he likes. Though he does not state this point, for him to take the woman out of time would be to destroy the natural order of the universe that seems to require death.[15] The existentialist worldview of the show requires that the Doctor do exactly as he had done.

The importance of the treatment of death in *Doctor Who* has everything to do with its primarily existentialist presentation. While it might seem that disbelief in the afterlife, coupled with a firm conviction that death is the end of the individual being, would lead to despair, "nothing to hope for," in the existential, Epicurean, and humanist views, that is not the case. Were it true that the natural or even correctly moral attitude toward life without a promise of an eternal afterlife is despair, then the Doctor's optimism, cheeriness, and *joie de vivre* would be cavalier at best and highly callous. Instead, appreciation of and for life is exactly the natural and correctly moral attitude to take.

English novelist John Fowles states the position eminently well: "*The more absolute death seems, the more authentic life becomes*" (37, emphasis Fowles'). Faced with as much death as the Doctor has faced, he does not despair. Rather, he enjoys life more highly than most the other characters in the series. He knows, as Fowles states, that "what makes our existence worthwhile is precisely that its worth and its while — its quality and duration — are as impossible to unravel as time and space in the mathematics of relativity" (35).

Doctor Who, Existentialism, and Humanism

To summarize, in questions of existence, *Doctor Who* takes a fundamentally modern existentialist perspective. This perspective is humanist in that it focuses on the reality of life in the material world and ignores or discounts ideas of a permanent afterlife. The Doctor is a kind of existentialist hero, whose life and exploits demonstrate key concepts of modern existentialist philosophy. As a person without a clear past or destiny, he exists only as a concrete duration, living in the moment and for the moment. He literally throws himself into whatever situation he finds himself in, and acts from the recognition that what he *is* can be nothing more than what he *does*. He knows that existence as a thinking person requires the recognition of other thinking persons, because *doing* is always for or to others, and not exclusively for oneself. He realizes that as an acting agent with limited free will, he must always act for humanity and not just for himself.

The program presents reality very closely to how modern existentialists describe it. This is a material reality. Those living in it are constrained by the laws of nature. Because people exist in community and not isolation, community also constrains the free agency of those living in it. Authentic existence, such as the Doctor's, means being both in and out of this community, of abiding by it rules when they affirm humanity, and of dissenting from its rules when they constrain or abuse humanity. Through this existential presentation, viewers of *Doctor Who* come to understand concrete definitions of *life*, *existence*, *freedom*, *free will*, and *death*.

CHAPTER 4

Knowledge

To the rational mind, nothing is inexplicable; only unexplained.
— The Doctor, "The Robots of Death"

Illusory Knowledge

In the backstory to the *Doctor Who* adventure "The Brain of Morbius" (1976), Morbius has concocted a brilliant scheme to elude execution. His follower Solon, a brilliant neurosurgeon, extracts Morbius's brain, preserving it in nutrient fluid and hiding it until Solon can find a suitable body into which he can put the brain. Though Morbius's brain has inputs for external audio stimuli, he has virtually no other existence or contact with the world outside his brain. To use his words, even a sponge in the sea has more life than he.

Morbius's condition replicates a philosophical riddle called "brains in vats." What if you were not actually living a full-bodied life, but instead were like Morbius? What if you were a brain in a jar connected to electrodes that fed you outside stimulation? All your experiences are simulated, but your brain has no way of telling that the experiences are not real. Can you prove that you are actually holding this book and reading it right now, and not merely receiving an electric simulation of the experience of reading?

There is an additional problem in the brains-in-vats thought experiment, which has to do with the nature of human brains themselves. The brain craves input, and requires a constant stream of information to work over, sort, analyze, evaluate, categorize, and interpret. Deprived of direct stimulus, or receiving only minimal stimulus, the brain starts creating imaginary input, illusory data to fulfill its need. Think of Morbius for a moment. Morbius has a conversation with Solon. How is he certain that this conversation is real? Could it not be the product of his under-stimulated brain as it tries to make a living experience? Could this conversation be only a dream?

66

Science writer William Poundstone calls the brains-in-vats thought experiment "the quintessential illustration of what philosophers call the 'problem of knowledge'" (8). Morbius's brain prompts us to think about how we receive information, and about our dependence upon one organ for transforming information into knowledge, in other words, for making information useful. Morbius's situation reminds us of the many ways that we can be deluded, that we may possess large amounts of false knowledge.

The spectrum of what is known or can be known is immense. The spectrum of what was once known and is no longer accepted as true is also immense. If knowledge changes, how can it be "known"? This problem only adds to the previous problem concerning whether what one "knows" is really a delusion.

Poundstone notes that the Renaissance philosopher René Descartes proposed some good solutions to the problem of illusory knowledge. In his *Meditation I*, Descartes recalls that fantastical paintings and dreams are still made up of representations drawn from reality. Neither the painter nor the dreamer ever creates an entirely novel form. So, even if one were being deceived by an evil demon (or by an electric simulation), the images and sensations being fed would be based upon the forms of real things. If what a person imagines as life is really a dream, then again the forms of experience correspond to an exterior reality that one still has access to (Descartes *Discourse* 103). In other words, even if, like Morbius, someone were rendered to being merely a brain in a jar, that brain would still have contact with some part of a true external reality, and therefore, that brain could *know* something about that external world. The world external to the self is known by a thinking brain.

Descartes says, "I am a thinking thing, a substance, that is to say, whose whole nature or essence consists in thinking" (*Discourse* 158). In other words, the essential nature of the human self is to think. What that self thinks is knowledge. There is individual knowledge, and there is collective knowledge. Individual knowledge includes all that a single person remembers plus all that that person accepts as "true." Collective knowledge includes the total of recorded information in print and electronic media, plus cultural knowledge carried through tradition and oral history.

Few things are easier than getting entangled in the strands of thought as one pursues the nature of knowledge, reality, perception, and meaning. Radical skepticism says knowledge is false. Radical essentialism says reality is plastic. Radical doubt says that perception is unreliable. Radical relativism says that meaning is impossible. However, most people live their lives confident in the belief that knowledge exists, reality is real, perception works most of the time, and meaning can be discovered. *Doctor Who*, being made for a populous and popular audience, sticks closely to the idea that the universe is real, knowable, and meaningful to perceptive, thoughtful people.

What Knowledge Is About

All that we know comes from the physical universe. At the level of human perception, this universe is made from things and the interactions of things. From this beginning, we may suppose one of two propositions. One is that whatever a thing is, it contains or has contact with the *essential* nature of itself in itself. In this proposition, Understanding is the attempt to apprehend the *essence* of whatever thing we are perceiving, and once we have perceived the essence, we can say that we have *knowledge* of that thing. According to this line of thinking, the essence of a thing is fully real and exists, not as a thing, but in its own space of ideas, which may be called ideal or the true or the spiritual reality of which physical reality is a pale imitation. Thus, this proposition of external essences is *metaphysical*, which means "beside the physical." This is the line of thinking that Plato develops in Book VII of *The Republic* (205–228). If we are to take the Doctor's TARDIS as a thing, for instance, then this proposition would say that it contains the essential concept TARDIS in itself and that what one tries to perceive when thinking about a TARDIS is the essence "TARDIS," which it gets from this realm of ideas.

The other proposition is that there is only the material existing universe. Such a proposition may be called *physical, empiricist,* or *material* depending upon degree, inclination of the definer, and so on. It eliminates most or all *metaphysical* notions. Any "essence" of a thing under study does not have its own existence as such, but is a construction of human intellect. Understanding in this case comes from defining by noting parallels, contiguities, and similarities in the patterns of interactions, the unfolding of events that we call "facts." All such definitions are contingent, not absolute, if or until a better definition can be formulated. "The world is all that is the case," Ludwig Wittgenstein famously wrote (1). Thus, the world as described in language, which is the repository of our knowledge, is the world of facts rather than things. To use the TARDIS example, there is, according to this principle, no "TARDIS" concept independent of a physical TARDIS in a universe of other physical things (which include all "things" from the minutest Planck unit of time to the grandest fabric of space-time itself) interacting with each other. What a TARDIS *is* can be understood only by what it *does*.

The discussion below will demonstrate that while sometimes *Doctor Who* will entertain metaphysical musings, it most often demonstrates materialist ideas about knowledge.

Thinking

Knowledge comes from the activity of thinking. If there were no thinking beings, there would be no knowledge, only disparate facts. But thinking itself is a tricky concept, and one can easily get lost in the hall of distorting mirrors that is the collection of theories about what makes thinking. To make matters worse, we know that a physical organ, the brain, performs this operation called thinking. We have already seen, using the Morbius example, that starting from merely these few facts can lead to most confusing ideas. So, there is a question about how to think about thinking. Does the investigator into this matter look merely at the physical operations of the brain, which would be a scientific approach to the question? Or does the investigator assume that while the brain does the thinking, thinking itself is an independent result of physical processes worthy of study separate from the brain that produced it, which would be the philosophical approach?

Obviously, for our purposes in this study we are concerned with the philosophical consideration of thinking. Some scientific justification for a philosophical consideration of thinking exists. Computer scientist and artificial intelligence expert Douglas Hofstadter argues that brain activity is hierarchical, producing levels. The base level is neuron activity, but this neuron activity is coordinated and comes directly from responses to external stimuli. Coordination of elements produces "higher-level" patterns, which themselves may be coordinated into even higher-level patterns. One higher-level activity produced from the relationship between external stimuli and neurons is *symbolizing*. Hofstadter calls symbols "the hardware realizations of concepts," which must be taken as real because symbols triggering other symbols "bears a relation to events in the real world — or in an imaginary world." Symbols allow for grouping of information that single neuron firing could not do (350). Another higher-level activity is categorization, or differentiating between *classes* and *instances* (351). As with symbolizing, categorizing involves grouping information that bears a relation to events in both the real world and imaginary ones, and so goes beyond what single neuron firing alone could do. Symbols and categories are overlapping patterns of neuron activity, during which one pattern stimulates another or several others, rather than one neuron stimulating another. Thus, when we are talking about thinking, we are talking about pattern interactions that can be expressed only in terms of symbols and categories, which is what philosophy is all about.

In more concrete terms, if "concrete" can apply to an imaginary world, it is wholly impracticable and beside the point to address how the Doctor thinks by trying to discuss neuron firings and brain functions. What we mean by "thinks" is the way that the Doctor uses symbols and categories.

Hofstadter calls the totality of neural patterns the "semantic network." This networking means that symbols and categories are never "on" or "off" in the way that neurons are either on or off. Each symbol has many ways that it may be activated, many "access points" rather than a singular in-out pathway. The number of symbol combinations and interactions is huge, occurring at multiple levels of the brain activity hierarchy. In a sense, as long as a brain is alive, that brain is always thinking. The huge number of symbol interactions also means that no two brains "think alike." There is no isomorphism (one-to-one mapping) of one semantic network to any other (Hofstadter 370–2). Instead, semantic networks are partly isomorphic, falling into a pattern with variations. Another way to think of it is that human semantic patterns, despite linguistic and cultural influences, are "globally" isomorphic, but not "locally" isomorphic. Hofstadter says that "the fact is that a large proportion of every human's network of symbols is *universal*" (376). At the level of thought, then, there are far more similarities between any two randomly selected people than there are differences. We tend to take the similarities so much for granted that the differences come to appear disproportionally large. The sum, however, is that human thought, the process of thinking, follows consistent and identifiable patterns that one can study, define, and explain in their own right entirely apart from the physical properties of the brain.

The concept of semantic networks helps explain why a new Doctor is not fully the same as a previous Doctor, and why each Doctor has distinct traits (apart from the fact that no two actors would play the role in exactly the same way). In the imaginary world of *Doctor Who*, it would be reasonable to ask why the Doctor's personality and thinking are not carried through from body to body. The answer would be that the regeneration process "shakes things up" in the brain, so that afterward the Doctor emerges with a slightly different semantic network than he had before the regeneration.

Types of Thinking

We have seen that there is a process called *thinking* that we can discuss in purely philosophical terms. The constituents of thinking are called *thoughts*, and *thought* is a category noun that applies both to any grouping of thoughts and the sum total of thoughts. We have suggested that there are multiple levels or types of thinking. So, the next step in this discussion is to categorize the types of thinking. Fortunately, in the early twentieth century, the American pragmatist philosopher John Dewey had already helpfully categorized the types of thinking.

Dewey identifies four ways in which the word "thought" is used. The first is "chance and idle thinking," defined as "that loose flux of casual and disconnected material that floats through our minds." Passing thoughts, daydreams, idle fancies, sudden recollections, all the random passing of things through the mind come under this first meaning of "thought." The second meaning of "thought" may be termed "imaginative thought." This sort of thinking refers to what people imagine to have happened, or can make up in imaginative stories. Such thought refers not to what is experienced, and does not aim at producing knowledge; instead, these thoughts enhance moods and rouse emotions. The third form of thought is what is popularly known as "belief." Such thoughts attempt truth statements about facts, and present themselves as "true." Yet these thoughts have few or no references to actual facts, and instead derive from tradition, "common knowledge," prejudice, and many similar sources. They are distinguished by the fact that the person who holds such a thought has not thought about the grounds on which it is based, but simply accepts the thought as "true." The fourth kind of thought, and the one that will most occupy the discussion to follow, is what Dewey calls "reflective thought." It goes by several names: logic, reason, critical thinking, contemplation, and so on. Its distinguishing characteristic is that such thoughts attempt truth statements about facts, but only after the thinker has considered the grounds for the belief and the consequences of it. Thus, this thinking produces reasoned conclusions, involving "active, persistent, and careful consideration" (Dewey 1–6).

Doctor Who provides multiple occasions for us to consider how reflective thinking works. In part, being a science fiction program, its very nature points viewers in this direction. That is, much of the plot of a typical *Doctor Who* story involves problems that require careful reasoning to solve. Such plotting rarely ends in the kind of ambiguity common in modern literature of the last century and a half. Instead, there is usually some kind of "answer" to the problem, and the answer comes only after considerable thinking about the problem.

We can take the plot of "The Ribos Operation" (1978) as a typical instance. In this story, the Doctor and his new companion Romana must track down a component of the Key to Time, which is disguised as a material object of some kind, and has special properties that impart the bearer with quasi-supernatural powers. Using a tracking device, they note two readings that indicate two locations, the second, more stable location being the planet Ribos, occupied by a medieval society. So far, the problem seems relatively simple, for the tracker will identify the correct object. However, the problem becomes complicated because the piece is locked inside a glass case containing the sacred relics of the planet, and can be in its disguised form any of the pieces inside this case. Numerous soldiers guard this case during the day and a large beast guards it at night. Furthermore, mixed in with these jewels is a large valuable stone called Jethryk, planted among the relics by a pair of con men using it to bait an interstellar tyrant into buying a planet the con men have no right to sell. So, the problem for the Doctor and Romana is to get to the jewels to find out which piece is the disguised segment to the Key of Time.

The resolution of the plot of "The Ribos Operation" comes down to a singular answer, one that can be rationally derived using Dewey's reflective thought, or what I call by the more common term used today, "critical thinking," about which there will be more to say later in this chapter. The first part of the problem is identifying which object is the disguised segment. Romana believes that the Great Crown of Ribos is the disguised segment because it is 9,000 years old and the natives believe that the wearer has the power to "call up the sun again at the end of each Ice Time." Since this folk belief sounds like the kind of power the segment might have, it seems a likely candidate for being the segment. However, the Doctor tells Romana, "Never jump to conclusions like that." Instead, the Doctor focuses his attention on the con men and not the jewels. His reasoning for this, which proves correct, is that he and Romana had taken two readings to find the segment, and each reading was different. This difference indicated that the segment had moved. Clearly, the Crown had not moved in centuries, perhaps millennia. The only object likely to have made a jump between planets was the Jethryk used to bait the con. The folk belief, it turns out, was not based on actual powers, and had Romana thought about the matter, in the sense of critical thinking, a little more, she would have realized that making the sun return at the end of the Ice Time is nothing more than the typical shamanic claim of being able to change the seasons and thus renew the world, a belief common to non-technological people such as the inhabitants of Ribos. "The Ribos Operation" is a simple example of how *Doctor Who* repeatedly demonstrates the process of critical thinking.

There are many more complicated issues to follow from this initial definition and demonstration of thinking. First of all, most problems in both *Doctor Who* and life in general are not as simple as that in "The Ribos Operation." We will need to look over the entire range of critical thinking, its components, its uses, and its advantages. Understanding of the totality of critical thinking will become very important in later discussions in this book, most especially when we consider science, ethics, and justice. Second, the answer to a problem is not necessarily the end of the whole matter. The goal of critical thinking is not merely to find immediate solutions to clearly defined problems, but is also to create meaning and to arrive at some understanding of truth. Therefore, we will need to consider both meaning and truth as fundamental to a better understanding of what knowledge is. Last, the means for conveying thought from one person to another is language. Thought probably does not happen entirely linguistically, but language is the only known way by which thoughts may transmit. Therefore, we must consider the role of language in the production of knowledge.

Meaning

Humans, like many species of animals, have thoughts, and "a thought is a logical picture of a fact" (Wittgenstein 5). Thus, thought always has a connection to the material world. "What is thinkable is also possible," says Wittgenstein (5). And where actuality and possibility connect, meaning lurks somewhere nearby.

If we were to enter the realm of pure thought, what might it be like? *Doctor Who* has a few times ventured into this territory, especially with regard to the "Matrix," which is a collection of Time Lord thoughts captured at the moment of death and used as a giant computer. This computer is thus a "thought machine." In two *Doctor Who* stories, "The Deadly Assassin" (1976), and "The Trial of a Timelord: The Ultimate Foe" (1986) the Doctor has actually entered the thought world created in this thought machine. In each case, the thought machine has been taken over and used by a Timelord, Chancellor Goth in the first story and the Valeyard in the second story. In the popular sense, the existence of this thought world would mean that "anything" is possible. As the Doctor says in the second story, "We're not dealing with reality." The Matrix is the place "where the only logic is that there is no logic."

However, this sense of total illogicality, of "anything goes," does not actually bear out. The problem is not merely a matter of limited production costs. It is a matter of the nature of thought itself. "You cannot speak as if reality is a one-dimensional concept," says the Valeyard, and he is right. Yet, that does not mean that it is possible to abandon reality even in pure thought, as Descartes stated in his *Meditation I*. It is not that "anything" is possible, but rather that "any thing is possible." In other words, we return to Wittgenstein's statement that a thought is a logical picture of a fact. These pictures can be true in the sense of agreeing with reality, or not true in the sense of disagreeing with reality, yet they still must be made from the things that exist and their interactions and changes (facts). Everything that exists in the thought world of the Matrix corresponds to (is a picture of) facts in existence. Whether these are a train, a swamp complete with swamp gas, poison, and so on in "The Deadly Assassin," or a Victorian factory with bureaucrats, a sea, poison gas that really is poisonous, and so on in "The Ultimate Foe," these things have their correspondences in reality and follow the logic of reality to some degree. To say that something is "possible" in thought is just to say that it has a potential to be true, but also a potential to be false. Thus, the Doctor's excursions into pure thought lead to the conclusion that thought is connected always to facts, and that thoughts exist on the possibility scale with "true" at one end and "false" at the other.

Broadly speaking, when someone connects material facts to thoughts about them, that person creates *meaning*. More specifically, the process of meaning "always consists in taking [objects and events] out of their apparent brute isolation as events, and finding them to be parts of some larger whole *suggested by them*, which, in turn *accounts for, explains, interprets them*; i.e., renders them significant" (Dewey 117–8). There are two types of understanding that are called *meaning*. One is direct knowledge of the thing, usually signified by applying a linguistic label to it: stone, Doctor, Timelord, TARDIS. Each label contains a realm of already known facts and signs. The other type of understanding involves conjoining different realms of direct meaning, usually through the process of careful critical thought, and expressed in sentences or groups of sentences. Whenever the Doctor says something like, "Of course, that means...," the viewer sees this second type of meaning. Thus, meaning in the first sense is applying what is already known or understood, while meaning in the second sense is discovering what had not been previously known or understood (Dewey 118–20).

Human Meaning

We can start with the fundamental problem that seems to be at the center of human endeavor — defining *human*. The problem of being human seems a strange problem. A cat knows how to be a cat. A toad has no difficulty understanding its toadness. Humans think of and account for themselves differently. They can do what, apparently, other living creatures cannot do, and that is to conceive of themselves in relationship to their surroundings, and not just exist in them. People each recognize their individuality. Thence come the theories.

There are the fundamentals, certain things absolutely clear about human existence. We have animal bodies with animal needs. These needs compel us to interact with the surroundings and the things in them so that they can help satisfy the needs. Humans are tool-making animals, and in this way *meaning* is determined by what is *useful*.

"Man is a political animal," says Aristotle, meaning a creature of the *polis*, of the city, from a time when cities generally contained a few thousand people or fewer, and a few large cities contained no more than a few hundred thousand. The human animal has communal needs, a desire and a place inside a society. In this way, *meaning* is determined by what is *social*.

As already mentioned, humans are symbol-making animals, seeing in one object the idea of some other object, act, or meaning. Without symbols, language and society and all that is consequent upon them would not happen. In this way, *meaning* is determined by what is *significant*.

The different types of meaning come about because humans have brains that perform exaggeratedly what many other animal brains do. Some animals can anticipate, but humans extend this ability to predicting. Some animals can remember, but humans extend this ability by writing, so that memory becomes thousands of years old. Many animals are curious, but humans extend curiosity beyond what is immediately around them and beyond what they might immediately gain from investigation. All these exaggerated animal mentations propel the human need to find knowledge and to make knowledge meaningful, yet none has as strong an influence as curiosity.

Curiosity

Humans are the only animals who retain the same level of curiosity, the same desire to explore, in adulthood as they had in childhood (D. Morris 130). According to zoologist Desmond Morris, the exploratory urge extends itself into the complex knowledge-making activities that help distinguish human behavior from that of other animals. Such activities as art, dance, music, writing, games, sports, even science, are extensions of infantile exploratory play patterns, done not merely as means to particular ends (such as fame and money), but for their own sakes as well. The function of heightened and extended exploratory play is "to provide us with as subtle and complex an awareness of the world around us, and of our own capacities in relation to it, as possible." In other words, humans are distinct in rejecting the conservative, territorial knowledge of other animals, even other primates. According to Morris, "What we acquire in this way can then be applied anywhere, at any time, in any context" (139).

Curiosity is not universally applied. Many people, perhaps even a slight majority, do not pursue their curiosity with much vigor. This is unfortunate, since the benefits of curiosity are overwhelmingly for the good. Curiosity increases awareness of problems and issues, keeps the mind dynamic, contributes to playfulness, and aids critical thinking (Ruggiero *Art* 161). John Dewey says that curiosity is the only true means for supplying material for meaningful thought. The "inert" mind merely waits for experiences to happen, but the curious mind actively seeks experience (Dewey 31).

Doctor Who affirms curiosity as a fundamental human virtue. In "Smith And Jones" (2007), the Doctor immediately chooses Martha Jones to aid him because rather than panic in a bad situation, she thinks and asks questions. In "The Keys of Marinus" (1964), when the Doctor is asked what he would most want in the world, he requests a well-equipped laboratory. The Doctor, of course, many times lets his tremendous curiosity lead him. Few characters in television have exhibited the level of curious fascination that the Doctor exhibits. For instance, in "Robot" (1974), the Doctor believes he has tricked a large killer robot to shut down. Though this robot had been trying to kill him, the Doctor now marvels at the ingenuity of its construction and immediately starts looking it over. It is a typical instance of the Doctor's almost compulsive habit of immediately studying and investigating whatever to him is novel or unexplained.

Of course, though acting on curiosity is the primary way to gain new knowledge and understanding, doing so can be dangerous. In the example from "Robot," the Doctor's fascination turns dangerous because the robot is only feigning deactivation, and immediately strikes him down. The old cliché that curiosity killed the cat may be old and may be a cliché, but it is often enough true to make curiosity a worrisome trait. Many of the Doctor's troubles would never have occurred had he not stopped to investigate this mystery or solve that problem.

However, mysteries would go unsolved and problems unfixed if no one sought to investigate them. "The seed of intellectual curiosity has to grow into a rugged tree to hold its own against the desires and fears, connotations and appetites, drives and interests, that inhabit the heart of man," says the modern Thomist philosopher Bernard Lonergan (285). If someone did not act upon the promptings of curiosity, very little would ever get better in general, and many things would become far worse. We are in a better position than our ancestors of old were largely because of the promptings of curiosity that drive the human species toward knowledge and improvement.

As stated earlier, *Doctor Who* repeatedly affirms the value of curiosity. Rarely does it go the "mad scientist" route, and even when it does, it is unusual that the program takes the old myth that there is knowledge best left undiscovered. "The Impossible Planet" (2006) tells of a group of investigators trapped in a decaying planetary base studying a black hole at absurdly close range. The Doctor calls this venture "brilliant" and human beings "amazing" even though for being on this venture they are, as he says, "completely mad." To study an unknown phenomenon, even when such study is perilous, is the brilliance of humanity's peculiar form of curiosity.

Language

Language is the means by which the promptings of curiosity and their resolutions become known to more than just the investigator, become "community property." The distinguishing characteristic of the human animal is language. In all other respects, humans are like other animals, though they may manage things more complicatedly than other animals. Language, though, is the differentiating characteristic. Language derives from the uniquely human ability to create *symbols*. Susanne K. Langer pointed out this distinction in her work, noting that all animals use *signs*, but only humans use symbols.

A sign is "anything that announces the existence or the imminence of some event, the presence of a thing or a person, or a change in state of affairs" ("Signs" 133). Dewey characterizes the matter typically well: "In the case of signs we care nothing for what they are in themselves, but everything for what they signify and represent" (171). Dewey notes that signification provides warrants for belief, and thus is the central factor of reflective (critical) thinking (8).

As Langer demonstrates, there is a second method of thinking in language, which is by using symbols. A symbol, unlike a sign, calls up the conception of the thing it means. This distinction does not lead to the conclusion that animals do not think, but rather that their thinking is much more limited than is human thinking. Animals may think *of* and *at* things, but they do not think *about* things ("Signs" 134).

Because of humans' symbol-making talent, people do not always react directly upon instinctual impulses. Rather, a person's reaction depends upon how that person conceives of the situation — as a moment for reflection, as a product of fate, as a manifestation of divine will, as part of the patterns of nature, and so on. Langer argues that humans must *construe* the events of their lives; they must *make* something of an event ("Signs" 135). The tool by which conceptions are moved from the experiencing mind into the physical world is language. All of human culture is possible only with language. The achievement of language is the ability to go beyond merely making signs by making physical representations of symbols and to place them into systematic constructions that are repositories of symbols. Language makes possible complex ratiocination. This ratiocination occurs mainly in sentences. "We use a sentence (spoken or written, etc.) as a projection of a possible fact" (Wittgenstein 5). We also use sentences, and not merely words, to make something of an event.

Sentences are more than just words. They are more than just collections of words, for "what constitutes a sentence is that its elements, the words, stand in a determinate relation to one another" (Wittgenstein 6). Neither is a sentence a collection of names. Only objects can be named, and the names of objects are therefore *signs*. Facts are relationships between objects, and therefore mere signs are themselves not enough to present our thought-pictures. Thus, to discuss facts, we need not just names, but also sentences, because "facts can be described but not named" (Wittgenstein 6). This is what we mean by speaking *about* objects. "Only sentences make sense; only in the context of a sentence does a name signify anything" (Wittgenstein 7). Thought has become inseparably bound to sentences in human mental processes. This bond has occurred because human thought has become direct communication, which means that the expression of one person's experience needs to correspond to the experience of another person's. Wittgenstein, whom I have been repeatedly quoting, states with characteristic succinctness: "A sentence that makes sense is a thought" (11).

As noted above, sentences provide the means for expressing one person's experience to another person. Sentences must do so according to rules for sentence-making on which both people agree. For humans, this process happens on the large, communal scale, so that "the totality of sentences is the language" (Wittgenstein 11).

The totality of language has greatly expanded what is possible with sentences. Eventually, someone had to start thinking that there must be a way to separate sentences that are true in the sense of describing accurately some actual piece of reality from sentences that are not true in this sense. Thus, philosophy and science were needed to make these separations. Sentences, as pictures of reality and our conceptions of reality, are either true or false. "The totality of true sentences is the whole of natural science" (Wittgenstein 15).

The Doctor is a great user of language, often the most eloquent character in any story. A sample of the Doctor's lines would probably reveal that about 50 percent of his dialogue involves explanations. Viewers see in these explanations the full symbolizing power of language in action. He makes sense of the perplexing events that baffle the other characters and the audience.

It is not surprising, therefore, that the Doctor is a scientist. If the totality of true sentences is the whole of natural science, as Wittgenstein maintains, then who better than a scientific polymath to separate the true from the false in the fictional world of *Doctor Who*? Because science is dedicated to the formulation of true statements, audiences see the Doctor as scientist possessing *truth* in the sense of an ability to create true statements about the universe *as it is*. Of necessity, then, the Doctor often symbolizes *reason*, the ability of using language to formulate new truths based upon previously established truths.

Reason and Knowledge

Philosophically, civilization takes a giant leap forward when *reason* is recognized as a fundamental human capacity and a good in itself. As far as we know, this recognition of reason's qualities first occurred in ancient Greece. Ancient Greeks, especially the Ionian Greeks, are unusual in the degree of intellectual curiosity deemed acceptable and even encouraged by the society of the time as compared to other civilizations in and around the Mediterranean. Many of the early philosophers contended that *reason* was a common possession of humanity that superseded all divisions between people and peoples. Democritus and Socrates held such views, and even more "conservative" philosophers such as Plato and Aristotle expressed the idea that no matter their divisions, people were united in having the ability to reason (Ibn Warraq 100–1). The Greek philosophies most influential and prevalent in pre–Christian Rome, Stoicism begun by Zeno of Citium and Epicureanism founded by Epicurus, likewise asserted the power of reason as a singularly important characteristic of human *being*. Such ideas can be found in the writings of the leading Roman exponents of these philosophies, Cicero the Stoic and Lucretius the Epicurean.

However, as Rome fell and the Dark Ages began, the valuing of human reason all but disappeared in the West, despite widespread popularity among the literate of the neo–Platonist Christian philosophers Augustine and Boethius. While popular history contends that nothing of intellectual importance happened between the middle 500s and the Italian Renaissance, in fact there was some intellectual activity that would help to make the Italian Renaissance possible.

A key moment prefiguring the Renaissance was the rediscovery of Plato's *Timaeus* in the later Middle Ages (Ibn Warraq 129). At the time, all matters philosophical were also matters theological, so that arguments in favor of reason and humanism were always placed in religious terms and took place within the doctrinal controversies of the time. The predominant mode of philosophy in the Dark and Middle Ages principally involved religious matters characterized by scholasticism, the belief that everything important had already been said and that all that was left to the learned was to work on pure understanding of a set of accepted texts. However, in the eleventh and twelfth centuries, a counter-movement took shape focusing on Plato's method of dialectic, of questioning and talking out a proposition rather than accepting it on authority. In the early 1000s, Berengar of Tours declared that reason was a better method of arriving at truth than was authority.[2] Other important thinkers of the period restated and clarified Berengar's idea that reason was the godly part of the human being. John of Salisbury in the 1100s called reason "the mother, nurse, and guardian of knowledge, as well as of virtue" (11). He further states, echoing Aristotle, that "man is superior to other living beings in dignity because of his powers of speech and reason" (27).[3] Ibn Warraq summarizes and quotes from a list of other noteworthy thinkers of this period who plainly argued that the world is rationally organized, that humans are endowed with the power of ratiocination, that reason is a superior virtue and divine gift, and that reason should be used to understand the rational order of the world (128–32).

The ideas of the medieval philosophers mentioned above would eventually become the dominant mode of Western thought once the Renaissance itself got fully under way in the 1400s, especially among those philosophers called the first Humanists. These philosophers called their studies "humanism" because they focused on human understanding and human nature. The philosophers Thomas More and Erasmus became prominent figures in the attempts to take the rediscovered classics of Rome and Greece and use them to move philosophy forward.

The historical development of ideas about reason aids in understanding how a modern Humanist view of human mental capacity came about. Before proceeding further, it was important to establish that (1) humans have reason; (2) reason has its own virtue and value; and (3) reason is the principal tool for acquiring knowledge. The third point needs explaining. *Knowledge* in the context of this work does not mean the collection of facts or data, but of collecting and using facts to derive new understandings.

An important step in this thinking about how knowledge comes about was taken in the late 1700s by the Scots philosopher David Hume in *An Enquiry Concerning Human Understanding*. Hume continues from John Locke's *An Essay Concerning Human Understanding* (1689). Locke shows that "ideas" come from either *sensation* (experience) or *reflection* (reason) or a combination of the two (Locke *Essay* 59–60). Thus, ideas are not, as Plato claims, ideals existing in a perfect realm of which reality is but a pale shadow. For Locke at the beginning of the Enlightenment, reality is primary, and ideas must be derived or discovered from living in the real world. Hume accepts Locke's view that ideas derive from living in the material world. Hume saw knowledge as having two sources that work together, which he called *Reason* and *Custom*. By Custom, or Habit, Hume refers to the drawing of a conclusion from *experience*. This experience is what most people mistakenly call cause and effect. When a person sees that event B happens after every instance of event A, then the person concludes by the principle of custom that the next time A occurs, B will follow, because experience has shown that always to be the case. Hume states that drawing conclusions by custom make experience "useful" and prevents ignorance of matters of fact. Hume calls *Belief* the anticipation that B this time will follow A this time because B has always followed A. However, Hume also points out that this manner of drawing conclusions is faulty reasoning, by which he means not that the belief is always wrong, but that it is not justified with absolute certainty because the future is never

100 percent certain. Reason starts from the recognition that every instance is unique. Thus, though B always happens after A, there is no *necessary reason* for B to follow A the next time A happens. Knowledge drawn from *Reason* occurs only when one can draw the same conclusion from every instance of A, that B is a *necessary* property or consequence of A. The difference is that there is always some amount of uncertainty in drawing conclusions by Custom, but no uncertainty when drawing conclusions by Reason (Hume 27–31).

An example of what Hume means by custom as separate from reason occurs in the episode "Dalek" (2005). Near the end, the Doctor has chased down a Dalek that seems to be holding his companion hostage and seems to be on the path to widespread destruction. The Doctor concludes this about the Dalek from custom because in his experience a Dalek is always a Dalek and thus any Dalek will act as all others act. In this instance, the Doctor mistakes custom for reason. The Doctor has not perceived a change in the Dalek brought about by its contact with the Doctor's companion Rose. Through this instance, one can see that custom, though generally reliable, is not always an accurate predictor.

This incident in "Dalek" reminds us that the Doctor is fallible, and that we are fallible in the same way. We are prone to act upon what we assume to be true. Reason works when one takes the humble approach to knowledge. Intellectual humility involves admitting when one does not know something, and in knowing that one can be wrong in almost any circumstance. Being reasonable means accepting new understanding when new or falsifying information comes to light. In "Dalek," the Doctor is ready to destroy the Dalek, but does not when Rose shows him that this Dalek is different. Though it goes against all his previous knowledge, every prejudice against Daleks that he has, and the emotional force of the memory of all the people Daleks have killed, the Doctor has the strength to say that he was wrong.

Audiences repeatedly see the Doctor as problem solver, and usually this problem solving involves the use of reason to work out the correct conclusion. At the end of "The Satan Pit" (2006), the audience can see the Doctor working through the information he has to determine whether the monster chained and growling before him is "the Devil" and what its plans have been. The audience follows the Doctor as he works through a series of if-then statements to conclude that this beast is probably not "the Devil" and that it is using another person's body to escape. The audience can see that this sort of reasoning is impossible without the language that allows for coherent strings of hypotheses and conclusions, as the Doctor must talk through the reasoning even when he is talking only to himself. This example from "The Satan Pit" is but one, and audiences can see similar instances of pure reasoning happening in "The Dalek Invasion of Earth" (1964), when he works out the Daleks' plan to mine the

Earth's core, "The Leisure Hive" (1980), when he figures out that Pangol is created and not born, and "The Twin Dilemma" (1984), when he works out Mestor's plan to colonize other worlds. These are just a few examples of how the show demonstrates the value of systematic, step-by-step ratiocination.

Unreason and False Knowledge

Given the above arguments about how knowledge is acquired, it must be admitted that people are stubborn and often refuse or fail to use their reasoning abilities to draw true conclusions. It could have been very easy for the Doctor to give in, to act upon *belief* as Hume defines it, to kill the Dalek in "Dalek" and satisfy his emotional mentality.

When we cling to ideas no matter what, we are self-deceived. The conditions for self-deception involve treating data in a motivationally biased way such that even when data provide greater warrant to believe a contrary or different conclusion, we still cling to the old belief (Mele 50–1; Williston 70). The method of justifying a self-deception can be that the desire that a belief be true is greater than the desire for Truth itself (personal bias). The method can also be a misinterpretation of the data against a belief (erroneous judgment). Another method is selecting only data for a belief or only the weak data against the belief as pertinent to the issue (selection bias). The Doctor in "Dalek" could have acted from personal bias and justified it using a selection bias, namely acted upon the conviction that a Dalek is always a "Dalek" despite appearances.

It also does no good to deny entirely the input from the senses. Such denial is another form of self-deception. Yes, the sensory organs may be deceived in any manner of way, by the refraction of light, by "smoke and mirrors," by apparent similarities, and so on. And yes, the brain is not in any sense a perfect and reliable recorder of sensory input. Yet, all these facts indicate only that one cannot rely upon the senses *alone* in order to determine truth. The reasoning mind is an aid that puts sensory data in context and makes "sense" of them (Hume *Enquiry* 104).

One can see in many *Doctor Who* episodes how the senses may be fooled, leading to erroneous judgment. In "Full Circle" (1980), the people called the Terradonians believe themselves to be descendants of the survivors of a starliner crash, and that the Marsh Men, as they call humanoid-amphibians who rise up to attack them every so often, are indigenous life seeking to destroy the Terradonians. Because Marsh Men do not much look like Terradonians, they fail to see that in fact the Terradionians are evolved Marsh Men. Another example comes from "Frontier in Space" (1973), which involves a plot to set the human space empire against the Draconian space empire through the use of a sonic device that makes humans see someone else as Draconians. Using this device, the Master can stage raids against human ships and make it appear that the Draconians are behind the raids.

The examples just described show the ease by which people fall into wrong beliefs. Let us classify and then exemplify various forms of wrong belief, using philosophers of old as guides. In the 1600s, Francis Bacon famously identified four "illusions" or "idols" of the mind that lead to erroneous judgment. These are idols of the tribe, idols of the cave, idols of the marketplace, and idols of the theater. Idols of the tribe are based upon what is natural to the human. It is the false belief that what is perceived is always true, and that one's judgment is infallible. Idols of the cave are errors that each person makes based solely upon his or her experience, the "it happened to me, so it is universally true" argument. Idols of the marketplace are common misunderstandings arising from human discourse. When one believes rumors, innuendos, the popular media, gossip, and so forth, one is succumbing to the illusions of the marketplace. Idols of the theater are false philosophical systems, believed on the basis of authority and tradition rather than on fact (Bacon 40–2).

Idols of the tribe occur fairly regularly. If people could not trust their senses and judgment, civilization would not be possible. Such trust becomes an illusion only when the trust is absolute. Numerous characters in *Doctor Who* die from believing that what they see and hear is real when it is not, or that something is what it appears to be. A less extreme example is in "Four to Doomsday" (1982), when the Doctor's companion, Adric, trusts the Obankan leader Monarch because Monarch appears to be wise, reasonable, and scientifically advanced. Of course, Monarch is in fact a tyrant with delusions of grandeur.

Idols of the cave happen to everyone, even the best of people. When Bacon says "cave" he is using the term metaphorically, arguing that often people live in the "cave" of their experience and prefer not to be aware of what happens outside the cave. An example is the character of Professor Hayter in "Time-Flight" (1982). Concorde aircraft have been hijacked and taken back in time. The passengers and crew are subjected to a powerful mental influence that forces them to labor on tearing down a wall while making them believe that they are still flying and performing their normal duties. Professor Hayter, an expert in hypnosis, was able to resist the mental influence, but not his own prejudices. Unable to accept the evidence of something beyond his experience, he firmly and wrongly believes that he and the other passengers aboard the plane were taken to the Soviet Union, Siberia to be exact. The Professor does come round about halfway into the program, but only after considerable amounts of evidence contradict his rather weak rationalizations for maintaining his belief.

Numerous instances exist of idols of the marketplace, but an easy example comes from "The Trial of a Timelord: The Mysterious Planet" (1986). In an underground habitat, the survivors of a fireball that wiped out most life on the Earth live under the control of a robot, whom they call "The Immortal." This robot conducts a series of tests to find the two cleverest youths, who will then serve him. However, the people in the station do not know what actually happens to the youths, and believe that the Immortal "eats" them. The Doctor replies to this statement, "Never believe what is said ... only what you know."

An example of an idol of the theater comes from "Genesis of the Daleks" (1975). The Doctor and his companions have arrived on the planet Skaro and are thus aliens. When the Kaled chief security officer Nyder questions the Doctor and he says that they are aliens, Nyder responds that Davros, the Kaled chief scientist, has stated that there can be no life on other worlds. When the Doctor challenges this statement, Nyder responds, "Davros is never wrong about anything." Nyder thus clings to a false philosophical system based solely on authority — Davros says it, so it must be true.

Later in the 1600s than Bacon, John Locke identified some further ways in which thinking can go astray, identifying them as types of personalities. The first kind of non-rational thinkers Locke notes are those people who "seldom reason at all." Such people are constantly following the examples of others and repeat whatever idea or fashion is directly in front of them. They are followers, perfectly willing to let others do their thinking for them. The second kind of non-rational thinkers are "those who put passion in the place of reason." Such people adhere to a singular belief set, repeating the platitudes and clichés belonging to that belief set, and stubbornly refuse to be reasoned or counseled. The third kind of non-rational thinkers are the shortsighted. Locke notes that everyone is prone to shortsightedness at some time or another, but some people believe in "reason" and believe themselves "reasonable" when they repeatedly leap to conclusions without obtaining all the relevant facts (*Conduct* section 3). Such non-rational thinking occurs, according to Locke, when people take heed of dogmatic principles, "that part of our knowledge which we have embraced, and continue to look on as principles." As Locke sees it, "The reverence borne to these principles is so great, and their authority so paramount to all other, that the testimony not only of other men, but the evidence of our own senses, are often rejected when they offer to vouch any thing contrary to these established rules" (*Essay* 601–2). Non-rational thinking also occurs from simple closed-mindedness, which often comes from the belief that one's person or reputation is at stake if one's beliefs are contradicted (*Essay* 602–3). A further source of non-rational thinking is a person's passions and appetites. Often, people cannot accept those things that would deny them what they want, so they rationalize their self-interest and justify in a mockery of reason whatever suits their beliefs (*Essay* 603–4). The last source of non-rational thinking Locke identifies is authority, "the giving up our assent to the common received opinions, either of our friends or party, neighborhood or country" (*Essay* 606).

An example in *Doctor Who* of a non-rational thinker who seldom reasons at all is the aforementioned Nyder from "Genesis of the Daleks." Nyder's unswerving loyalty to Davros leads him to reject irrefutable evidence and never question the ethicality of what Davros does. When Davros plans to destroy his own people, Nyder asks, "You would go that far?" Davros replies, "Did you ever doubt it?" This reply demonstrates the unreasoning commitment Nyder has to ideas and values not of his own making.

Examples of those who would put passion in place of reason are common in *Doctor Who*. One example comes from "Planet of the Spiders" (1974). The giant mutated spider calling herself the Great One plans to use a device that will amplify her will until it encompasses the entire universe. Refusing to believe the Doctor that the device will cause a positive feedback loop that will consume her mind, the Great One activates the device. The Great One exhibits non-rational thinking not strictly because she does not believe the Doctor, but because her description of what she thinks will happen actually corresponds to a positive feedback loop. However, the Great One is so entranced by her own ideas and desires that she does not recognize the problem and ignores the evidence.

Plenty of examples also exist in *Doctor Who* of shortsighted non-rational thinkers. Companions are often leaping to conclusions. We noted earlier how Romana in "The Ribos Operation" uses some reasoning to arrive at a wrong conclusion about the identity of the segment of the Key to Time that they were looking for. Another example comes from "Logopolis" (1981), when Adric wrongly assumes that the mysterious figure in white watching him and the Doctor is the Doctor's arch-enemy, the Master. While there are some grounds for this belief, they are not sufficient grounds to warrant the conclusion.

There are many other ways to describe how thinking can go wrong. The most important lessons to get from these descriptions involve identifying the sources of bad judgment and false knowledge. These sources are egocentric thinking (false justification of what suits one's beliefs and desires), sociocentric thinking (false belief in the collective wisdom of groups such as nations, regions, religions, organizations, families, and traditions), over-reliance upon authority (false belief that an authoritative or powerful individual is never wrong), and assigning emotion a higher place than reason (false belief that *feeling* defines "human" and is more "genuine" than reasoning).

Skepticism

Overcoming idols of the mind, egocentric thinking, and other sources of poor judgment leads people significantly closer to truth. Human intellect has created tools for recognizing bad thinking and for increasing good thinking. Using the tools of experience, curiosity, language, and reason, humanity has created the arts, sciences, and philosophy.

The humanist conception of Truth, or at least of the search for it, derives from the precepts stated above, of eschewing bad thinking and of using the arts, sciences, and philosophy to find truth. Putting together these habits of mind creates *skepticism*. This skepticism is not to be taken as simply denying for the sake of denying. Nor is it the impossible task of ridding one's mind of all that one has learned or currently experienced, as Descartes claimed he did or as Buddhists seek to do. It does involve first ridding the mind of prejudices. Hume defines this sort of skepticism very well: "To begin with clear and self-evident principles, to advance by timorous and sure steps, to review frequently our conclusions, and examine accurately all their consequences; though by these means we shall make both a slow and a short progress in our systems; are the only methods, by which we can ever hope to reach truth, and attain a proper stability and certainty in our determinations" (103). This skepticism is not the radical skepticism of denying entirely either the input of the senses or the ability of reason to create understanding. Humanistic skepticism is a moderate skepticism that advises caution before deciding upon a conclusion.

The Doctor is just this sort of skeptic. When he cautions Romana in "The Ribos Operation" against leaping to conclusions, he demonstrates this skepticism. We have seen the Doctor using reason to solve problems, and reason is the skeptic's principle tool. The true skeptic avoids reaching conclusions without enough evidence to justify them.

The episode "The Keys of Marinus" contains an interesting exchange in which the Doctor admonishes an investigator to study Pyrrho, whom he claims to Ian to have met.[4] Pyrrho of Elis lived in the third century B.C.E. and founded one of the major schools of philosophy in ancient Greece, a generally materialist and skeptical outlook based upon three questions: (1) What are things by nature?, (2) How should one be disposed toward each thing?, and (3) What will be the outcome of the disposition one takes? The question of disposition is the central concern because in it one recognizes that attitude affects judgment, which then determines outcomes. The investigator whom the Doctor admonishes had seen Ian lying unconscious next to a dead body and thus assumed (disposed himself) that Ian had done the slaying. This disposition toward Ian's guilt instead of toward curiosity about the circumstances led to

Ian's arrest and conviction upon false charges, a bad consequence of an ill-chosen disposition. Pyrrho, as best as one can tell from the scant documentary evidence that exists, argued that senses are not trustworthy, so that one should not assume either that they lie or that they tell the truth, and so one should usually adopt an unopinionated position as a first response. The investigator did not adopt this neutral position, and so let both his senses and his judgment mislead him about the nature of the facts. Because of this bad attitude, the investigator "knew" Ian was guilty, but this knowledge was false.

Theories of Knowledge

Platonic theories of knowledge state that knowledge derives from apprehension of "higher" or "ideal" forms, while material objects are merely shadows or poor imitations of the ideal forms. We can call this a top-down theory of knowledge. Aristotle argues the reverse, that knowledge derives from apprehension of the material world, and it is from this "empirical" knowledge that one may intuit higher or ideal forms. We can call this a bottom-up theory of knowledge.

Theories of knowledge, of what it is and of how one acquires it, are in philosophy called epistemology. One of the major schools of Aristotelian epistemology is Thomism, derived from the philosophical works of Thomas Aquinas. A leading modern Thomist is Bernard J.F. Lonergan, who argues that Being itself is inextricably tied up in knowledge. According to Lonergan, being "is the objective of the pure desire to know" (348). This "notion" of being is "all-pervasive" because it involves all aspects of thinking and judging (356). The notion of being is prior to thinking (the act of applying the desire to know) and prior to judgment (the act of determining meaning). Since it is a desire, it is an orientation toward the objective of knowing, and its characteristics are intelligence and reasonableness, which Lonergan also calls rationality (354–5).

Kant, a different sort of metaphysician from the Thomists, argues that "pure reason" organizes and unifies data taken in by the senses and fits the data into *a priori* "categories." Such categories are roughly equivalent to Plato's ideal forms with the difference that the categories are not actual superior things occupying a heavenly realm.

On the other hand, existentialist philosophers of the late nineteenth and early twentieth centuries contended that "knowledge" is the active, intuitive mind of the perceiver, sometimes called a "subject," that projects itself onto the blankness of reality, or that calls reality into existence (Patka "Five" 26–7). Indeed, the existentialist view of knowledge is a kind of reformulation of that of the Sophists, a group of itinerant teachers for hire who nevertheless became a strong enough force in ancient Athenian thought and society that both Plato and Aristotle devote pages to impugning them. "Rejecting traditional religion as an explanation for natural phenomena, they evinced a special interest in human perceptions as the only source of knowledge in all fields, including nature, and emphasized the significance of language in constructing that knowledge" (Jarratt xviii). The belief that knowledge derives from personal experience revealed through the tools of language, especially rhetoric, completely contrasts with Plato's contention that knowledge is inferior material perception of superior ideal forms. It is no wonder that Plato had it in for the Sophists.

Doctor Who at various points entertains most of these theories of knowledge. However, the program fundamentally takes a humanist perspective on knowledge that derives from Enlightenment philosophy mixed with both the existentialist view of knowledge as what the individual perceiver discovers and the scientific method of learning about the world. The starting point for this is the maxim "our understanding of the world in which we live is fundamentally flawed." This statement by the financier and philanthropist George Soros derives from his studies with the philosopher Karl Popper, who proposed the model of the "open society" as the best solution for human social organization. Soros uses this statement to differentiate between social situations and natural phenomena (191). As we shall see in subsequent chapters, this is a key distinction for understanding the philosophy of *Doctor Who* in general and for distinguishing between the Doctor's outlook and those of his opponents.

In brief, the Doctor assumes the truth of flawed perception and proceeds from it. Thus, a typical story is also an exercise in gradual "correction" of initially flawed perceptions. The process mimics the scientific method by presuming that through observation, logic, and analysis people come to fuller understanding. The assumption accepts the existentialist belief in the centrality of the perceiving individual. The position necessarily leads to a view of limited cultural/moral relativism, since it starts from the proposition that one's own convictions and ideas may not be right and must constantly be checked against the ever-changing social reality.

The principle that Soros calls *radical fallibility* (from Latin *radix*, the root, and not meaning politically radical or anarchic) is the recognition that social reality directly involves thinking participants who influence events by being thinking participants (192–3). Thus, social reality is markedly different from natural reality, which follows fixed laws discoverable through scientific method. Social reality does not have fixed laws of the same kind, and attempts to establish these "laws" of society or politics or economics have universally failed because of it. Later in this book, I will discuss the flawed view that there are social "laws" that one can scientifically determine, a position that Popper calls *historicism* and one that almost inevitably leads to totalitarianism. At this point, it is sufficient to note that the Doctor's perspective is that of radical fallibility, not of historicism, and that generally speaking his opponents follow the latter philosophy.

The characteristics of radical fallibility are that since scientific knowledge is self-correcting and always subject to being falsified, it is always hypothetical and never 100 percent predictive. "Only testable generalizations qualify as science" (Soros 194). Soros observes, "There is bound to be some divergence between reality and our view of the world, and this divergence is itself part of reality" (192). In other words, one's perception is always implicated in whatever process is going on and full disentanglement to gain a fully objective perspective is impossible. One can come to a better understanding, but never to a complete one.

This latter conclusion differentiates existentialist/humanist relativism from the current vogue of *postmodernist* relativism, which assumes *absolute subjective relativism* and thus concludes that understanding of any kind is impossible. *Doctor Who* has so far avoided postmodernist relativism. The difference is that in postmodernist relativism, radical fallibility leads to the conclusion that because total knowledge of a given concept is impossible, no true knowledge of any kind can occur. In existentialist/humanist terms, though, radical fallibility simply means that *absolute certainty* is impossible. Understanding is corrected over time so that one may get closer to absolute certainty. However, one must remain humble before the facts. Total certainty cannot occur, and there must be room in theory for further correction. We can see from what I said about the "typical" pattern of a *Doctor Who* story that the program assumes an existentialist/humanist conception of understanding by demonstrating the process of correction.

When moved to the social realm (including the political, economic, and psychological), the principle of radical fallibility becomes more uncertain because the acts of perceiving, testing, corroborating, and falsifying affect whatever is under study. In *Doctor Who* terms, this is called *interference* or *involvement*. In "The Trial of a Timelord," this point is the central case against the Doctor. By being in a situation, he affects a situation. Pure observation from the inside cannot happen and entanglement is a necessary result. The only correction for a bad situation is, therefore, piecemeal interference (again borrowing from Popper) rather than global or total "solutions."

The Doctor is the piecemeal solver *par excellence*. His opponents tend to the global view and hence toward totalitarian solutions that become even worse problems than those they would resolve. Thus, *Doctor Who* constantly displays the difference between the best possible solution for a social problem and the ideal solution for that problem, with the Doctor consistently choosing the path of the best possible solution.

In terms of more general concepts to understand, especially what is broadly called "scientific" knowledge, we may add another dimension to a humanist perspective: wonder. According to physician and humanist writer Lawrence Rifkin, wonder is what prevents the humanist from concentrating overly much on the void between what we know and potential total knowledge (49). The problem is in understanding the nature of meaning. Does this gap or void signify lack of meaning? Looking at it as "lacking" creates the desire to fill the void, and such fills are products of the brand of wishful thinking known as "faith." On the contrary, a humanist view is that a meaning need not be meaningful *for all time*, that it need only be meaningful *now* (Rifkin 49). The result is not to approach the universe with awe and fear generated by "forever" meanings, but to approach the universe with wonder (Rifkin 50). This wonder is a form of appreciation of the larger view. In particular, it is an appreciation of existence itself: "To be conscious, to experience life as a human, to create our own meaning — these are unparalleled wonders" (Rifkin 50).

The Doctor certainly appreciates the universe and its inhabitants with wonder. He consistently pauses to marvel at this thing or that thing, to praise life for its own sake, to enjoy a newly found or newly formed meaning. His sensibility moves toward a bonding between the self and the other by realizing that both are part of the same reality, connected by the same wonder that is existence. There is no better way to unite with something than to understand it, and no better way to understand it than to appreciate it with scientifically-informed wonder. The more one knows about it, the more wonderful the thing becomes. Thus, the Doctor interacts with reality.

Critical Thinking

So far, we have identified the components of thought for producing knowledge as *Doctor Who* demonstrates them. To summarize, these are language, logic, an active and intuitive perceiver, radical fallibility, and a sense of wonder. Language is the tool for making meanings, which are statements about reality, using signs and symbols. Logic is the process of applied rational judgment, placing together meaningful statements to create new meanings. An active and intuitive perceiver uses his or her brain in curious contemplation of the ways of reality. Radical fallibility, or skepticism, is the assumption that meaningful statements ought not to be accepted as 100 percent certain. A sense of wonder motivates the perceiver in using the previously discussed tools. Putting all these components together, we arrive at *critical thinking*.

A leading contemporary theorist of critical thinking says that thinking is "purposeful mental activity over which we exercise some control" (Ruggiero *Art* 4). Such mental activity includes both conscious and unconscious components. What is often called intuition or "gut" feeling is really thinking at a level below conscious awareness. It is still directed to a purpose and the conscious mind still exercises control over the outcome. Typical goals for thought include solving problems, making decisions, developing understanding, and searching for meaning.

Good thinking requires intellectual work, but once that process starts it becomes relatively easy to maintain a high level of thinking (Paul and Elder 9). Gaining a command of the principles of critical thinking involves keeping these principles firmly in mind and then applying them to the circumstances of one's life (Paul and Elder 10). Becoming a thinker involves explicitly noticing what and how one is thinking and recognizing both the strengths and weaknesses of one's thinking (Paul and Elder 11).

Successful thought contains two components: factual knowledge and proficiency in thinking (Ruggiero *Art* 5). According to Paul and Elder, the "well-cultivated critical thinker" is able regularly to perform the following mental tasks:

- Raise and formulate vital questions and problems, using precise and clear language.
- Gather, assess, and effectively interpret relevant information.
- Come to well-reasoned conclusions and solutions, testing them against relevant criteria and standards.
- Think open-mindedly within alternative systems of thought.
- Communicate effectively solutions to complex problems [15].

The standards for assessing one's reasoning are Clarity, Relevance, Logicalness, Accuracy, Depth, Significance, Precision, Breadth, and Fairness (Paul and Elder 97–8).

Dewey, in talking about training children to become better thinkers, identifies characteristic traits, what we might call "habits of mind," that a good thinker, or in our terms a critical thinker, possesses. The first of these is ease or promptness of thinking. A critical thinker perceives problems to solve and connections to make faster than most other people. One should not suppose that ease of thinking by itself is an absolute indicator of quality thinking, nor that slowness is a certain sign of stupidity. Few people are "quick" on every subject, and most people are "quick" on subjects that interest them. Plus, many people possess other mental habits of critical thinkers and can be good critical thinkers without the need for being swift critical thinkers. In general, though, ease of thought tends to indicate what Dewey calls a "bright mind." The second habit of mind for the critical thinker is range, or breadth. The critical thinker tends to see connections well beyond the immediate problem or issue, and is better able to follow multiple courses of thought. The third habit of mind is depth or profundity. Critical thinkers are better able to see the difference between the significant and the meaningless. They are better able to get to the roots of the matter, and thus are more likely to produce significant, meaningful, and useful conclusions. Two additional characteristics are orderliness and continuity. That is, the critical thinker can organize courses of thought and make clear the connections, and the critical thinker is more likely to pursue a difficult matter to its conclusion. The critical thinker is not merely thinking for the sake of thinking, but is thinking to accomplish or produce something novel or useful (Dewey 34–41).

Following from Hume's definition of belief, several things can be said to clarify the fundamental processes of critical thinking. Hume, as we have seen, defined belief as the expectation of an effect based upon experience of common conjunctions between types of events. I hear the TARDIS noise and believe that the TARDIS will presently materialize, because I have experienced multiple instances in which TARDIS materialization followed from TARDIS noise. Even if I do not see the TARDIS actually materialize, I believe with certainty that it has materialized and I will find it soon enough. The critical thinker, however, pauses before accepting the belief as true. Something might prevent the TARDIS from materializing (which has happened), or something may sound like a TARDIS but not be one. Thus, if I am a critical thinker, I will hold judgment in abeyance until I can obtain the ocular proof of TARDIS materialization. According to Dewey, the process of critical thinking (what he calls reflective thinking) involves two steps: (1) a hesitation, perplexity, or doubt; and (2) an act of search or investigation for further facts to corroborate or falsify a belief (9). Thus, a situation in which there is some ambiguity gives rise to perplexity, which then demands a solution. All this means that "*the problem fixes the end of thought* and *the end controls the process of thinking*" (Dewey 11–2, italics in original).

Both recent psychological and neurophysiological research have led to the determination that the brain has two phases of thinking, a production phase and a judgment phase (Ruggiero *Art* 7). The production phase resembles what is popularly called creative thinking: developing ideas, solving problems, aesthetically exploring. The judgment phase resembles what is popularly called critical thinking: examining, analyzing, evaluating, and refining what has been done in the production phase.

Good thinkers are proficient in both phases. They produce multiple ideas and solutions to problems rather than just automatically acting upon the first idea that comes along. They take intellectual risks, consider alternative ideas, and imagine possibilities and implications. They take their time before coming to judgments, use and double-check logic, and actively attempt to eliminate prejudice, bias, and predisposition from the thinking process (Ruggiero *Art* 7–8).

Bad Thinking

Ruggiero identifies six habits that hinder thinking. These are:

1. The Mine-Is-Better Habit — the preference for "self-flattering errors" rather than for unpleasant truths.
2. Face Saving — defense mechanisms such as shifting the blame and rationalizing behavior so that a person can maintain his or her self-image despite truth to the contrary.
3. Resistance To Change — the habit of rejecting new ideas out of hand.
4. Conformity — going along with crowd opinion or fearing being considered different.
5. Stereotyping — extreme and irrational generalizing of people.
6. Self-Deception — ignoring unpleasant facts and altering memories to suit prejudice or self-definition.

All these habits are widespread and often nearly impossible to extricate once embedded in a person's mind (Ruggiero *Art* 46–53). The ideas above clearly relate to "unreason" discussed earlier in this chapter.

Creative Thinking

Ruggiero has identified five characteristics of creative people. Creative people are *dynamic* in that they like to keep their minds active. They are often playful with ideas. Creative people are *daring* because they do not accept matters on the basis of authority or tradition, but instead challenge conventional wisdom and face unpleasant truths. Creative people are *resourceful*, able to apply what materials are at hand, and knowing where to look for quality research elements. Creative people are *hardworking*, not merely resting on the promise of an idea. Creative people are *independent*, not needing the approval of others (Ruggiero *Art* 84–5).

In problem solving, creative people will do such things as take a novel approach, modify a process or system, invent, find new uses for existing things, improve things, and/or redefine a concept (Ruggiero *Art* 86–8). We find that, with the possible exception of inventing, the Doctor qualifies as a creative thinker in all the other categories.

The creative process itself has distinct stages that show that creativity comes from applied thinking and not from nature or inspiration. The stages are searching for challenges, expressing the problem or issue, investigating the problem or issue, and producing ideas (Ruggiero *Art* 88–90).

Travel Broadens the Mind

The Doctor as an example of a curious, creative, critical thinker, makes his companions into better thinkers, and because the companions often stand in for the audience, the Doctor indirectly teaches the audience as well how to think. The character of Donna Noble most dramatically illustrates the process. First appearing in "The Runaway Bride" (2006), Donna is a rather loud, irritating, and some might even say ignorant person. She does not keep up with facts on the news, disregards what does not fit her experience, and lacks self-awareness. When Donna reappears in "Partners in Crime" (2008), she has dramatically changed since her contact with the Doctor. Dissatisfied with her boring life of temp work and package holidays, Donna actively investigates mysterious occurrences on her own. As her time with the Doctor proceeds, Donna becomes more confident, more self-aware, and more attentive to problems and how to solve them. The change has become very dramatic by "The Doctor's Daughter" (2008). The example involves a set of numbers stamped onto plates on every level of a colony complex. Donna keeps track of these numbers, writing them down, eventually figuring out by relying on her skill as the "best temp in Chiswick" that the numbers are date stamps, a piece of information vital to the discovery of what went wrong on this colony. The Donna of "The Runaway Bride" would not have bothered with the problem, and would have spent the time shouting at the Doctor to take her home.[5]

The truth is that the Donna Noble of "The Runaway Bride" is a very ordinary person, stuck in being ordinary. And like too many ordinary people, she does not really use her intelligence to guide her through life. Too many people, like Donna, lack the example and training of truly good critical thinkers. Without this contact, such people, like Donna, react rather than act, address their problems emotionally rather than rationally, and repeatedly make poor judgments that leave them feeling victims of fate. They need exposure to good critical thinking so they can see how to take charge of their own mental lives. The *Doctor Who* example demonstrates the beneficial results from seeing how critical thinking is actually done.

Insight

We have seen how the process of critical and creative thinking operates. The question remaining is how they may be put together. In other words, what are the ingredients necessary for a demonstration of critical creative thought, of insight? The question is relevant partly because the Doctor is almost always the most insightful character in a given program. The reason for this is that the Doctor combines the necessary characteristics.

Isaac Asimov, in his usual clear, direct method, identifies five criteria for a "crazy idea," an insight. According to Asimov, a creative person is "(1) broadly educated, (2) intelligent, (3) intuitive, (4) courageous, and (5) lucky" (150). The Doctor, whose title comes from a doctorate degree specializing in thermodynamics,[6] also possesses tremendous knowledge in astrophysics, chemistry, history, literature, sociology, and philosophy; few could be said to be as broadly educated as that. The many demonstrations already given of the Doctor's intelligence certainly establish that trait. The Doctor is also intuitive, which enables him to choose the right path of inquiry. Courage is a necessary trait of an action-adventure hero. Finally, the Doctor is certainly lucky, at least in so far as improbable coincidences happen to him quite regularly. So, the Doctor has all the personality traits needed for the insights to come to him. The stories themselves require that the insights do come to him, but possessing the right traits makes his having the insights believable.

Conclusion

We may now conclude that in *Doctor Who* the main method of acquiring knowledge is *scientific naturalism*. Philosopher Paul Kurtz characterizes scientific naturalism as "looking to the sciences to understand nature" (*What* 26). Scientific naturalism involves a *materialist* understanding of the universe, which means that there is nothing but matter and energy, at least as far as understanding how the universe works. Scientific naturalism also involves a systemic understanding of the universe, which means that complex properties emerge from the ways that matter and energy organize.

Watching *Doctor Who*, viewers do not receive propaganda. The program does not tell its audience what to think. Instead, through the character of the Doctor, the program shows viewers how to think. The attitude is that knowledge is incomplete, that survival and happiness depend upon acquiring more knowledge, plus a fuller understanding of the universe and its complexities. The Doctor demonstrates that critical and creative thinking are the only means by which to acquire understanding and true knowledge.

CHAPTER 5

Archetypes and Mythology

Professor Rumford: The Cailleach? The Witch-Hag? That's only a legend.
Doctor: So was Troy till Professor Schliemann dug it up.
—"The Stones of Blood"

Myth Defined

"Myth," like many old words, has come to mean so many things that in ordinary conversation people may use the word, but no two use it in the same way. We often find ourselves at cross purposes when discussing myths because while I have one meaning in mind, the person to whom I am talking has another meaning. Further compounding the problem, I think that the other person is using my definition and she thinks I am using hers; or worse, each of us believes that the other is using the "wrong" definition.

Consider the many ways that "myth" may be used. The word derives from Greek *mythos*, meaning speech or story, and thus embodies the fact that the first myths were spoken. In our times, "myth" may mean a story about gods, which is how the literary critic Northrop Frye defines it (33). "Myth" may refer to a person or object thought to have mystical or supernatural characteristics. "Myth" may refer to a universal idea, which we shall see is more properly called an archetype. "Myth" may refer to a popular idea or cultural value, such as the "myth of the individual" in the United States. "Myth" may mean a widely held but false belief. Using this definition of myth as false belief and adding European linguistic theory to it, the semiotic literary critic Roland Barthes in 1957 stretched the definition of myth to be any set of associations attached to a sign (a unit of language either spoken, written, or gestured) used to convey or reinforce culturally accepted ideas.

Therefore, it will be important to specify just how one should use the word "myth." For the purpose of discussing *Doctor Who*, I will use the first two definitions of myth stated above, namely "a story about gods" and "a

96

person or object with supernatural qualities." Using "myth" this way, I will show how *Doctor Who* uses myths and the concept of myth, and I will prepare the ground for the discussion of religion in the next chapter.

The famous twentieth-century myth scholar Joseph Campbell identified four functions of myths. The first of these is "to waken and maintain in the individual a sense of wonder and participation in the mystery of this finally inscrutable universe." The second function is "to fill every particle and quarter of the current cosmological image with its measure of this mystical import." In other words, myths give meaning to whatever understanding a culture has of the way the universe works. The third function, according to Campbell, is "validating and maintaining whatever moral system and manner of life-customs may be peculiar to the local culture." The fourth function is "conducting individuals in harmony through the passages of human life" (*Historical* 8–9). To summarize, myth functions to give meaning and shape to the cosmos in terms an individual person can understand given his or her culture and historical setting.

The Thomist philosopher Bernard Lonergan holds that the "primary field" of myth consists of "affect-laden images and names." Images develop in a process from image as image to image as symbol to image as sign. This movement is the development of myths. The image as image contains those things sensed and experienced. Image as symbol stands in "correspondence with activities and elements on the intellectual level." Image as sign is linked with some interpretation that gives import to the image (533). Thus an image, such as that of a warrior, turns into a symbol, such as a representation of the tribe to which the warrior belongs, and then turns into a sign, such as the warrior's victory demonstrating the benevolence of the gods upon the people. Lonergan's explanation corresponds to Campbell's view that the principal method of mythology is analogy (*Historical* 9). Mythology links pieces of the universe by similarity, instead of explaining pieces of the universe by causality.

An example of this associative method comes in the *Doctor Who* story "The Stones of Blood" (1978), which centers on the Celtic goddess Cailleach. The Doctor is told that the Cailleach is goddess of war, death, and magic. In myths, a supernatural being is often a god *of* something, associating the deity with an idea. The Doctor is also told that the crow and raven are the Cailleach's "eyes." Being carrion birds, the crow and raven become naturally associated with death and thus by commutation with the Cailleach, goddess of death.

One can also see in various examples how believers of a mythology find structure, meaning, and purpose from the myths in which they believe. In "The Stones of Blood," the Cailleach's high priest, De Vries, finds a power and confidence through his belief that he would not have in the de-mythologized society of the 1970s in which he lives, represented by Professor

Rumford, who studies the mythology surrounding a stone circle instead of being part of the mythology. Within the mythological system that De Vries mentally occupies, everything "makes sense," even when to an outsider such as the Doctor belief in an ancient Celtic goddess makes no sense. It is apparent, then, that a myth's properties and effects are largely psychological, as Campbell, C.G. Jung, and others have argued.

Doctor Who and similar programs such as *Star Trek* and *The X-Files* exist in the de-mythologized modern world, and thus stand in an awkward relationship both to specific myths, and to myth as a concept. Myth becomes employed in distinct ways. One is as material for making stories. Another is as a subject for study. A third is as a set of symbolic properties demonstrating a very particular understanding of humanity, the universe, and how they fit together.

Science Fiction and Myth

The literary writer, says Frye, imposes the same recognizable mythic forms onto the content of his or her work, no matter what the mode of that work (63). The same process is at work in *Doctor Who*. As we will see, science fiction and *Doctor Who* are amenable to using and replaying myths and mythic elements. Individual stories in *Doctor Who* follow recognizable ancient patterns of mythic storytelling.

At least one school of thought is that science fiction itself is a kind of replacement myth. "For those sophisticated souls," says cultural historian William Irwin Thompson, "who are closed to religious imagery but have a strong faith in science and technology, a new way has been opened to the old truths of myth, and that is the way of science fiction" (37). Science fiction author and editor Ben Bova has said that science fiction corresponds to the four functions of mythology that Joseph Campbell postulates. Science fiction often relies on a "sense of wonder," which corresponds to Campbell's first function, the sense of awe about the universe. Science fiction generally upholds a scientific view of the universe and how it works, which corresponds to Campbell's second function, providing an explanatory system for the universe. Science fiction, as Bova characterizes it, "almost invariably backs a basic tenet of Western civilization ... the concept that the individual man is worth more than the organization — whatever that may be — and that nothing is more important than human freedom," which corresponds to Campbell's third function, supporting the social structure and ideology. Science fiction also appeals to the young and has gained a strongly loyal and dedicated fan base, which corresponds to Campbell's fourth function, supplying emotional support to the individual (Bova 10–1).

As science fiction, *Doctor Who* follows the functions of myth after the manner of Bova's description. Audiences get a taste of the "sense of wonder" common to science fiction through the Doctor's omnivorous curiosity. The sense of wonder was enhanced through the character of Wilfrid Mott, grandfather of the Doctor's companion Donna Noble. An amateur astronomer, Wilf finds exciting the idea of life on other worlds. Audiences see the scientific worldview upheld through the Doctor, a scientific generalist and admirer of scientific endeavor. Audiences also have their Western values validated through *Doctor Who*, which pushes hard the concept of individual freedom. Finally, *Doctor Who* is science fiction phenomenon that, like most of them, greatly appeals to the young and has a strongly dedicated, worldwide fan base. Thus, *Doctor Who* is a phenomenon of science fiction mythology. This phenomenon, though, is a complicated matter of multiple dimensions.

Using Mythic Material

The most basic relationship that a modern story has to myth is through borrowing. The writer takes elements from ancient stories and places them in a modern setting. James Joyce did this famously with his novel *Ulysses*, while William Faulkner took the tale of Jesus' last few days and set it in World War I in his novel *A Fable*. Science fiction writers find the magical elements of myths amenable to transformation. Roger Zelazny in *Lord of Light*, for instance, retells the genesis of Buddhism from Hinduism by placing it in the far future and supplying scientific rationales for such things as reincarnation and divine powers. Done well, such transformations spark our understanding of the mythic patterns operating on human experience.

David Rafer identifies several ways that *Doctor Who* contacts mythic material. One is the creation of a kind of mythic structure in the program itself. The Doctor's mysterious background makes part of the mythic structure. Most of it, though, comes from the Doctor's quasi-divine characterization (124), his superhuman abilities such as withstanding extremely cold temperatures, hypnotic powers, limited psionic abilities, mental control of metabolic functions, super-encyclopedic knowledge, and extreme intelligence.

Another mythic contact is through Roland Barthes' identification of myth with ideology (Rafer 124–5). This is the view that myths are explanatory systems that tame the more chaotic elements of reality, making the contingent seem eternal and historical outcomes seem natural (Barthes 142). The Doctor's power of regeneration, for example, makes the contingent (life) seem eternal. The story "The Reign of Terror" (1964) affirms the notion that history will always be what it was no matter what time travelers do in it, thus affirming a naturalistic cause-and-effect view of history.

Still another contact with myth in *Doctor Who* is the use of mythic patterning in narrative development. Rafer notes, for example, that the Doctor's own personal history corresponds to parts of Joseph Campbell's "monomyth," a grand narrative template that fits all heroic myths (125). Thus, the Doctor has clearly gone through a "separation" from home, heeded the "call to adventure," and undergone several "trials." Particular adventures, to be discussed in further detail below, follow this mythic pattern, as do the personal stories of some of the companions, notably Ace and Rose.

Another contact with myth occurs where mythic structures are a way of life. This is the point at which myth slides into religion, so the issue will be discussed in depth in the next chapter. For now, we can note a couple of points regarding myth as a way of life as it is portrayed in *Doctor Who*. The first point is that the program's ethos in general, based as it is on science, Enlightenment values, and humanist ethics, places the privileged point of view oppositional to the mythic/religious one. A case in point is "The Aztecs" (1964). Barbara, mistaken for a reincarnated priest, tries to use her status as "voice of the gods" to change Aztec civilization a century or so before it will be wiped out. Her main objection is the use of sacrifice in religious ceremonies. She fails in her quest because, as Ian says, she cannot fight a whole way of life. That it was wrong for her to try is clear. However, *that the whole way of life needed fixing* is also clear as it is presented in the story. Thus, a modern rationalist perspective is shown to be greatly superior to an ancient mythical perspective. The second point is that the Doctor's rationalist, scientific outlook is in all cases (with the notable exception of "Kinda" [1982]) shown to be better than the mythical outlook.

Additionally, *Doctor Who* contacts myth by building its own mythic system (Rafer 127–8). Viewers have gotten increasing amounts of information about the Doctor's background, though not about his personal history. The Time Lords, the nature of Gallifrey, the "dark times," and so on, gradually build up an "other realm" where "great things" happen that cause chaos, death, and generally apocalyptically scaled disaster when intruding upon the "ordinary" realm of mere human beings. This background provides a constant reference for new stories, allowing the setting of *Doctor Who* to become a kind of closed universe.

The most common contact *Doctor Who* has with mythic material is also the simplest and most easily recognized — borrowing it from other myths. Several stories self-consciously retell ancient, mainly Greek, myths by resetting them in a science fiction universe. *Doctor Who* also borrows from more recent cultural products that have gained mythic status. Thus, both *Frankenstein* and *The Mummy* get the *Doctor Who* treatment. Other stories borrow elements from myth and folklore, often "explaining" them in science fiction terms. Still others capture the "spirit" of myths and mythic systems, but do not retell myths.

Retelling Myths

Some *Doctor Who* stories take a well-known myth and recast it as science fiction. For example, "Underworld" (1978) retells the story of Jason and the Argonauts, renaming its elements so that Jason becomes Jackson, Hercules becomes Herrick, the Golden Fleece becomes the golden cylinders carrying the race banks of the Minyans, and so on. "The Horns of Nimon" (1979–80) retells the story of how Theseus conquered the Minotaur. As in "Underworld," characters are renamed: Theseus becomes Seth, Daedalus becomes Soldeed, the Minotaur becomes the Nimon. Similarly, details of the story receive a science-fictional spin. The annual tribute Athenians had to pay to Cretans becomes a powerful energy source called hymetusite, and the youths who bring it are not merely killed, but provide food for the Nimon. These transformations, though, are more clever than insightful.

A step up in use of mythic elements involves treating them as though real, and then "explaining" them in science-fictional terms. For instance, "The Stones Of Blood" features the Celtic goddess Cailleach[1] and ogres given the misleading names of Gog, Magog, and Ogros.[2] The goddess in the story is really a humanoid alien given special powers through a device she wears round her neck, and the ogres are really silicon-based lifeforms from the planet Ogros.

The story relies upon the myth and folklore of the British Isles to broaden its range of reference. The woman posing as the Cailleach calls herself Miss Fay, "fay" being an old word for sprite. The story's setting is a Neolithic stone circle. Such circles are common in Britain and popularly thought to have magical ancient properties. Miss Fay has some control over the crows and ravens, birds traditionally associated with the Cailleach. In addition to being the "old woman," the Cailleach is also called "the veiled one" (from a different Gaelic root) who brings winter and death. Miss Fay veils her identity through most of the story. Through giving rationalistic justifications for these elements of folklore, the story makes such elements palatable for the enlightenment-minded modern audience of *Doctor Who*.

"The Stones of Blood" and similar stories operate by rationalizing mythic elements. In "Underworld" and "The Horns of Nimon," the transformed story elements are analogous to the originals. However, in "Stones of Blood" the alien is not merely an analogue for the Cailleach, she really *is* the Cailleach. The theory in such stories is that the impetus for the myth is some part of the material universe unintelligible to primitive humanity, who then converts it into something that "makes sense" in their credulous, magical thinking. The theory in such a story derives from the "myth as bad explanation" view of mythology, and implies its more radical form, the "myth as bad science" view. However, such a theory of myth also derives from Arthur C. Clarke's famous dictum that a sufficiently advanced technology is indistinguishable from magic. Thus, if an escaped criminal named Cessair of Diplos comes to prehistoric Britain bearing a staff through which she can change shape and live practically forever, the local people are hardly likely to view the stick as a perfectly natural piece of technology, or her as a material and limited being.

Other stories offer similar explanations for mythic creations. In "The Dæmons" (1971), an alien that once landed on Earth hundreds of thousands of years in the past has been reawakened. This alien, a daemon from the planet Dæmos, and others of its kind have been pushing along human development as an experiment. They gave humanity both fire and the wheel and have been "coming and going ever since." One result of these visitations is that many powerful, masculine gods and demigods were created as a reaction to contact with the Dæmons. In the middle of the story, the Doctor presents a slideshow of various gods "with horns" to show the influence that these Dæmons have had on human imagination as well as human history.

In all the stories that borrow from existing mythological material, the mythical elements really are material and not much else. They have a use in giving a pretext for the plot and in providing ready-made plots and structures. By being turned into material, whatever imaginative or psychological power the myths themselves may have had now becomes only spectacle. Some *Doctor Who* stories, though, work with myth on a deeper, archetypal level.

Archetypes

The term "archetype" refers to certain "universal" symbols, those that appear in various guises repeatedly in stories, rituals, and dreams across cultures and historical periods. The archetypes symbolize the primal experiences of all people. The theory of archetypes received its first formal treatment in the writings of the psychoanalyst Carl Gustav Jung, still the most influential voice on the matter. Jung argues that the archetypes manifest the basic psychic matter that creates a personality. The archetypes are projections, images that one sees in myths, fables, fairy tales, rituals, and so on. The more fabulous the story, the more likely it is to involve archetypes.

In Jung's theory, there are fundamental pairs of archetypes that operate in each person, a conscious power and an unconscious one. The most primal pair is the ego/shadow. Ego is the balancing of the personality. According to Jung, "The ego is never more and never less than consciousness as a whole" (*Aion* 5). Its dark side is the shadow, the basic instincts and drives that the ego tries to hide. Jung says, "On this lower level with its uncontrolled or scarcely controlled emotions one behaves more or less like a primitive, who is not only the passive victim of his affects but also singularly incapable of moral judgment" (*Aion* 9). However, the shadow is not always evil, and each person needs it for survival.

The next pair is persona/soul. The persona is the conscious mask that people use to negotiate their way through the world. Jung divides the soul into two types — the anima, which is the female part of the male personality; and the animus, which is the male part of the female personality (*Aion* 10). Each person contains some aspects of both the anima and animus; thus, Jung calls this pair the *syzygy*, since they are inseparable. The anima seeks connectedness. Its positive properties are tenderness, forgiveness, patience, and compassion, while its negative properties are moodiness, vanity, and oversensitivity. The animus seeks knowledge. Its positive properties are assertiveness, control, and ratiocination, while its negative properties are dominance, ruthlessness, and prejudice.

These archetypes combine to produce the *self*, the archetype of wholeness and totality, the square formed by the four aspects of the personality. As Jung postulates it, all other archetypes, such as the Trickster, the Princess, the Magician, the Devouring Mother, etc., are projections of one of the four primary archetypes.

Archetypes in *Doctor Who*

It is the nature of fantastical tales, such as the various adventures of *Doctor Who*, to present a self in action, split into various manifestations of its personality. For example, the original crew of the TARDIS is four, the square that represents the personality. While archetypal roles switch somewhat based upon need, in most cases the four correlate to the primary archetypes as follows: The Doctor (ego/shadow), Susan (anima/shadow), Ian (animus), Barbara (ego/anima). When the Doctor is the shadow, Barbara becomes the ego, and when the Doctor becomes the ego, Barbara becomes the anima while Susan becomes the shadow.

One can most strongly see this interplay of primary archetypes in "The Edge of Destruction" (1964). This story involves only the four cast members, trapped in the TARDIS. The TARDIS is trying to warn them of impending disaster and affects their minds in the process, so that much of the civilized polish is rubbed off. Through most of the story the Doctor takes the shadow aspect. He distrusts the others, threatens Ian and Barbara, and even drugs them. Susan modulates between anima and shadow, being vulnerable and emotional, but also accusatory and distrustful. At one point, her shadow self comes out fully when she grabs a pair of scissors, threatens Barbara with them, and then violently attacks a chair with them. Ian remains the animus, approaching the situation through both rational logic and by directly confronting the Doctor. Barbara provides the unifying elements, having some aspects of the anima, but most often acting as the central ego. It is Barbara, when challenged with annihilation, who proves her value by setting the Doctor on the right path to solving the problem. Barbara is always sympathetic to the others, and is the one most emotionally hurt by the disharmony among the crew members. In a sense, the TARDIS in this story becomes the "head" in which the four aspects of the personality enact a psychodrama.

"The Edge of Destruction" shows that this original TARDIS crew is the best configuration for demonstrating the idea that in storytelling of a fabulous nature, the various characters combine into a single personality. Such stories are psychodramas according to both Freud and Jung, and symbolize the dynamics of the individual personality. Since the personality in question is almost always the "hero" of the fabulous psychodrama, we may call the self in question by that hero's name. Thus, in the first season of *Doctor Who*, the Doctor, Susan, Barbara, and Ian combine to become the self called "Doctor Who."

The Doctor, as a combination of ego, shadow, and sometimes animus (Doctors 3, 4, 5, 6, 9, and 10), represents another common archetype, the artist-scientist, sometimes called the Magician. The artist-scientist, according to Campbell, "is the hero of the way of thought — singlehearted, courageous, and full of faith that the truth, as he finds it, shall make us free" (*Hero* 24). One sees in the Doctor's actions the impulse to discover and use parts of the material world.

However, the Doctor may shift into other archetypes. A common one for the Doctor is the Trickster (Rafer 124). The Trickster is the inverse of the Magician, each the shadow of the other. The Trickster combines high culture polish with childlike curiosity, and may freely move between the rational and irrational. In combining extremes, the Trickster upends convention and tradition, deflates pompousness, defuses social tension, and brings leaders down a little from their high perches. The dark side of the Trickster can be chaos for its own sake, as well as lies and deception as a way of life. The Trickster is able to change shape (Jung *Four* 136), like the Doctor does through regeneration. Also like the Doctor, the Trickster "approximates" the figure of a savior (Jung *Four* 135).

The connection of the Trickster to the Doctor is obvious in many places throughout the series. In "The Romans" (1965), the audience gets the spectacle of the elderly Doctor besting a bigger, younger Roman assassin. The Doctor laments that he has become so used to outwitting his opponents, that he had forgotten the joys of "the gentle art of fisticuffs." The second Doctor, called "Chaplinesque," often sets off a chaotic furor the moment he enters a room, and his first incarnation calls him a "clown" in "The Three Doctors" (1972–3). The third Doctor spends part of one story, "The Green Death" (1973), in drag. The fourth Doctor became famous for his incongruous behavior, sudden fascination with trivia, and confrontations of dangerous enemies by offering them jelly babies. The fifth Doctor gets called an "idiot" in "Kinda." The sixth Doctor wears garish, mismatched, piebald clothing. The seventh Doctor began in his first season as very similar to the second Doctor, generally causing chaos and playing mix and match with aphorisms. The next three Doctors have not shown much of this Trickster aspect, with the new producers playing up the Doctor's romantic and heroic aspects. The eleventh Doctor brings back some of the trickster characteristics. With his thoughts often running far ahead of his actions, this Doctor can at times appear clumsy, and often out of touch with social norms.

The Doctor's companions always work archetypally, even when producers consciously choose them for modern and realistic reasons. Most of the companions have been female, and most fit into a recognizable role. The simple formula, as Tulloch and Alvarado devise it, is female companion = intuition, Doctor = reason (213). The result of the formula is that female companions who have been originally written as extraordinary in some way, often degenerate into screamers. Zoe (1968–9) was originally conceived as a kind of human computer, but that did not last long. Jo (1971–3) was more consistently like the hip and independent young woman of the 1970s, but she was still scatterbrained and emotional. Sarah (1974–6) was the "women's lib" companion, and being a journalist she was meant to recognize the entry of women into professions. In her case, there was more consistency regarding the character, due in large part to the acting skill of Elisabeth Sladen, which has made Sarah one of the most popular of the companions. Nevertheless, many of the old "dependent female" characteristics slipped into stories late in her run. Two later companions, Peri (1984–6) and Mel (1986–7), brought back some of the old dependent female stereotypes. Mel in particular screamed her way through many episodes. Ace (1987–9), Rose (2005–6), Martha (2007), and Amy (2010–1), however, were standout examples of companions who preserved their throats and faced danger in an often traditionally "masculine" way. Even so, though neither Ace nor Rose is prone to screaming, both are highly "emotional" and so preserve the archetypal formula. Other companions have done some screaming, but have been unfairly criticized for screaming. While Victoria (1967–8) and Zoe, in particular, had to produce some unrealistically wild, hysterical screaming, Sarah's "screams" were more like panicked yelps of the kind naturally produced in such circumstances. There are few who would not make some noise after being temporarily blinded and then rolled down a flight of stairs. The issue of screaming is important because it symbolizes the degree to which the characters are traditionally feminized.

The one consistent exception to the intuitive female archetype among the companions was Romana I (1978–9). Played by the strikingly regal Mary Tamm, often dressed in white, and when not dressed in white still wearing severe and aristocratic garments, Romana I was fashioned out of a different female archetype, the "Ice Queen." Cool (naturally for an Ice Queen), intellectual, and ironic, Romana I became almost a female Doctor, lacking only the Doctor's vast experience and considerable skills of situational improvisation. However, after her regeneration into Romana II, things returned to form a little. Played by the more waif-like and vulnerable Lalla Ward, Romana II gets swiftly brought down from the regal position of Romana I in her first story, "Destiny of the Daleks" (1979), when under interrogation by the Daleks she panics and screams. Though neither panicking nor screaming would become habitual with Romana II, she is by comparison with both Romana I and the Doctor a more emotional character.

It is not as though the writers and producers of *Doctor Who* are unaware of the archetypal formulae operating in the series. "The Dæmons," for example, opens with a discussion between the Doctor and Jo about magic, the supernatural, and the "age of Aquarius." While Jo wants to believe in such things, and at one point later in the story is convinced that people really saw the Devil, the Doctor despairs that he will never turn Jo into a scientist. The five-minute exchange early in the story establishes the archetypal roles.

One of the sources for female archetypes becoming female stereotypes is that the stories often require a companion brave enough to go adventuring through the universe, but also vulnerable enough to need regular rescuing, and so companions are prone to a "traditional" interpretation of gender roles. This can often cause confusion about the behavior and function of the companion. In "Genesis of the Daleks" (1975), writer Terry Nation has Sarah very bravely and rationally plan an escape from a forced labor facility, but become inexplicably paralyzed by fear and vertigo during the actual escape. Thus, the production brief that Sarah be a strong character conflicts with her archetypal role as dependent female.

The few male companions in the series have been even more restricted in narrative function than the female companions. In general, their job has been to be the muscle. This was true with Doctor 1, an old man who could not reasonably be expected to fight his way out of problems. Therefore, he gets a series of fighting men to do the work for him: Ian (1963–5), Steven (1965–6), and Ben (1966–7). Attention gets drawn to this Doctor = brain, male companion = brawn formula in "The Romans," a story played mostly for laughs. The Doctor and Ian are separated for almost the entire story, so that when the Doctor, mistaken for a bard and assassin, gets attacked by a would-be assassin, as mentioned before, he has to fight his own way out. In general, though, Doctor 1 rarely gets involved in a physical struggle and often exhibits physical weaknesses, such as swift exhaustion.

Doctor 2, though younger and more physically active than Doctor 1, also rarely got into physical scrapes. His typical reaction to danger is to run from it, and his typical method of overcoming the enemy is to out-think and out-maneuver it. These tendencies get taken to absurd levels in "The Mind Robber" (1968), in which the puny Zoe must fight the massively muscled comic strip character Karkus while the Doctor watches on. Doctor 2 needed Ben and then Jamie (1966–9) to do most of the physical work.

Male companions in the usual sense disappear with the arrival of the physically vigorous practitioner of "Venusian Aikido," Doctor 3. Though he spends much of his time assisting the military force of U.N.I.T. (United Nations Intelligence Taskforce), Doctor 3 does most of the direct person-to-person fighting on his own. This general raising of the testosterone level led to the Doctor's repeated criticisms of U.N.I.T.'s "big booted soldiers" and their "clumsy" ways. Though they have an obvious respect for each other, the Doctor and U.N.I.T.'s leader, Brigadier Alistair Gordon Lethbridge-Stewart, often argue and rarely see eye-to-eye on anything. Because of the heightened masculine tension in Doctor 3's period, his favored companion, Jo, was highly stereotypically feminine in numerous ways and thus provided a counterbalance. Doctor 3's other two female companions did not fit quite so well with him. Liz was a brilliant scientific polymath, too much like the Doctor, while Sarah was better able to take care of herself than was Jo.

Since Jamie departed the show in 1969, the few male companions have often served other archetypal functions than as a warrior. Harry (1974–5) was originally intended to be a typical "muscle" type, but when Tom Baker took the role as Doctor 4, he proved more than capable of handling himself in such situations, and so Harry became a foil for the two main characters: an ignorant traditionalist against Sarah's "women's lib" persona, and a bit thick-headed against the Doctor's intellectualism.

When Adric (1980–2) came onto the program, he first was a kind of young protégé for Doctor 4, who naturally fit into an indulgent tutor role in his dealings with Adric. When the younger Doctor 5 took over, the relationship became more like siblings, with Adric taking the annoying younger brother role.

Turlough (1983–4) was a marked contrast to all other companions, not just the male ones. His archetypal role is the "sly fox," what Jung would call an "imago" of the shadow. Originally, he inveigles his way onto the TARDIS to murder the Doctor. In his first story, "Mawdryn Undead" (1983), he is immediately shown to be devious, callous, and wholly untrustworthy. Though he eventually gives up his attempts to kill the Doctor by his third story, "Enlightenment" (1983), he never sheds the sly fox image. The stereotypically female companion, Tegan, never learns to trust him. His cunning leads him to manipulate people regularly, while the audience never truly gets to know how he thinks or feels about anything. As with Harry, Turlough acts as a foil to the other main characters. In his cool arrogance, Turlough is a foil against Tegan's brash candidness. Turlough's devious selfishness is a foil against Doctor 5's honesty and willingness to place himself in danger rather than place others in danger.

Turlough is the last male companion of the first sequence of the program. With Tom Baker having established a pattern of Doctors played by actors in their 30s and 40s, the Doctor becomes enough of a physical character that he no longer needs a "warrior" along with him. Experiments with different kinds of male roles for companions beyond the "warrior" archetype just never worked well in narrative terms. The Doctor 5/Adric dynamic demonstrates this point very well. While Adric and Doctor 4 harmonized to a high degree, since Adric becomes slightly feminized in his role as dependent protégé, Adric and Doctor 5 spent most of their time arguing and competing. There was just not enough animus in the Doctor Who personality to be split two ways. The two characters were simply too close in age and manner for them to harmonize. The result was that Adric's character changed from willing student to petulant younger brother. He became more childish, such as being always hungry and persistently complaining about being left out. It became apparent that Adric had to go.

The revived series has had only one male companion for a brief stay with the Doctor. Three other male characters become semi-regulars. In two of these cases, their role is to defuse the building sexual tension between the Doctor and Rose. Mickey Smith, who appears semi-regularly in the first two seasons with a few guest appearances later, is Rose's "official" boyfriend, whose presence makes her feel guilty for preferring the Doctor. Mickey is a kind of jester archetype who would rather not be. He must suffer repeated jibes from the Doctor. His role seems to be to get it wrong, whatever the situation may be, ineptly crashing about. This ineptitude is endearing, since it comes not purely from stupidity, but from an overwhelming and childlike desire to please others while proving himself worthy in his own eyes. Like other post-1960s male companions, Mickey functions as a foil, his incompetence highlighting the Doctor's savvy.

Captain Jack Harkness (2005) is on for about half a season, with some cameo returns in later seasons. Though bisexual strongly leaning in the homosexual direction, Jack is still primarily coded in the action hero mode, and draws on many filmic "signs" of masculinity, especially from American films — military officer's rank, deal making, sexual promiscuity, "classic" good looks, and cockiness. With these attributes, Jack interferes with Rose's increasing sexual attraction to the Doctor by being a more standard object of sexual desire. Jack also allows the very physical working-class Doctor 9 to be more intellectual than he was in his first few stories.

The case of Rory Williams (2010–1) is much more complicated. There seems to be an attempt to some degree to rewrite the Doctor-Rose story, and so Rory fits into the same position as Mickey Smith, with some vital differences. The Doctor-Rose story became an unconsummated love affair in which the two become separated and Rose finally gets a substitute Doctor for herself.[3] Mickey was gradually pushed aside and then later rewarded with an apparent marriage to a later companion, Martha. Rory, on the other hand goes from boyfriend to fiancé to husband of Amy. The series plays on Amy's conflicted feelings: she loves Rory, but desires the Doctor more. In this case, though, the Doctor scrupulously avoids emotional entanglement with Amy even when she sexually offers herself, and instead invites Rory to join them for the purpose of preventing the kind of relationship that had developed with Rose. Rory, like Mickey, is dedicated to his beloved, endearingly, desperately in love with a woman who does not love him with the same intensity. Like Mickey, Rory is something of a clown figure, charmingly inept at the heroics displayed around him and repeatedly in need of rescuing as though *he* were the female companion. His presence on the TARDIS fosters a kind of guilt in Amy that Rose really did not show with regard to Mickey. Rory's archetypal position is as a feminized male, just as Amy's archetypal position is as a masculinized female. Rory possesses traits commonly associated with male characters — loyalty, dedication, an unswerving sense of what is morally right — but also some traits associated with female characters — vulnerability and sensitivity.

A much discussed question among fans and critics regarding *Doctor Who* regards the gender of his companions, who have been overwhelmingly female. These numerous females, most of them young and "available," are usually desexualized in relation to the Doctor even when they are sexualized for the audience, with the exceptions of Rose, Martha, and Amy as discussed both above and below. Jo Grant (Katy Manning) spent much time in miniskirts and other "revealing" garments. The savage Leela, played by an athletically trim Louise Jameson, spends most her time in brief leatherwear of a vaguely "jungle queen" sort. The voluptuous Peri (Nicola Bryant) is regarded a sex symbol among male fans more than any other companion. Yet, there has always been a fast rule in *Doctor Who*: no hanky-panky in the TARDIS. The renewed series teased at this rule like a small child stepping over a line he is told not to, but in the end stuck to it. Why?

One answer to the female companion conundrum is strictly practical, dealing with the designation of *Doctor Who* as "family" viewing contrasted against the need for any television program to attract viewers. Thus, beautiful women regulars attract a male audience, but the Doctor's disinterest in these women as sexual objects keeps the program on a "family" level. However, there are also archetypal reasons both for having mainly female companions and having a no hanky-panky rule. Consider again that the Doctor and his companions combine to represent a unified self that one can call "Doctor Who." Since the Doctor is heroic animus but also generally both the ego and shadow of this self, it is naturally going to be masculine in characteristic. This is why the Doctor has traveled with only a male companion just four times, in "The Massacre" (1966), "The Evil of the Daleks" (1967), "The Keeper of Traken" (1980), and "Planet of Fire" (1984), and in each case has picked up a new female companion at some point in the program. There always needs to be an offsetting female presence, the anima of this self, to balance the personality equation.[4] The Doctor and his companion, whoever she may be or however many there may be, are *one person*.

Focusing on archetypal roles of the companions in *Doctor Who* draws attention to the problematic position of archetypes in modern society. In the technological, rational, and functional society of England in the last half decade (and the rest of Europe, America, Australia, Canada, and New Zealand), archetypes lose much of their power. They still have a presence, still push their way into the collective narrative consciousness. However, sophisticated audience members quickly spot and analyze them. Other audience members may find the archetypes "cheesy," or "unbelievable," or old-fashioned and melodramatic. The matter is one of belief. When people stop believing in the reality of the archetype, the archetype loses much of its ability to convey cultural values.

Writers may even be aware of the rationalist audience response to archetypes. In "Kinda," Dr. Todd of a high-tech colonizing team remarks on the "clown stroke jester" figure and his function in primitive societies. Similarly, in "Snakedance" (1983), Lon, the bored son of a prominent politician, stops an elaborate ancient ritual in which he is taking the starring role, and points out that the whole thing consists of just props and costuming, entirely lacking any of the "hidden depths" promised in the ritual. These two scenes occur in two strongly, almost self-consciously archetypal stories and demonstrate the author's awareness of potential audience skepticism. Though ultimately the audience is meant to think of Dr. Todd's and Lon's views on this matter as somewhat limited, these two scenes in their larger contexts do invite the audience to see archetypes as having a strong culturally unifying function, though not necessarily a spiritual one.

Archetype into Mythology

Once the static archetype is set into narrative motion, a myth results. In the nineteenth and early twentieth centuries, many literary scholars noted that stories tended to fall into recognizable patterns, most of which are traceable to the earliest myths known. So persistent are these patterns that the American scholar of comparative religion Joseph Campbell identified a "monomyth," a single pattern identifiable in part and whole throughout world literature (*Hero* 30–40). The fundamental aspects of this pattern are *separation-initiation-return*, corresponding to the basic rites of passage found in all cultures and religions. Campbell describes it thus: "A hero ventures forth from the world of common day into a region of supernatural wonder: fabulous forces are there encountered and a decisive victory is won: the hero comes back from this mysterious adventure with the power to bestow boons on his fellow man." Campbell identifies various sublevels and common plot elements in each of the three main stages, but the main stages remain throughout.

Campbell's monomyth corresponds to the archetypal genre that Canadian literary critic Northrop Frye called *Romance*. Frye identified four such archetypal genres: *Comedy, Romance, Tragedy,* and *Irony*. This last term never became popular, and most subsequent critics have preferred *Satire* as an appropriate name for the fourth mythic genre. These genres correspond to the four seasons (Spring, Summer, Fall, Winter) and to the four major stages of life (Childhood, Adolescence, Adulthood, Senescence). These genres also cycle through, so that one can a see a unitary archetypal "hero" who goes through all these stages, dying in Satire and being reborn again in Comedy (Frye 131–239). Campbell characterizes this monomythic Romance as a constant cycle of Comedy to Tragedy back to Comedy (*Hero* 28).

Campbell's monomyth is Romantic in Frye's terms. A romance "is nearest of all literary forms to the wish-fulfillment dream," says Frye (186). Campbell begins his discussion of the monomyth with a correlative comparison of dreams and myths, noting their similar symbology and interpretation (*Hero*

3–25). These connections had been noted by the great psychoanalysts Freud and Jung, and the connections between dream and myth led to Freud's designation of the "Oedipus complex," as well as both analysts' extensive writings about mythology and folklore. According to Frye, the essential plot element of Romance is the quest, the climactic adventure usually announced from the beginning that drives the hero through the sequence of little adventures in between (186–7). The quest has three stages: conflict, death-struggle, and discovery (recognition of the hero). This pattern corresponds to the rituals of death, disappearance, and revival. One can see that Frye's tripartite structure of Romance plot is essentially the same as Campbell's tripartite monomyth, just with different thematic emphases.

Typical of the Romance genre is the focus on two principle characters: protagonist and antagonist. Frye notes, "The enemy may be an ordinary human being, but the nearer the romance is to myth, the more attributes of divinity will cling to the hero and the more the enemy will take on demonic mythical qualities" (187). One can see these properties in *Doctor Who*, in which the Doctor has superhuman status and increasingly mythic attributes, especially in the revived series, while his enemies have equally impressive powers and abilities.

The imagery of Romance is typically fantastic, ranging from the supernatural in myths to the exaggerated character types and heatedly emotional activities of Gothic Romance. *Doctor Who* has tread into all these realms. Fantastical stories such as "The Celestial Toymaker" (1966) and "The Mind Robber" (1968) move like dreams, involving almost a free play of archetypes. *Doctor Who* went through a distinctly Gothic period from 1975 to 1977, reconfiguring famous Gothic Romance stories and story types: *The Tempest* ("Planet of Evil"), *The Mummy* ("Pyramids of Mars"), *Frankenstein* ("The Brain of Morbius"), "Masque of the Red Death" ("The Masque of Mandragora"), *The Hands of Orlac* ("The Hand of Fear"), *The Phantom of the Opera* ("The Deadly Assassin"), "Sherlock Holmes" ("The Talons of Weng-Chiang"), the "Haunted Lighthouse" tale ("Horror of Fang Rock"), and the "Ancient Evil" tale ("Image of the Fendahl"). In essence, *Doctor Who* has traversed the various Romance genres, bringing forth archetypal and mythic structures.

Thematically, the Romance or monomyth enacts "the victory of fertility over the waste land" (Frye 193). Campbell characterizes this as "the unlocking and release again of the flow of life into the body of the world" (*Hero* 40). It becomes important within mythic tales, therefore, that the forces that threaten the central personality be ultimately defeated. At the same time, such stories also contain recognition that these forces can never be fully defeated, and more often than not are simply contained.

Many critics have noted how science fiction often fits into the patterns described above. The prominent science fiction writer Brian Aldiss defines the genre as a derivation from Gothic Romance, using "Romance" in Frye's sense (25). Mark Rose states that "science fiction is a version of romance" (8), and that its characteristic opposition is "a struggle between good magic and bad magic" (9). In Chapter 2, I argued that these definitions of science fiction are insufficient in the larger sense; however, for the purpose of the current discussion they are basically sound.

The story "Kinda" provides a good example of these Romance-myth-archetype patterns at work in *Doctor Who*. "Kinda" relies on two mythical narrative patterns — The Fall from Innocence and The Cycle of Renewal, which are two phases (beginning and end) of Campbell's monomyth. The story places the second myth in the context of the "wheel of history," in which civilization goes from primitive but content society living peacefully within nature to depraved, technological, warring society that destroys itself and returns civilization to its primitive, natural roots as the aftermath of that destruction, only to repeat the cycle many times. The cycle of history is an analogue of the cycle of nature, moving from Spring to Spring, renewal to renewal. The Fall from Innocence is most commonly known through the Garden of Eden story, repeatedly referred to in "Kinda." The myth presupposes a pure state of natural humanity that gets tainted through the introduction of some kind of "knowledge," which then propels the protagonists out of the garden (the symbol of their innocence) and into the world of change and death.

Such myths dramatize the desire for spiritual and mental community. The word community derives from Latin, and originally means roughly "performing services together, or in unison," or alternatively "giving together." Community on the mythic level occurs when the whole of a society shares precisely the same beliefs, and has the entire culture in common (another word deriving the same Latin root). Religious rituals serve the purpose of focusing the minds of the believing community until they join as one common mind, or when they link with the mind of a deity. Supposedly, once cultural, spiritual, and supernatural community exists, evil vanishes and strife disappears.

"Kinda" plays out these myths of community by positing a society that has already achieved it. In such a society, everyone is content, no one wants, and no disharmony occurs. Into this perfectly innocent communal society comes a group of highly "civilized" colonizers. Additionally, the Doctor and his companions stumble in, bringing with it their own problems caused by their various versions of civilized disharmony.

The force that drives the Kinda people out of their idyllic state is language. The logic behind this is that the Kinda, being a perfect community, can think to each other, since they share one mind. They have no need of language since there is nothing happening in one mind that is unknown to another within the Kinda community. Literally, there is nothing to reveal, nothing to explain. Language is part of the fallen state. Thus, one who has "voice" will take control of the Kinda people and begin the cycle of history by creating, in essence, individualism and the isolated, alienated person.

The Garden of Eden symbolism runs throughout "Kinda." Evil, in the form of language, control, and militarism, takes the physical form of a snake. This snake is the manifestation of an enemy to humanity, named the Mara in this story. Evil enters the physical world first through temptation of a woman, the Doctor's companion Tegan. Driven nearly to madness by the Mara's lies and tricks, Tegan agrees to allow it to use her body temporarily. Thus, as in the Bible, evil enters the world through a woman. Possessed by the Mara, Tegan then drops an apple on the head of a troubled Kinda man, Aris. When the possessed Tegan tempts Aris to allow her to "read" him, the Mara then passes on to him, thus beginning the process of the fall of the Kinda by starting the wheel of history because Aris obtains "voice" (i.e., language, but also knowledge) and so a power that other Kinda do not possess. As in the Garden of Eden story, evil is symbolized in the snake, temptation in the apple; dangerous knowledge passes from woman to man, and all of this occurs in a "paradise."

"Kinda" is a particularly rich story in terms of its mythical and archetypal structuring. In addition to the biblical allusions and the fall of evil story, "Kinda" also includes multiple references to Buddhist concepts, becoming a kind of Buddhist allegory on the strengths of meditation. Much of this must be inferred, since some characters are not specifically named in the teleplay itself, only in the actors' credits. The names of various characters from the planet Deva Loka stand for specific ideas. The evil entity in the story is the Mara, which is a demon in Buddhist mythology. The word "mara" is etymologically related to the root—*mare* in "nightmare." Nightmares were originally thought to be visitations by demons and imps; thus, it makes sense that Tegan contacts the Mara in a dream. Dukkha, the Mara that first takes over Tegan and then Aris, is suffering and insubstantiability, the world's sickness that can be cured by Jhana (meditation) represented as the box of understanding that allows outsiders to partake of the Kinda communal mind (Tulloch and Alvarado 270–1). "Aris" is the name of a heretical early Buddhist cult that sanctified killing, so that it is appropriate Aris gets "voice" and turns the Kinda people away from their true nonviolent path. The name Deva Loka itself comes from the Hindu Upanishads, and means the celestial realms.

While the Mara occupies Tegan's mind, it torments her with visions, including an old man and old woman playing chess. Annica (impermanence) and Anatta (egolessness) make a game of identity and perception, the first step in showing that "self" is an illusion (Tulloch and Alvarado 271). The next step is self confrontation, which occurs when the Mara creates a double of Tegan and the two argue over who is the "real" Tegan. The answer is that neither is the "real" Tegan because both are merely mental conceptions. However, since Tegan's is an "unshared" mind, she is unprepared by meditation to deal with the Mara's conundrums, and thus allows the Mara to use her.

Suffering in "Kinda" comes about through knowledge of the world, represented in the misuse of language (voice) and in the attempt control and manage the natural order, the attitude of the colonial force that threatens the Kinda way of life. Thus, the Kinda are threatened in two ways: from the inside in the form of the Mara and from the outside in the form of militaristic colonial power.

Contrary to the destructive force of the Mara Dukkha are a woman and a girl, Panna and Karuna, who have "voice," but who employ it for the good of the community while living outside the community. Panna is wisdom and insight, in the story a wise old woman who understands the situation and its dangers and thus feels compelled to "show" to the colonials why they must leave the Kinda alone. Her assistant is a girl, Karuna (compassion), who can "read" the feelings of others through touch. Notably, Karuna's ability is inversely mirrored when the possessed Tegan "reads" Aris and finds a weakness to exploit rather than to heal. Karuna also implies love and becoming (Suzuki 38). Thus, when Panna dies in "Kinda," her wisdom is passed on to Karuna. Panna and Karuna possess the Box of Jhana, the power of true insight through meditation. It is important to note that jhana (sometimes spelled dyana) is *silent* meditation, and directly translates as "a quiet state of mind" (Suzuki 67; 96). Buddhists distrust language, often referring to it as a "prison." For this reason, the Kinda do not speak, and those who do are mostly corrupt and dangerous.

In Buddhist thought, the physical world and its needs disturb the mind, thus preventing the quiet state of jhana necessary for insight. When the mind is disturbed, "there is no time for it to be quietened" (Suzuki 96). In "Kinda," the Mara works to disturb Tegan's mind in this way, and later the minds of the Kinda people themselves when it uses Aris to stir up an attack against the colonizers' dome. This disturbance causes the wheel of history to spin, to create awareness of past and future rather than just a *now*, and brings with it suffering. Additionally, two of the colonizers, Sanders and Hindle, are unbalanced and disturbed. Both are obsessed with protocol and military regulation. Both see the planet's paradise and people as threats to themselves and their way of life. For instance, Sanders is afraid of feeling too much "at home," which is contrary to his colonizer's sensibility. Hindle is paranoid, fearing that "out there" will get in, and so plans to destroy all of "out there."

Their reactions to the Box of Jhana, then, are instructive. The Zen master D.T. Suzuki writes that "the aim of dhyanna is to attain a quiet, tranquilized equilibrium" (97). The Box of Jhana drives both Sanders and Hindle literally out of their minds. The process brings both men a peace with themselves. They freely wander outside the dome, Hindle with his shirt partly unbuttoned. Sanders remarks, "I never read the manual," indicating that he has abdicated the entire system of military procedure by which he has run his life for at least 40 years.

Christopher Bailey, author of "Kinda," returned to *Doctor Who* a year later with a kind of sequel, "Snakedance." This story is much less allegorical than its predecessor, and drops much of the specifically Buddhist philosophy for a more synoptic, comparative religion perspective. In "Snakedance," Tegan has not been freed of the Mara, which still resides in her subconscious and uses her to get back to its home world, Manussa. Once there, the Mara contrives to arrange for a new manifestation, which will allow it to destroy the current civilization. Manussa is in the midst of its festival celebrating the Federation's defeat of the Mara. This decennial celebration involves the representatives of the current Federator's family, his wife, Tanha, and his son, Lon. In charge of the festival is the museum curator and expert on ancient Manussa, Ambril, who has taken over the post from his predecessor Dojjen. Dojjen has gone off to become a religious hermit among the Snakedancers, a sect that believes that the Mara was not destroyed and so prepare themselves for the Mara's return.

Many Buddhist concepts help structure "Snakedance." However, Bailey has decided to play down the connections between character names and concepts they are supposed to represent. Tanha in Buddhist thought is "thirst," the desire for the things and attainments of physical reality (Suzuki 45). Dojjen, sometimes spelled Dogen, was a great Chinese Buddhist master and influential writer on Buddhist matters. In Tibetan medicine, Lon is "air," which drives the circulation of breath, blood, and the life energy known as *chi* in Chinese Buddhism and *prahna* or *prajna* in Indian Buddhism. Manussa is a Sanskrit word meaning "humanity," and is related to both "man" and "mind," a reminder that even ancient peoples understood that the key quality of humanity is mentation. While Mara is used in the sense of demons in general in "Kinda," in "Snakedance" the name refers specifically to the powerful demon who tried to temp Buddha through sensual pleasure.

Bailey has incorporated a few ideas from "Kinda" into "Snakedance." For instance, the Mara causes the historical cycles of rise and fall. Manussa is the homeworld to two former empires, the Manussan and Sumaran, both now destroyed. The Mara seeks to return to destroy the current society on Manussa. Thus, as in "Kinda," suffering derives from the vicious circle of birth and death (called *samsara* in Buddhist terms) as applied to societies, which is driven by the chain of causes and effects (called *karma* in Buddhist terms) (c.f. Capra 85).

Similarly, wisdom and understanding are displayed by not talking. Dojjen never says anything, and though his mind does speak to the Doctor's it is important that this happens without voice. This distrust for language is typical of Buddhism, Zen Buddhism in particular, so it is not surprising to find it again in "Snakedance." Suzuki says, "Language is very fine and we cannot exist without it, but at the same time it is the worst thing man has invented." According to Buddhist thought, language functions to define everything and thus blocks understanding. Furthermore, language is the source of quarrels, which mainly happen over definitions (Suzuki 38–9). One can see this fixation for things to be absolutely what the name says they are when Ambril, the Director of Historical Research on Manussa, ridicules the legends of the Mara by noting that a mask referring to the Six Faces of Delusion has only five faces. Ambril becomes very cross when the Doctor points out that the sixth face of delusion is the wearer's own. In turn, this idea that one's own face is a delusion is typical of Buddhist thinking, which states that personal identity is another falsehood caused by language (Capra 85).

These Buddhist ideas become tied to a more synoptic view of mythology and its functions. The synoptic mythological points include an intriguing inversion of the hero's journey as Joseph Campbell describes it. Like the typical mythical hero, the Mara is of mysterious birth and is fostered away from a biological mother and father. The Mara travels away from home to prove its power, enlists the help of agents and assistants, then returns home for a triumphal welcome. This inversion of values demonstrates the old notion that every villain is the hero of his own story.

Other synoptic points of interest include the celebration of the Mara's defeat. The part of the Federator, who defeated the Mara, includes a kind of sun god costume. Typically, sun gods are those who defeat the dark forces, just as the sun dispels night. The Federator is the "hero" of the Romantic drama being enacted, and Frye is quite clear about the strong relationship between Romantic heroes and solar deities (188). The litany of the celebration includes paraphrases from T.S. Eliot's "The Waste Land"—"I offer you fear in a handful of dust"—and Emily Brontë's "Death"—"I offer you despair in a withered branch" (Brontë's version is "Time's withered branch"). The dust, the withered branch, and the skull from which the dust is poured are all archetypal symbols. These occur in Christianity, for example, as in the liturgical phrase "ashes to ashes, dust to dust," and in some depictions of the cross on which Jesus was nailed as a dead tree. Similarly, the ceremony itself involves a typical trio of temptations that the solar-powered hero must overcome to defeat evil: fear of death, despair about aging and accomplishing nothing, and greed for knowledge as symbolized in the Great Crystal. Jesus and Siddartha Gautama (the Buddha) are both assigned properties of sun gods and both undergo similar abstract temptations when faced with evil.

The ceremony resembles many rituals from around the world that involve the public expulsion of evil. For instance, the ceremony happens in a cave that contains the jewel symbolizing knowledge. Typical of such rituals, the driving idea is renewal of civilization through banishment of the evil force, which must repeatedly be banished "to the dark places of the inside" according to Manussan legend because it cannot be destroyed.[5] The perceived need for such rituals has been the belief in the omnipresence of demons. In the Manussan celebrations, for example, people dress as "attendant demons," who touch various members of the crowd, symbolically cursing such people who can remove the curse only through forfeiting a coin. Frazer notes that in societies that practice such rituals, "They think that if they can only shake off these their accursed tormentors, they will make a fresh start in life, happy and innocent; the tales of Eden and the old poetic golden age will come true again" (547). Frazer notes that often such ritual expulsions are periodic (551), as is the ceremony on Manussa, which occurs once a decade. Frazer recounts as an example an Incan ceremony in which "messengers of the Sun" banish the evils from their city (554).

Intriguingly enough, even in "Snakedance" some of the Western ideas that characterize science fiction and *Doctor Who* come through. For instance, in "Kinda" the Mara seemed to be a supernatural force of some kind. However, in "Snakedance" Nyssa intuits that the Mara is manmade. Thus, the story demonstrates how people create their own evil, both collectively and individually. One notes how the Mara exploits individual weaknesses to acquire its goal: Tegan's fear, Ambril's Faustian greed for knowledge, Dugdale the showman's ambition, Lon's aristocratic arrogance. When these weaknesses combine to create the circumstances under which evil may gain a larger power within society, one can see at work a kind existential notion of evil as a product of human activity rather than as something external and inimical to humanity.

"Kinda" and "Snakedance" exemplify the most sophisticated uses of mythical elements in *Doctor Who*, demonstrating the continued functioning of myth and archetype at both psychological and social levels. While the majority of *Doctor Who*'s viewing audience is unlikely to pick up most of the specific allusions in these stories, they will, nevertheless, respond to the interplay of symbols. Much of the "action" of these stories happens "at the edge of consciousness," so to speak, where the audience is likely to sense the meaning without being wholly aware of its happening. In today's society, these mythical and archetypal events happen most often in popular fantastic entertainment, where they can be kept distant, with far less effect than they would have in previous historical periods. Nevertheless, the mythical and archetypal elements encode common patterns of experience: birth, death, and the wish for rebirth.

Regeneration and Rebirth

Jung identifies five forms of rebirth in mythology and ritual: *metempsychosis*, which is the transmigration of souls from body to body; *reincarnation*, which is the idea of a constant personality that moves from a dying body to a new one at birth; *resurrection*, which is the re-establishment of existence after death either in a new location (such as heaven) or in a new body; *rebirth*, which is the idea that through a ritual a living person becomes a different "born again" person; and *participation in the process of transformation*, which is the witnessing of or partaking in a ritual of rebirth (*Four Archetypes* 47–9).

One can see *Doctor Who* toying with versions of these rebirth forms. Metempsychosis occurs in "New Earth" (2006), when the consciousness of the devious "last human," Cassandra, jumps from Rose's mind to the Doctor's and back several times. Reincarnation occurs in "Kinda" when the consciousness of Panna transfers to Karuna after Panna dies. Resurrection occurs in "Forest of the Dead" (2008) when characters who have died physically are given new lives in a computer-created virtual world. Rebirth occurs in "The Pirate Planet" (1978), in which Queen Xanxia uses time dams in a technological substitution for a ritual so that she can make a projected image of her younger self into a fully corporeal person. Many characters act as witnesses, in the sense of testifying to the truth of, to rebirth transformations throughout the series. Of course, the Doctor's power to regenerate is the series' pre-eminent example of rebirth. Given Jung's definitions, it is perhaps proper to say that the Doctor's process of regeneration is a kind of resurrection, in which the dying body and personality are transformed into a "same but different" constitution.

According to Jung, through archetypes of rebirth, people experience the "transcendence of life," by which he means a revelation of "the perpetual continuation of life through transformation and renewal" (*Four Archetypes* 51). Early humans saw that the sun rises and sets, the day is "reborn," plants lose their leaves and then come back to life. Naturally, people would like to be like these things that apparently do not die, or simply die and return. Participation in rituals of rebirth "give rise ... to that hope of immortality" (*Four Archetypes* 51).

Myth Without the Mythic Worldview

Though interesting and thorough, the synoptic criticism of Campbell and Frye is much better when focusing on literature of the past than on that of the present. As the social standing of the hero comes down and as the details of the stories approach realism, mythic criticism loses much of its explanatory power. The focus has shifted. This is why, for instance, Campbell in later works went into gushing detail about the first three *Star Wars* movies, but had little to say about most of the contemporaneous literature and film of significantly higher quality than the rather trite and clichéd *Star Wars* films. So, Campbell can see in modern literature only stories that seem "bleak" and "pitiful" in comparison to the world-saving myths of ancient times (*Hero* 27–8).

Additionally, the mythic perspective in criticism tends to view all artistic production in terms of the primal symbolism of early myth. Myth critics of this kind tend to think that every system of knowledge, every formal activity is myth. William Irwin Thompson says that both science and history (the two most common building blocks of *Doctor Who* stories) when "wrought" to their uttermost become myth[6] (3). Such thinking so generalizes the term "myth" that it comes to mean anything the writer wants it to mean. Additionally, such thinking fails to take into account that the evolution of society has meant that people have become greatly detached from those early symbolic meanings, or, if this detachment is recognized, it is counted only as a loss to the human "spirit," not as a maturation of human understanding. Campbell, especially, relies upon Jungian dream interpretation to try to reestablish a modern link with primal symbolism, arguing that it is still a part of the collective unconscious, and thus still has a "power" over our lives. However, modern dream study shows that dreams are not what the psychoanalysts thought that they were. Furthermore, modern scientific understanding dispels conscious interpretation of the world in terms of ancient symbology. When we know that the sun is just a big nuclear fireball of completely natural origin and finite duration, we no longer give it the same kind of awe and reverence that our ancestors devoted to it when they believed it was a supernatural entity, but an entirely different kind of awe and reverence.

Additionally, mythic criticism treats symbols as static archetypes. For them, such symbols cannot fundamentally change value or meaning, and so they assume that most modern symbols must relate to the mythic archetypes. The Italian novelist Italo Calvino has discussed this problem in regards to Frye's work. He notes for instance that conceptually "city" has changed its connotations since the Industrial Revolution, "changes in the arrangement and attribution of values that ought to be looked into both on the imaginary-literary and the social levels" (53–4). Frye, however, designates the symbol "city" as part of the *mineral* set of symbols, and thus ignores the important changes in common understanding of "city."

The *Doctor Who* approach to mythic symbolism is generally modern and ironic. For instance, *Doctor Who* demonstrates a modern perspective of the city as symbol. As in a large amount of English science fiction, *Doctor Who* often focuses on cityscapes as the appropriate setting to evaluate the modern human condition. This starts from the very first season, with the city of the Daleks a prominent feature in "The Daleks" (1963–4) and the cities of Morphoton and Millenius in "The Keys of Marinus" (1964). Also, a typical pattern emerges of having a single city or portion of it act as a synecdoche for an entire planet. Thus, in "The Sensorites" (1964) the Sense Sphere, the home planet of the Sensorites, is wholly represented by the few city settings the TARDIS crew get to see. The implication is that this city *is* the planet. This relationship runs straight through the program, and a prime example of it is "The Armageddon Factor" (1979), where the twin planets of Atrios and Zeos are wholly depicted in terms of their urban centers. In the typical *Doctor Who* story, the modern human is an urban human and needs to be understood in that context.

Doctor Who often relies upon the modern understanding of life, not on the ancient. Its symbolism is often more modern and its outlook contrary to ancient mythic views. When it is working well, it bypasses the faux mythology of a *Star Wars* for a more mature, enlightenment view of humanity's place in the cosmos. However, the mythic functions still operate, providing organization and structure to the stories, plus a handy set of quick references to convey themes.

Mythic and archetypal thinking rest upon premises, one could even call them prejudices, about the relationship between people and the environment. High amongst these premises is the differentiation between the "eternal" and the "transient." The belief is that those things that are "eternal" are also "perfect." That which is transient, or changes, is "imperfect." The prejudice extends very far, so that the Greek philosopher Plato, for instance, respects only that which is "eternal and subject to no deviation" (222).

Doctor Who repeatedly rejects the notion that "eternal" and "unchangeable" are synonyms or synecdoches for "perfect" and "good." In "Brain of Morbius" (1976), a cult called the Sisterhood Of Karn guards an "Elixir of Life," formed by the Sacred Mountain that produces a Flame of Life. The Elixir keeps the sisters alive and bodily preserved for centuries, maybe even millennia. Yet, the sisters' lives have not changed in the passing years. They remain as they were: unlearned, paranoid, and stultified.

The Sisterhood's entire way of life is threatened in the story because the

Flame is dying and without the flame, there is no elixir to preserve the sisters. They will age and die like everyone else. The Doctor, as representative of science and the humanistic worldview, demonstrates to the sisters that there is nothing at all "sacred" about their flame and elixir. Both are formed as part of a natural volcanic process, and a good chemist could "synthesize the stuff by the gallon." The Doctor openly criticizes the sisters' way of life: "Death is the price we pay for progress."

Thus, "Brain of Morbius" shows that immortality is a trap and eternity a delusion. Instead of the perfection usually associated with what is unchanging and eternal (or close to it), the story depicts such traits as a source of stagnation. Instead of bliss and happiness as outcomes for eternal life, there is only endlessly repeated ritual and constant fear that someone might steal the secret.

Another story dealing with immortality is "Enlightenment" (1983). The story involves "Eternals," immortal beings of immense mental powers, but no imagination or enjoyment. They need the proximity of the ever-changing minds of those they call "ephemerals" to give their existence any sense of meaning. So they use the imaginations of humans to conjure a boat race in outer space. One of the Eternals becomes quite attached to Tegan, one of the Doctor's companions, because of the passionate energy of her mind. The main problem that the Eternals must overcome is boredom. Apparently, eternal existence requires changeable life to have any meaning. Eternity, it turns out, is nowhere near perfection.

While *Doctor Who* repeatedly demonstrates a belief in a human *spirit*, this spirit is not the same as the religious and mythic concept of the soul. The human spirit in *Doctor Who* is that of Gwyneth in "The Unquiet Dead" (2005), the will and intention to do good, preserve life, and prevent catastrophe. Gwyneth's personality keeps her body going after it is already dead, so that there is perhaps some suggestion of an eternal spirit. Yet this is temporary only, and the end of the story makes clear that she dies a complete death. The "spirit," such as it is, becomes something more like abstract will or vital force. As such, it coincides with a consistent portrayal in *Doctor Who* of soul as a non-eternal will to live, or a personality that can be construed as a mental force. Such a will or force might outlive a physical body, but it does not last eternally.

Myth, Archetype, and the Worldview of *Doctor Who*

Beginning with the early psychoanalysts, research has shown remarkable correlations between dream content and myth content. This relationship is what makes myths and folktales so amenable to analysis as symbolic representations of common fears and desires.[7] This connection made by Freudian psychoanalysts led to Jung's concept of archetypes, the universal symbols appearing in both dream and myth. To his credit, Campbell makes this very point, arguing not that dreams are myths recast, but that myth is "psychology misread as biography; history, and cosmology" (*Hero* 256).

However, Campbell and other myth critics are all too ready to leap back out and argue that mythic structures were "the support of all human life" and that "the visible structures of the world ... are the effects of a ubiquitous power out of which they rise, which supports and fills them during the period of their manifestation, and back into which they must ultimately dissolve" (Campbell *Hero* 257). This is having the matter both ways, arguing that myth is just desire and fear symbolized, but also arguing that myth is the ultimate spiritual power that shapes all human endeavor. Such contrary thinking leads to illogical conclusions about just what the "power" of myth is. Campbell, for instance, says this power "is known to science as energy" (*Hero* 257). Thus, for the myth critic, the myths and archetypes are immanent in literature, philosophy, indeed the entirety of human history. However, one ought not to take such a view as wholly accurate if it leads to a counterfactual statement such as the one that the power of myth is the same as what scientists call energy. It is not. Advancement into modern life, buoyed by Enlightenment inquiry into every aspect of nature and human activity, has increasingly led to the conclusion that power of myth is in its psychological effects, its giving symbolic structure to common psychological needs, and not in any transcendental properties that it really does not have.

As a product of Enlightenment humanism, *Doctor Who* gathers and tames the transcendental attributions of mythic materials. Again and again in *Doctor Who*, as with most science fiction, the supernatural resolves into the natural. Gwyneth's angels are not angels because there are no angels. Peladon's Aggedor is no myth, just "solid hairy fact." No matter how powerful or awe-inspiring the entity, its final explanation is not as a force above (super) Nature, but as a part of nature as yet unexamined by human inquiry.

Similarly, drawing upon recent scientific discoveries and theories, *Doctor Who* denies the reality of what Campbell calls "the universal round" and the "cosmogonic cycle" of birth–death–rebirth "repeating itself, world without end" (*Hero* 261). Stories such as "Kinda" and "Snakedance" are aberrations in this regard, since their author draws upon similar sources and similar conclusions as myth critics like Campbell. The wheel of history in "Kinda" is very similar to Campbell's "universal round." However, it is also an evolutionary nowhere, a dying niche wholly resistant to the process of change that is the true driving force of the universe. "Death is the price we pay for progress," says the Doctor in "Brain of Morbius." Change and Life are interchangeable concepts he tells Light in "Ghost Light" (1989). The world does end, finally and completely, as the Doctor shows Rose in "The End of the World" (2005).

Thus, I must agree with literary critic Darko Suvin in arguing that though science fiction contains mythical elements, it is not as some critics have argued, a substitute mythology, but something else quite apart. As we have seen in the above analysis of *Doctor Who*, the humanistic and materialist worldview of science fiction prevents it from being mythology. *Doctor Who* shows that this worldview is "diametrically opposed" to myth, as Suvin states. "Where myth claims to explain once and for all the essence of phenomena, SF posits them first as problems and then explores where they lead to; it sees the mythical static identity as an illusion, usually a fraud, in the best case only as a temporary realization of potentially limitless contingencies" (Suvin "On" 61). For viewers of *Doctor Who*, in most cases myth gives way to science, spirit gives way to life, and the ancient knowledge of archetypes becomes only the structural base for a story.

CHAPTER 6

Religion

Doctor: You know, I had a feeling that Niever was actually expecting to hear an answer to his prayer.
Leela: There wouldn't be much point in praying if you didn't.
Doctor: I could quote you a few theologians who'd give you an argument on that.

—"The Face of Evil"

The Question of Religion

Doctor Who is placed in the dilemma that religion poses for the modern era. As scientific knowledge advances and no supernatural beings are discovered, there are fewer grounds on which to secure the contents of religious belief. Additionally, advances in technology and society have replaced or obviated many of the functions that religion once served. As science fiction, *Doctor Who* tends to lean toward acceptance of this modern worldview. On the other hand, contrary to the predictions of Nietzsche, Marx, and others, religion and faith have not vanished from modern life. This fact has led some to view faith as fulfilling a need that cannot be satisfied in any other way. *Doctor Who*, depending upon the writers, script editor, and producer at any one time, pulls back and forth between these two views about the value of religion and faith.

The Origin of Religion

Religion is a varietal experience. It has multitudinous ways of practice and systems of belief. There are religions professing many gods, religions professing one god, religions professing one god with many faces. There are even atheistic religions, such as Buddhism, that profess to no gods at all. Some religions or sects require large numbers of congregants; some insist on lone asceticism. Some proclaim that followers enjoy the bounties of the world, while others require followers to reject everything in the world as wicked. Despite these varieties in religious expression, all religions derive from a small set of foundational ideas and what might be called "initial conditions."

The French philosopher Michel Onfray is blunt about the origin of religion — fear of death. The Epicurean philosopher Lucretius offers a similar reason for what he calls "superstition," which he defines as the mistaken belief that gods are concerned in human matters (67–9). Almost no one wants to die, and no one enjoys seeing loved ones die. The thought of the absolute end of personal existence can be overwhelming. How much nicer it would be if it did not happen. So, "*Homo sapiens* wards off death by abolishing it" (Onfray 2). Thus, a cognitive disconnection exists between the fact of death as finality and the desire that it be not final. Religion covers the disjunction, provides "mental help." Because of its origin, religion is a "death fixation" easily exploited by those seeking or holding power (Onfray 3).

In *Doctor Who*, one can see this common refusal to accept death in the story "Army of Ghosts" (2006). The Doctor and Rose return to Earth to find that the entire world is experiencing regular visitations of hazy, shimmering anthropomorphic manifestations. These are being taken as ghosts by the general population. Thus, Rose's mother, Jackie, believes that the one appearing in her flat is the spirit of her late father. She can even smell the smoke of his cigarettes, so she thinks. Rose, having traveled with the Doctor, is more skeptical. She cannot smell the smoke and does not really believe in ghosts. The manifestations turn out not to be ghosts; instead, they are Cybermen trying to break into this world from another universe. Jackie's overwhelming desire for the comfort of her father returned leads her first to imagine its occurrence, then to accept the falsehood as real, and even to conjure nonexistent evidence for it. Since the belief that these manifestations are just friendly ghosts or otherworldly guardians is nearly universal, few question the assumed interpretation. The situation demonstrates the psychological process that Onfray claims is the origin of religion.

Religion has additional psychological functions. Sigmund Freud, the founder of psychoanalysis, places the origin of religious feeling in the feeling of helplessness that all people have as children, and the subsequent need for a father's protection (11). Later theorists would argue against the notion that the symbolic protector needed to be specifically a father. There is even some claim, though the historical evidence for this is tenuous, that the original religions posited the divine mother as protector, and a few religions exist today focusing on the divine mother instead of the divine father. Whichever kind of protector a religion may believe in, most theorists on the psychology of religion would acknowledge that protection is a key appeal of religion.

Religion has from its beginning exercised a political function in addition to its psychological one. Zoologist Desmond Morris, who specializes in human and primate behavior, speculates that religion arose in human communities because the leader of a community was not the tyrant that his counterpart among gorillas and horses, for instance, would be. Unlike the communities of our ape ancestors, human communities do not orbit around a single dominant male, but require far greater degrees of cooperation. The result is that no leader actually has the god-like status that other primate leaders or pack-animal leaders have. Nevertheless, human evolutionary inheritance includes a deep need to be subordinate to some all-powerful figure. Belief in some sort of being beyond nature that lends its power to its believers and protects them is a natural response to this need for submission. Indeed, if one strips all religions of their superficial differences, one is left with the same basic pattern: "the coming together of large groups of people to perform repeated and prolonged submissive displays to appease a dominant individual" (Morris 178–9). *Doctor Who* has multiple examples of these submissive religious displays, from the acceptance of ritual slaughter in "The Aztecs" (1964), to obeisance to an alien artifact as a divine object in "Meglos" (1980), to a computer becoming high priestess of a theocracy in "Underworld" (1978).

Because the powerful god-leader is not actually there to do the protecting and empowering that most people require, some real person has to stand in as a proxy for that power. Thus, the priests come about. Priests function as interpreters and executors of divine will, the administrators of the god's supposed judgment. Other kinds of proxies also develop, such as "divine" kings and queens, prophets, and self-declared avatars. These people wield immense, sometimes nearly absolute, power within their communities, and command or influence almost all aspects of social life: education, military arrangements, marriage and mating, social standing, and so on. Those religions with powerful priesthoods anathemize, demonize, and often execute those who would seek a religious path apart from the organized structure of a church or temple. Whatever the reason for it, churches, temples, and clergy predominate in most of the world's religions.

Viewers of *Doctor Who* see at various times these political and psychological functions. Just as a starting point, one may look at the episode titled "The Dæmons" (1971), regarded as a classic episode among *Doctor Who* fans. In this story, the Doctor's rival, the Master, has taken the guise of a substitute vicar in a small-town English church, presumably within the Church of England. Being vicar gives the Master many advantages. One is the political power he holds within the community, so that he can talk with the town squire as a political equal. He can call meetings with prominent citizens. As a political leader, the Master can use this position to call for the people's "obedience" to his "will." He can also, therefore, fulfill the psychological function of "protector," letting the people know that he is the one controlling the "powers" let loose at a nearby archaeological dig and convincing them that they have "nothing to fear." In his speech to the collected people of the village, the Master can also operate at the social level, using the local "network" to maintain an uneasy unity. Thus, he knows many of these people's secrets, though he has been in his position only a few weeks. He has easy access to this information because the church is a center of local activity, where the community interactions transfer and transpire. Watching this story, viewers can see the foundational functions of religion operating in a community.

From its origins as a communal and personal method for satisfying psychological needs of reassurance, protection, and social hierarchy, religion spreads to other social and psychological functions. It gains political functions, works to bind communities, and influences multiple social systems. Religion is one of the longest-lasting products of human social organization.

The Evolution of Religion

Clearly, from its beginning religion requires more than fear of death coupled with political expediency to develop. In the first part of the twentieth century, Susanne Langer put together a theory of religion's origin based upon its linguistic, i.e., symbolic, characteristics. Langer's theory includes the fear of death and the political expediency theories of religious origin and places them into a larger framework. She proposes an evolutionary theory of religion. She is not the first. In 1757, David Hume offered *The Natural History of Religion*, which states that religion begins with polytheism and then follows religion's functional and historical development. In focusing on religion as a development of the human propensity for symbol-making, Langer develops a more complete theory. It is important to keep in mind through the discussion that follows that new forms in an evolutionary process do not replace and erase older forms; rather, the older forms become incorporated into the new ones, and one may see the design and properties of older forms in the operations of the newer.

Langer writes that religion begins when humans imbue objects with the powers of dream symbols. Such objects carry an emotional importance far beyond any practical value they may have. In the beginning, such objects have two functions: life-giving and death-giving. These symbols represent the power that the gods have over life and death. Thus, the snake-god does not prompt the thought in early religious minds that snakes are gods, but rather the snake symbolizes the god's power, and an object such as a statue that can recall the snake to memory can likewise be invested with this power.

These objects are passive, and serve no function other than to convey the idea associated with a particular god (*Philosophy* 132–3).

One can see the process that Langer describes as the development of early religion in the *Doctor Who* story "Meglos." In this story, on the planet Tigella thousands of years before the story's events, a mysterious object of power fell from the sky. This dodecahedron, which came from a neighboring planet, is a machine for generating power. However, primitive Tigellans turned it into an object of worship. Now, after millennia, Tigellan society is split into two main factions centered on the dodecahedron — the Savants, scientists who want to study the object, and Deons, worshippers of the object as a gift from the gods.[1]

The example of Langer's description of early religion fits the behavior of the Deons. Here there is an object, which because of what it is lends itself to interpretations of divine origin. Therefore, the object gets imbued with supernatural power. It is either a god or metonymically attached to one. While this object is used as a practical device for powering a city, its worshippers revere it quite separately from this practical function and would worship it even if it performed no such function. The Deons do not worship the dodecahedron as much as they do the *idea* that they attach to it: "source of life." Thus, their dismay at the "heresy" of the Savants, who argue that the dodecahedron is a manufactured object in need of study, does not come from a fear that the object will become offended, but instead from the challenge to the idea that the Deons have so thoroughly invested into the object. The Deons demand death for those who would dissociate the object and the idea, those who would make the object again just an object among objects.

The next phase of development for religion, according to Langer, occurs when holy objects become sources of contemplation. Such contemplation takes the form of sacred rites combining imitation and supplication, through which the supplicants attempt to move the god to act (*Philosophy* 139–40). The item's use will go in two directions from here: one toward magic, which is the belief that there is a direct causal connection between mimicked action and desired result, and one toward totem, which comes from the idea that the object is a personality taking part in the ritual (142). Once a culture has identified itself as the idea they have attributed to a holy symbol, the next step is for this culture to view the symbol as progenitor of the people (143). The people consider themselves solid, like the stone, and so call themselves the stone-people, descendants of the stone god; or, they are cunning like the coyote, so call themselves coyote-people, descendants of the coyote god. Belief in magic does not lead to religion, though it may form part of a religion's ideas. Totems, on the other hand, are the first step toward theology.

In "The Underwater Menace" (1967), the people of lost Atlantis worship the fish-goddess Amdo, being themselves "fish" people,[2] living entirely off the sea. A giant statue of Amdo Goddess of the Sea is their totem, the center of their rituals and the power to whom they look for guidance. The Trojans in "The Myth Makers" (1965) see themselves as the people of the Great Horse of the Plain. In "The Curse of Peladon" (1972) and its sequel "The Monster of Peladon" (1974), the people of the planet Peladon worship and identify themselves with a powerful mountain beast, Aggedor, which is something like a cross between a bear and a boar. It does not matter that the animals have been hunted to near extinction, for Peladonians see the power resting not in the animal but in the ideas that it has come to symbolize for them. This is the power of the totem and what makes it the first step toward theology, that it abstracts any natural relationship and symbolizes it, removing the concept to the space of contemplation and ideation away from nature.

From totemic religion comes the development of religious story, or placing the symbolic object in action and making it function in the world of experience. According to Langer, symbolic material transforms into three story types: fairytale, which is the wish-fulfillment of the individual who identifies with the protagonist; legend, which is history converted into abstract themes; and myth, which is presentational thought that attempts to understand the general truths of existence (*Philosophy* 148–74). Fairytales take realistic materials and convert them into fairyland, and are thus closest to dream-narrative. Legends begin with history, converting the historic figures into culture heroes who symbolize the aspirations and achievements of an entire culture. Neither of these two symbol-narrative forms is either theological or metaphysical. Neither attempts to *explain* anything. Instead, they are purely presentational. Myths, however, encode the first attempts to understand natural conflicts, especially conflicts between human desire and nature, which constantly thwarts that desire (Langer 153).

Typical *Doctor Who* adventures may be seen as something like fairytales. They have the requisite otherworldly or fairyland symbolism. In "Terror of the Autons" (1971), plastic chairs, dolls, flowers, and even telephone wires come to life. "The Web Planet" (1965) features intelligent, human-sized insects. "The Trial of a Timelord: Terror of the Vervoids" (1986) has talking carnivorous plants. Two stories in particular, "The Celestial Toymaker" (1966) and "The Mind Robber" (1968), expressly take place in malleable fairylands where rules of causality are suspended. Similarly, many *Doctor Who* stories follow the wish-fulfillment structure of fairytales, in which "good" conquers "evil" and the viewer is expressly drawn to identify with the "good" characters. Most producers chose the Doctor's companions precisely so that the companion could fill the role that the viewer would occupy within the story, drawing viewers, especially young viewers, to see themselves as triumphing over those things that would threaten their existence and from which many phobias derive: technology, insects, authority figures, foreign places, unspecified "others," and so on.

These fairytale qualities, however, do not rise to the level of theology. Good and evil do not come from theological concepts in fairy stories. Good is that which the protagonist desires. Evil is that which prevents the protagonist from obtaining his/her desire or threatens his/her life. There is no *reason* for evil to be evil in fairytales, or the reason is simply envy and hatred of the protagonist and his/her values. There are no gods directing events, dispensing roles, ruling over lives. While characters may have supernatural properties, they are not divine nor are they meant as stand-ins for divine entities.

The next level of abstracting story telling is legend. *Doctor Who* has properties associated with legends. The Doctor may at times appear to be a kind of culture hero, a symbol of "English" preserving English identity against the forces that would destroy it. The revived series beginning in 2005 decidedly pushes this idea to the foreground. Certainly, most of the alien invasion stories from the entire series have this property. The characteristics of the culture hero who is the protagonist of legend fit the Doctor quite well at these times, for despite his being a Time Lord from Gallifrey, he is distinctly English, enough so that the TV movie "Doctor Who" (1996) makes a joke out of it. Langer says of the culture hero that he has "a somewhat vague, yet unmistakable historical relation to living men, and a tie to the locality on which he has left his mark" (*Philosophy* 157). The culture hero also tends to be multifaceted, being a trickster, or a magician, or a warrior, or a child, so many diverse personalities that it would seem the only constant is the name. The Doctor who "regenerates" and develops new personality characteristics, yet is intimately tied to Earth history, especially English history, certainly fits the description. Stories accrue to the culture hero. The legend of King Arthur perfectly exemplifies this as materials from disparate sources, such as the Grail legend, the fisher king legend, and Celtic mythology, gradually attach themselves to the culture hero and become his story. The Doctor's participation in the events of history works in a similar way, taking apparently unrelated elements and linking them through the culture hero.

The culture hero may also be a topic for contemplation in *Doctor Who*. Such is the case in "Paradise Towers" (1987) and the character who calls himself Pex. Paradise Towers is a luxury high-rise complex cut off from the outside world because of a war. Living inside are old women, girls who have joined into gangs, and a few male "caretakers" to maintain law and order. Pex is a young man who as a boy stowed away to go to Paradise Towers because he did not want to fight in the war. As compensation, Pex has styled himself in the form of an action hero, a Rambo type who wanders around in a cutoff shirt searching for people to rescue. Clearly well-built and muscular, he nevertheless trembles at the thought of danger and runs at the sight of it. Because he is basically a coward, Pex's "rescues" amount mainly to breaking down doors and destroying equipment. Pex desires more than anything to be viewed as a culture hero, to be revered for his manliness and bravery, yet he is infamous for being a "cowardly cutlet."

The story of "Paradise Towers" from this perspective is the story of how Pex in a single instant overcomes his fear and transforms into the culture hero he always wanted to be. Pex dies rescuing the Towers and its inhabitants, bringing its diverse parts together into one culture. The final shot of the program shows a graffiti design declaring "Pex Lives." Thus, the story shows that the person who will become a culture hero cannot be one while he or she is alive. Pex's foolish desire to be perceived as a culture hero leads to wholly inappropriate reactions, silly bravado, and ridiculous self-definitions. The culture hero is always a distorted memory, an idea symbolized, whose status is "legendary" in the popular sense of being part of the "old times."

Here again, though, with legends and culture heroes we have yet to arrive at theology. The culture hero is a stand-in for an idealization of a culture's self-definition. The culture hero may be demigod by birth, yet the culture hero is not a god. Instead, the culture hero is a part of history, of particular times and places, often long ago enough that no storyteller recalls the exact date or generation. He or she may contend against gods, but that comes from a process of joining legendary and mythological elements much later than the origination of the legendary material.

I have discussed the fairytale and legend characteristics of *Doctor Who* because mythology does not leave behind these forms. *The Iliad* and *The Odyssey*, for instance, are principally legends of culture heroes that then have mythological elements attached. Or, the system may work in the other direction. As in the case of King Arthur stories, when the myths no longer have value in a given culture, they devolve to the nearest appropriate legend.

In myth, the next level of abstracting story telling, the tendency is to generalize symbolic representations, to take the path of legend one step further. Legends generalize historical personages and events into symbolic substitutions for an entire people and culture. In myth, the totemic symbols similarly generalize. A bear does not symbolize a single person's father (as it would in fairytale) but that person's *fathers* to the beginning of time, and a cow image may become Great Mother. Additionally, cosmic forces such as weather, Earth, and sky become symbolized. Such mythic figures are "super-personal," deriving from "social insight" rather than particular experience (Langer *Philiosophy* 155).

Doctor Who does not present myth in its socially functioning capacity. As we have seen in previous chapters, various myths from ancient times can be recast into *Doctor Who* stories, but such recasting is really based on what we might call "data mining," where the author digs for storytelling ore from which to fashion a story. While the Doctor himself has some quasi-mythic functions, such as comparisons to "fire" and some hyperbolic characterization, he more generally operates at the level of culture hero as described earlier. As we shall see later, those beings that have godlike properties in *Doctor Who* are not generally referred to as "gods" and lack the invulnerability and awesomeness often associated with gods.

The closest *Doctor Who* comes to a truly religious myth is in "Last of the Timelords" (2007). In this story, the Doctor has been trapped by his old enemy the Master, who has established a cruel and despotic regime over all of Earth. The Doctor is now a withered, ancient gnome-like figure, powerlessly held in something like a bird cage. In this arrangement is the ancient story of the sun-god (the Doctor is variously associated with fire and light) captured by the night-demon (the Master characteristically wears black). The Doctor's companion, Martha, has been left with the task of freeing the Doctor and defeating the Master, which is to say of bringing the sunrise and dispelling the night. Although she appears to be wandering the world as a warrior gathering troops and finding a secret weapon, it turns out that her real function is to act as wandering priest. She tells stories of the Doctor, in other words myths and legends, to build the faith of the remaining populace so that at the crucial moment they will all concentrate in unison on just his name, creating a psychic force that will turn the Master's power against him and restore the Doctor renewed to his full self. The Master mockingly calls this mass concentration "prayer," believing in its ineffectuality. However, the program pulls back a bit from becoming overtly religious or mythical by having the Doctor explain that he has been attuning his mind to the Master's global communication system so that the Doctor can harness its power and so reconstitute himself. The Doctor manages to bring back to life all those whom the Master has killed by resetting time itself, thus renewing the world, though of course only a few remember the dark times of the Master's rule.

"Last of the Timelords" replays long standing myths and gives them a religious character. The great early twentieth-century collater of legends and myths, Frazer, tells of various peoples around the world who would perform rituals and communal prayers during solar eclipses to bring back the sun. Others perform morning prayers, something like a kind of encouragement, believing that without these prayers the sun would not rise (Frazer 78–9). The story also imitates the rituals and myths of Egypt and Rome of the first through third centuries C.E., especially the rituals and myths of *Sol Invictus*, the "Invincible Sun," whose effigy or likeness as a baby was brought forth from a dark room or cave on the winter solstice to mark the "birth" of the sun and thus the renewal of life (Frazer 358).

Still, unusual as it is in its creation of a Doctor mythography, "Last of the Timelords" takes the typical *Doctor Who* cast of mythic and religious elements. The makers of the program *use* these elements to fashion a story, but do not insist upon their being taken either as myth or as religion, and expressly include a quasi-scientific explanation of the process to deemphasize the religious overtones of the story. The Doctor is not used as a stand-in for any particular god or religious figure, but is used only as analogous to any solar deity whom one may choose to compare. Likewise, there is no theological message in the story, no assurance that there really is a Doctor out there looking after humanity and maintaining the balance of the universe, or that the Doctor is the agent of a deity. Analogy rather than equation is the *Doctor Who* means for treating mythical-religious matters.

From Mythology to Religion

Totem is the first step toward mythology. Then, mythology is the next development toward theology. "Mythology projects itself as theology," says the literary critic Northrop Frye (64). The forms of mythology are narrative, but the themes are religious.

Theology is a systematized set of religious ideas. That is to say, theology is the religious attempt at philosophy. The purpose of theology is to demonstrate the truth of some set of religious ideas. Theology answers the questions about the legitimacy, function, and purpose of religious practice. It also answers questions about the truths of the myths, legends, and fairytales that are the first means for conveying religious ideas. The information of theology comes from the myths, legends, and fairytales, and from the experiences of the community of believers. Fundamentally, theology asserts that the ties between the community of believers and their gods are real. Anyone practicing theology assumes that there is a real foundation for his or her religion and that there is some genuine justification for the form that the religion has taken. Thus, theology always works from the inside out and tends to promote the creation of insiders, people trained in and devoted to the subtleties of the religion that pass by the common believer unnoticed. The conclusions of theological thinking are that either some belief, ritual, or custom of the religion is true, or it is not. The implications are to affirm the religion as it is or to effect change in the religion, either in practice or in thought.

Doctor Who itself is not a theological program. It presents few affirmations of or challenges to existing religious practices. Occasional reflections on religious ideas in general do, however, have a part in *Doctor Who*. One can see ideas being worked over about the existence and nature of deities, the role of priests, the value of belief, and the function of religion itself in a rationalistic, materialistic, and scientific cultural climate.

The Gods

Because of the Enlightenment and humanist intellectual ground on which it stands, *Doctor Who* usually discounts the concept of supernatural entities that guide humanity and intrude on human affairs. There is a similar idea in Epicurean philosophy from ancient Greece and Rome. Lucretius argues that *"nature is free and uncontrolled by proud masters* and runs the universe by herself without the aid of gods" (64). Epicureans believed that whatever gods may exist, they are made of god stuff, atoms entirely different from those comprising the ordinary material world. The gods are perfect and serene, and have neither desire nor need to interfere in human affairs (Lucretius 64). One of Lucretius' translators states that the Epicurean gods "are ideals of contentment and serenity who by definition cannot be bothered with human beings" (Godwin xvi). The idea of perfect gods who do not meddle in human affairs can also be found in Plato's writing, although in other respects Plato's philosophy scarcely resembles Epicurean philosophy. Such ideas espoused by a few ancient writers presage Enlightenment deism, which similarly posits a wholly aloof deity.

In *Doctor Who*, whatever has what could pass for supernatural and godlike abilities acts more like traditional Olympian and Pagan gods than like the wise, patient, and benevolent father-figure of modern liberal Christianity, or the aloof beings of Epicurean philosophy. These godlike beings in *Doctor Who* are self-centered, capricious, indifferent to human fate, and in some cases actively hostile toward humanity. A few such super-powerful beings do have something of the Epicurean aloofness, such as the White Guardian in "The Ribos Operation" (1978), careless and content, sipping a cocktail in a tropical setting. Yet even the White Guardian can be menacing, threatening the Doctor with banishment from existence if he does not perform the Guardian's quest. Mainly, the super-powerful in *Doctor Who* regard humanity as "puny" and "ephemeral," as "toys" and "playthings," or as "willing servants" and "slaves." Never is it in their minds to look after and protect humanity or the Earth. Most importantly, all of them are *naturalized*. They are all explained as a part of the physical universe, not as above and beyond it.

In "Pyramids of Mars" (1975), for example, the viewer learns that the whole of Egyptian culture and mythology was based upon the culture of ancient extraterrestrials, the Osirians. The Egyptians took the battle between contending factions of Osirians, one led by Horus and the other by Sutekh, who becomes the god Set in the Egyptian mythology, and fashioned their mythology and culture around the alien ones. These Osirians have immense mental powers, live for thousands of years, and possess a highly advanced technology, all of which would make them appear to be gods to the early Egyptians. When the Doctor traps Sutekh, the last of the Osirians, he tells Sutekh, "The time of the Osirians is long past." The statement and story join many in *Doctor Who* that place godlike beings in the far ancient times of the universe, when it first began, and that assert that modern people can do without such beings. In essence, the assertion is that civilization has outgrown or evolved past the concept of gods, which are merely vastly powerful and ancient parts of the material universe anyway.

"The Dæmons" provides an example of a godlike being who guides human history, yet is indifferent to human fate. Most importantly, though Azal "looks like the very devil," he is only an alien being, mortal and vulnerable, possessed only of superior technology rather than superior essence. He is subject to perfectly natural scientific forces, and his apparently supernatural abilities, such as they are, derive from a "secret science," not from genuinely supernatural forces.

Similarly, in "City of Death" (1979), the main alien of supernormal ability, Scaroth last of the Jagaroth, possesses only superior knowledge and technology. Like Azal, Scaroth has pushed human history in particular directions mainly for his own ends. However, Scaroth has a particular goal. Like Sutekh and Azal, Scaroth has become mythologized in human cultures, but is in reality little like the myths.

The story "Enlightenment" (1983) concerns "immortals," beings who can create minor alterations of reality and who "occupy" eternity. While this would seem to make them equivalent to a god, their power is somewhat limited. They themselves lack personality and find eternity boring. They require contact with the minds of "ephemerals" to give their own existences some kind of value.

In "The Time Monster" (1972), viewers get the closest portrait of what could be a "god" according to normal definitions of the word. This being is Chronos, the ancient Greek Titan who represents time. Yet this Chronos through most of the story is a beast, not a god, and the Doctor's enemy the Master can capture and control Chronos for a time. When Chronos gets released and finally appears as a kind of goddess, there is no assertion that Chronos actually *is* a god of some kind, or that it is precisely what the ancient Greeks made it out to be.

The theme from all these examples comes through repeatedly. In *Doctor Who*, what might be called "gods" come from the early times, even the origin of the universe, characterized as a dark, chaotic period. These "gods" derive whatever powers they have from the universe itself, not from outside it, and these gods are not creators of the universe. These gods are aloof, capricious, warmongering, and unsympathetic. In short, "gods" are not to be trusted, and humanity is better off without them.

Faith

Because gods perform their miracles in secret or only in the deep past, people have no direct experience of them. Their experiences are mediated through the priests and other church functionaries. People may experience states of mind that they believe to be divine contact. However, for most people, belief in the supernatural comes down to matters of *faith*. While many among the religious laity and the theologians object to the definition of faith as belief without proof, in religious matters this is really what it comes down to. The faithful often feel they do not need proof as such, since their personal experiences and their cultural traditions uphold their beliefs and supply what they think of as sufficient proofs. Most of the time, faith is devotion to things unseen.

Sometimes, the portrayal of religion in *Doctor Who* can appear to be an incoherent misunderstanding of devotion. "Planet of Fire" (1984), for instance, centers in part on the religion of a group of inhabitants of the planet Sarn. The story gradually unveils the sources of this religion, unknown to the people of Sarn. This religion centers on the nearby volcano, which is worshipped as the executor of the fire god Logar. The priests of Logar, known as Elders, hold tremendous political power, most of which centers on the "chosen one," who bears a special tattoo. There is also a figure they know as "the Outsider," who appears in different guises from time to time bearing gifts to the followers of Logar. As is often the case in such societies, there is a small group of dissident unbelievers who risk death for their questioning of the religion and the authority of the Elders. These Elders do not work or contribute to the physical well-being of the culture, but live principally off the tithes that they demand from their community. The high priest Timanov has tremendous influence over the current young chosen one, Malkon, so that, although Malkon is the official spokesman for Logar's will, Timanov actually has nearly total say in interpreting Logar's wishes. Most manifestations of this religion come through Timanov's interpretations of various "signs" given by Logar. Throughout the story, these interpretations swing wildly.

An extreme example of these incoherent interpretation/reinterpretation jumps comes when the Doctor's arch enemy, the Master, uses a chameleonic robot, named Kamelion, to pose as the Outsider to convince Logar's followers to execute the Doctor. The execution involves a flame sustained by primordial gas pushed up by the volcano; thus, the flame is to Logar's followers a manifestation of Logar's will.[3] When Malkon, the chosen one, defies the false Outsider and the Doctor points out that this Outsider cannot even identify the Chosen One, Timanov blithely overrules Malkon.

The situation becomes even more complicated. In the confusion over authority between the Chosen One and the Outsider, Malkon gets shot down, and most of Logar's followers believe him to be dead. When the Doctor's companions manage to shut off the gas flow to the sacred fire before the Doctor is sacrificed, Timanov immediately interprets this as a sign that Logar "rejects" the sacrifice in anger for violence against the Chosen One. The Doctor and the Master then have a mental battle over control of Kamelion, the robot pretending to be the Outsider. During this struggle, Kamelion, controlled by the Master, orders the Doctor to be killed, but a confused Timanov decides to wait for Logar's "sign" to determine his course of action. As the two Time Lords struggle for mental control over Kamelion, the robot shines, which Logar's followers take as the "sign." When the Doctor loses control over Kamelion, Timanov orders him and the dissidents helping him imprisoned. One elder threatens to kill the Doctor's companion, Peri, but Timanov declares that there had been "too much killing" already.

It may seem as though "Planet of Fire" is rather casually dismissing religion as an incoherent system of *ad hoc* interpretations void of logical and moral content. Timanov sways this way and that, at first appearing rather blood thirsty, and then suddenly weary of killing. Logar's followers view every unusual event as some sort of divine "sign" and conclude numerous nonsequiturs from these signs.

However, the story had earlier prepared the viewer for these disturbances in Timanov's mind. Very early in the story, Timanov and Malkon had discussed the practice of burning unbelievers. Malkon calls the practice "barbaric," but Timanov calls it merely "over-zealous." Timanov, trying to persuade Malkon of his religious duty, states that it is "a wise precaution to send the occasional free thinker to the flame" because "burning encourages faith in our traditions." Timanov believes that their people and way of life are in danger, and that securing absolute faith in their traditions is the only means to save them: "For our people to survive, we must have faith." He further believes that all in the community, even unbelievers, profit from the burning of heretics: "It can be a rewarding experience for those consumed in the flame; unbelievers are such ... such unhappy souls." As Timanov sees these matters, unbelief endangers the entire society and threatens to destroy what small level of civilization they have. These pressures partly explain why Timanov is so desperate during the community's encounter with the Master.

Another way to understand Timanov's behavior is to ask what is in his religion for him. Langer, in writing about the linguistic origins of religion, argues that the point of rituals is not immediate instrumental value, nor is it fun. Rituals make it possible for people in a community to achieve the right *attitude* as that community defines it. The principal achievement of a ritual is *morale*. Rituals are not normally meant to produce a specified material effect (such as rain or striking down an enemy); instead, they are meant to have participants interact with the important forces of their existence. As far as the participant is concerned, if a ritual does not produce the expected result, that simply means that the ritual has not been *consummated*. A failure in getting the expected result usually means for the believer that something has gone wrong, that some unforeseen influence has interfered, but that the next performance of the ritual could produce a correct result and consummate the relationship between the believer and the supernatural (Langer *Philosophy* 139–41).

Timanov and his followers have had their comfortable world disrupted. Elements outside of their world of well-known rituals have destroyed the balance of their civilization and disrupted the followers' morale. Timanov's flailing for reasons derives from a simple desire to return things to as they were. From Timanov's perspective, if the strangers and all they bring can be fit into the mythology, then the world can return to its orderly system. Like other believers, Timanov turns to explanations for why a ritual has gone wrong. He can never see in a ritual's failure disproof of his beliefs. Thus, Timanov exhibits self-deception as discussed in Chapter 4, based upon personal bias (the overwhelming wish for his beliefs to be true) and misjudgment (wrongly interpreting the facts against his belief).

Despite whatever sympathy a viewer may have for Timanov's conflicted emotions, the story's portrayal in fact reflects much of the dark side of religion. Lucretius noted that "superstition is the mother of impious and sinful deeds" (12). Ethics professor Gabriel Palmer-Fernandez has discussed religion's "constructive" role in the creation of violence. He says that religion "provides an interpretive framework through a system of narratives and symbols that make possible extreme violence." He goes on to note that killing in God's name "as an act expressive of religious devotion" is both an "enduring and universal" characteristic of religion. Killing for the so-called glory of a deity is not limited to any religious group or type of religion, and very few religions, not even Buddhism, go without it (28). Even a religious philosopher, such as the Jesuit Lonergan, can recognize the problems that arise from the mythological aspects of religion. Lonergan calls these the "confines of mythic consciousness which operates without the benefit of distinctions that are generated only by the critically reflective process that is aware of myth and goes beyond it." The trouble with mythic consciousness, as Lonergan sees it, is that it fails to distinguish between experience, imagination, understanding, and judgment (538)[4]. Thus Timanov's inability to remain consistent in his judgment derives from his inability to distinguish between what he experiences and what he imagines his experiences to mean.

Additionally, Timanov's initial siding with what he believes to be the Outsider against the Chosen One demonstrates a historical truth of religion, that *interpreters* rather than prophets more often than not set the rules. "All religious notions are founded solely on authority," says the Romantic poet Percy Bysshe Shelley (39). Lucretius argues that the fear of eternal punishment after death keeps most people from questioning the "blood-curdling declamations of the prophets," who through "hocus-pocus" and "intimidation" can conjure up "phantoms" that will "overturn" one's life and "wreck" people's happiness (13). If a person is established, or establishes him or herself, as *the* authority on the deity's will, then prophets and supposed incarnations of divine spirits operate only as ciphers and objects to be worshipped and interpreted.

One reason that a living symbol of a myth, such as Malkon in "Planet of Fire," does not get to make pronouncements of his or her own regarding doctrine is that as symbols, such people lose their wills and identities as far as those around them are concerned. How is it that Timanov can override the wishes of a "chosen one"? It is precisely because "chosen one" is a concept inhabiting human form, a symbol in flesh. Symbols do not get to interpret themselves. Only humans can interpret symbols. That a human symbol has little say in his or her interpretation explains why Buddha (the Awakened One) and Christ (the Anointed One) can endure hundreds of diverse and contrary representations. They are simply symbols, archetypes even, in human form of the concepts "Enlightened" and "Anointed." They and others like them embody the abstractions identified by the labels attached to them.

Because religious symbols, personified or otherwise, cannot sustain a *single* interpretation for very long, disagreements and divisions among believers must inevitably follow. The formation of sects within various religions happens for this very reason, as people struggle over various "correct" interpretations of the words and deeds of the prophets. Often, these divisions happen almost immediately when a church is established. The biblical book Acts recounts various attempts by "apostles" to unify disparate collections of Jesus' worshippers, most of whom had not even yet begun to call themselves Christians. The book recounts disagreements between Greek speaking followers and Hebrew speaking followers, questions over how Jewish the Christian church is to be, and arguments over whether to include gentiles. The "apostles" are interpreters, men who claim to have spoken with God or Jesus or to have seen various signs of divinity's will, and thus also claim to have the authority to push the fledgling churches one way or the other. Although the writers of Acts attempt to portray a church gradually coming together, historical fact shows that there has never been a unified Christian faith, in part because charismatic and authoritative figures repeatedly reinterpret the words and acts of its central figure.

Additionally, throughout history, the devout have interpreted unusual events as signs from a deity. They see on a wall a stain vaguely shaped like a woman and imagine it to be a manifestation of Mary, mother of Jesus. American minister Jerry Falwell claimed that the devastating terrorist attacks of September 11, 2001, were proof of God's anger with an "immoral" America. Repeatedly, the devout take unusual events and normalize them within the interpretive framework of some religion. Given a rapid sequence of unusual events, such people will naturally sway, just as Timanov does, while trying to place the whole sequence into what to them seems a reasonable narrative.

"Planet of Fire," however, goes further in demoting religious authority. Not only does it expose the irrational and dark side of religion, but it also shows that religion derives from the imposition of symbolic narrative onto a sequence of natural events. The religion of Logar, it turns out, is based upon the arrival of members of a high-technology civilization from the planet Trion. The religious members of the low-technology civilization on Sarn have built up a mythology to account for technological marvels that they do not understand. The Chosen One, for instance, is a member of the high-tech society whose tattoo actually marks him as a prisoner. The vision of Logar is actually a man wearing a protective suit against volcanic heat. The Outsider is a member of the high-tech society whose job is to aid the low-tech society to a small degree. The people of Sarn, then, act out Shelley's characterization of religious belief: "Every time we say that God is the author of some phenomenon, that signifies that we are ignorant of how such a phenomenon was able to operate by forces or causes that we know in nature" (37).

As the story of "Planet of Fire" unfolds, Timanov and the Elders receive proof after proof of the purely material origins of their religion. The one they believe to be the Outsider tricks and belittles them. The various icons and relics of the religion are shown to be remains of high-tech man-made objects. The leading unbeliever, Amyand, proves to Timanov that his youthful vision of Logar is nothing more than a man in a heat-resistant suit. The ruins of the sacred ancient city are just the remains of an old Trion colony. The forbidden lands from which the Chosen One came, where Logar's followers saw a great fire, a sign of Logar, contain nothing more than the remains of a crashed spaceship, the source of the fire. At the end, the Trions themselves arrive to evacuate the Sarns before the volcano's imminent eruption. Not one piece of this religion has a supernatural origin. Here again the story demonstrates an idea articulated by Shelley: "If ignorance of nature gave birth to the gods, knowledge of nature is made for their destruction" (38). Thus, the freethinking unbelievers can see and understand the origins of their culture's faith once a character from a more technologically advanced culture shows what those origins really are.

"Planet of Fire" demonstrates another truth about religion: "Rational arguments have little impact on the true believer" (Koestler *Ghost* 255). This explains, in part, the willingness of many to die for their religions. In "Planet of Fire," the high priest Timanov, having been given complete proof that his religion of Logar the Fire Lord is a concoction of myths, chooses nevertheless to remain with a few other true believers and die in volcanic destruction. To him, physical proof is irrelevant, since the "real" Logar is in the hearts and minds of true believers and cares for them alone. Such action mimics the mass suicides committed by followers of the Russian Orthodox Church in the 1600s. These "Old Believers" refused to accept liturgical changes and preferred martyrdom, usually burning themselves to death. Nearly 20,000 such believers killed themselves in one century.

The demonstration of the limitations of religious belief in "Planet of Fire," and as we shall see in other *Doctor Who* stories as well, leads to the conclusion that Freud succinctly states in an essay on the origins of religious belief: "The religions of humanity ... must be classified as mass-delusions." These delusions stem from the desire to retreat from reality, the perceived source of all suffering, and substitute another reality that eliminates and replaces the painful aspects of lived experience. The retreat can be the idea that there is another, better reality somewhere else, or that this world of material reality is not "real" and that "spiritual reality" is the true reality. In whatever form the retreat takes, religion occurs when large numbers of people attempt together to "obtain assurance of happiness and protection from suffering by a delusional transformation of reality." Freud concludes this line of reasoning by noting that "no one who shares a delusion recognizes it as such" (22–3).

The religion of Logar follows Freud's mass-delusion theory of religion. The people of Sarn have placed a narrative on top of the natural phenomenon of a volcano. Through this narrative, which has very little correspondence to reality, they hope to ensure peace in this world by appeasing the god Logar, taking eruptions and earthquakes as signs of the nonexistent god's will. Through appeasing Logar, they try to ensure themselves of the protection from the elements they desperately seek, and simultaneously assure themselves peace forever after death, secure in the power of Logar. A viewer of "Planet of Fire" can simply substitute the name of any god he or she chooses, or substitute the mythic narratives and rituals of any religion he or she chooses, and end with the same conclusion: the religion is a mass-delusion as Freud describes it.

There is no doubt that the principal writer of "Planet of Fire," Peter Grimwade, has all religions in mind in this portrait. The story begins with an American archeologist looking for ancient artifacts off the coast of a Mediterranean island, remnants of a culture whose religion is now dead. In his novelization of "Planet of Fire," Grimwade makes several biblical references, for instance comparing Timanov's vision of Logar, which made the young man into a true believer, to Saul's vision of Jesus on the road to Damascus, which turned him into Paul the apostle. In an earlier story, "Time-Flight" (1982), Grimwade has the Doctor ridicule Bishop Berkeley's theory of perception, on which Berkeley had based his proof of God's existence. In short, Grimwade is perhaps the most openly dubious about supernatural providence of the *Doctor Who* writers,[5] and his skepticism is abundantly apparent in "Planet of Fire." He shows faith to be without foundation, a delusional and largely destructive psychological state.

Few stories in *Doctor Who* address the issues of faith and the foundations for religious belief quite as thoroughly as does "Planet of Fire." Many stories, such as "The Underwater Menace" and "Meglos," offer more basic and less detailed critiques of faith that still draw viewers to the same types of conclusions about it. Many other stories, particularly in the revived series since 2005, take a less harsh view of faith, as we shall see below, replacing the traditional faith-reward system of religion with a social-functional system. In all, *Doctor Who* demonstrates a skeptical view of religious content, and an uncertain view of religious functions.

Doubt

The opposite of faith is doubt. Throughout history, the faithful have viewed doubt as an intellectual enemy. "Faith in a shared belief-system is based on an act of emotional commitment; it rejects doubt as something evil" (Koestler *Ghost* 259). This idea that doubt is evil appears more often when religion is a group phenomenon. That is, on a person-to-person basis, the faithful can be on very good relations with the doubters. However, collectively, the view is quite a bit different, as Koestler makes clear:

[W]ithout a transcendental belief, each man is a mean little island. The need for self-transcendence through some form of "peak experience" (religious or aesthetic) and/or through social integration is inherent in man's condition. Transcendental beliefs are derived from certain ever-recurrent archetypal patterns which evoke instant emotive responses. But once they become institutionalized as the collective property of a group, they degenerate into rigid doctrines which, without losing their emotive appeal to the true believer, potentially offend his reasoning faculties [Koestler *Ghost* 260].

Because faith appeals to the emotions and contradicts the intellect, the devout must use a kind of double-think to ward off doubt. The defenses include official censorship, fear of contamination through contact with heresy, avoidance of forbidden information, classification of evidence contradictory to the belief as unreal or outdated, classification of evidence favoring the belief as glorious proof, interpretation of all facts of life solely in terms of the belief, and seeing the belief system and its leaders as infallible. The result is that what is a purely emotional response appears reasoned because it fits into a consistent pattern. This is the double-think, in which the belief system becomes a closed system through which all data are reinterpreted and relabeled, so that black can be white, right can be wrong, fact can be fiction.[6] The belief system pretends to offer a universally valid truth that explains "everything" and can cure all one's problems.[7] Adhering to the belief system involves tremendous distortions of logic and consistent use of the *ad hominem* counterargument, especially by attacking the motive of whoever disagrees with what one believes (Koestler *Ghost* 260–5).

One problem of trying to wrestle conceptually with religion is the complexity of the phenomenon. Stories such as "Planet of Fire," "Meglos," and "The Underwater Menace" demonstrate the rationalist view that religion is a kind of mass-delusion, a set of ignorant interpretations of natural phenomena, a means of political power, and a reactionary institution of oppression. The psychologist C.G. Jung has argued that such rationalist critiques of religion miss a fundamental component of religion, its *psychological* validity. Religion provides its adherents with the comfort of community, a reference to an external authority, and a secure fate, all of which, Jung argues, satisfy primal psychological needs and keep people in general functioning (*Undiscovered* 29–39).

To account for the destructive attributes of religion, Jung separates the concept "religion" from the concept "creed." Religion to Jung is the personal attitude of the believer toward the extramundane authority and irrational impulses of the psyche that constitute the believer's religion. A creed, according to Jung, is a set of doctrinal beliefs asserted by tradition and made necessary for participation in both the religious community and the society that holds the religion (*Undiscovered* 31–2). Thus, the rationalistic attacks on religion that one often finds in *Doctor Who* would actually be attacking the creeds and not the religions that give rise to them.

According to Jung in *The Undiscovered Self*, religion becomes creed when it conspires with the State, when its functions become as much political and social as they are religious. The creeds codify themselves into doctrines and customs, and "in so doing have externalized themselves to such an extent that the authentic religious element in them ... has been thrust into the background" (31). Creeds form established churches and public institutions that define what qualifies as belief (32). One can see in such *Doctor Who* stories as "Planet of Fire," "Meglos," and "The Underwater Menace" that religious figures have a great amount of political power in their communities, even when they are not the titular political leaders. This is the power of their creeds, which provide religious authority to support the positions of the rulers.

But it is hard to see how a religion would ever remain purely religious in Jung's terms and never fall into a creed. While religion may be a matter of a personal relationship between a believing individual and his or her chosen god, as Jung argues, it always requires diminution of the individual person. The religious person assumes that he or she is *less* than the gods and that his or her fate is in the control of these gods. Only the creed would provide the necessary narrative and ritual by which the believer could make sense of his or her feeling of inferiority in relation to the deity. By performing the right rituals, one points one's life in the right direction, gains the favor of the deity(ies), and fulfills the promise of the mythic narrative through making the narrative come alive again via reenactment.

There are two incidents in *Doctor Who* that give approving recognition of religious belief. The incidents are noteworthy because they are quite contrary to the general skepticism regarding religion that permeates the program. One may also note that both incidents occur early in the program's run, during the time of the first Doctor, when England was still a "religious" society, though already religion was a waning influence.

The first incident occurs in "The Romans" (1965). The story is set during the reign of Nero, ending on the day of the great fire of Rome, July 19, 64 C.E. The particular incident involves the slave buyer for the royal family, Tavius. He buys the Doctor's companion, Barbara, whom a slave trader had abducted. However, he treats her very well and in the end helps her to escape during the confusion of the fire. Barbara is perplexed by Tavius' concern. It turns out that Tavius is secretly a Christian. Thus, the story's ending contrasts the charity of the Christian against the barbarity of the rest of the Romans. At least in theory, that is what it sets out to do. In fact, Tavius is also the head of a plot to assassinate Nero, a strange thing for a "good" Christian to be doing. The contradiction undermines the warm feelings the audience is expected to have regarding Christianity as a source of moral conduct, though it is likely that most viewers never paid attention to the contradiction.

The second incident, which is subtler, occurs in "The Time Meddler" (1965). The story takes place in northern England in 1066 a few weeks prior to the invasion by the Viking king Harald Hardrada. The Doctor's companions, Vicki and Steven, both from the Earth's future after space travel is common, have been taken to a Saxon village, but then are released when they prove to be harmless. As they leave, the Saxon woman Edith tells them, "God be with you." The expression surprises Steven, who pauses before replying in kind. The pause suggests that in Steven's time of the high-tech far future, religious expressions of good will do not exist, or are at least extremely rare. The incident itself, like that in "The Romans," acts as a small reminder of Christian charity.

The historian Jennifer Michael Hecht in her history of doubt shows that there are actually several varieties of religious doubt. There is the rationalist materialist and purely atheist sort of doubt; the atheist "with a pious relationship to the universe" kind of doubt; the agnostic kind of doubt; a nonmaterialist moderate doubt; and belief (Hecht xi). There are certainly other ways to categorize doubt and belief, but this system serves my purpose because we can see that *Doctor Who* runs the spectrum from rationalist materialist to nonmaterialist moderate (rarely), but never to religious belief. In general, the usual stance for *Doctor Who* is atheist with a pious relationship to the universe. Such a stance accords well with the program's overall secular humanist orientation.

"Planet of Fire" demonstrates, among other things, that technological achievement and the knowledge accompanying it dispel mythic and religious thinking to a high degree. Religion is constructed on the grounds that a god or gods or life-force or ancestral spirit has powers beyond human ability and that these powers are manifested mostly in control of nature. The supernatural forces use the powers to dispense collective beneficence or damnation in the form of natural phenomena. Science and technology, along with the culture and civilization that go with them, have given people the powers that once only the gods supposedly had. However, the apotheosis is never complete, because god-like powers are achieved through artificial enhancements (Freud 33–5).

The result, as we see in "Planet of Fire" and other *Doctor Who* programs, is that the god-figure gets pushed further and further away into abstraction. At one time, God was the sky. However, once people learned that the sky was in some way natural, God becomes merely a dweller in the sky. English speakers may call this dwelling place "Heaven" and separate it from its sky-bound residence, but in most other languages there is no such distinction: "Heaven" and "sky" are the same word. Additionally, many documented religions clearly place their gods in the sky, Christianity among them. However, once science and technology teach us that the sky is just a collection of gasses and that there are other worlds and vast distances separating them, then the sky cannot be a dwelling place. Heaven must be pushed into some abstract realm, literally otherworldly, and the gods go right on into it. The gods become distantly removed from people, and division occurs between people and gods. Are the people to assuage their uneasiness and regain their lost celestial father or mother through strict devotion, strict adherence, and reactionary values? Such is the life of Timanov, ever chasing the harsh volcano-god-father's good will. Or, are the people to accept the provisional nature of material reality as the guiding principle? Such is the way of Amyand the Unbeliever.

As society becomes materialist and scientific, so does its education. As education becomes materialist and scientific, it loses its religious function. Nietzsche argues that the most important task of schools is to teach "rigorous thinking," which excludes the teaching of religion. Citing the biologist Karl Ernst von Baer,[8] Nietzsche notes that the emphasis on reason in education was what made the intellectual superiority of ancient Greece and later of Europe. The problem with Asian and Medieval European cultures, according to Nietzsche, was that they did not differentiate between "truth and poetry" (56–7). Ignoring the Eurocentrism of the argument for a moment, one can see that what Nietzsche argues is that the mythological-poetic view of religiously dominated cultures made it impossible for them to discern the true form of nature, to develop a scientific method, or to develop the benefits of a technological society.

The story "Meglos" provides an example of the science/religion split common to modern societies. The story "Meglos" places the science vs. religion conflict in very similar terms as the Intelligent Design debate does in the U.S., and more starkly than in any other *Doctor Who* story brings the clash to the center of the action. However, from the outset, the scientific elite of Tigella, known as Savants, come across as reasonable and reality-minded people, while the religious elite, known as the Deons, come across as small-minded, irrational fanatics with little regard for any truth that they do not believe they already possess.

The scientific, materialist, existentialist, and humanistic orientation of *Doctor Who* means that it must come to doubt the validity of religious ideas. The "null hypothesis" operates here. That is, in science "lack of proof is effectively disproof" (Ellis 20). Even to consider a hypothesis requires grounds for doing so. Thus, for instance, in "The Satan Pit" (2006), the Doctor entertains the idea that there really is a Devil trapped in some sort of Hell, for at least on first observation there is some evidence for it. However, he comes to reject the idea on rational and scientific grounds. He must conclude that absent positive evidence for a Devil hypothesis, he has not found the Devil and that there probably is not one.[9]

We can go even further along these lines. Commonly, because "super-natural" phenomena, such as gods and devils, are by definition above or beyond nature, they may be, as many religious philosophers claim, beyond the scope of reason. They are beyond detection, requiring, therefore, only belief. And that is the point. From the scientific standpoint, anything that is undetectable cannot be considered (Ellis 21). Furthermore, if it is outside of nature, yet somehow operates on nature, then that would make scientific inquiry impossible, because science requires natural regularity, and such regularity would be utterly disrupted. Hypotheses about a natural regularity that could be turned upside down at any moment would make doing science impossible (Ellis 21). Any intrusion by a "super" natural entity into nature would necessarily make it part of the natural order. It would produce observable effects and obey observable laws and thus would never be supernatural at all. Therefore, it is utterly logical, and not just a product of a particular worldview, that all entities that appear to be supernatural are naturalized in *Doctor Who*.

As a final consideration on the matter of doubt, one must face the truth that whenever one is talking about "religion" or presenting "belief" in a story, one almost never means these terms in the abstract. For Timanov and other true believers, the source of their belief is fact. As facts, they can be tested. Testing belief is the function of doubt. *Doctor Who* consistently exposes and undermines the habit of using abstract religious terms but meaning or implying specific ideas attached to them. In "The Dæmons," Jo is convinced that people have seen "the Devil" because their descriptions fit her received ideas about it. The Doctor sets her straight on the matter, though, identifying the creature as an alien with advanced technology that could be interpreted by early human society only as a malevolent supernatural force. Similarly, when the Doctor scares off a demon-statue brought to life, he does so by holding up an archaeologist's trowel and reciting nonsense words. When Jo asks him how he scared off the beast, he notes that iron (in the trowel) is commonly regarded as magical protection. "I thought you didn't believe in magic," states Jo, perhaps thinking she has caught the Doctor in a logical contradiction that would force him to accept the supernatural. "I don't," replies the Doctor, "but he did." The theme is kept going when the Doctor corrects the local white witch, Olive Hawthorne, about the powers of the alien. She assumes that "black magic" is in operation. The Doctor tells her that the rituals are part of the "secret science" of the Dæmons (the aliens in question), who harness the "psychic energies" that such procedures create. Miss Hawthorne persists by saying that the explanation defines "black magic." The Doctor, though, corrects her: not magic — science. "The Dæmons" provides several useful examples of a process repeated throughout *Doctor Who*. Because not even one of the particular god-beings stands up to scrutiny as being a god, one is led to conclude that in the universe of *Doctor Who* there is no god, no devil, no supernatural. What is left is the scientifically based view of the Doctor.

Religion as a Social Function

So, if *Doctor Who* both implicitly and explicitly rejects the *contents* of religious belief, denying the reality of the object of belief, then what is there left for religion and faith? The revived series under the guidance of producer, script editor, and principal script writer Russell Davies for five years, and now under similar guidance from Steven Moffat, has trended toward showing the positive value of religion and faith as personal anchor and social glue. In this view, the specific content of faith is irrelevant. One could believe in anything, and the value would still be there. That value comes in the form of *thanks*, *hope*, and *communion*.

"Planet of the Ood" (2008) provides a model of this conceptual triumvirate. The Ood share a telepathic connection, forming a mental communion. This mental connection takes the form of song, which conveys whatever mental state an Ood or group of Ood happen to be in. The song as rendered in the program for the audience sounds chorale-hymnal in a Church of England fashion, sung in Latin. When a group of Ood form a communion, they stand in a circle touching hands. They then raise their hands as in supplication to something in the sky. They use their "song," which is constant, as a method for storing history, much as the major holy books contain passages used to store history. The song they sing at the story's end is of thanks to "the Doctor-Donna" for freeing them from slavery. Nowhere in the story is there any statement that any of the Ood behavior is at all religious, yet the makers of the program have peppered extra-narrative religious signs throughout. In this way, the story avoids any complications from bringing in specific religious content. There is no mythology, no religious symbolism, no theology, no sense at all of what the Ood believe or that they have any beliefs or faith. Instead, what corresponds to human religious activity is made purely functional for social and psychological purposes.

With "Gridlock" (2007), the audience gets a view of faith as it bonds people into a society. The people in question are trapped on the city's motorway, spending their lifetimes going round and round without knowing that everyone else in the city is dead. What keeps these people going, keeps them alive and sane in the sense of socially functioning is a sense of community. They are bound by "friends" networks, by the daily broadcasts of a cheery hologramatic news reader, and a daily ritual of mass singing, in this case a cosy American hymn called "The Old Rugged Cross." At the end of the show, when the Doctor has released all the drivers to repopulate the city, they sing in unison another hymn, "Abide with Me," which often gets sung in part at English sporting events. At the times these hymns are sung in "Gridlock," the importance is not really on the content of the hymns, but on their power of social bonding, of providing hope in troubled times, and cementing faith in the community. Thus, the Doctor's companion, Martha, lists the hymns as one of several things these people have to keep them from despairing. What the hymns are about is not nearly as important as their social function, and really the songs could be about almost anything and serve the same function as long as the message is uplifting and encouraging.

The Religious Challenge in *Doctor Who*

In *Doctor Who*, the story that comes closest to bringing together these various arguments on the nature and value of religion is the two-part adventure "The Impossible Planet" and "The Satan Pit." In this story, the Doctor and Rose become trapped on a scientific research station. This station resides on a planet orbiting a black hole. The system of planet and black hole turn out to be a prison for an ancient powerful creature identifying itself as "the Beast." The Beast is now using the human base as its escape route.

The story itself resembles to a high degree the "return of the devil" sub-genre of horror films, movies such as *The Exorcist*, *The Omen*, *The Devil's Advocate*, and most particularly *Prince of Darkness*. In such stories, there is an evil figure identified with the figure called "the Devil" as characterized in extra-biblical Christian mythology.[10] This Devil seeks a bridgehead into the world so that it can take over the whole universe, and has chosen a single weak person and/or small community in an isolated environment as an access point. "The Impossible Planet" and "The Satan Pit," like these diabolical films, have numerous references to the Devil strewn throughout the story. When the Doctor and Rose arrive, for example, they see a sign saying "Welcome to Hell." References to the Book of Revelation, the biblical text that talks most about the Devil, include the name "The Beast," and use of the number 666 (the gravity funnel beamed from the planet requires "an inverted power index" of six to the sixth power every six seconds). The Beast claims to be the dark, evil power located in every religion, and to have been imprisoned since "before time." There is also what seems to be a deliberate misquotation from the biblical Book of Revelation, where a character called "the Beast" features prominently.[11] Other religious references recur throughout the story, from the station's being called a "sanctuary base" to common oaths such as "my God" and "godspeed." Two of the story's characters have nearly alle-gorical names, acting captain Zachary Cross-Flane and archaeologist Toby Zed[12], the weak person whom the Beast takes over. The black hole around which the planet orbits looks like a giant eye, similar to the giant eye of the evil Lord Sauron in the film version of *Lord of the Rings*, which likewise has a "return of the Devil" sensibility. Placing such a story in *Doctor Who* inevitably brings a clash of worldviews — the religious worldview in which a Devil is a reality, and the Doctor's scientific humanist worldview in which a Devil is not possible.

From early in the program, the Doctor takes the role of skeptic, bringing people back to reality, the empirical and *material* universe, whenever they start to turn toward religious interpretations of what is happening to them. When Rose asks if the Beast is the Devil, the Doctor tells her, "Keep it together." When the Beast tries to incite fear among the station's crew, the Doctor reassures them by telling them that the Beast is simply playing upon basic fears and that its apparently supernatural understanding of individual crew members' anxieties and disappointments is nothing that a good psychol-ogist could not produce. The Doctor points up a common phenomenon of religion, the tricks of prophets and charlatans to appear to have "secret" knowl-edge gained by only supernatural power. The Doctor points out that this is really a trick, not at all beyond human means. Additionally, in his first speaking encounter with the Beast, the Doctor notes that if the Beast had been trapped since the early days of the universe, it could not possibly have been available to inspire the religious ideas of evil that it claims to have done. Repeatedly, by use of Reason, the Doctor strips the Beast of supernatural power, a power that exists only to the extent that people believe it does. By taking away the *super* and leaving only the *natural*, the Doctor makes the danger the Beast poses into something manageable, inspiring the humans not to quit.

The program goes even further into the idea of evil as it is religiously characterized. Evil according to this line of thought exists as a supernatural, nearly all-powerful being that seeks to do harm to humanity by exploiting the weak and easily tempted. In "The Impossible Planet" and "The Satan Pit," the Beast takes control of the two psychologically weakest entities on the station, the highly insecure Toby Zed and the alien servant race known as the Ood, who have no individual consciousness or identity to withstand a mental takeover. In a program that takes extraordinary mental abilities for granted and reassigns them to the natural world of measurable and controllable phenomena[13], the Beast's ability to take control of some minds only appears to be an ability of supernatural evil. That the Beast can control some minds, and those of only the weakest individual identity, and not *all* minds of the people on the base, shows that the power is not supernatural. This fact of the story points out a fundamental flaw in the religious characterization of evil as a supernatural being. If the Devil had the power to take control of any human mind, being so much more powerful than humans, why doesn't he? Debates about free will or the protection of a more powerful good force as answers to this question involve far too many *ad hoc* arguments to go into here. Many of these issues will be discussed in subsequent chapters. The relevant answer to the problem is the *Doctor Who* answer: the problem does not exist because there is no Devil to cause it.

Characters in the story discuss the matter at various points. The conversation between the Doctor and the scientist Ida Scott is the most philosophical and involved. Scott, like an increasing number of people in Christian dominated countries today, occasionally goes to church out of habit and belongs to the denomination of her mother, but does not actually believe most of the church's teachings. Shortly, there will be more to say about the Doctor's beliefs, but it is easy to see that he does not believe in a "Devil." Their conversation comes down to this question: what *is* the Devil? Their two answers are entirely secular. The Doctor calls the Devil "an idea." Scott says the Devil is "the evil that men do." Thus, the Devil is not a thing utilizing a flaw in the human design, not an external force of any kind. Either answer leads to the same conclusion that the Devil is simply a label placed by humans onto some of their own activities.

In the end, if logically and empirically there is no justification for thinking that the supernatural exists, then what is left is *belief.* The question of belief also gets taken up in "The Impossible Planet" and "The Satan Pit," and focuses primarily upon the Doctor. It first comes up in the initial verbal exchange between the Doctor and the Beast. The Doctor rejects the Beast's claim that it has been locked up since "before time," saying that it is impossible. Given what audiences know of the character, it is reasonable to assume that the Doctor's claim of impossibility rests upon his scientific knowledge and experience. The Beast counters the Doctor's claim with the question, "Is that your religion?" This question mimics the often-made claim by the religious that any statement counter to religion is itself religious. The Doctor's reply, "It's a belief," actually reveals much.

One may take the Doctor's scientific and secular outlook as a worldview. The claim often made by the religious is that since religion is a worldview, every worldview is a religion. Logically, this claim is a category confusion, mistaking the smaller category, religious worldview, for the larger category, worldviews. The claim rests on a further logical fallacy, equivocation. It goes like this: Since religions are based upon belief, all beliefs are religious. However, the argument rests upon ignoring different definitions of "belief." The Doctor means by "belief" the trust that a conclusion derived from empirical knowledge and logical procedure is very probably true. One may take the Doctor's use of the word "belief" as similar to Hume's definition of the term, which is that experience of patterns of the past lead one to expect that pattern to carry over into the future (Hume 30). This expectation is *belief* when one discounts almost entirely the possibility of the pattern's not continuing in the future. For instance, since one has in the past always found that heat increases the closer one gets to a fire, if that person sees a fire at a distance, he or she *believes* that approaching the fire will increase the sensation of heat because he or she rules out based upon experience the possibility that no heat increase will occur coincident with increasing proximity to the fire. Religious "belief," though, requires the "leap of faith," the trust that a statement is true apart from any evidence or reason in its support. The religious point of view is that if a belief is held strongly enough, it is true. The secular point of view is that the religious view is wishful thinking. Thus, the Doctor's response that his claim is a "belief" validly counters the argument implied by the Beast's question. The Doctor's is a scientific belief, not a religious one.

Other things that the Doctor says in the story confirm the superiority of his secular view in the conception of the program. Unlike the religious, who claim to have the single answer for everything, the Doctor welcomes the fact that he does not. He states that the "belief" that motivates him "to keep traveling" is "to be proved wrong." He paraphrases this statement several times in the story. The statement itself summarizes quite well the difference between scientific and religious belief.[14] Scientific belief is the idea that being proved wrong brings one closer to truth. Religious belief is the idea that one already possesses absolute truth.

The Doctor's own belief is more than just belief in science. It is also a humanist belief. This comes through at a couple of points in the story. The Beast, as representative of certain religious strains if not of religion itself, relies upon fear to generate belief. The Doctor counters this fear with hope based upon human achievement. He assuages the crew's doubts and anxieties by pointing out their "amazing" accomplishments, such as getting to the "impossible planet" in the first place. His "belief" rests upon the fact of people who conquer their fears and discover and explore simply because something is there to be discovered. He implicitly believes that acquiring knowledge and meeting new challenges furthers the advancement of humanity more than does the religious view, which rests upon the *status quo* or even upon taking humanity backwards, as shown in the multiple references to the Beast as "ancient" and "old."

The Doctor has defied what philosopher Paul Kurtz calls "the transcendental temptation." The Beast says, "I am the temptation," a statement that catches the Doctor's attention enough for him to repeat it. The Beast also has the controlled Ood say, "You shall worship him." When the Doctor reaches the pit that turns out to be the Beast's prison, he describes "the urge" and "the itch" and a "little voice" saying "go down, go down." The "temptation," then, is to descend into the pit of darkness (identified with "fear" and "basic emotions") to release the beast (by definition, unreasoning) that demands worship because it can instill fear and guilt. The "transcendental temptation," according to Kurtz, is that "one may barter one's life to destiny, affirming that because of the limits of knowledge and the need for something more the transcendental stance is a meaningful response" (*Transcendental* 26). The agencies of the temptation are magical thinking, which is the belief that in the absence of a known physical cause for something an unknown supernatural cause must exist (454–5), the power of imagination to fill gaps left by limited knowledge (457–8), the need for rules and commandments to guide conduct (467–8), plus various social functions.

One can see the Beast in these two stories as symbolizing this transcendental temptation. Various characters are astounded by the Beast's apparent ability to see their minds and to affect events by broadcasting its thoughts. Since no "normal" answer seems to account for these abilities, characters are tempted to opt for a mythic-religious interpretation that would satisfy their need to know by providing an answer, even if it is the wrong one. Thus, for example, Rose seeks assurance from the Doctor that there is no such thing as "Satan." The Beast's ethical world is one of commands: you will worship, you will all die, don't turn around, and so on.

Contrasted against this transcendental temptation is rational skepticism, what Kurtz calls "selective positive skepticism" (*Transcendental* 27). This skepticism is part of critical inquiry, the search for *the* answer to a problem or question rather than *an* answer. One embarks on this inquiry aware that there are great possibilities for error and revision in whatever answer one finds, that knowledge has not ended and is in no danger of ending. Rational skepticism proceeds with a recognition that there are degrees of doubt and probability. It also proceeds with a recognition of the burden of proof, a need for evidence and corroboration (Kurtz *Transcendental* 34–40).

The Doctor's behavior demonstrates the superiority of this skeptical method for encountering the universe. The Doctor is not willing to accept an answer merely because it seems to fit. He questions his own beliefs, such as when he questions whether he was right to reject the Beast's claim that it existed since "before the universe." The Doctor welcomes the chance to be proved wrong. He recognizes the error of coming to a conclusion when not enough information exists to justify it. Thus, the Doctor refuses to state just what the Beast really was, saying merely that he does not know. This rational skepticism leads the Doctor to make the correct decision about what to do when he faces the Beast.

The binding up of these various ideas comes when the Doctor has come face to face with the Beast and finally realizes the trick it has used to effect its escape. This situation mimics a typical religious concept embedded in theology, the sacrifice of one so that all might be saved. In this case, the Beast has transferred its mind into the body of Toby Zed, now on an escaping spaceship with Rose. If the Doctor destroys the prison containing the Beast's body, now functioning as "just beast," he will kill Rose in the resulting gravity collapse. The Doctor's monologue at this point reveals the humanist answer to the religious problem: "But that implies in this grand scheme of gods and devils that she is just a victim. But I've seen a lot of this universe. I've seen fake gods and bad gods and demigods and would-be gods, and out of all that, out of that whole pantheon, if I believe in one thing — just one thing — I believe in her." The Doctor says that the one thing he believes in most is his assistant Rose, in her humanity, specifically in her courage and reason. He trusts her ability to reason her way through the problem, to see the trick, which in fact she does. The situation and the speech also recognize an aspect of religion, which the story and the Doctor both reject as invalid, which is that people are "victims" whose fate is in the control of supernatural beings. Whether the benevolent god Logar or the evil Beast is in charge, the problem is still the same — a person is victim of the choices the deity makes. The Doctor and *Doctor Who* defy this line of reasoning. The best that is in humanity can overcome the narrow strictures of a theological view that portrays the universe as the playground or battleground of supernatural forces, with people being merely pieces to be manipulated. Curiosity and Reason stand as the two pillars of the Doctor's *positive* humanism, which when applied with courage allow one to overcome the transcendental temptation.

So, we have seen in *Doctor Who* that religion and the supernatural are largely rejected as meaningful or valid ways of encountering the world. Though the program never outright attacks either any one religion or religion in general, it does repeatedly demonstrate flaws in the religious worldview. It also demonstrates that a *positive humanism*, a secular worldview based upon science, reason, and the desire for truth, is a superior worldview to religion, which is based upon emotion, faith, and the desire to isolate oneself from the unknown rather than to investigate it.

CHAPTER 7

Science

Tish Jones: He's a science geek, I should've known.
Doctor: Science geek, what's that mean?
Martha Jones: That you're obsessively enthusiastic about it.
Doctor: [*grins*] Oh, nice.

— "The Lazarus Experiment"

Defining Science

Signs and symbols of science surround the Doctor. The third Doctor had a regular working laboratory. The TARDIS provides occasion for numerous theoretical discourses on the nature of time. In itself, it is a technological marvel clearly from a more advanced science than Earth's. The Doctor's name/title itself suggests science in general, just as the Doctor is himself a scientific generalist. "Science" as a concept, an abstract noun full of promise, so pervades the series that one cannot ignore its impact upon the viewer.

Science as it is generally understood and practiced today arose and developed in tandem with Enlightenment philosophy and the Industrial Revolution. So intertwined are these three paths of knowledge that one cannot really follow the course of one without somewhere crossing the other two. In turn, these three paths of knowledge — science, Enlightenment, and technological evolution — combine to help form the modern humanistic outlook that *Doctor Who* espouses.

Carlo L. Lastrucci defines science as "an objective, logical, and systematic method, analysis of phenomena, devised to permit the accumulation of reliable knowledge" (6). In turn, a deeper understanding of science involves a fuller sense of the terms used to define it. *Objective*, for instance, Lastrucci defines as "attitudes devoid of personal whim, bias or prejudice, and to methods centered around ascertainment of the publicly demonstrable qualities of a phenomenon" (6). *Systematic* means that science has orderly methods and procedures (10). Scientific processes are logical, internally consistent, and thus

156

self-correcting. *Reliable* means dependably predictable (15). To be dependably predictable, science must be precise and exact.

As a science fiction series, *Doctor Who* often shows science in action. Audiences regularly see scientists experiment and study. These activities help provide the objective position to phenomena that science needs. Scientists gather facts and withhold judgments. In "Planet of the Spiders" (1974), the Doctor engages in an experiment to discover the extent of human psychic abilities. The subject sits in a chair and the Doctor uses various measuring devices to test responses. The Doctor is not seeking confirmation of a result he wants to get; instead, he tests to see what the result will be. The measurements are necessary for publishing and repeating results, which are the means for determining the reliability of the experiment.

Science is a set of practices using a particular general method (discussed later) to establish what is true about the material universe. It also has other features. Among these is a constant state of doubt. Scientific truths are tentative in the sense that they are not 100 percent confirmed, nor can they be because prediction is part of the scientific method. A predicted result may turn out to be wrong, which is itself data for further investigation.

One must also have a solid understanding of the terminology used in describing scientific conclusions. In science, a *fact* is a carefully observed instance, what has been found to be the case. A *law* in science is a rule found always to be the case describing specific kinds of phenomena. Thus "angle of incidence equals angle of reflection" is a law. A *theory* in science is an explanation of facts and laws. One must therefore distinguish between the popular conceptions of these terms. In popular thought, a "fact" means whatever is widely accepted to be true, and a "theory" is whatever is speculated (Carrier 219). In science, as we shall see, the popularity of a belief has no bearing upon its truth and thus no relevance concerning its standing as a fact. Additionally, in science speculation is merely an early stage in a mental process producing theories in the scientific sense.

How Science Is Done

Previously, we reviewed the modes of thinking and how they produced knowledge, and then arrived at the conclusion that *critical thinking* was the most reliable form of thinking for producing new ideas both true and useful. There are two different levels of critical thinking, though, and in discussing *science*, we will be discussing the higher order of critical thinking. John Dewey makes a useful distinction between these two, which will aid understanding of the scientific difference.

The first order Dewey calls *empirical thinking,* which is the perception of associations and connections. To use Langer's linguistic terminology, this level of thinking is the perception of *signs.* Or, to use Hume's terminology, this level of thinking is pure *belief.* One notes that B often happens after A, and therefore anticipates B's occurrence every time A happens. Thus, A becomes a *sign* of B. The person *believes* that B will happen every time he or she experiences A. However, the person using only empirical thinking does not inquire after *why* A and B are so associated. That is, the person fails to make the *connection* (Dewey 145).

Empirical thinking is quite useful. A large amount of what we call "practical knowledge" comes from empirical thinking. Mastery of agriculture derives from empirical thinking. Noting the changes in the position of sun, moon, and stars provided humanity with reasonably reliable signs for knowing when to plant which crops, and when to harvest them. The ancient calendars of the Mayas and the Anasazi are marvels of empirical thinking. The accuracy of observation astounds the modern mind raised to believe in the "primitive" ways of ancient peoples. Yet, as magnificent as these accomplishments are, they were made entirely without looking into *why* they worked. The only concern was *that* they worked. They are demonstrations of skill, but not of knowledge in the advanced or scientific sense.

The disadvantages of purely empirical thinking glare when we consider the *why* question of phenomena. The trouble with empirical thinking if one goes no further is that it leads to stagnation. Repetition is the conclusion of empirical thinking. From it, one gets general rules and first principles, but beyond this no progress occurs. Empirical thinking leads to logical fallacies. Hasty generalizations commonly follow, where one expects that the rules one has learned apply in multiple areas to which they do not. Empirical thinking leads to causal fallacies (in logic known as *post hoc, ergo propter hoc*— after this, therefore because of this) when someone assumes that an event that precedes another causes the other, and so looks no further for the true connections between events. For instance, one can conclude, as is often the case (especially since the 1980s) in *Doctor Who,* that because the Doctor commonly appears where there is trouble, that he must be the cause of the trouble, that the trouble is his fault. Clearly, though, it is not the case that merely "being there" is a cause, and if one traces the effects back to their origins, one will see that in most cases the Doctor is not the cause of whatever trouble is happening.

A quick example from "The Pirate Planet" (1978) demonstrates the limitations of purely empirical thinking. The Captain, who rules the planet, regularly announces a new Golden Age of Prosperity. He gives the people great wealth in the form of rare gems and minerals. Also, the lights in the sky change; i.e., the pattern of stars forms a new arrangement. The people in general note that these two events always happen together, yet few to none inquire beyond this. What is happening to make both the bounty of gems and the change in the constellations?[1] One inhabitant, Kimus, intuitively senses that something is wrong with the constant new Golden Age announcements, prompting the Doctor to call it "an economic miracle." He says, "Of course it is wrong." To ask a question such as what links the Golden Ages and the change in constellations and to pursue it to its conclusion is to take the next step toward scientific thinking.

To summarize the disadvantages of purely empirical thought, we can list its defects. Empirical thought as an end often leads to hasty generalizations, and by extension lazy thinking in general. Empirical thinking as an end often leads to assuming false causes. Empirical thinking as an end cannot account for novel events. Empirical thinking as an end leads to traditional and conservative thinking, whereby a person will disregard the new or disconfirming, and overestimate that which confirms the old ideas. Therefore, purely empirical thinking often leads to "fantastic and mythological explanations" (Dewey 148). Finally, in its worst form, empirical thinking as an end leads to dogmatism, the belief that a tradition or an "established body of knowledge" must remain always intact, and must be guarded by authorities who cannot be questioned. Through empirical thinking alone, one can easily fail to recognize that what used to work no longer works, and that yesterday's knowledge could be false.

Scientific thinking fixes the problems of empirical thinking. To use scientific thinking, one does not discard empirical thinking; instead, one begins from empirical thinking. The rules of the past are not merely accepted, but are tested to determine their validity, worth, or truth. With scientific thinking, new rules, or *theories*, come, but only after old rules have been questioned. It is not enough to know *that* B follows A; the scientific thinker looks for *why* B follows A. Thus, scientific thought is always flexible because with it, one does not assume that what was will be, nor does one accept that what is currently known is all that is knowable or is entirely correct. The advantage of scientific thought is best expressed by the nineteenth century English philosopher W.K. Clifford, who said, "Skill enables a man to deal with the same circumstances that he has met before, scientific thought enables him to deal with different circumstances that he has never met before" (88).

Science is not merely the kind of thinking just described; it is the application of that kind of thinking. Thus, science is creative. A scientist does not merely think at or about a problem; a scientist attempts to solve that problem. The means of solving problems is called "scientific method." It is much misunderstood through popularizations of scientists as pedantic, lonely nitpickers. At other times, dedication gets mistaken for obsession, leading to the "mad scientist" parody.

During the run of Doctor 3 (1970–4), viewers got a look at the Doctor practicing science more often than at any other time in the series. There is both truth and popular misconception in these portrayals. On the one hand, viewers could see how a scientist uses study and experimentation to solve clearly defined problems. On the other hand, the program often showed the Doctor and other scientists as lone workers in small laboratories kitted out far too similarly to a high school chemistry lab.

A clarification of what "scientific method" actually means is needed. Scientific method, according to Theodore Schick, Jr., and Lewis Vaughn is the system of overcoming conclusions based purely upon personal experience (80–1). In the scientific method, one does not take matters on authority. Measurement, calculation, and logic substitute for personal reports and "the great person says so" claims. For this method to work, scientists accept one proposition as given, namely "that the world is *publicly understandable*" (Schick and Vaughn 176). The proposition has three parts: "(1) The world has a determinate structure; (2) we can know that structure; and (3) this knowledge is available to everyone" (Schick and Vaughn 176). This public aspect of science is part of what makes it *objective* in Lastrucci's terms. For science to work, publication is essential to the process. The scientific method does not in itself make a scientific statement fully reliable, but it does provide the means for finding out whether a statement is reliable and the degree of its reliability. Only publication makes this self-correcting method possible. Publication means not only to print in obscurely technical scientific journals, but also availability to anyone who wants the information. A scientific statement's reliability comes from its ability to withstand the toughest criticism and closest scrutiny.

When one takes the idea that the world is publicly understandable, one arrives at how scientific statements actually get made. The popular conception has science working according to the procedure of observe-hypothesize-deduce-test, where a scientists observes phenomena (or collects data), makes hypotheses about the observations, deduces the conditions under which the hypotheses would be true, and then tests the deductions through experimentation and/or further observation. This is called the *inductive method* of science because data supposedly leads to hypothesis. Viewers of *Doctor Who* see the Third Doctor regularly working in this manner of the popular understanding of scientific method. It is not the only method, though. Historian and philosopher Richard Carrier notes that though science may follow this general procedure, there are many methods by which one may perform any of the steps. Many of these more particular methods come from carefully finding out which works and which does not. Furthermore, the methods are field specific, so that methods that work in biology do not necessarily work in physics (Carrier 215).

Several philosophers of science have noted that this popular conception of scientific method has a major flaw, namely beginning from "observation." If observation is taken to be the collection of data, then the data observed are meaningless without an already formulated hypothesis to guide the observer. In short, the observer has first to know what to look for before he or she begins looking. "Scientific investigation can occur only after a hypothesis has been formulated, and induction is not the only way of formulating a hypothesis" (Schick and Vaughn 178).

As an example of the problems of trying to observe without placing observation within a context, one can consider what happens in the *Doctor Who* story "The Moonbase" (1967). The Doctor finds a problem: moonbase crew are getting sick and dying seemingly at random. The Doctor must find the cause of this disease. To do so, he takes samples of just about everything on the moonbase, with no result at all. Finally, in a brilliant flash of insight, he hits upon the sugar that the men take in their coffee as the source of the illness, which is really a poisoning, since sugar is the only substance with which only some of the men come into contact. This point about the role of observation needs to be stressed. The examples show that observation without context makes scientific activity hit-or-miss. Though lucky coincidences that produce positive results happen in *Doctor Who*, in reality such coincidences are highly unlikely. In reality, observation without context is very difficult. To return to "The Moonbase," the Doctor surmises early on that the disease affecting the men "isn't really a disease at all." This observation comes from experience with diseases, which informs the Doctor about the ways diseases ought to behave. The observation does have a context and becomes the source of the suddenly intuited solution. However, the Doctor fails to follow through with this initial observation, and instead takes a "data overload" approach to solving the problem, hoping that somewhere in the almost randomly collected overflow of data is a secret to the problem's solution.

So, taking out "observation" as necessarily the first step of the scientific method, one must revise the thinking about how science is really done. A scientific hypothesis can sometimes arise from observation. However, it can also refer to concepts that are not in the data. A famous example is the atomic theory of matter, which rests upon data that one can describe without reference to atoms. Thus, a scientific hypothesis may come from pure inference, or from imaginative "thought problems," or even from intuitive leaps such as the Doctor's sudden realization of sugar as the source of the poison. A large amount of hypothesizing is highly creative. However, this creativity is not purely making things up, nor just guesswork. In hypothesis formulation, specific criteria guide a scientist, such as testability (can one formulate a test or experiment for it?), parsimony (is this the simplest answer to the problem?), practicality (is there a useful result?), reasonability (does one have to formulate too many extra hypotheses to prove the one hypothesis in question?), and so on.

Another popular misconception of scientific method exists in the common phrase "Science says...." Such misconceptions presume that in science, one comes to final answers. In reality, though, "no scientific hypotheses can be conclusively confirmed because the possibility of someday finding evidence to the contrary can't be ruled out" (Schick and Vaughn 182). Scientific hypotheses both *retrodict* (explain previously observed data or problems) and *predict* (guide a scientist about what to expect in the future). Since no prediction is guaranteed when it is made, no final confirmation can occur. On the other hand, one cannot absolutely confute a scientific hypothesis either. One negative result cannot disprove a scientific theory since there could always be outside factors influencing the result. Rather, probability and preponderance of evidence determine what becomes scientific "fact." Even then, no fact in science is absolutely certain.

In fact, the more one looks into the matter, the more complexified the scientific method becomes. In the early 1900s, Adam Leroy Jones published an introductory textbook on the scientific method identifying several mental activities in the process, because the scientific method actually involves most of the processes of good reasoning. Thus, he discusses the use of classification, labeling, inductive logic, proof, falsification, statistics, averages, probabilities, explanations, hypotheses, and reference to existing systems of knowledge as all being part of what is generally called the scientific method. The great utilitarian philosopher of the nineteenth century, John Stuart Mill, had identified a similar set of mental activities involved in scientific method. Both Jones and Mill categorize scientific method as a species of logic. Put more precisely, Mill argues that logic is the "science of science" (*John* 12), that it is the means by which a scientist moves from data to theory. Mill says, "Logic is the common judge and arbiter of all particular investigations. It does not undertake to find evidence, but to determine whether it has been found" (11). Because these logical mental activities are so important to both the process of formulating hypotheses and of drawing inferences, both Mill's and Jones's works are primarily explanations of logic.

We need not review all the systems of logic for an understanding of scientific method. It is enough to see the Doctor at work on a scientific problem to see the role of logic in the process. The logic comes into play in the Doctor's habit of reserving judgment. Repeatedly, companions and other characters ask the Doctor for enlightenment about a novel situation. Repeatedly, the Doctor refrains from making an absolute statement that might mislead people. It is logical to avoid hasty generalizations. Additionally, the Doctor uses hypothetical syllogisms, "if ... then ..." statements leading to definite conclusions.

The importance of scientific method to every other aspect of science is so great that Friedrich Nietzsche claimed the methods were "at least as important as any other result of research: for it is upon the insight into method that the scientific spirit depends: and if these methods were lost, then all the results of science could not prevent a renewed triumph of superstition and nonsense" (63–4). However, as Karl Popper has demonstrated, following the scientific method all by itself is not the qualifying factor for determining when someone is "doing" science. Put another way, what most people assume is the "scientific method," probably including Nietzsche, is not the entirety of the scientific method. Science cannot be done by the lone person tirelessly toiling away to unlock the secrets of the universe. This picture is really a kind of mysticism associated with alchemy. True science is a social enterprise existing in a community.

The fundamental terms for communication within this community are "replicability" and "falsifiability." For any scientific discovery to be meaningful it must be submitted to the scientific community for evaluation, i.e., be published. There now comes a debate phase, in which the scientist's or team's conclusions are evaluated. For these conclusions to be validated, they must first be tested. That means that the methods by which the scientist or team derived the conclusions must be replicable. A scientific study must have clear instructions for how to produce the result. The study must also state the criteria necessary for refuting the conclusion; in other words, the study must be falsifiable.

This explanation of the community aspects of scientific method is the contribution of Popper, and represents one of the two great advancements in the philosophy of science in the twentieth century.[2] Popper shows that scientific objectivity does not rest in the observation-hypothesis-experiment-conclusion process, which is liable to suffer from individual prejudices, personal biases, and external pressures. Rather, "objectivity" comes from the examination of results in the scientific community. Scientific social institutions such as laboratories, universities, and journals provide the objectivity, not the individual scientist or scientific team, no matter how hard one tries to be logical and objective (*Open II* 217–20). The individual scientist can succumb to egocentric biases and fallacies, while the scientific team can easily become trapped in groupthink.

One may identify the characteristics of science as methodological naturalism. In general terms, methodological naturalism means commitment to the hypothetical-deductive method of acquiring knowledge. That involves, roughly, imagining an explanation for a phenomenon, then testing this explanatory hypothesis by means of controlled experiment and by prediction. Tested hypotheses are then integrated into more comprehensive theories, primarily mathematically expressed. Theories and results may be reviewed by anyone, and independently corroborated or disproved (Kurtz *What* 23–4).

Several *Doctor Who* stories demonstrate the community aspect of science at work. One is "The Claws of Axos" (1971). In this story, an alien has landed on England, bringing with it Axonite, a substance that can grow and shrink matter. The Doctor wants to analyze a sample of Axonite, but to do so he must secure the cooperation of the scientist in charge of the local particle accelerator. Science in this case, as in the real world, is not a matter of backyard tinkering. It involves a giant, highly technical, nuclear-powered apparatus run by a team of scientists and technicians with a lead scientist in charge. Another example comes in "New Earth" (2006), in which a large hospital also contains a secret research project into the curing of all human disease. This project is large, probably expensive, and operated by a large team, not a lone scientist hidden under the facility like the Phantom of the Opera.

Real dangers exist when scientists do not follow the processes of science. A subplot from "The Leisure Hive" (1980) demonstrates some of the bad consequences of not following scientific procedure. The people of Argolis are dying. A war has left the race sterile, and now almost all are old and moribund. An Earth scientist named Hardin has been working on the problem by experimenting with tachyons, trying to reverse the aging process. However, his machine does not actually work. Convinced that he will succeed despite contrary evidence, but lacking funds to continue his experiments, Hardin does not publish his negative findings and fakes his results. The faked video of the experiment convinces the Argolin leadership to back Hardin.

Hardin's deviations from scientific method are independence and secrecy. He works alone and restricts knowledge about his process. The consequence is fraud. Additionally, Hardin risks exposure as a fraud should an expert in tachyonics see his faked video. In fact, an expert does see it, the Doctor's companion Romana, who kindly takes to helping Hardin rectify his errors instead of exposing him. In the end, though, the process never does work. Viewers do not learn of Hardin's fate, but in the real world Hardin's behavior would lead to expulsion from the scientific community at the least and possible criminal charges. Hardin forgets that the goal of science is not being right, but discovering truth, even when the truth is that one's theory is false.

When a scientist is "doing science" correctly, that person performs a specific set of mental tasks in a specific way. Science, then, is a form of critical thinking. It starts from empirical thinking, the perception of associations and connections, and proceeds through the testing of ideas derived from empirical thinking. Science is a community activity usually performed by teams and managed within the larger community of scientists. Scientific procedures and results need to be public to ensure honesty, relevance of scientific applications to the public good, and proper scrutiny of scientific results. The goal of all these processes is objectivity, the best assurance that results are as true as possible.

Scientific Truth

Conclusions of the scientific method are always tentative. This is not to say that they are therefore untrue or without foundation or merely "hypothetical" or "theoretical." Rather, it is to say that science arrives at statements that are *probably* true. Put another way, for any scientific theory to be considered valid, it must account for the phenomena it describes with a high degree of accuracy. However, at any time any theory is a "best determination" based upon the observations and tests of the time. A scientific theory is valid when it routinely turns out to be correct. Thus, a scientific theory is a *belief* in the sense that David Hume meant belief, meaning an expectation of a future consequence based upon previous experience.

Good scientists welcome challenges to current theories and findings. To them, such challenges mean that science is *working*. However, challenges they accept need to be reasonable, meaning that they need to come from an understanding of the relevant scientific principles, or from experience of phenomena contrary to what a scientist would expect given the current theory. For a scientist, the challenge presents a new problem to be solved, a new area illuminated. A brief example of the enthusiasm for challenges comes from "The Three Doctors" (1972–3). When the physicist Dr. Tyler gets whisked off to another world seemingly instantly, he does not panic. He does not ignore what has happened. Instead, he draws equations in the sand trying to work out the physics of an event that totally contradicts both theories of relativity.

In popular opinion, scientific tentativeness is seen as a flaw. If theories are constantly overturned, if scientists are constantly wrong, then what good is science? Contrary to this belief, though, this tentative quality of science is one of its great strengths. A scientific theory does not change as a matter of fashion, nor as a matter of doctrine. Rather, scientific theories change because of *better* observations and *better* theories, where better *always* means "more accurate." As Carrier says, in science "evidence is king" and the "dogmas of science will ultimately bend to its will" (216).

Thus, no theory that is widely accepted in the scientific community is "just a theory," as popular opinion would have it. The theory of universal gravitation and the theory of evolution by natural selection hold because they are well-supported; there is little contrary evidence against them, and that evidence is highly suspect. A scientific theory remains accepted because the huge preponderance of evidence overwhelmingly corroborates it, leaving only a very minute chance of its being in error. In science, a hypothesis gets counted as a theory only when it has repeatedly withstood the tests of doubt and rigorous review.

Science and the Public

The existentialist philosopher Jaspers states, "*Science* has gained an ever-growing overwhelming importance; by its consequences it has become the fate of the world" (139). The question of the degree to which one can live one's life by and for science is constantly with those who live in the modern technological world, from the nineteenth century forward in the industrial societies. We are surrounded by its products, the technology that makes our lives possible and is so inextricably part of the fabric of culture. We are constantly reminded of new aspects of existence, once marvelous, now made material and controllable through science. The average person is bombarded by statistics, while it seems that every intellectual endeavor aspires to the condition of science. None of this is necessarily bad or wrong. However, too many people are ignorant of the ways and means of science, and so see it either as a kind of menace to the knowledge and lifestyles they grew up with or a cure-all for every social ailment.

Since genuine scientific inquiry began in earnest during the late Renaissance, the discoveries of science have turned "common" knowledge upside down and erased much of what seemed certain. Jaspers notes that these "inversions cause scientific superstitions and a desperate hatred of science" (139). For these reasons, it is quite common for philosophers to try to limit the intellectual scope of science. Jaspers, for example, thought of science's role as the beginning of philosophy, providing the data upon which philosophy must be based. One source who summarizes Jaspers puts it this way: one must overcome science's apparent omniscience to become one's transcendent self (Gallagher 118–9).

However, this understanding of science as a source of oppression stems from a misunderstanding that the Thomist philosopher Bernard Lonergan explained. This confusion derives from thinking that scientific explanations and common experience naturally conflict. As Lonergan describes it, the problem stems from confusing what Renaissance philosophers would distinguish as primary and secondary qualities of nature, the difference between what something actually is and what it appears to be. More complexly, science, and its related mode of discourse, concerns a "comprehensive, universal, invariant, non-imaginable domain" of the thing itself, which is to be *explained*. Common sense, or common experience, and its related mode of discourse, concerns an "experiential, particular, relative, imaginable domain" of the thing for us, which is to be *described*. These are methodological differences that help one understand why so many scientific explanations run totally counter to our common experience of the way the world works (Lonergan 293–6).

As an example, we can consider the Doctor's time traveling. Time travel is theoretically possible, at least at the very boundaries of current scientific speculation. Let us say that it is in fact possible and that the Doctor defies no scientific law by traveling to and fro in history. Scientific theory thus *explains* the Doctor's time traveling in terms of laws, postulates, and formulae. However, time travel violates commonsense experience because it creates cause-effect paradoxes. Common experience is life understood as cause-effect sequences along a single temporal direction. Common experience thus *describes* the Doctor's time traveling in terms of adjusting the cause-effect sequences so that a clear order is once more established. So, for instance, in "The Visitation" (1982), the Doctor's presence in seventeenth-century England becomes part of what has been described elsewhere in the series as the "web of history" when he *causes* the Great Fire of London.

One problem in the popular conception of science, which has been seized upon and exaggerated in postmodernist culture criticism and philosophy, is the notion that when a scientist makes a public pronouncement, he or she speaks with the voice of science. Put another way, if a scientist makes a political statement, it is assumed that this is the political stance of science. To complicate matters, many scientists themselves have fallen into this fallacy of making unscientific pronouncements using science as their justifications.

However, as Lastrucci points out, "a scientist, as a scientist, does not advocate any values" (8). This is not to say that scientists as scientists do not have values. As scientists, they value what belongs to science, such as pursuit of knowledge for its own sake, pioneering research, or scrupulous and thorough work. Such values are not to be confused with the values of whatever culture to which the scientist belongs. Culture may influence areas of research or even the choice to be a scientist, but scientific values are not necessarily cultural ones. To be more precise, political, social, and moral pronouncements are not in themselves scientific, nor do they originate in science. Thus, even when asked to give an opinion in such matters as an "expert," a scientist is really in no better position than any other citizen in making such pronouncements.

Nevertheless, there exist repeated demands that science be put to "practical use" for the "public good." An example of this public face of science comes from "The Mind of Evil" (1971), when early in the program a rather self-satisfied scientist demonstrates the Keller Machine for extracting negative emotions from a criminal's mind, supposedly to render the criminal into a "productive, if lowly, member of society." Another example comes from "The Green Death," wherein Global Chemicals has produced a method for converting oil that will produce cheap fuel and plenty of it. Intriguingly, these and other examples from *Doctor Who* of science in the public good end up being disastrous. There are examples of "applied" science that actually are in the public interest, such as Professor Jones' Wholeweal community in "The Green Death." These contrasts no doubt come from the basic need for there to be an evil for the Doctor to fight. However, they also demonstrate the general ambivalence of the public toward science. On the one hand, there is appreciation for all that science in the public good has done; on the other, there is the fear that such applications may go "too far."

Reductionism

Another argument that has some popularity among the public is that science "reduces" interesting, amazing, extraordinary, beautiful things and events into just the changes of matter and energy. Physicist and ecologist Fritjof Capra has devoted several books to the task of demolishing what he considers to be predominant reductionist, linear, Newtonian (his terms) strain in science. Theologian David Ray Griffin has taken a similar line of argument, stating that the principal theme in modern science has been "the idea that science requires a reductionistic account, and rules out all downward causation from personal causes and all action at a distance" (4). The English naturalist and anthropologist Gregory Bateson wrote a whole diatribe against "linear" science, arguing among other things that there is no "objective" experience, that science never proves anything, but only formulates perceptions, and that every scientific theory needs to account for the personal subjective perspective of the person or people making the theory (27–71). What bothers these and other writers on the matter is that scientific reductionism seems to rule out any consideration that cannot be made in terms of strict physical laws regarding only the interactions of matter and energy.

Doctor Who has picked up this perspective from time to time. In "The Dæmons," the Doctor and Jo have a running conversation about whether there is "magic" in the world, or phenomena inexplicable to scientific investigation. Jo brings up such "New Age" ideas of the 1960s and 1970s as "The Age of Aquarius." The Doctor, however, demonstrates how "magic" is about appearance. The Doctor makes his car move and respond to his commands without a driver. He does so by remote control, thus demonstrating that what is currently inexplicable will not necessarily always be so, once the key piece of evidence is found. The debate gets carried forward between the Doctor and Olive Hawthorne, the local white witch of a small English town. The Doctor has the last word in this debate by declaring, in essence, that "magic" is simply an application of science unknown or unclear to the observer. By the end of the story, though, the Doctor admits that there is "magic" in the world. However, this magic is the resiliency of people, who can pick up their lives after great trouble and celebrate life despite the troubles, the celebration in this case being a traditional English May Day.

Another *Doctor Who* story takes a different approach. "The Mind of Evil," as stated earlier, opens with a demonstration of a machine that supposedly extracts the negative emotions from criminals, leaving behind a healthy, well-adjusted member of society. Of course, the machine actually does nothing of the sort. However, the idea behind the machine is consonant with many theories popular in the mid-twentieth century, theories that supposedly quantified and regulated human behavior. The story takes up the idea mainly to reject it. The problem with attempts to place behavioral science on the same level as physical science is that the two areas do not correlate. At least, that is how one of the leading philosophers of the twentieth century, John Searle, sees it. The problem, says Searle, is a matter of "grounding." Physical sciences are grounded in simple phenomena the interactions of which can be predicted with high accuracy according to a formulated "law." Even though human behavior has its origins in the same physical phenomena, by the time it has attained the level to manifest as human behavior, its complexity has far outreached simple prediction according to mathematical or statistical laws (Searle 71–7).

The historian and philosopher Richard Carrier has taken up this issue of reductionism in science and demonstrated that the common view rests upon a set of misunderstandings regarding how scientific explanations work. Reductionism is the argument that everything in a defined field can be explained by one thing. In this sense, science in the last hundred years has been reducing, or converging, upon the laws of physics as the foundation for explanation, and physics is the study of the transformations of matter and energy. Thus, it would seem that "everything" can be explained in these terms. Thinking along these lines produces the Keller Machine of "The Mind of Evil," premised on the belief that complex human behavior such as criminality reduces to elementary particles, described as "negative emotions" in the story.

However, the reality is that the pattern of arrangement for any set of material objects has as much or more to do with the nature of those objects as does the "stuff" the objects are made of (Carrier 130). The two-part story "The Empty Child" and "The Doctor Dances" (2005) provides a good demonstration of this argument. In this story, a boy wearing a gas mask has been killed by a bomb during the London blitz of 1941. A set of nanogenes, microscopic medical robots, has come across the body and tried to put it back together, but does the job wrong because the nanogenes have never encountered a human before. Thus, they fuse the gas mask and the flesh and provide the reanimated brain with only a limited set of responses. The result, as the Doctor characterizes it, is human DNA that has been "rewritten by an idiot." Even though the living boy and the reanimated corpse are made of exactly the same "stuff," they are clearly quite different things. The pattern of arrangements, including causes and circumstances, accounts for these differences.

Carrier notes an additional mistake critics of scientific reductionism make, which is to confuse reduction of substance with reduction of method. Carrier gives the example of psychology, which is rapidly reducing to biology in terms of identifying the causes of mental distress. This reduction does not, however, make the practice of psychology meaningless because mental states are emergent properties of patterns of arrangement, and these emergent properties are too complex for people to throw away psychological explanations of them. As Carrier states, "The higher science of psychology is needed in order to simplify and analyze aggregate phenomena, focusing on larger patterns rather than the myriad smaller ones that compose them" (131). Thus, higher-order sciences studying epiphenomena, those that emerge from the interactions of baser components, will continue to have an important place in science.

Part of what drives the campaign against reductionism is the false popular sense that because science relies upon skepticism and logic, that scientists are dour, destructive people with no sense of wonder and little imagination. In reality, no description of scientists could be further from the truth. The Doctor demonstrates that wonder and imagination are integral parts of a scientific worldview.

One example of this wonder comes from "The Ark in Space" (1975). When the Doctor is dissecting a giant insect carcass, he marvels at the creature's "superb adaptation." In "The Green Death," the Doctor pauses to admire a giant insect even after he had to kill it to preserve his own life. Time and again, the Doctor pauses to marvel at the beauty and intricacy of the natural universe. The desire to understand is not the same as the desire to control, and those who view science as "reductionist" in this sense can learn from the example of the Doctor that their opinion is faulty.

Good Science and Bad Science

Like most science fiction, *Doctor Who* is generally approving of science, though with some ambivalence. The mixed feelings come from the larger cultural attitudes about science and from the realization that, like every other human endeavor, science has produced some terrible things. Philosophically, there is a tug-of-war between the Enlightenment's almost totally affirmative attitude toward science, and Romanticism's anxieties about dangerous industrialism and technology that seem to come from what scientists discover. Typical of the push me/pull you between Enlightenment and Romanticism, *Doctor Who*'s humanism finds its expression in contrasting types of science. Science is a tool, and as such in itself morally neutral. Its use becomes the important issue for future humanity.

In the case of *Doctor Who*, setting often functions to demonstrate one or the other interpretation of the modern scientific enterprise. Tulloch and Alvarado note that bad science (in terms of its devastating results) gets symbolized in caves and tunnels and blasted landscapes. On the other side, symbols of benevolent scientific progress frequently appear as space stations and research establishments (69). For instance, the Cyberman story "The Invasion" (1968), which involves the use of a corporation so that the scientifically antihuman Cybermen can insert themselves into human society, takes place in numerous tunnels and sewers, which create an oppressive and claustrophobic atmosphere, enhancing the "something is wrong" ambience of the story. Contrarily, "The Wheel in Space" (1968), another Cyberman story, takes place almost entirely on a space station on which valiant scientists and technicians fight off a Cyberman invasion. Though realistically a space station would probably be nearly as claustrophobic as a tunnel, the Wheel is rather spacious and open.

In plot, too, *Doctor Who* often displays the disparate interpretations of science within the same story. An example of the contrasting bad and good science is "The Green Death." In this story, "bad" science is characterized in Global Chemicals. Alternatively, "good" science is characterized in Wholeweal, an independent research establishment commonly referred to as the Nut Hatch. "The Green Death" has the strongest pro-environmental message in *Doctor Who*, but one can hear echoes of this story's sentiments throughout the program's history.

Global Chemicals is a secretive for-profit corporation. Its purpose seems mainly to supply petroleum-based products, or to devise petroleum alternatives using a similar product. It promises abundant, inexpensive power. And that is indeed a worthy endeavor, which Global Chemicals plays to its full potential in terms of public relations.

The story itself opens with the manager of Global Chemicals, Professor Stevens, promising a group of Welsh coal miners "wealth in our time." However, from the beginning, a viewer will note something seriously wrong with Global Chemicals. Stevens' opening speech mimics Neville Chamberlain's famous statement that his agreement with Hitler brings "peace in our time." Thus, an alert viewer will spot right away that Global Chemicals is not to be trusted. Being a for-profit government contractor, Global Chemicals is obsessed with security, complete with locked gates and armed guards, a sure sign in *Doctor Who* that something very wrong is happening that the evildoers do not want known. The very coal miners to whom Stevens speaks were put out of work by Global Chemicals. Finally, the process that Global Chemicals uses produces a highly toxic waste sludge that causes monstrous mutations in the local insect population. The manager and the computer that runs the company know of these problems, but do everything possible to hide the evidence, even at the expense of human life, in order to preserve the status of Global Chemicals.

Wholeweal is a very different place. It is important that the viewer not mistake the contrast, or, as Professor Jones, who runs the Nut Hatch warns, think of the Nut Hatch as an asylum for dropouts. All the members are scientists and academics who have decided to bypass the usual systems of approving projects and experiments. The Wholeweal community itself is dedicated not to making itself rich and powerful, but to putting science to use in solving world problems. Professor Jones himself is taking on the problem of famine in underdeveloped countries through cultivation of high-protein fungus. Wholeweal is an open community rather than a high-security factory.

The contrast of the two views of science as two different ways to "do" science makes "The Green Death" the most explicit portrayal in *Doctor Who* of debates about what science should be. It mimics a popular sentiment that science in the employ of government or corporations is always suspect. It also supports the idea that science is best practiced separate from the forces that would compromise scientists' consciences.

More commonly in *Doctor Who*, bad science is often a matter of bad scientists. These can range from the over-the-top hysterics of Professor Zaroff in "The Underwater Menace" (1967) to the obsessive dedication of Professor Lasky in "The Trial of a Time Lord: Terror of the Vervoids" (1986). The former simply wants to blow up the world because he can do it. The latter sees her work as more important than nearly all other considerations, though near the end of the story she does admit that her professional ambition blinded her to the implications of her results. In part, stock characterizations of the "mad scientist" have something to do with this. However, the mad scientist is also a symbol of the fear that science may destroy people's ethical sense.

Good science in *Doctor Who* follows the Wholeweal ideal of intrepid, independent investigators. These are like the research team in "The Impossible Planet" (2006), whom the Doctor admires because they risked their lives living in danger to study a planetary anomaly simply because "it was there."

There are also the scientists such as Dr. Tyler in "The Three Doctors," determined to discover new information and to solve problems. These portrayals show that "good" science in the *Doctor Who* universe is always a matter of expanding knowledge.

It is true that applied science has been the single most important contributor to general prosperity, well-being, and cultural advancement in the modern era. As scientist, commentator, and novelist C.P. Snow put it, "We cannot avoid the realization that applied science has made it possible to remove unnecessary suffering from a billion individual human lives" (*Naturalism* 73). Because science provides the means for relieving mass suffering and deprivation, Snow contends that the scientific revolution needs to spread across the world. However, the cost to the planet for unchecked development, for the spread of technology without guiding conscience must also be recognized. *Doctor Who* stories such as "The Green Death" demonstrate this need for conscience to accompany scientific advancement.

Scientism

A curious phenomenon common to science fiction is that scientists are often portrayed as overzealous about their work, and thus as dangerous. *Doctor Who* sometimes follows this pattern, as seen with Professors Zaroff and Lasky. Another example comes from "Power of the Daleks" (1966), in which Lesterson, the chief scientist of a human colony in space, has found a crashed space pod with what he takes to be robots inside it. He believes that these robots will revolutionize society, and so pays no heed to the Doctor, who warns him that these are dangerous creatures known as Daleks and not servile robots. Even after Lesterson receives more than enough proof that his robots are really something else, he pursues his program of reactivating Daleks and treats the Doctor as a rival. Lesterson is overly possessive of his lab and keeps secrets. Of course, Lesterson's actions lead to the almost complete destruction of the colony. Lesterson's attitude may be summarized as follows: the scientist always knows best because science always knows best.

The attitude described above is "scientism," which ecology professor Massimo Pigliucci defines as "an ideological position implying that science is the only key to solve any problem worth addressing" (21). The naturalist philosopher Kai Nielsen defines scientism as "the belief that what cannot be known by science ... cannot be known" (26). At its furthest extent, scientism involves the kind of unification of all knowledge into the physical sciences that the controversial biologist E.O. Wilson attempted in the book *Consilience: The Unity of Knowledge*. Pigliucci criticizes Wilson's sort of unified theory of everything by characterizing it as mainly "a program of academic imperialism" (21). Scientism confirms the fears of those who see science as reductionist in the wrong sense of that word.

Another common form of scientism is the notion that society should be led by science, or more specifically by scientists. In this view, one replaces Plato's "philosopher kings," who would run his idealized republic, with scientist kings. A *Doctor Who* story that critiques political scientism is "The Savages" (1966). In this story, a future society seems completely utopian, where no need goes unmet and science has provided nearly total material comfort. However, this entire system works by the scientists' extracting the life energy from people who live abject lives in prehistoric conditions. The scientist kings regard these "savages" with utter contempt, and completely ignore that they are capable of both art and compassion. Based upon cruel exploitation, this scientific utopia is false to the true aims of science and civilization.

Almost every mad scientist in fiction, including in *Doctor Who*, follows scientism. Of course, one need not be dangerously insane to practice scientism. Being merely eccentric or loopy is enough. For instance, noted American skeptic Michael Shermer reports in one of his books on the Extropians, members of the Extropy Institute founded in 1988. Extropians fervently believe that because science and technology have significantly improved everyday lives and vastly expanded human collective knowledge, science and technology will go on to solve the most fundamental problems. Cultural disharmony, disease, even death will all be cured in the foreseeable future, according to the Extropians. Indeed, many well-known scientists agree with or are sympathetic to Extropian views, at least if one is to judge by the list of speakers at the Extropian conventions. One might call this version of scientism a "faith" in science, a belief based on scant evidence and numerous hasty generalizations that science will solve all the problems that religion has not (Shermer 59–61).

Pigliucci asserts that scientism also gives bad publicity for science and skepticism (22). Scientism leads the general public to believe that all scientists are arrogant, presumptuous, and dismissive. One can see this in the character of young genius millionaire Luke Rattigan in "The Sontaran Stratagem" and "The Poison Sky" (2008). Rattigan has turned his home into a kind of science cult compound, a sort of Extropian boot camp, where he has young geniuses work on various projects while living separated from their normal lives. Rattigan expects devotion to his ideas and himself, and gets easily upset, as the Doctor points out, when someone says "no" to him. Firmly believing in the superiority of scientific genius, Rattigan is completely surprised that his protégés abandon him when disaster threatens their families. For Rattigan, anyone not a scientific genius is a lesser being unworthy of sympathy. Rattigan, then, exemplifies many of the problems of scientism.

Science vs. Religion

Another area of public concern is that science is the enemy of religion. Given that much of the public believes that scientists are mad or eccentric, anti-social, and driven by reductionist scientism, it is little wonder that the anti-religion perception holds much sway in the public mind. Certainly, when a popular program such as *Doctor Who* depicts scientists in this manner, it upholds some of the public discomfort with science. The belief is that science precludes religion, or that expanding scientific discovery diminishes faith and hence diminishes religion itself. Since the 1700s, many thinkers have attempted either to widen the divide or mend the fences between science and religion. However, it may turn out that the public is right and that more science means less religion.

The poet Shelley conjectured, "If ignorance of nature gave birth to gods, knowledge of nature is made for their destruction." He further notes that human "terrors dissipated in the same proportion as [human minds] became enlightened." As Shelley states it, "The educated man ceases to be superstitious" (38). While *Doctor Who* never goes fully so far in this regard, it does favor the idea that science pushes back religion and that most religion is superstition.

The examples in support of these ideas are plentiful, and have in many ways already been discussed in Chapter 6. "Planet of Fire" (1984) demonstrates that religious belief is founded upon incorrect interpretations of nature. Natural phenomena are attributed to supernatural beings, but instead are purely natural. Knowledge about how and why things are as they are favors the rationalist doubter over the religious believer.

Similarly, "The Underwater Menace" works through the contention between science and religion, and ends by favoring science. The story pits the mad scientist Zaroff, absolute believer in scientism, against the nearly as mad high priest Lolem, absolute believer in his fish goddess Amdo, both fighting for influence over the king of Atlantis. Lolem is all too willing to use human sacrifice. He is credulous, and thus easily fooled into believing that almost anything unusual is a manifestation of Amdo. Lolem does bring to the Atlanteans a sense that they are protected and special, a psychological and social comfort. In the character of Zaroff, science appears to hold a similar position. On the one hand, Zaroff is too willing to perform something like sacrifice himself, by turning lost travelers into human fish. Zaroff fools the king of Atlantis into believing that he can make Atlantis rise from the sea, when in fact Zaroff plans to destroy the world. On the other hand, Zaroff's technological improvements to the Atlantean way of life provide the people with material abundance. It would seem inevitable that the two extremist antagonists would come to a physical fight to the death, symbolically enacting the religion versus science motif that had run throughout the story.

It would seem equally inevitable that the story would settle for some sort of "balance" between science and religion, recognizing in the two personalities the extremes that should be thrown off so that the good can come through. However, this is not quite how "The Underwater Menace" resolves the issue. The balance might be seen in the character of Damon, a native Atlantean whom Zaroff has provided with a scientific education, a character who might be taken as symbolic of the two sides of post–Zaroff Atlantean life. However, the story resists this "balance" symbolism. In the end, when Zaroff's madness has nearly destroyed Atlantis, Damon does not really embrace this middle path that the story heavily implies as a resolution. Instead, when the surviving King Thous offers to raise a stone in the new temple of Atlantis, Damon rejects the idea. Having the final word on the matter, Damon says that the temple should remain buried and that there should be no new temples. The way forward, says Damon, is to take the knowledge Zaroff gave the Atlanteans and build a new Atlantis without either temples or fish people. Thus, the middle way, the rational way, is not to reconcile science and religion, but to take the best from science, and throw out the worst of it and the religion too.

Science and Humanism

As we have seen, *Doctor Who* plays out a debate concerning the nature of science, a debate that characterizes the whole of post-1950s science fiction. On the one hand, there is the Enlightenment conviction about the benefits of science and knowledge, a belief in progress, and hope for humanity to throw away the chains of religious superstition. This conviction has never vanished, and was strong enough to influence the romantics' Romantic, Percy Shelley. On the other hand, there is fear that scientific and technological progress may remove the "essence" of humanity and replace it with a machine essence (Tulloch and Alvarado 70). Blake's "dark Satanic mills" become Global Chemicals in "The Green Death," International Electromatix in "The Invasion," Think Tank in "Robot," Cybus Industries in "Rise of the Cybermen" and "Age of Steel."

However, *Doctor Who* also takes the more realistic and rational view of science, that science is a particular domain and method of understanding. Science does not need to compete with common sense. It does not need to be tamed and subsumed into philosophy or metaphysics. One should not see it as an exercise in oppression and control. These false views come from misunderstanding the nature and function of science, and perhaps from some envy of science's successes and wide-ranging effects.

Science is methodical application of intelligent inquiry. It stems from the nearly universal human trait of curiosity, and turns that curiosity into structured acquisition of empirical truth. Lonergan contrasts this methodical curiosity with that of the child, who would have all questions answered at once even when bursting forth in a flood of questions. As Lonergan states,

> [The child] does not suspect that there is a strategy in the accumulation of insights, that the answers to many questions depend on answers to still other questions, that, often enough, advertence to these other questions arises only from the insight that to meet interesting questions one has to begin from quite uninteresting ones. There is, then, common to all men, the very spirit of inquiry that constitutes the scientific attitude. But in its native state it is untutored. Our intellectual careers begin to bud in the incessant "What?" and "Why?" of childhood. They flower only if we are willing, or constrained, to learn how to learn. They bring forth fruit only after the discovery that, if we really would mast the answers, we somehow have to find them out ourselves [173–4].

The Doctor's childlike wonder and curiosity, then, are simply emergences of the primal basis for the scientific attitude.

CHAPTER 8

Good and Evil

Doctor: What is the one thing evil cannot face, not ever?
Tegan: What?
Doctor: Itself.

—"Kinda"

The Language of Good and Evil

In the 1980s, the controversial American political theorist Allan Bloom identified what he thought of as "*the* most important and most astonishing phenomenon of our time," which was "an entirely new language of good and evil" that attempts to go beyond these very concepts and thus prevents people from talking about the concepts with any consistency (141). Bloom identifies the source of this phenomenon as German Romanticist philosophy, culminating in Nietzsche's demolition of nineteenth-century verities. "God is dead," Nietzsche has his fictional prophet Zarathustra declare, and so he declares as a corollary the death of all values commonly thought of as "eternal." After Nietzsche, the simple language of eternal verity gets devalued in favor of the complex language of relative values (Bloom 141–7).

In Western cultures, a struggle has developed between the two conceptions of good and evil: eternal vs. relative, or essentialist vs. relativist. On the one hand, an essentialist view of good and evil is easy to grasp and provides ready measures and standards upon which to found judgment. However, essentialism when mishandled leads to stereotyping, egocentrism, and the worst forms of nationalism. On the other hand, relativism requires careful assessment and understanding. However, relativism when mishandled leads to the absurd positions that *all* points of view are equally valid and that every matter is negotiable. The result is often stagnation and inaction in the face of gross injustice.

One can view this struggle in conception throughout *Doctor Who*. As a science fiction program, *Doctor Who* is built upon mythic story apparatus, which includes recognizable monsters, allegorically depicted characters, and truly villainous villains, all "evil" mainly because that is how the story defines them. There is little to assess or understand about such characters; they have no psychology apart from the label "evil." Nevertheless, many *Doctor Who* stories take an alternative position, getting "inside the heads" of the villains, to use a cliché, and showing them as misguided or misunderstood, often following the wrong course for the best of reasons.

Despite the conflicting conceptions of good and evil in both *Doctor Who* and Western culture in general, a careful analysis reveals that the program has reasonably consistent definitions of both "good" and "evil," and that these definitions correspond to the humanist and existentialist philosophies that form the program's intellectual foundation.

Static and Dynamic

One answer to the question of what good and evil are comes from Plato. He argues that good is the "saving and improving element," while evil is the "corrupting and destroying element" (303). In short, Plato sees that which is eternal and unchanging, in other words static, as good, and that which is malleable and changeable, in other words dynamic, as evil.[1] Plato repeatedly uses the words "corruption" and "degeneration" to describe change.

In *Doctor Who* some characters take up ideas similar to Plato's. In "Ghost Light" (1989) the creature Light is a kind of galactic encyclopedist who tries to catalog all life on planets. Light is obsessed with change, which renders his catalog obsolete, and desires to arrest change, to make everything be always what it is, and never become what it will be. However, "Ghost Light" demonstrates that the typical *Doctor Who* position on the matter is contrary to Plato's. Light, as stated earlier, is obsessed, fixated on what he perceives to be the terrible mistake of change, of evolution. Obsessions of this kind are these days thought to be signs of an unstable mind or personality. Unable to accept reality, the obsessive character loses flexibility and demands that the world conform to a single ideal. At the show's end, the Doctor taunts Light with constant reminders of change, so that Light's power to fixate small patches of reality turns inward; he gradually becomes stone, a symbol of both permanence and inflexibility.

"Ghost Light" ties this critique of Platonic idealism with the fight over evolution. Set in the late 1800s, the story includes the character of Reverend Matthews, an opponent of evolution who claims, "Man has been the same ... since he stood in the Garden of Eden." The opposition to evolution, then, stems from a belief in the permanence and perfection of the creation, and the admission that life evolves is an admission that the creation is less than perfect. Light, too, opposes the concept of evolution, though not on the same grounds as Matthews. For Light, evolution is an inconvenience that makes his cataloguing work impossible to finish. The Doctor's response to Light is simple: "That's life."

"Ghost Light" most forcefully demonstrates a running theme in *Doctor Who*: rejection of equating change with corruption. Instead, the story demonstrates the idea that change leads to improvement. This idea is embodied in the character of Control. Originally, Control is a genetically created early human meant to be used as a standard to assess the characteristics of the human species. However, the Doctor and Ace accidentally release Control, who over the course of two nights swiftly develops into a very good replica of a Victorian lady. In "Ghost Light," civilization is an evolutionary development, and evolution creates greater scope for mental, emotional, and ethical development of the individual human. The idea runs wholly counter to the Platonic theory that human civilization has been successively degenerating through a series of ages. The idea of evolution in "Ghost Light" stresses *development*, an important concept in the *Doctor Who* version of good vs. evil.

Virtue and Vice

In *The Republic*, Plato has Socrates consider the nature of judges in an ideal society. Socrates concludes that a good judge must have a good nature, and must, from birth, not know vice. The argument seems to be that virtue and vice are permanent qualities of the "soul," which are imbued in a person congenitally. Plato also has Socrates say that virtue, being "good," is permanent, true, and unchanging; vice, however, is "corrupt," by which Plato almost always means changes. Since the material world is similarly corrupt, the vicious see only reflections of their own behaviors and thus cannot intuit virtue when they find it. The virtuous, however, seeing vice in action, will eventually understand its nature, though never succumb to it. Thus, according to Plato "vice cannot know virtue too, but a virtuous nature, educated by time, will acquire a knowledge of both virtue and vice" (99).

It is clear that Plato has a strict idea of human nature. Given a definition of "good" as "that which does not change," he cannot help but come to false conclusions about a person's "good" nature. In particular, the Platonic definition rules out the possibility of free will. If a person is virtuous or vicious from birth, then that person cannot help but act out his or her nature.

In *Doctor Who*, whether someone is good or evil from birth, that is naturally and inescapably good or evil, does not get much consideration, but where it does get consideration, the program goes out of the way to reject it. An example is the Doctor's arch-rival and "evil" double, the Master. Whenever he appears, the Master seems to delight in causing harm through an egocentric idea that one must rule or be ruled. Yet repeatedly, the Doctor treats the Master as though he can change, mainly through the power of reasoning. Since the Master seemingly does not change, the question remains open: is he simply unwilling to change or is he naturally incapable of change?

The question comes to a head in "The End of Time" (2009). In a prior episode, "The Sound of Drums" (2007), the Doctor reveals that when potential Time Lords are eight years old, they are shown the Time Vortex, and that a child's reaction to that experience will determine whether he or she will become a Time Lord. He hints that the Master as a child saw the Vortex and went insane. The conjecture is brought back in "The End of Time." If it is true that the Master *became* evil through some outside influence, then he probably was not *born* evil. Because he is not born evil, his behavior can change. This line of reasoning explains why the Doctor persists throughout the story in trying to persuade the Master to give up his way of life.

It turns out, though, that the Master is more a victim than a master, and not just a victim of a childhood mental breakdown. All his life since seeing the Vortex, the Master has had an incessant four beat pattern pounding in his mind like a drum line. This beat was actually implanted by the Time Lords to provide them with a homing signal by which they could return their planet and themselves from a time trap the Doctor had placed them in. Thus, the Master believes that his plan to replicate himself in the entire human race is his idea, but in fact some such idea was inevitable to provide the amplification of the signal in his mind for Gallifrey's return. In a way, the audience and the Doctor are placed in the position of feeling sorry for the Master. His evil is the acting out of his misery forced upon him since childhood. Once more, *Doctor Who* rejects Platonic idealism and essentialism, and embraces a purely material explanation for vicious behavior.

More often than not in *Doctor Who*, and even in "The End of Time," vice is a choice. Even if the Master is both insane and manipulated, he is nevertheless intelligent enough and self-aware enough to realize it. Thus, the Doctor never sees it as futile to argue the Master out of whatever he is trying to do, from the early days of the character in such stories as "The Time Monster" (1972) up to his last appearance (so far) in "The End of Time." Indeed, the idea of choice associated with vice is a running motif of the revived series from 2005 onwards. Repeatedly, the Doctor asks or attempts to persuade wrongdoers to stop their vicious activities. Choice is a vital concept in this regard because it precludes the possibility in the Doctor's mind, and thus in the viewers' minds, that viciousness is inevitable.

Viewers have seen that some characters in *Doctor Who* do not merely choose vicious action, but actually cultivate vice as a habit. By the same token, virtue may also be cultivated as a habit. This idea, too, is advanced in *Doctor Who*. Time and again stories show characters who use reason or conscience to impel them to do the right thing. Furthermore, characters will often find that doing good leads them to doing more good in the same way that many of the villains will feel that they have gone so far in doing evil that they cannot turn away from it. In "The Next Doctor" (2008), Jackson Lake, an ordinary Victorian mathematics teacher, accidentally becomes a heroic adventurer after his brain is inundated with information pertaining to the Doctor. However, after Lake learns of his true identity, he does not immediately go back to his old, staid life, nor wallow in self-pity for the loss of his wife and son. Instead, he rescues the Doctor and aids him in defeating the Cybermen. Even after this adventure is over, the program strongly hints that Lake is a much better man for having played the Doctor.

In promoting the idea that vice and virtue may be cultivated, and that acting virtuously or viciously can become self-perpetuating habits, *Doctor Who* takes a more Aristotelian view of vice and virtue than a Platonic one. In the *Nicomachean Ethics*, Aristotle argues that actions that produce virtue increase virtue (27). By implication, actions that produce viciousness increase viciousness. In other words, to be virtuous, one must consciously act virtuously. Furthermore, the sources of virtue are identifiable, namely: "First, with knowledge, secondly, from rational choice, and rational choice of the actions for their own sake, and, thirdly, from a firm and unshakeable character" (28). It follows, then, that a virtuous character can come about only through *practice*, both in the sense of application in the world and in the sense of making it a habit. Aristotle argues that "virtue of character ... is a result of habituation" and that what arises from a person "naturally" must first be acquired as a capacity and then exhibited in activity (23). A virtuous character is one who makes it a habit to be virtuous. Aristotle makes it clear that the labels "virtue" and "vice" can apply only to *voluntary* actions.

Doctor Who clearly lays out a formulation for understanding vice and virtue very similar to Aristotle's. The key to this formulation is mainly through the Doctor's character, which follows the model of voluntary virtuous action made into a habit. Similarly, vice is mostly the choice to act viciously, which itself can become habit. Because these are voluntary habits, it is possible for a "vicious" character to change his or her ways. Sometimes persuasion and example do work. It works with the arrogant and ambitious Professor Lasky in "The Trial of a Timelord: Terror of the Vervoids" (1986) when she realizes the terrible results of her attitude and sets out to rectify the problem. Another example is the self-absorbed young genius Luke Rattigan in "The Poison Sky"

(2008). Rattigan has allied himself with the warrior race known as Sontarans to allow them to take control of the Earth, destroying all but a few specially chosen humans. When he finally realizes just what his plans really mean, he decides to take the Doctor's advice and "do something clever" with his life, in this case sacrificing himself to save both the Doctor and the Earth.

So, while *Doctor Who* does have its share of stock villains who seem to be evil because the story requires them to be so, a good portion of the stories, and most of the better ones, take a more nuanced and realistic view of vice and evil. This view recognizes that where vicious action is clearly voluntary, the fault lies not with a person who *is* vicious or evil, but with a person who *chooses* to be vicious or evil.

Enemies

Characters designated as "evil" in stories often function as scapegoats, repositories of unwanted social and personal iniquities that can be banished through destruction of their container (Burke 34). This, at least, has been the mythical function of evil characters. It has also noticeably operated in much of science fiction. In the Cold War days, many Americans feared the collectivist "menace" of the USSR and China, believing them to be opposed to every value Americans used to define themselves. Alien invaders became "containers" for these fears. Novels such as Jack Finney's *The Body Snatchers* (1955) and Robert Heinlein's *The Puppet Masters* (1951) embodied the collectivist "nightmare" as stealth invaders who could pose as ordinary Americans and take control from within. Defeat of these aliens from outer space with evil collectivist ambitions symbolically destroyed the imagined threat from overseas.

Doctor Who has not been immune to the pattern of containing evil, in both senses of the word, that much other science fiction has used. The two great alien menaces from the early days of the program, the Daleks and the Cybermen, embody the fears that many in the UK still had of a totalitarian takeover of Europe. The Daleks and Cybermen, with their jerky mechanical motions, their "soulless" drive to conquer and destroy, their singular obsession either to wipe out everything that is not like them or to make everything become like them, and their belief in their racial superiority, symbolize Nazism and the terrors of a war that most of the population in the 1960s still vividly remembered. Indeed, one story, "The Dalek Invasion of Earth" (1964), drives home this connection quite clearly by turning the story of the underground resistance against Nazi occupation as portrayed in such films as *The Moon Is Down* (1943), *A Generation* (1955), and *Kanal* (1956) into a story about the Earth's underground resistance against Dalek occupation. The story "Remembrance of the Daleks"

(1988) returns to this territory by having two Dalek factions using the Earth of 1963 to fight a war of "racial purity," with one faction recruiting a secret Nazi sympathizer in England to help them. Similarly, "Silver Nemesis" (1988) has an escaped Nazi official living in exile in the 1980s mistaking the Cybermen for Wagner's "giants" from Teutonic mythology, the idea being that to him the Cybermen are the next phase in the development of the master race.

Not all *Doctor Who* stories present the moral universe in such clear good vs. evil terms, but enough do that one might worry that *Doctor Who* simplifies a real problem too much, and too often, in the manner of the melodrama and popular fiction that form a basis for much of its storytelling style. However, the containers of evil do not merely embody what writers and viewers fear or detest; they also reflect what writers and viewers believe are valuable concepts worth fighting for and keeping.

Doctor Who's creators have brought awareness in the series that what one rejects often demonstrates what one values. There is also recognition that in the conflicted, complex, and dangerous world we live in, good must be fought for. Each time the Doctor appears on the TV screen, he lives out the precept set down in the *Tao Te Ching*:

> There is no greater misfortune
>   than not having a worthy foe;
> Once I believe there are no worthy foes,
>   I have well-neigh forfeited my treasures.

Therefore,

> When opposing forces are evenly matched,
> The one who is saddened will be victorious
>   [verse 34/69].

Publilius Syrus, a Syrian writer of Latin maxims, put it more succinctly: "It is an unhappy lot which finds no enemies." In "Remembrance of the Daleks," the Doctor remarks that one can tell the quality of a man by the quality of his enemies.

It is in the nature of the Doctor's enemies that one can begin truly to understand the humanist philosophy at the center of *Doctor Who*. The *Tao Te Ching* has an observation that dead things are stiff, straight, dry, and withered, while living things are soft, supple, and fragile. The observation extends not merely to dead and living things, but also to the human mind, saying:

> The rigid person is a disciple of death;
> The soft, supple, and delicate are lovers of life
>   [verse 41/76].

The "villains" of *Doctor Who* are nearly all "rigid" disciples of death. They are single-minded, determined, self-centered, uncompassionate, and power-hungry.

Indeed, their thirst for power fuels the other rigid traits. When they rage in groups, these enemies are most often fascistic, especially the Daleks and the Cybermen. So ruthless and motivated are these enemies that they bring death with them and dispense it with terrifying lack of concern. Being anti-life, these enemies are the very definition of anti-humanist.

Why are the Doctor's enemies as they are? At least one answer lies at the very core of human nature — egocentrism. As American philosophy professor Joseph K. Hart put it early in the twentieth century:

> [W]e identify the "good" with the "real": what is "good" to us is "real" to the universe; or at any rate, "it ought to be"; and "if we work at it hard enough we can make it so"; or at least, we can make ourselves believe it to be so. Eventually, therefore, most of us have come to assume, quite without thinking, that our world is the world; that our values are universal values; that our goods are the Ultimate Good. Hence, we feel justified in trying to impose our values on other people, in trying to make them good according to our ideas of good, and in denouncing all their divergences from our own ways as bad [165].

This egocentrism is particularly noticeable in the singular villains of *Doctor Who*: The Master, the Rani, Sutekh, Professor Zaroff, Salamander, et al. These villains often justify their behavior by arguing that they are being "realistic," and that "everyone knows" that only the strong survive. Sutekh in "Pyramids of Mars" (1975) states, "Your evil is my good." These villains take their "realistic" views to be part of their natural "superiority" over those whom they destroy. Davros, creator of the Daleks, offers an especially exemplary version of this line of reasoning, saying that because the Daleks are programmed to survive and dominate, they will eventually eliminate war, conquer disease, and thus through wiping out virtually every living non–Dalek thing will be "a force for good." The Cyber Controller in "The Age of Steel" (2006) echoes Davros' sentiments: "I will bring peace to the world. Everlasting peace. And unity. And uniformity."

Typically, the egocentric view of the villains, whether they be singular or collective villains, results in two lines of action in treating others: to dominate through murder or enslavement, or to convert all others into their type. "You belong to us. You shall be like us," says the Cyber Controller in "Tomb of the Cybermen" (1967). In "The Happiness Patrol" (1988), Helen A, leader of the Earth colony Terra Alpha, forces her people to behave according to a superficial view of happiness that she has concocted. She makes it illegal to express sadness, sorrow, loss, or pity. She outlaws forms of music such as the blues. Conversation gets reduced to trite expressions: "I am happy that you are glad," and "I am glad that you are happy." The Cyber Controller and Helen A typify the conjunction of egocentrism with power. As Hart indicates, most people assume that their definition of "good" is the same as their definition of "real." Given enough power, a person who uncritically accepts that his or her "good" is also what is "real" or "right," will inevitably try to force others to accept the same premise. An equally inevitable consequence is that such egocentric people believe only in their own free will, not in the free will of others. Thus, to the powerful egocentric, those who do not conform to the "plan" deserve whatever horrible fate they receive. Often in the *Doctor Who* universe, conjoining egocentrism with power *is* the definition of evil.

A consequence of extreme versions of the egocentric view of reality is the notion that people must subordinate themselves to supposed unchanging absolutes. The powerful egocentric unquestioningly assumes that his or her "good" is not only "real," but also "true" in the absolute sense. Such people propagate and promote whatever ideal label they have attached to their notion of the good. When they are powerful, charismatic, and determined, they bring others under their sway, for the human animal is a contradictory animal. As much as there is an egocentric component, there is also a hierarchical component, a tendency to submit to a "top dog" and follow the pack. The psychoanalyst C.G. Jung argues that such group experiences take place on a level below the individual psyche.

> If it is a very large group, the collective psyche will be more like the psyche of an animal, which is the reason why the ethical attitude of large organizations is always doubtful. The psychology of a large crowd inevitably sinks to the level of mob psychology [*Four* 59].

Thus, the powerful egocentric uses his or her self-assertive tendencies to prey upon other people's self-transcendent tendencies. The result, historically, has been destruction on an immense scale.

> No historian would deny that the part played by crimes committed for personal motives is very small compared to the vast populations slaughtered in unselfish loyalty to a jealous god, king, country, or political system. The crimes of Caligula shrink to insignificance compared to the havoc wrought by Torquemada. The number of people killed by robbers, highwaymen, gangsters and other social elements is negligible compared to the masses cheerfully slain in the name of the true religion, the righteous cause [Koestler *Janus* 77].

Doctor Who contains plenty of examples of those who would gladly sacrifice others in the name of some "cause." The cause itself becomes the justification for the killing. "Underworld" (1978) pits two such groups. On the one hand, there is the team from Minyos led by Jackson. This group has traveled for millennia searching for the race bank of their people, going on and on because "the quest is the quest." While this team might be lead to do just about anything to fulfill their quest, they take a somewhat honorable path. However, at several points the Doctor must pull them onto that path. Their adversaries, however, are quite different. This is the society set up by the computer charged with protecting the race bank, Oracle. This computer has established a theocracy with itself as the god-queen. The elite classes of Guards and Seers obediently follow every direction Oracle hands them and willingly subjugate those not part of their inner circle, the Trogs.

In "Kinda" (1982), the normally peaceful Kinda people readily give up their ways to start a war because one man has apparently fulfilled a prophecy by acquiring "voice." In "The Aztecs" (1964), the Doctor's companion, Barbara, tries to change the Aztec religion's reliance upon human sacrifice, but instead finds that only one man is willing to make the change. "The Massacre" (1966) concerns events around the St. Bartholomew's Day Massacre in France in 1572, a result of Catholic and Protestant clashes in which Catholic followers of the "prince of peace" murder hundreds of Protestants. When the abstraction fought for is not "God's will," it is something equally vaporous, such as "survival" in the case of the Daleks and Cybermen, "power" in the case of the Master, "science" in the case of the Rani, or "revenge" or "profit" or a "golden age." *Doctor Who* repeatedly, shows that rigid adherence to some abstraction produces warped thinking, immoral mistreatment of others, torture, enslavement, and war. The adherents to the cause lose sight of their victims' humanity, and lacking compassion they bring only harm and destruction rather than the "good" they suppose will come of their activities.

Another answer to the question of why the Doctor's enemies are as they are comes from the modified psychoanalytic perspective of Jung. According to Jung, modern Western humans live mostly in a profound state of ignorance about themselves. Because of the apparent sureties afforded them by science, technology, and rational philosophy, people forget the *shadow* of the unconscious, the instinctual nature of the human and remnant of humanity's primordial existence. Instead, people identify with the fiction of their conscious, rational selves. This unhealthy split in the personality has dire consequences. It leads to *uprootedness*, a restless sense of a missing component that people then seek in some place other than themselves. One need only note that the common desire to "find" oneself is a wholly modern phenomenon. Jung explains that "the forlornness of consciousness in our world is due primarily to the loss of instinct" (*Undiscovered* 97).

The need to fill the gap felt by estranging one's shadow regularly leads not to the autonomy that people often believe they have, but to association with mass groups and a giving up of large portions of that autonomy in order to feel *community*. Jung argues that because the instinctual side has not vanished, but merely been suppressed, the struggle between conscious and unconscious inevitably can neither be neglected nor avoided. "The accumulation of individuals who have got into this critical state starts off a mass movement purporting to be the champion of the suppressed" (*Undiscovered* 93). Because the members of the mass movement are in psychological denial, they seek the source of their alienation in the world and not in themselves. Thus is born the desire to stamp out *en masse* whatever "evil" the group or its leaders have determined is causing their misery. In this way, the shadow makes its way out from under the suppression of the conscious ego, and since it is "always chaotic and turbulent" ends merely by replacing one oppressive evil with another one (*Undiscovered* 93–4).

The last result from suppression of the shadow is projection of it onto some person or thing that can act as repository, symbol, and often scapegoat. Whatever received the shadow projection is made into a "spiritual and moral opponent" (*Undiscovered* 95). These outer representatives of the inner psyche are then held responsible for one's decisions, either because one feels the need to counteract them if the projection is deemed evil, or to follow them in the form of "leaders" who do all one's thinking if the projection is deemed good (*Undiscovered* 97). This process of projection is as much a social phenomenon as an individual one, and to see how projection operates at a social level one need look only at the way "communists" or "terrorists" or "immigrants" or "Jews" or any other entity or group one could name become imbued with powers grotesquely disproportionate in the popular mind from their true status and import.

In *Doctor Who*, one can see the psychic forces Jung describes operating among those characters deemed evil, or those perpetrating wrong doing but not considered evil. Often these characters are uprooted and restless in Jung's sense. One such is General Carrington, from "The Ambassadors of Death" (1970). In this story, aliens, having previously encountered humans on a Mars expedition, have come to Earth seeking contact and diplomatic exchange. Unfortunately, the aliens are not fully aware at first that their touch is instantly lethal to humans. Thus, when contacting humans on Mars, they accidentally kill members of the Mars team. Among the survivors of that team is General Carrington, who conducts his own covert operation using his authority to sway the opinions of both government officials and the general populace that the aliens are hostile, and "alien," and should be destroyed. Carrington pits one group of the British army against another, with loss of life. He convinces a space scientist to threaten people so the scientist can protect a secret, manipulates a politician into keeping the whereabouts of kidnapped aliens secret so that the politician may make the claim of having negotiated diplomatic relations, employs criminals to hide evidence of his activities, and uses copied alien technology to control the kidnapped aliens and make them appear to commit crimes. Carrington convinces himself he must do all of this because it is his "moral duty." Thus, Carrington is alienated from his shadow, unable to see that his motivation is fear. Because he cannot face his personal dilemma, he projects his fear onto the aliens. Characterizing them as monsters, he sets out to prove to himself that they are monsters, and so, in a vicious circle, justify his own monstrous behavior.

General Carrington is somewhat unusual in *Doctor Who* in that he is a complex villain sympathetically characterized. The audience is able to understand him, even though he cannot understand himself. More often, *Doctor Who* villains take the form of symbolized social evil, and do so in one of two ways. If we follow Jung's theory, we see that modern restless humanity finds itself in an unbalanced state. One way of helping to restore balance is through stories that dramatize the psychic conflict. Rational, enlightened, scientific humanity in these stories becomes threatened by the psychic projections of its shadow. Since the sane person is an autonomous being that has come to recognize and understand its shadow, the insane will be unbalanced. This unbalance will move either to extreme over-identification with the ego or to the dissolution of the ego in mass movements. In other words, one gets the egotistical villains, such as the Master, the Rani, Professor Zaroff from "The Underwater Menace," and so on; or, one gets the mass identity villains, such as the Daleks, the Cybermen, the Sontarans, the Dominators, and so on. The result is either domination of everything that is not "me" (egotism, Koestler's self-assertive drive) or destruction of everything that is not "us" (cultism, Koestler's self-transcendent drive). These extremes represent two of the great fears of modern humanity — the ego run amok in powerful and charismatic individuals who can dominate and destroy the weak willed (which would be most of the rest of us), and the ego lost in mass movement juggernauts of destruction such as Nazism, fundamentalist religion, and racism.

The Master is a perfect example of ego out of control. He constantly seeks to dominate the universe, everything that is not "me" from his perspective. He divides the moral universe into a simple false dilemma, one must rule or be crushed. The charisma of the egotist in the Master takes the form of his formidable hypnotic powers, by which he can control most people, making them go against their own personal best interests and personalities. Only the very strong-willed, people fully confident in their personhood, can resist his hypnotic power. He considers all others to be his inferiors, and deems his own survival to be the greatest moral imperative.

The other extreme is the cultist mind, best represented by the Daleks. Like most mass movements, Dalek society is extremely hierarchical and functional. Leaders have absolute authority over subordinates. Each Dalek performs a specific function, and any individual identity it has comes solely from the function it performs. Daleks, like most groups, are also extremely xenophobic. All mass movements define themselves in relation to some "other" that must be beaten or annihilated if "we" are to remain safe. With the Daleks, "us" versus "them" gets taken to its extreme, for "them" includes all non–Dalek life.

As with the egotist, the rationale for brutal behavior is "survival," a shadow urge turned into moral absolute. The Daleks' creator, Davros, programmed them with his belief that conflict is the sole truth of life, that one species must dominate all others if it is to survive. Thus, there is a twisted logic that controls Dalek destructiveness: one must use war to end war, kill to end killing. As in most mass movements, members of Dalek society require constant pep talks and need to work themselves into a mass hysteria, chanting phrases such as "Daleks conquer and destroy." Daleks repeatedly stir themselves into collective frenzy, which presumably keeps them focused on the major purpose of their existence, eradication of all other life. These demonstrations are similar to the organized public hatings described in George Orwell's *1984*, and serve the same function of energizing collective unity while suppressing individual identity. Like all members of mass movements, Daleks see themselves as champions of the suppressed — themselves, threatened by all the rest of life.

Megalomania

Undoubtedly, the most typical *Doctor Who* villain is the megalomaniac. It is the source of most satires about the program. The psychopath desiring either power over all others or destruction of all others, or both, seems wholly contradictory to modern experience. The Nuremberg Trials of Nazi leaders created the impression of the banality of evil, to use Hannah Arendt's famous phrase, that inside every seeming human monster is really a whimpering victim screaming for help, that perpetrators of evil do so for reasons of duty rather than of fanaticism, that the leaders who lead to destruction know perfectly well what they are doing.

So if the would-be dominators of the world today do not go about ranting deluded speeches declaring how they will "rule the world," then why are there so many who do so in *Doctor Who*? Could it be that portraying evil in this way makes it safe? That the audience can easily dissociate itself from the megalomaniacs they see raving on the TV screen? This assessment seems an uncharitable view of the program and does not explain its popularity if its vision of evil is so out of touch with the popular conception of evil.

While there are the occasional melodramatic villains in *Doctor Who*, most are actually more subtly drawn. More importantly, such symbolic characters serve psychological and philosophical functions. The person ruthless in acquisition of power and heedless of the destruction left behind in acquiring power is the shadow of modern mass humanity. Jung has argued that the emphasis on mass movement, mass commitment, on belonging either to an institutionalized state or an institutionalized church, on suppressing individuality for the "good" of the many, reduces most people to zeroes within their own societies. This banding together of a million zeroes that still add to zero, of people without the objective tools necessary for expression of individuality, makes this society "succumb so readily to a dictator" (*Undiscovered* 67). Despite the lessons of the first half of the twentieth century, people mostly believe that the answer to mass action is more mass action. "People go on blithely organizing and believing in the sovereign remedy of mass action, without the least consciousness of the fact that the most powerful organizations can be maintained only by the greatest ruthlessness of their leaders and the cheapest of slogans" (*Undiscovered* 68).

Jung's answer to this state of affairs is religion. Jung carefully distinguishes *religion*, by which he means a collection of symbols allowing one to attain personal individual salvation through understanding his or her life-affirming truth (i.e., religion as a collection of archetypal symbols and tales), and *creed*, by which he means a set of doctrines made official by an institution claiming religious or analogous authority (*Undiscovered* 30–1). As I have argued in Chapter 4 of this book, it is hard to see how the one does not inevitably become the other. However, even ignoring that problem for a moment, as Jung himself does, Jung's real solution here is not religion, for he also argues that properly administered psychotherapy performs a similar function (*Undiscovered* 64–6). Jung states, "*Resistance to the organized mass can be effected only by the man who is as well organized in his individuality as the mass itself*" (*Undiscovered* 72, emphasis in original). Thus, Jung does not see religion as inherently accurate or right or good in the usual theological sense, a point with which he and the creators of *Doctor Who* agree. Instead, Jung sees the virtue of religious symbols "properly understood" and psychotherapy properly administered because both raise the person's individual truth to consciousness. "*Consciousness is a precondition of being*," he writes, and by "being" he means conscious awareness of one's full individuality (*Undiscovered* 58–9, emphasis in original). The person who succumbs to the mass mentality is not *being* in Jung's sense. Such a person is ruled by the animal urges that a ruthless dictator of any sort in any institution can easily manipulate.

The megalomaniacs in *Doctor Who* are counterpointed by their willing followers. The blustering Captain of "The Pirate Planet" has his assistant, the fawning Mr. Fibuli, but he also has the willing submission of the entire population of Zanak, persuaded by the mineral wealth he gives them never to question. The leader Salamander in "Enemy of the World" plots his way toward the political top by using blackmail over weak men such as Controller Fedorin, threats such as over his assistant Fariah, and public opinion by manipulating situations to make himself appear to save people from disasters he has secretly engineered.

Doctor Who's megalomaniacs actually symbolize fears of political and social power. Every popular democracy runs on the popularity contests called elections. The danger is always present that people seeking public office do so because they need the ego-raising experience, not because they are the most competent people for these jobs. If that is the case, then acquisition of power to enhance a person's self-worth always factors as a risk within the political system. In short, there is always the fear that the political leadership are megalomaniacs of some kind.

Insanity

Repeatedly in *Doctor Who*, the villains are described, characterized, or labeled "insane." This may be seen just as a simple way out of a moral dilemma — the insane cannot be wholly conscious of the danger of their actions, nor can they be seen to be fully in control of them. This displacement of responsibility may be true of the "insane" villains of *Doctor Who*. On the other hand, these villains represent certain strains in the human character taken to extreme. It is important to distinguish "insane" from "psychopathic." In other words, these are not characters for whom harming of others is their principal means of pleasure or satisfaction. Thus, harming people is not their goal, merely a means to some other goal. *Doctor Who* villains are rarely psychopathic. David Whitaker's scripts, especially "The Power of the Daleks" (1966) and "The Ambassadors of Death," take the position that the perpetrator of evil is not psychopathic, but psychologically damaged. The damage causes extreme behavior. The egocentric megalomaniac is one extreme, and the fascistic mass mind is the other. But what makes such behavior "insane"?

One answer may be in the writings of humanistic psychoanalyst Erich Fromm. Fromm's theories start from the premise that humanity is presented with a problem. Being removed from the pure union with nature that all other animals retain, humans have reason and imagination and thus must push themselves forward to make a new home since they cannot in reality return to a purely natural state. Humans are aware at some level of being alone, separate, powerless, and ignorant; they know that their births and deaths are accidental. In this state, satisfaction of physiological needs is not enough to keep people sane. Therefore, they seek new ties with other people to replace the old ties to nature. Thus, to be sane, people seek *union* (Fromm 29–30).

There are two basic answers to the problem that Fromm defines. I have already defined these as *cultist* and *egotistical*, or to use Koestler's terms *self-transcendent* and *self-assertive*. Fromm describes the situation slightly differently. According to Fromm, people "can attempt to become one with the world by *submission* to a person, to a group, to an institution, to God," or people "can try to unite [themselves] with the world by having *power* over it, by making others [parts of themselves], and thus transcending [their] individual existence by domination" (30–1).

What makes extreme submission and domination *insane* is that people controlled by these impulses "have lost their integrity and freedom." If the submissive or domineering passions were realized, still these people would never be satisfied.

> They have a self-propelling dynamism, and because no amount of submission, or domination (or possession, or fame) is enough to give a sense of identity and union, more and more of it is sought. The ultimate result of these passions is defeat. It cannot be otherwise; while these passions aim at the establishment of a sense of union, they destroy the sense of integrity. The person driven by any one of these passions actually becomes dependent on others; instead of developing his own individual being, he is dependent on those to whom he submits, or whom he dominates [Fromm 31].

Ultimately, says Fromm, both behavioral extremes are forms of *narcissism*. Such insane people lose "contact with the world" and cannot see reality as it is, but only as it appears processed through the distortions of their minds (36).

One need only look at the behavior of the best-known *Doctor Who* villains to see that they are insane by Fromm's definition. It is easy enough to see how a megalomaniac such as the Master is purely narcissistic, seeing in the universe only things to be made into reflections of himself. Thus, in "The End of Time" it is both logical and consistent that the "Master plan" is for the Master to turn all humans into versions of himself, the "Master" race. The submissives are likewise narcissistic, though, because they see in the universe only things to be made into reflections of the ideas they have borrowed from the group or leader with whom they identify. Thus, while Daleks seek to conquer and destroy, they do so always from a submissive position within the Dalek group, so submissive that individual Daleks do not even get names. Since the singular idea for Daleks is to turn the universe into Dalek-universe, they too are narcissistic.

Since both submission and domination stem from the need for transcendence, they provide an answer, but a wrong answer, to the problem of human existence. Humans are aware of their creative potential. Creativity is a result of love. However, submissive and domineering individuals are narcissistic, incapable of love, and so incapable of creation. These people choose the second answer to the problem of human existence. Since they cannot create, they *destroy*. By destroying, the narcissistic person gains the feeling of transcending life. The "will for destruction" is enormously powerful, but ultimately not satisfying, since the destroyers suffer along with those whom they would destroy (Fromm 37–8).

Violence

Another important factor in the humanist vision of good and evil displayed in *Doctor Who* has to do with weapons. The Doctor is a highly unusual hero in that he almost never uses weapons, certainly never carries weapons, and almost always rejects weapons when someone offers them to him. In his actions and statements regarding weapons the Doctor firmly agrees with the following Taoist assessment: "Weapons are instruments of evil omen;/Creation abhors them." According to the *Tao Te Ching*, "Weapons are not instruments of the superior man," and "are to be used only when there is no other choice" (verse 75/31).

In "Mark of the Rani" (1985), when offered a gun to protect himself, the Doctor rejects the offer, saying that guns are very bad for one's health. Such is typical behavior for the Doctor. The rare times the Doctor uses weapons, it is as stated in the *Tao Te Ching*, when the occasion is forced upon him and he has no other choice. In "Genesis of the Daleks," the Doctor cannot bring himself to blow up a room full of incubating Daleks, even after he has set the explosives. Only at the end of the program when the Daleks have been fully unleashed and have started a killing rampage, does he set out actually to blow up the incubator, and even then, it is a Dalek's accidentally setting off the explosion that does the job.

The issue of using weapons plays a prominent part in "The End of Time." Wilfrid Mott repeatedly offers his old service revolver to the Doctor, who repeatedly rejects it. Finally, when he feels he has no other option, the Doctor takes the gun. Even then, when it appears he will use it to kill either of two villains, he instead uses it to destroy an important piece of machinery, not to take life. "Day of the Daleks" (1972) is highly unusual for showing the Doctor using a gun on an attacking opponent.

For the Doctor, using a weapon comes from two necessities — self-defense or defense of others. In the first case, the Doctor never makes it a plan to kill the opponent(s) who threaten him, though on occasion he has seemed very tempted to do so. In "The Curse of Peladon" (1972), the Doctor is forced to defend himself in gladiatorial-style conflict, but having defeated his opponent refuses to kill him. In the second case, in the Doctor's mind the situation becomes a matter of choice on the part of his opponent. In "The Next Doctor," when he faces Miss Hartigan, who has control of the Cybermen's great battle robot and is threatening to destroy all London with it, the Doctor gives her the choice, go away or face the consequences. Even then, Miss Hartigan's death is an indirect consequence of the Doctor's action, and he states that his intent was not to kill her.

The Doctor's good is visible in his repeated attempts to find any means other than killing to stop ongoing evil. Sometimes avoiding killing is easy, other times it is almost impossible. Either way, violence in defense of oneself or in defense of others is not always wrong.

The Doctor's opponents, on the other hand, are all too willing to use violence. Most often, they are the initiators of the violence. Their evil often comes from their belief that weapons make them superior. The thinking is that superior force creates personal, moral, or social superiority. They see their victims as inferior precisely because their victims are victims. Unable to assert the control they seek over their surroundings, they see weapons and violence as the primary means to gain this control. Repeatedly, *Doctor Who* shows that the will to violence stems not from strong people, but from weak people who must borrow the strength that weapons appear to give them. It is characteristic of *Doctor Who* that the personal weakness of the evil character is the symbol for the weakness of the evils for which they stand.

Three Kinds of Evil

To wrap up the discussion of the nature and definition of evil in *Doctor Who*, we can look at different manifestations of evil and how characters respond to them. The English philosopher Bertrand Russell identified three kinds of evil: *physical evils*, such as death and natural disaster; *evils of character*, such as ignorance and violent emotions; and *evils of power*, such as government-sponsored oppression (188).

Physical evils can be temporarily avoided and partially controlled, but life will always involve some encounters with them. The treatment for physical evils is science, in the broad sense (Russell 189). Thus, for instance, in "Planet of Fire" the people of Sarn suffer the physical evil of the erupting volcano. Their suffering is alleviated by the science of an advanced civilization, which uses technology to tame the eruptions and to provide survival materials for the people.

Evils of character, says Russell, are often created or exacerbated by physical evils and evils of power. The treatment for evils of character is education, in the broad sense (Russell 189). Even psychological treatments are largely forms of education, in which a patient must first learn the source of his/her distress and then learn the methods for combating it. The matter of education differentiates the evil characters of *Doctor Who*. Some, such as the Master, refuse to be educated out of their evil behaviors. The example of Captain Jack Harkness serves here. At the end of "The Doctor Dances" (2005), having learned that his selfish con has potentially led to the whole human race's turning into zombies, he sets out to correct his mistake, even risking his own life to do so. After this epiphany, Jack gives up his ways as a con artist.

Evils of power derive from inequalities and injustice within the social system. As long as one person has *more*, all others will want it while that person seeks to keep it. The person with more usually has significant influence within the social system, and thus can arrange matters to ensure that his/her interests are always maintained. Russell's treatment to evils of power is socialism (191). More broadly speaking, the treatment would be devolution of power. The resolution for oppressive political-economic system on Pluto in "The Sun Makers" (1977) is to remove the chair of the company running Pluto, dissolve the company, and turn the running of Pluto over to the workers. Always in *Doctor Who*, concentrated power is an evil to be changed.

Good

So far, I have been discussing only evil. While evil is a difficult concept, good is an even more difficult one. It is not as simple a matter as defining good as the opposite of evil. When evil is viewed as the product of psychological and social conditions, and not as an absolute or ideal that occupies some otherworldly realm and occasionally intrudes into reality, then good must be considered in similar terms.

For instance, identification with a crowd, as Jung notes, is not always bad. "The group can give an individual a courage, a bearing, and a dignity which may easily get lost in isolation" (*Four* 61). *Doctor Who* contains many examples of this sort of rising to the occasion. In "Paradise Towers" (1987), a young man who calls himself Pex desperately wants to be a hero, but cannot overcome the cowardice that is all too apparent to the others within his society. When the Doctor pulls together the disparate groups of Paradise Towers in order to defeat that which threatens them all, he forces these groups to accept Pex. Now part of a larger entity, Pex is able to be the hero he always wanted to be, eventually sacrificing himself so that the rest of the society of Paradise Towers can go on.

However, it is important to note that such self-transcendence through the group is more often a source of a dangerous mob mentality. The euphoria and sense of heroic energy that comes from a crowd usually gets turned to the purposes of the crowd. It is what Jung calls a "participation mystique," which diminishes the individual psyche, making it dependent upon repeated participation in crowds to regain the euphoria (*Four* 60). Furthermore, such positive enthusiasm that may arise from identifying with a group is an "unearned gift" of the moment, and people tend to take such gifts for granted, to demand them as a right rather than making an effort to obtain them. Thus, members of groups who share some common identity not only seek euphoria, but also come to expect it as their due, demanding constant renewal of the euphoria from the group as a "right" of participation. Through this arises the cult hero, who will give the group "purpose" at the expense of demanding all rights and powers for himself (*Four* 61–2). Clearly, then, in the long run any good that comes out of the group mentality is fleeting and accidental, and fails to counterbalance the overwhelming harm that comes from groupthink. Furthermore, since in the case of group identification, the good and the evil derive from the same sources of the human psyche and the human "condition," and so are not easily extracted and isolated from each other. They operate as potentials, triggered by the right sets of conditions.

Love

According to Fromm, "There is only one passion which satisfies man's need to unite himself with the world, and to acquire at the same time a sense of integrity and individuality, and this is *love*." Fromm defines love as "*union with somebody, or something, outside oneself, under the condition of retaining the separateness and integrity of one's own self*" (31, emphasis in original). Love as Fromm defines it, prevents the tendency to extreme that leads to the insanity of egotistical domination or of total submission because through love one can find communion yet retain individual identity. Love is one aspect of the "productive orientation," the "active and creative relatedness" of people to each other. In this sense, the object of love is not nearly as important as the *quality* of loving. Neither can love be restricted to one person; when it is, this is pathological fixation and not true love (32).

The components of love in Fromm's terms are *care, responsibility, respect,* and *knowledge* (33). Care is concern for the growth and happiness of another. Responsibility involves responding to the needs of others. Respect involves objectively looking at another as that person is, undistorted by the viewer's wishes and fears. Knowledge involves the union of people from the cores of their being.

These definitions clearly apply to the Doctor as a character. Central to the Doctor's ethos is his concern for the well-being of others. The Doctor's altruism demonstrates his sense of responsibility. He solves problems that often are not really his own personal problems. The Doctor's respect is displayed mainly in his open-mindedness. The Doctor repeatedly looks at matters from how others look at those matters. Knowledge, in the sense Fromm uses it, does not come much into play. There is a psychological unity the Doctor sometimes reaches with his companions, but mostly the Doctor is aloof, avoiding getting too close.

Why Evil Exists

A curious commonality, even among philosophers, is for people to ask the question, "Why does evil exist?" This is curious because rarely does anyone ask the corollary, "Why does good exist?" Taken as it is, though, the question of the existence of evil has gone through multiple permutations over the centuries. I will not here go over them all because doing so is irrelevant to *Doctor Who*. The question of *why* evil exists does not come up. Instead, *Doctor Who* seems to accede to the position stated in Ecclesiastes, namely that evil simply exists, there is no explaining it, and the best one can do is deal with it when it happens but otherwise get on with the business of living and enjoying one's life.

Written in the 400s B.C.E., Ecclesiastes is unique in the Bible in terms of outlook, and is the most philosophical work collected into the Bible. The central theme of Ecclesiastes is usually translated as "vanity." The actual Hebrew word, "hevel," can be variously translated as "emptiness," "absurdity," or "uselessness." Its etymological meaning is of a vanishing mist, so that the key idea to an ancient Hebrew speaker would be something like "ephemeral" (Ehrman 191). The main point in its famous opening, that all is "vanity," ephemeral, and that time and nature march on regardless of what people do, establishes the central point: life is short, death comes to everything, bad things happen.

This idea that evil simply *is* and that life is a fleeting phenomenon is central to the understanding of how the universe works in *Doctor Who*. Though the program and the Doctor come to different conclusions from those the writer of Ecclesiastes comes to, they start from the same premise. This sense that evil simply is and always will be gets driven home in the Dalek stories from 2006 and 2007. In the revived series, the Timelords and the Daleks engaged in a last great time war that appeared to wipe out both races. However, it turns out that some Daleks survived. These Daleks had been seemingly erased from existence at the end of the 2005 series, "The Parting of the Ways." However, the Daleks re-emerge at the end of the 2006 series, "Doomsday," and again in the middle of the 2007 series, "Daleks in Manhattan." Their mere continued existence makes the Doctor furious. He loses everything, they keep living. His anguish at the unfairness of this situation is palpable. Yet, the Doctor does not pause to ponder *why* it should be so. It simply is so.

Another key similarity between the view in Ecclesiastes and the view in *Doctor Who* is that there is no comfort in thoughts of an afterlife.

> The hearts of men are full of evil; madness fills their hearts all through their lives, and after that they go down to join the dead. But for a man who is counted among the living there is still hope: remember, a live dog is better than a dead lion. True, the living know that they will die; but the dead know nothing. There are no more rewards for them; they are utterly forgotten. For them love, hate, ambition, all are now over. Never again will they have any part in what is done here under the sun [Eccl 9:3–6].

The Doctor *never* comforts himself with thoughts that his dead companions and friends are somehow alive somewhere else. He always proceeds on the idea that dead is dead, and that to kill without just cause is a great moral evil because death is a final absolute.

The conclusions that differ between the writer of Ecclesiastes and those shown in *Doctor Who* involve what to do about evil. The writer of Ecclesiastes concerns himself mostly with what might be called petty or localized evil, the evils that people do to each other. He does not concern himself with the great evils either of humans or of nature, the genocides and other such actions on the one part, and the catastrophic disasters on the other part. So, looking at the localized level of evil, the Ecclesiastes writer gives the advice, seven times, to enjoy life's simple pleasures, to take from it what one can. Clearly, *Doctor Who* does not follow this line of reasoning.

In *Doctor Who*, the Doctor is a man of action, one who sees that evil must be fought. The point is made at the end of "The War Games" (1969) when the Doctor defends himself to the Timelords, and gets variously repeated throughout the series. In some sense, the presence of evil is the answer to the question of why there is *good*. Good in *Doctor Who* is not merely the opposite of evil, though the idea has been considered in "The Key to Time" series (1979) and in "The Curse of Fenric" (1989). The conception is not a "two sides, can't have one without the other" perspective. In *Doctor Who*, Good does not exist as opposite of Evil, it exists in active opposition to Evil.

Why Good Exists

In *Doctor Who*, Good exists to combat Evil. More precisely, "good" is the name for actions that reduce suffering and increase happiness. Good is not an abstract, pure essence. If there is a cosmic battle between good and evil in *Doctor Who*, its form is the struggle of those who do good against the products of a universe indifferent to the fate of the living, naturally hostile to life in many areas, and rewarding in many ways to those who pursue evil ends. Good makes life bearable. By demonstrating this concept and entertaining its audience in the process, *Doctor Who* does good.

CHAPTER 9

Ethics

The Master (offering the Doctor "a half-share in the universe"): One must rule or serve. That is the basic law of life. Why do you hesitate? Surely it's not loyalty to the Time Lords, who exiled you to one insignificant planet?
Doctor: You'll never understand. I want to see the universe, not to rule it.

— "Colony in Space"

Ethics Defined

Ethics is the area of thought devoted to the assessment of choices in situations requiring determinations of value. Vincent Ryan Ruggiero, a leading writer on the subjects of ethics and critical thinking, identifies two kinds of ethics: *normative ethics* and *metaethics*. Normative ethics involves "determining what is reasonable and therefore what people should believe" (*Thinking* 6). Metaethics is the practice of comparing ethical systems to determine their logical bases and consistency. Philosophy professors Thiroux and Krasemann place these two fields under the general category of *philosophical* approaches to ethics, as opposed to the *scientific* approach to ethics one finds in anthropology and sociology, which simply describes the ethical rules of given cultures (6).

"Value" is a widely used and misused term. In human behavior and ethics, defining value is highly valuable. As a working principle, Charles Morris's three aspects of value work well in clarifying the concept for ethical behavior. The first aspect involves *operative values*, "the actual direction of preferential behavior toward one kind of object rather than another" (Morris 10). In other words, when the Doctor chooses one corridor to run through over another, the Doctor is practicing an operational value, putting preferences into practice. The second aspect involves *conceived values*, or acting upon an idea of receiving a particular outcome (Morris 10–1). So, when the Doctor

201

manipulates the TARDIS controls expecting to take his companion to some special location, he is acting according to conceived values regarding the pleasure to be derived from being at that location. The third aspect involves *object values*, "concerned with what is preferable (or 'desirable') regardless of whether it is in fact preferred or conceived as preferable" (Morris 11–2). Thus, when the Doctor arrives at location X and it is a cauldron of danger rather than a resort paradise, the place's object value is its level of danger. Ethical behavior involves the decisions for action in situations regarding negotiating between different value aspects. What should the Doctor do if the object value of location X is danger, but his conceived value of it was paradise?

An ethical outlook, a system of decision-making "rules," provides guidance for negotiating conflicts between value aspects. Within the broad scope of philosophical ethics, there are four fundamental precepts or orientations that in some degree make up any system of ethical outlook. These precepts in definition make two pairs of binary opposites. One pair is consequentialist and nonconsequentialist ethics (in modern philosophy known as teleological and deontological theories). *Consequentialist* theories focus on the results of actions — who benefits, in what manner, to what degree — in determining whether an action is ethical or not. *Nonconsequentialist* theories focus in whether an act is "right" regardless of the consequences of the act. The other binary opposing pair is absolutism and relativism. *Absolutism* is the belief that moral rules pre-exist humanity either by nature or by divine command, and thus are unchanging and irrefutable. *Relativism* is the belief that all moral rules derive from individual or cultural circumstances and are "moral" only within particular and specified conditions. The relativist position is that what is moral for one person is not necessarily moral for another, and that there is no universally binding way to determine whether one ethical statement is superior to another. All ethical theories play within the field of these four positions.

Consequentialism

If a theory focuses on benefits as the determining factor for ethics, it is consequentialist. There are several consequentialist ethical theories, but the most widely known is Utilitarianism, the fundamental premise of which is that an action that produces the greatest good for the greatest number of people is the ethically right one. It can seem, when put this way, to be "moral calculus" or "ethics by numbers." In *Doctor Who*, viewers see numbers ethics whenever the Doctor weighs the saving of one life versus saving an entire species or planet or even the universe.

Utilitarianism and other consequentialist theories can be more subtle than this. John Stuart Mill called Utilitarianism "The Greatest Happiness Principle" (*Utilitarianism* 9). He saw Utilitarianism as a descendent of the philosophy of Epicurus, who argued that pleasure was the indicator of happiness, and that which brings the greatest pleasure brings the greatest happiness. It may seem as though this position is equally facile as the moral mathematics. However, such a view follows from a false idea of what "pleasure" means to Epicureans and Utilitarians. For them, pleasure means simply retreat from or escape from pain. Both Mill and the great Epicurean philosopher Lucretius point out that "pleasure" in this case does not mean what Mill calls "swinish" pleasure of bodily sensations. Instead, pleasure in Utilitarianism refers to well-being. People get pleasure and feel happy when their livelihoods are secure, their health is optimum, and their affairs are in their own control. Thus, for the Utilitarian, an act is ethical when it increases well-being. An act is unethical when it decreases well-being.

In *Doctor Who*, these sorts of considerations do come up from time to time. Mostly, one can see that the villains of *Doctor Who* almost always seek the selfish pleasure over spreading happiness. For them, their personal well-being supersedes that of all others, and if increasing their happiness requires destroying the happiness and lives of others, then so be it. The Doctor, on the other hand, takes the position that personal well-being does not exclude increasing the well-being of others.

A modern modified version of Utilitarianism focuses not on consequences as determining the ethicality of an action after the fact, but thinking about consequences before the fact as determining ethicality. In other words, the focus shifts to thinking about what qualifies as a "good reason" for a particular action. Kai Nielsen, for instance, argues that there are cases in which thinking about consequences will cause a decision that abandons or overrides commonsense morality (*Ethics* 152–8). These situations happen when conflicting commonsense moral obligations force a person to rank obligations, a process Nielsen calls the "equitable or fair adjudicating of interests" (197).

Such a situation occurs in "The End of Time" (2009). The Doctor has just resolved a major conflict, saved the Earth once again, and seemingly averted his own death. Then, however, the elderly Wilfrid Mott is trapped inside a control booth for a nuclear reactor going critical, which would flood the booth with lethal radiation. The only way to save Wilf is to swap places with him. The Doctor finds himself confronted with a moral dilemma requiring the ranking of obligations. Wilf tells the Doctor to leave him to die, that he is old and has had his time; the Earth needs the Doctor, but not Wilfrid Mott. The Doctor, tempted to accept this rationale, fights with himself. Would he be the Doctor that everyone knows if he left Wilf to die? Are there circumstances in which one life is in fact more valuable than another? Is a life with the potential for years of continuation more valuable than one nearing its end? The Doctor opts for saving Wilf because the Doctor's body will be able to absorb the radiation and will keep him alive long enough to fix some other remaining problems, while Wilf would simply die outright. The determination of which action to take, then, rests upon thinking about the consequences *before* taking the action.

Nonconsequentialism

Many philosophers do not favor consequentialist theories. The principal objection is that if results determine ethics, then that does not rule out accidental ethics. In other words, one's intention could be to do harm, but the act could accidentally produce happiness instead, and thus the act would be considered ethical if viewed with a Utilitarian perspective. Furthermore, there is no way to see from merely looking at outcomes whether any action can be repeated or generalized into a rule. Therefore, some philosophers have argued that there must be a standard outside of the consequences that can determine whether a particular action is ethical.

The focus upon standards, rules, obligations, and duties is broadly called nonconsequentialist, and its most potent form is called *deonotological* ethics, or ethics that focuses on obligations and duties. The most significant deontological ethical theory is Immanuel Kant's. There will be more to say about his ideas further on. Kant's principal idea is that absolute moral rules do exist, but that they must be abstracted from experience through the exercise of reason. Situations act as precedents, which one can then generalize. If the generalization produces a logically sound moral rule, one without contradiction, then the rule becomes imperative.

Rule-based ethics do appear in *Doctor Who*. In its base form, it appears as an obligation that one may have to act a certain way. In many cases, the Doctor mentions his duty or obligation as a Time Lord. Such duties, though, are at the simple level of ethics, and really amount to a kind of legalism, following the law because it is the law and not necessarily because the law is morally justified. Perhaps the most significant test of rule-based ethics in *Doctor Who* comes in "The Waters of Mars" (2009). In this story, the Doctor arrives on a Martian science station only to discover that it is a doomed expedition and everyone in it is fated to die. The Doctor knows this from his knowledge of the future. He immediately realizes that he is under obligation to leave the station, because from his perspective these people are already dead and to interfere would be to risk changing history as he knows it. The obligation to preserve the timeline conflicts with the Doctor's instinct to aid people in trouble. The Doctor does decide to try to help the people instead of leave them, going against his obligation and setting in motion catastrophic changes to history. Thus, the obligation not to interfere with what one knows to occur proves a rationally sound one that should be pursued regardless of the immediate apparent bad effects it may have, such as the deaths of the crew.

Absolutism

Ethical principles are often stated as *moral laws*. When people think of them as such, they tend to view ethical principles as absolute and inviolable. They act according to the law because they think of it *as a law*. This point of view is moral *absolutism*.

Doctor Who rarely takes anything like an absolutist stance when it comes to ethics. Often the *villains* are those who believe in moral absolutes. This is especially true of those misguided people who do the wrong thing for the right reason.

One trouble with absolutism is that it tends to reflect an inflexible and egocentric perspective. Few are ready to recognize that their own value systems may be inferior or inadequate. The absolutist, however, is firmly convinced that he or she has the one true system of values. Such perspectives lead to self-serving justifications for wrongdoing. "My motivation is good, based upon what I perceive to be sound universal moral principles, and therefore anything I do motivated by these principles must also be good." So goes the thinking in a classic kind of circular argument.

An example is the character of Taren Capel in "The Robots of Death" (1977). Raised among robots, Capel comes to believe that robots are superior to humans since robots do not lie and are always reliable. Capel sneaks aboard a mining vessel posing as the ship's robot technician Dask, and programs the robots on board to start killing the humans. Capel justifies murder through a strict moral code — humans are inferior to robots, so robots should rule and not be slaves. Another example of a similar line of thinking is that of Harrison Chase in "The Seeds of Doom" (1976). Chase's superiority complex revolves around plants instead of robots, but it takes on the same kinds of absolutist and murderous characteristics as Taren Capel's complex. Chase believes that the beauty and serenity of plants makes them superior to people. Again, an inflexible and absolute value system leads to the devaluation of human life when humans do not conform to the ideal.

Even apparently benign ethical codes can become twisted by the moral absolutist. In "The Happiness Patrol" (1988), Helen A, the leader of a human colony in space, instigates a police state because she wants everyone to be "happy." Tlotoxl, the High Priest of Sacrifice in "The Aztecs" (1964), schemes, plots, and undermines because he believes absolutely in preserving the ancient Aztec ways, including and especially human sacrifice. Preservation of culture usually counts as an ethical good, but not when its form is the consumption of its own human life.

These examples demonstrate how in *Doctor Who* absolutism in ethical matters is tied to inflexibility of judgment and self-serving value systems. In these value systems, preserving life is secondary to maintaining and implementing the value system. For the moral absolutist, the rule is more important than the person.

Relativism

Mostly, what people refer to as "relativism" is *cultural relativism*, the belief that while value judgments are fair within a culture they are not fair when made about other cultures. According to this perspective, ethics is entirely culturally determined, and so all culturally derived ethical systems have equal value. One problem with this view is that it greatly exaggerates the differences between systems of ethical value (Ruggiero *Art* 33). Another problem with cultural relativism is that it elevates cultural needs above individual human needs. Implicit in any cultural relativist position is the notion that because some rule is part of an identifiable culture, that makes the rule right, regardless of whether that rule denigrates whole classes of people and denies them rights afforded to others.

The opposite of cultural relativism is *sociocentrism*, the habit of viewing ethical choices entirely through the values and ideals of one's own culture. Since science fiction stories are often about conflicting cultural values that emerge as cultures contact each other or as novel situations arise with new technology, science fiction stories often challenge sociocentric views. These challenges occur repeatedly in *Doctor Who*. In the story "The Unquiet Dead" (2005), for instance, the Doctor proposes that an alien race he presumes to be threatened can use human cadavers as temporary hosts. The proposition instantly offends Rose, his companion. "Seriously, you can't," she declares. "Seriously, I can," retorts the Doctor. He continues, "It's a different morality. Get used to it or go home." This different morality conflicts with Rose's conventional view that cadavers were once people, so using their bodies is "just wrong." Interpolating the Doctor's attitude in this regard, we may safely assume that he thinks of Rose's conventional views as provincial and sociocentrically small-minded, hence the "go home" comment.

The ethical systems at work in *Doctor Who* are relativistic, but not the kind of absolute cultural relativism that leads to the absurd view that everything is right as long as it has the stamp of "culture" on it. Instead of upholding cultural relativism, *Doctor Who* tends to uphold *situational relativism*.

The Foundations of Ethics

Doctor Who works within the range of humanistic philosophy, which usually uses a *blended* approach to ethics that especially avoids the problems of strict absolutism and strict relativism. A basic assumption in *Doctor Who* is that *some* morals are culturally determined, but that *some* moral standards are universal across cultures. Humanistic ethical theories are especially opposed to extreme relativism, which is all too often self-serving and impractical.

If ethics are not merely matters of subjective preference, then, according to Paul and Elder, there are five foundations by which to understand ethical reasoning:

- Ethical principles are not a matter of subjective preference.
- All reasonable people are obligated to respect clear-cut ethical concepts and principles.
- To reason well through ethical issues, we must know how to apply ethical concepts and principles reasonably to those issues.
- Ethical concepts and principles should be distinguished from the norms and taboos of society and peer group, religious teachings, political ideologies, and the law.
- The most significant barriers to sound ethical reasoning are the egocentrism and socio-centrism of human beings [Paul and Elder 205].

Understanding ethical principles requires separating the concept of ethics from those areas with which it is commonly confused: social norms, religious rules, and laws (Ruggiero *Thinking* 9; Paul and Elder 207). "People ... have a strong tendency to confuse what they believe with the truth" (Paul and Elder 208). The result is the desire for indoctrination. The true path of ethics, though, is a process of education.

Kant provides another way to look at the matter, which is that an action is not "good" *because* it conforms to an ethical principle when viewed after the fact. A selfish or evil motivation can produce effects that conform to a moral law. However, the result is from mere accident. Ethical thinking involves imagining the principle first, then acting in accordance with it, a process Kant calls *duty* (*Foundations* 13–7).[1] As a practical consideration, Kant provides a simple method of ethical reasoning for determining the good. If one takes a particular course of action and turns it into a maxim, could that maxim apply as a universal law? If it cannot apply as a universal law because it would immediately create an unlivable contradiction, then the motivation, if not the action itself, could not be ethical (*Foundations* 39).

To see how Kant's method works, we can look at two examples from *Doctor Who*. In "Gridlock" (2007), a desperate couple kidnaps the Doctor's companion, Martha, so that they can bypass a traffic block so massive that it takes years to travel only a few miles. With a third person in their party, the couple can get to the fast lane. The couple intend no harm to Martha, threaten with only toy guns, and plan to take care of her for the comparatively short six months that she will have to stay with them. Since no "harm" was done, and the couple receive a potential reward for their action, was it moral for them to have kidnapped Martha?

Kant's method of answering this question would be to take the action and turn it into a maxim. If it is a universal law for any people who want access to the fast lane to be able to kidnap harmlessly anyone they choose, what would result? Everyone for him/her self and all against all would be the result. Whatever social order is left on New Earth would totally break down as kidnappings multiply. The fast lane would become clogged. Harmless threats of violence would escalate to real threats, and inevitably someone would be hurt or killed. Thus, the action of harmless kidnapping to attain a personal goal fails as a moral standard, and must be deemed unethical.

Another example involves the ethics of time travel itself. In "The Aztecs," the Doctor comes into conflict with the companion Barbara over whether one should try to change the course of known history. Barbara, mistaken for a reincarnated priest, wants to use her status to move the Aztec civilization away from human sacrifice and direct it toward emphasis of its better qualities. The Doctor, however, insists that a time traveler's responsibility is not to interfere with known history, but allow it to unfold as one knows it to have happened. Barbara's motivation is clearly "good" and if she were successful, many terrible early deaths would be avoided. Is the Doctor's position in this matter ethical? Applied as a maxim, the position would be that all time travelers should never attempt to change the history they know to have occurred, or to shape history according to their own ideals, no matter how noble those ideals appear to be. Such a maxim is effective as a universal moral law because it prevents the disasters of the typical historical paradox that time travel involves, and allows those living in the past to live their lives according to their values and not be coerced into conformity to what only appears to be a "superior" vision.

One can see that, simple as Kant's method of ethical evaluation is, it nevertheless requires good ethical reasoning, in part because, as the examples above show, actual moral rules are very rare. Good ethical reasoning requires certain mental abilities. One must be able to identify the ethical principles involved in any situation requiring ethics (Paul and Elder 209). One must be able to state these principles clearly and precisely (Paul and Elder 211). One must also be able to assess the relevant facts needed to make a proper ethical determination. There is further discussion below of various ethical orientations, their relative strengths and weakness, and what one can reasonably say are the core ethical values.

The Individual and the Universe

In *Doctor Who*, there are characteristically three positions a character may take in defining the relationship between the individual and the universe:

- I think; therefore, I am.
- I will; therefore, I am.
- I do not think; I obey.

Characteristically, the Doctor takes the first, the villains take the second, and various subordinate characters take the third (Tulloch and Alvarado 73–4). The Doctor's privileged position as moral center of the program encourages the viewer to accept his attitude as fundamentally "correct." Furthermore, adopting the "I think; therefore, I am" perspective is a necessary component to the humanist and existentialist ethics consistently at work in *Doctor Who*.

I Think; Therefore, I Am

Humanistic psychoanalyst Erich Fromm states that ethics "is inseparable from reason" (172). Human existence is thinking existence. When Descartes declared *cogito ergo sum*, he not only founded modern philosophy by placing the perceiving individual mind at the center of the philosophical universe, he also established a new path to ethics. Because reason requires a thinking person, it requires a *self*. So, too, does ethics, which Fromm designates as the application of reason in the course of judgment and action (173).

A beginning point for the humanistic view of ethics comes from John Locke's *An Essay Concerning Human Understanding* (1689). Locke shows that there are no "innate" principles in the mind (12). One can see that there are no innate principles because if there were, children would not need to learn them, and adults would not need to use reason to state them (12–14). Thus, ethical principles as much as any other are not stamped upon a person's mind, but must be learned through experience and reason. Each person must discover ethical principles.

I Will; Therefore, I Am

The Doctor consistently belittles the will-to-power extremism of the villains he encounters. In "The Armageddon Factor" (1979), the Doctor makes a mockery of the various speeches villains have made to him, rolling his eyes in mad-dog fashion and proclaiming, "As from this moment there's no such thing as free will in the entire universe. There is only my will...." This speech mimics the more melodramatic villains of the series, but also highlights the program's aversion to the desire for power.

I Do Not Think; I Obey

There are many forms of obedience, but they all fail as standards of moral and ethical understanding. A common form of obedience is following majority opinion. The idea stems from a misunderstanding of democracy. The thinking goes that if the majority states its opinion either through a vote or through social rules and agreed-upon laws, then that opinion is right. Even in non-democratic societies, this idea of the authority of majority opinion is common. The problem with deriving ethical principles from majority opinion is clear. Majority opinion is as often that of the mob as that of a collective of rational individuals. Majorities often "think" in terms of prejudices, biases, and self-serving rationalizations. Majorities are often swayed by media and unreliable presentations of "public opinion."

A good example of these sorts of problems is "Vengeance on Varos" (1985). The social system on Varos is based upon apparent majority rule. The Guard Elite chooses a governor (similar to a parliamentary system whereby the majority political party chooses the political leader instead of the populace choosing one), who then submits his policies to popular vote, a referendum. Each governor must submit himself to judgment during this vote by being strapped to a chair to await the outcome. If the vote is favorable, he receives a soothing bath of light. If the vote is unfavorable, he receives a bombardment from a cell destructor beam. The idea is that the "people" are always right, and that a governor under such restrictions will find solutions both practical and popular.

Of course, the system does not in any way work according to the ideal. First of all, it shields from public censure the true power on Varos, namely the Guard Elite. The Chief of Guards can do whatever he likes because the governor will always receive the blame for bad policy. Second, the social system of Varos is both hierarchical and unfair. The elite enjoy power, luxury, and virtual legal immunity, while the rest, the majority, toil full days for scraps of food. The populace are never properly informed about what the government is really doing. Instead, the populace are fed a steady diet of televised torture and entertainment to keep them distracted. An ignorant and ill-informed populace can never come to a truly logical or rational decision.

As "Vengeance on Varos" shows, the people are likely to see politics presented on television as either part of the show or a distraction from it. Voting is a matter of popularity, a vote against the person and not against the policy. Voters are likely to vote no just to see the torture of the governor. Thus, popular vote does not produce truly ethical political policy, and the inequities of society remain or worsen as a result. The program demonstrates John Stuart Mill's conviction that if a society through the will of the majority "issues wrong mandates instead of right, or any mandates at all in things with which it ought not to meddle, it practices a social tyranny more formidable than many kinds of political oppression since, though not usually upheld by such extreme penalties, it leaves fewer means of escape, penetrating much more deeply into the details of life, and enslaving the soul itself" (*Liberty* 13).

Freedom and Ethics

The contrasting thought that the Doctor always substitutes for obedience is *freedom*: freedom of thought, freedom of action, freedom of expression. We might think of the *Doctor Who* variety of freedom as corresponding to Immanuel Kant's definition of freedom: "independence from being constrained by another's choice" (*Metaphysics* 30). For instance, in "Ark in Space" (1975), the Doctor "forced the people of the Ark to stop obeying rules for the rules' sake and instead act in a way conducive to their own survival" (Gregg 652). The story involves a group of humans specially selected to repopulate the Earth after it has been ravaged by solar flares. An insect life form has invaded their orbiting space station, called the Ark, before they were revived, and is now preparing to use the Earth as a new home and the survivors as food. The people of the Ark come from a very rule-bound and stratified culture in which each person has a specific "function" and is not allowed to act beyond that function. When that social order gets placed under stress, it quickly becomes dysfunctional. For instance, the Doctor, Sarah, and Harry are allowed to wander around the Ark even when suspected of sabotage and kidnapping or murder because there are no people available qualified in guard and defense functions. By the end of the story, the Doctor has persuaded the acting commander, Vira, to break out of her habitual patterns several times, usually by using the argument that such action is for the sake of her people. Had Vira obeyed her social conditioning, she and all the survivors would have been dead. Only a mind free from social boundaries is flexible enough to respond logically to danger.

However, the Doctor is fully aware that freedom is won, not granted. In "The Sunmakers" (1977), for instance, the Doctor helps to foment a human rebellion against the oppressive Usurians by telling the rebellion's leaders: "I want you to scatter through the city and tell the people what's happened. Remind them that they're human beings, and tell them that human beings *always* fight for their freedom."

Fromm places the matter in a rhetorical question: "How ... can ethics be a significant part of a life in which the individual becomes an automaton, in which he serves the big It?" (173). Clearly, *Doctor Who* portrays a similar perspective. A "human being" in *Doctor Who* is not a servant of anything. *Freedom* means not only political freedom, but freedom of the mind, "freedom to think" as Kimus says in "The Pirate Planet." This freedom must be fought for as much as any other freedom, with the difference that the oppressor is as likely to be the self as any external factor.

The need to conform prevents development of a conscience, which, according to Fromm, "by its very nature is nonconforming" (173). One cannot have a conscience and lack the ability to say "no." Conscience requires the personal capacity to judge and to act accordingly. If judgment is left up to the system, to anonymous authority or distant authority, then ethical action cannot occur.

Free Will

Another way to look at the concept of freedom as it plays in *Doctor Who* is to address the question whether such freedom exists at all. Individuals can be *free* only if, as a precondition, they have some degree of autonomy. Put another way, for a person to be able to make free personal, political, and ethical choices, that person must have sufficiently *free will.*

In the popular mind, free will is a given. People generally act in the belief that they make free choices about whether to act or not. This belief, however, is mitigated by a countervailing belief that some choices (usually the wrong ones) happen because of overwhelming forces — biological, social, divine — that compel people to act in particular ways. At one end of this rationale, the argument of compelling force leads to rationalizations and cheap excuses for self-serving behavior. However, there are strong arguments favoring the idea that some, maybe even all, of human behavior is compelled or predetermined. The theory that for whatever reason humans are largely incapable of independent choice is called *determinism.*

Viewers of *Doctor Who* see examples of crude sorts of determinism in action every time a character's mind is taken over by some stronger alien force. In "The Hand of Fear" (1976), the Doctor and Sarah discover the remnant of a powerful alien creature in a quarry. The remnant has the ability to influence human minds, to drive people to take it to a power source where it can renew itself. So strong is the influence that it even drives ordinarily plain and passive people to murderous action, as when the physician Dr. Carter under the alien's influence attacks the Doctor with a wrench. Carter clearly did not choose to attempt murder, so in an ethical sense cannot be held responsible or accountable for this action.

Scenes of this kind demonstrate rough approximations of determinist theories. One can see that if in fact all behavior is determined by a demonstrable cause of some kind, then choice is removed from considerations about the value of an action. No normative rule could ever be formulated or applied since a person, according to determinist theories, is not in control of his or her own mind, but simply acting out a predetermined set of operations. If determinism is true, there is no ethics.

However, in *Doctor Who* extreme determinism of this kind does not fit the worldview of the program's makers. Rightly so, since extreme determinism is always inconsistent and absurd. We can take as a test the concept of religious determinism, or *predestination*. The argument as some monotheistic theologians formulate it is that an all-powerful and all-knowing god must, by definition, know everything that will happen and have made it to happen that way. The problem with this theory is intuitively obvious. How or why hold anyone accountable if that person is simply obeying divine will? And what of that divine will itself? If it created everything, then it created evil, pain, suffering, and so on. Furthermore, rewards for good behavior and punishments for bad would be solely determined by this deity, and for humans to evaluate any activity and act upon it would be presumptuous, even if it were possible for humans to so evaluate and act, the possibility of which extreme predestination would deny (Thiroux and Krasemann 106–7).

Doctor Who does not dive too often or deeply into the waters of predestination, partly because it does not dive too deeply into religious and theological considerations at all. The program presumes some degree of human autonomy and free will. In those cases where the powers of aliens mimic those of deities, people under the influence are forgiven for their actions. Repeatedly someone, usually the Doctor, reassures other characters and the audience that a person like the suddenly murderous Dr. Carter is being "controlled" and is "not himself" and "could not help" acting as he did. Such statements presume that ordinarily these people would have a choice and would choose not to commit violence.

The rejection of the theory of predestination is further confirmed when the program distinguishes between those totally under an influence and those willingly under an influence. Often, those under an influence will struggle to break out of it, as some characters will do when under the Master's influence. The mind struggles to assert itself. Those who willingly submit to such influence, though, receive little pity or understanding. In "Ghost Light" (1989), Mrs. Pritchard and Gwendoline, under the influence of Josiah Smith, the product of a biological experiment that has assumed the role of a Victorian gentleman, gleefully send people "to Java," that is kill them with formaldehyde. After the two women are partly restored to their minds, Mrs. Pritchard admits that the two of them are "lost," implying moral responsibility for their actions. After the two are turned to stone, the Doctor makes an even harsher judgment, saying that he could have forgiven the trips to Java if the two had not enjoyed it so much. Willingly submitting to a controlling power is an ethical wrong in *Doctor Who*.

A different form of determinism from the religious one is scientific determinism. There are two varieties of this determinism — physical and biological. Physical determinism is not much in favor any more, but from the late 1600s and the theories of Isaac Newton through the early 1800s it had many adherents. The argument is that all physical phenomena are effects of traceable sequences of causes. The human being is a physical phenomenon and, therefore, whatever a person does is traceable to sequences of causes. Biological determinism takes a similar line, but focuses primarily on physical characteristics of the human animal, and since the mid-twentieth century more particularly on genetics. The main argument is that biology is destiny and that human behavior is always preconditioned upon biological imperatives such as survival and procreation.

The problems with these positions are many, but there are some notable ones. One reason that physical determinism no longer has much influence as a theory is that modern science shows that physical phenomena are in many key areas more probabilistic than deterministic. Since probabilities allow for greater diversity of "effects" than do deterministic chains of causes, the argument is put forward that free will exists within the probabilities.[2] Biological determinism seems more firm, especially given the magical thinking popularly applied to genetics over the last few decades. However, its problems are similar to those for physical determinism. It provides too much of an all-explanatory answer used to dismiss objections and cut off inquiry into other possibilities. It is artificially reductive, ruling out without consideration the possibility that mental phenomena may be significantly different from physical phenomena (Thiroux and Krasemann 108). Even if the sources of mental phenomena are all biological/physical, yet they may transcend their origins through numerous means.[3]

Since belief in physical determinism would make fiction of any kind utterly meaningless, *Doctor Who* simply ignores its possibility. Biological determinism, though, does deserve closer scrutiny. Fundamentally, the argument would be that standard natural imperatives (eating, procreation, sleep, dominance, self-preservation, etc.) can account for all human behavior. No matter what we do, it is a response to a biological imperative, or a group of imperatives operating in concert. If I write a book, it is nothing more than a bid for some kind of eminence/dominance, and/or perhaps eating and self-preservation if the book sells enough copies. The key is in the phrase *nothing more than*.

A counter-argument to biological determinism is that these impulses may indeed play a part in my writing a book, but they are not the only and may not even be the principal factors determining whether I do or do not write one, let alone the choice of topic, perspective, and so on. We will need to take a look at some of *Doctor Who* to provide scenarios to help determine whether I am wrong and that biology alone accounts for all human behavior.

Some creatures most definitely operate at this purely biological level. Take, for instance, the drashigs from "Carnival of Monsters" (1973). Huge worm-like creatures whose primary imperative is to eat, drashigs are so mindlessly persistent in this endeavor that they are behaviorally uncontrollable. The drashigs, like most other creatures in the story, live in a miniature environment inside a technological traveling menagerie called a miniscope. The controller can adjust the machine so that the creatures inside will behave in different ways. This includes the humans inside. All creatures, except the uncontrollable drashigs, perform the same routine over and over, apparently incapable of realizing their trap. Drashigs are uncontrollable because their biological imperatives are greatly reduced. In the same way that one cannot train a worm, one cannot make a drashig do anything other than be hungry.

But what about the rest? Is it any better for the humans if they can be made aggressive or mild by the mere turn of a dial? Is it possible that having more imperatives operating makes such manipulation possible, simply by enhancing one and suppressing the others? Does it not seem that humans are just as much slaves to their biology as are drashigs?

The answer to this set of problems lies in the fact that in order for the miniscope effect to work, the humans and other thinking creatures must be kept in a constant state of deception. They must be made to believe that their existence is perfectly normal and that they are not part of a sideshow. When the Doctor and Jo are captured inside the miniscope, they have behavioral independence; they have not gone through the processing and so do not succumb to the miniscope's effects. Even the processing itself is not 100 percent effective, since one of the humans, Clare Daly, is constantly on the verge of realizing that something is not quite right in this little world.

The argument from biology would be that human mental phenomena are simply "more complex" versions of animal behavior, but are nevertheless only responses to internal biological drives. The counter-argument is that "more complex" is precisely the point at which free will develops. It is at least possible that a complexity threshold exists over which the human animal has definitively crossed and around which a few others (apes, dolphins, whales, pigs, cats, dogs) hover. Complexity does not logically or empirically rule out independence from biology. "Carnival of Monsters" asserts that people do have free will and are partly independent from basic biological drives.

The point of this digression on free will is that it is the fundamental principal of ethical thinking. Ethics is not possible if free will does not exist. Therefore, if we are to proceed in discussing ethics in any context, we must establish the existence of free will. We can then evaluate choices made either constrained or freely.

Temptations

Epicurean philosophy assumes that people are motivated by pursuit of pleasure and avoidance of pain. This argument has often been misinterpreted as pursuit of pure self-satisfaction. One can see *Doctor Who* villains often acting in this fashion, pursuing what pleases them regardless of how their actions affect others and often getting their pleasure from the pain of others. However, far from seeing pure self-satisfaction as the best result of pleasure-seeking, Epicureans equate "pleasure" with physical well-being. Similarly, Epicureans mean more than just physical pain when they say that a good life involves avoiding pain. They mean also the pain that derives from need. Therefore, beyond merely physical pleasures, which can be temporarily satisfied and lose appeal when appeased beyond satisfaction, there are the more important pleasures of serenity and contentment, which come from satisfying both need and desire. While the things that produce physical pleasures can also produce the pain of frustration and loss, the higher pleasures of serenity and contentment do not produce pain. Therefore, these higher pleasures are the ethical goals of life (Godwin xviiff). It is also important to note that contentment and serenity do not mean wallowing in luxuries, power, or fame. Far from it. The Epicurean philosopher Lucretius tells us, "If a man would guide his life by true philosophy, he will find ample riches in a modest livelihood enjoyed with a tranquil mind" (157).

It may be seen that to some degree the Doctor is an Epicurean in the true sense. Whereas his various foes seek money, power, or fame, the Doctor seeks only to go on in his content, peripatetic way, happy enough to have what he has. Furthermore, the Doctor finds it difficult to understand why other people should not share this view. Thus, for example, in "The Visitation" (1982), the Doctor finds it difficult to reconcile the Terileptils' love of beauty with their violence and cruelty. In "The Enemy of the World" (1967–8), the Doctor pauses to contemplate that people take time to make pretty things only to have those things smashed in an instant of violence. For the Doctor, the villain's desire to control, possess, or destroy just does not make sense, nor does it have any appeal to him.

The Epicurean rejects seeking after fame and power as the way to produce contentment. Lucretius calls this pursuit "an idle dream." He states that those who seek power "beset their own road with perils." He further mentions the "wearisome unprofitable struggle along the narrow pathway of ambition." He even goes so far that it is better to lead "a quiet life in subjection than to long for sovereign authority and lordship" (157). In *Doctor Who*, one clearly sees a more modern understanding that rejects totally the notion that to live in subjection is better than seeking power. Later in this chapter, there is more discussion about why that is not a particularly ethical position. One should note, however, a constant in *Doctor Who* is that the villains constantly "long for sovereign authority" and in doing so, fulfill Lucretius prophecy that they "beset their own road with perils."

Epicurus and his followers were not the only ones to reject desires for luxury and power as both inferior and potentially painful. The early Christian neo–Platonist Boethius writes at great length of the misery that people bring to themselves and to others when pursuing total control of material things. Epicureans such as Lucretius argue that there is a simple, practical reason for this misery, which is that seeking such power is a desire that cannot be satisfied. Furthermore, seeking power tends to spread pain, since spreading pain is the only way to get the power. Boethius, however, sees the matter not as a practical reality of the material world, but as a matter of mistaken judgment. As Boethius sees it, those who seek power do so because they mistake good things for the Good. Money, fame, and power are in some ways good, or at least appear good. However, no matter how many good things one may acquire, they cannot add up to produce the Good.

Boethius relies upon a religiously-based definition of "the Good,"[4] but such a definition is inconsistent with the *Doctor Who* universe. There is one point of agreement, though, regarding the Good, and that is that whatever the Good is, only if one possesses all the things that are good might one possess the Good (Boethius 57). Yet, it is impossible to possess all that is good. Also, pursuit of control over all that is good brings at best only fleeting happiness (Boethius 58). Inevitably, the company that such pursuit brings is misery.

The Greater Good

One of the most common ethical arguments is that the quality of an action is determined by the number of people it benefits. This idea has been discussed earlier as the "moral mathematics" argument, but it may also be called the "greater good" argument. Holders of this view would quantify the ethicality of an action by focusing on its results. Most commonly, this argument is attributed to the founder of Utilitarianism, Jeremy Bentham. In 1822, Bentham defined *the principle of utility* as "that principle which states the greatest happiness of all those whose interest is in question, as being the right and proper, and only right and proper and universally desirable, end of human action" (11n). He goes on to state that *number* is the key concept to understanding the ethical principle of utility. Bentham's godson John Stuart Mill reformulated Bentham's theory into a tight construction: "The creed which accepts as the foundation of morals, Utility, or the Greatest Happiness Principle, holds that actions are right in proportion as they tend to promote happiness, wrong as they tend to produce the reverse of happiness" (*Utilitarianism* 9–10).[5]

The *Doctor Who* story "New Earth" (2006) puts the utilitarian theory of ethics to the test. In the far future, a hospital on the planet New Earth can cure all sorts of diseases thought to be incurable. The Sisters of Plenitude, evolved cats who run the hospital, have devised a secret method to make this "miracle" of science happen. They grow thousands of human clones specially cultivated to host every disease that affects humans. The Sisters then extract the immunities these clones develop and use them to treat ill patients. The clones, however, are developing self-awareness and language. Whenever this happens, the specimen is incinerated because of the trouble he or she causes.

Clearly, the Sisters' keeping this process a secret indicates knowledge on the Sisterhood's part either that the practice is unethical or that the humans they treat will think it so. The Doctor, when he discovers this enterprise, is outraged. The clones are human beings in pain, no matter their origin, and thus deserve the right not to have pain inflicted on them, certainly not without a say in the matter. Nevertheless, the Sisterhood have convinced themselves that they are doing the right thing. They feel overwhelmed by the amount of disease humans bring, and see this plan as the only way to meet the demand for healing. Novice Hame of the Sisterhood defends their actions. "It's for the greater good," she declares. About the clones, she says, "They are not real people.... They have no proper existence."

The situation presents the viewer with a utilitarian conundrum. Clearly, the procedures produce a good, quantifiable in the number of cured patients. However, the procedure could be seen to be causing pain to the clones carrying the diseases. Thus, the Sisters think of the matter in terms of qualitative good as well, namely that the good done to freely born humans living full lives is high enough to warrant whatever they do to clones who do not deserve the same consideration as free-born humans.

The Doctor's understanding of utilitarian ethics seems to be closer to Karl Popper's formulation, which is not "maximize happiness," but "minimize suffering" (*Open I* 235). Reformulating the concept in this way resolves the conflict demonstrated in "New Earth." What the Sisterhood does is wrong because they try to maximize some people's happiness through increasing the suffering of others whom they define merely as "flesh" and "specimens." Since their plan for healing does not minimize suffering, but instead makes more of it, the plan as ethical healing fails.

Doing Good

Fundamental to ethical thinking is the question of how one can tell when one is doing Good. In his defense of himself before the people of Athens, Socrates, as reported in Plato's "Apology," states, "A man who is good for anything ought not to calculate the chance of living or dying; he ought only to consider whether in doing anything he is doing right or wrong — acting the part of a good man or of a bad" (458). Socrates' opinion on the matter is that one can tell when one is doing right by comparing the action to what an ideal "good man" would do. Ethical thinking along these lines involves imagining this "good man" and using him to make an imaginary test run of a possible course of action.

Socrates' idea as expressed in the "Apology" runs into trouble, though, when one realizes that determining Good depends upon an individual's imagination and intellect, not only the power of each but also the type of each. Doing Good itself can be a temptation to step beyond ethical boundaries. The desire to see wrongs righted and to undo or redress errors can lead those who otherwise lead lives of virtue to commit heinous and immoral actions. The Doctor, as a doer of Good, is a likely target for such temptations. The headnote to this chapter derives from one such example. The Master has apparently gotten his hands on a doomsday weapon capable of wiping out solar systems. The Master offers the Doctor coequal rule over the universe. He says that the Doctor can "reign benevolently" and ensure that societies do not become corrupt or violent. This is the mythical devil's bargain, the offer of "the world" now expanded to a size appropriate for modern scientific awareness. The forces of evil tempt the mythical hero, knowing that the power to control humanity's destiny inherently corrupts the wielder of that power.

When the hero accepts the temptation, the result is inevitably a tragedy, as in *Macbeth* or the tale of King Minos. However, when the hero refuses the temptation, as in the relevant tales about Buddha and Jesus, the result in terms of the story is the safety of the world. Thus, it is only right that as Romantic Hero, the Doctor in "Colony in Space," refuses the Master's deal.

The Doctor receives a similar deal and, unlike in "Colony in Space," seems genuinely tempted to take it in "School Reunion" (2006). In this story, a group of aliens called Krillitane have taken over an English high school, enhancing the children's mental abilities so that the children will be able to break the Scasis Paradigm, a code that unlocks the secret to manipulation of the universe's building blocks. The lead Krillitane, Headmaster Finch, explains the purpose of this endeavor: "With the Paradigm solved, reality becomes clay in our hands. We can shape the universe and *improve it*" (emphasis added). Thus, the first part of the temptation is announced. The second part comes from what the Krillitane have learned about the Doctor, namely that he is the last of the Time Lords, a lonely, homeless wanderer with a deep need to see justice done. Finch offers the Doctor the chance to reshape the universe to his liking, to become God at Finch's side, and thus reverse all the terrors that plague him. The Doctor can make it so that the Time War that destroyed his home would never have occurred, can make anyone he wants practically immortal, and can regain all the losses he has ever suffered. Placed in these terms, the temptation is not so much one of power, as in "Colony in Space," but of healing. No one really wants to feel pain, and the ability to make the pain go away can appear to be a Good of such overwhelming value that one can very easily overlook the obvious — that one can never make things better for *everyone*, and that making things better for one person will most likely mean making it worse for some other person.

These devil's bargains just discussed call up a fundamental question. What does it really mean to "play God"? The problem in the show's humanist terms is really this: In a universe in which no god is apparently taking enough interest to prevent catastrophe and suffering, for after all were such a god to exist there would be no apparent need to play one, and in which the intelligent beings feel the gap between harsh reality and their desire to see justice in the form of reduced pain, is not the ultimate temptation the power to end all suffering?

It becomes clear as one thinks about these matters that the power to redress all wrongs, while seeming good, is really the corrupting power to end choice. It is not the dream of the ethical person, but of the megalomaniac. The Doctor himself reveals this truth while mocking Finch as Finch offers his power-sharing deal. The Doctor ridicules Finch's plan for a new universe by noting that its "face" would be Finch's. However, the Doctor does pause over the offer to fix what most troubles him. This pause draws viewer attention to the second problem in humanist terms to this offer of "the universe." If the Doctor has a desire to fix all the problems causing him pain, then though it appears that he is doing Good for others, he is in fact making things good only for him. Just as trying to order people to be good under the threat of a gun, as in "Colony in Space," robs people of free will and individual dignity, so too does trying to fix their problems through the selfish desire to make oneself feel better. It still robs those people of free will and dignity. If the Doctor uses such a power, he acts as though he is changing things *for* them, without, however, consulting them. Additionally, it only appears that he is making things better for them; in reality, he is making things better only for *him.* The Doctor's old companion, Sarah Jane Smith, realizes this in "School Reunion." She thwarts Finch's tempting plan by stating, "The universe must move forward. Pain and loss, they define us as much as love." Sarah here refers to *dignity*, the right and ability of all people to improve themselves through surviving, understanding, and transcending that which hurts them.

So, we can see in the examples from *Doctor Who* the limitations of doing Good. One ought not to presume what is good for others. One ought not to act so as to remove or invalidate other people's free will and dignity. One ought not to be so caught up in the idea of relieving one's own personal griefs that one fails to see the harm that might come from trying to right the wrongs of the past.

Science and Ethics

Since the late nineteenth century, there have been many attempts at creating ethical theories from scientific knowledge and practice. In the late nineteenth century, Herbert Spencer attempted to use Darwin's theory of evolution to determine what socially ought to be. In the late twentieth century, philosophers such as John Searle and Paul Churchland used brain anatomy and cognitive science as bases for determining philosophical and ethical principles. However, in general popular conceptions (most of them misconceptions) of the relationship between science and ethics have persisted for the last 150 years. An example of a common popular misconception about science rests on an equivocation involving the word "relativity." Einstein's theory of relativity, which has to do with explaining gravity, is taken as saying or implying that all values are relative. It is seen as scientific validation of moral relativism. The novelist Italo Calvino is among many who reject this mistaken notion (35). Fortunately, *Doctor Who* generally avoids some of the more egregious errors in relating science to ethics.

The Doctor is one of the most ethical characters in fiction. A distinctive feature of his ethicality is its source — the Doctor's scientific worldview. At first, this may seem to make no sense. It is popular, even among practicing scientists and moral philosophers, to believe that science is mostly a matter of applied study and logical thinking to specific empirical problems and mysteries. Science, so the thinking goes, deals with what *is*, while ethics deals with what *ought to be*. The Doctor's adventures, however, demonstrate that there is a deeper relationship between science and ethics that goes beyond even the ethics of science to encompass ethical behavior in general.

As a starting point to understanding the way a scientific outlook leads to certain ethical positions, we can consider what it means to have a universal perspective. A thought experiment can help here. This one was proposed by Ann Druyan and recorded by her husband, the physicist Carl Sagan. One can look at the Earth from the vantage point of a spacecraft. We have the pictures that spacecraft have already taken to guide us. What do we see? From the distance of Saturn, the Earth is just a pale blue dot hanging in space, barely visible. Even from as close as inside the Moon's orbit, there are no signs of human impact on the Earth. Sagan notes, "From this vantage point, our obsession with nationalism is nowhere in evidence." He also notes something "well known to astronomers," namely that "on the scale of worlds — to say nothing of stars or galaxies — humans are inconsequential" (*Pale* 3). Druyan takes these musings even further. She asks that one take a good hard look for a long time at the inconsequential dot that is the Earth in photographs taken from space, and then try to convince oneself "that God created the whole Universe for one of 10 million or so species of life." After this, she suggests that one pick another dot, any other dot, and try convincing oneself of exactly the same thing, that God chose it out of all inhabited worlds for special dispensation, and that only one species on that one dot is to receive all the benefits of the Universe (Sagan *Pale* 8–9). The logical result of such musings is to reject the ideas that humanity occupies some special sacred location, that we are "the center" of the universe, either physically or spiritually.

This particular thought experiment should shake one from the conceit of human superiority. One sees in *Doctor Who* just this sort of idea. Both "Remembrance of the Daleks" (1988) and "Rose" (2005) begin from this outer space perspective of the Earth, vulnerable and small when viewed from the beyond its atmosphere. "Remembrance of the Daleks" involves several scenes in which humans must abandon their self-centered views. Group Captain Gilmore must realize that the universe contains far more destructive powers than he could ever hope to defend against militarily. Professor Rachel Jensen faces the humbling prospect that her scientific knowledge is primitive compared to that of both "a bunch of tinplated pepperpots" and a "wandering space tramp."

Another view of these matters comes in "The End of the World" (2005). The Doctor takes Rose five billion years into the future to witness the destruction of Earth. They meet the last human, which upsets Rose greatly. However, this upset derives from that automatic response that "human" outweighs all other values. What she learns is that humanity has moved on evolutionarily. More to the point, she presumes that the end of biological humanity really means the end of the Earth. However, she learns that other Earth species have moved on and developed starfaring civilizations of their own, including the trees. Rose must step outside the limitations of human conceit, must see that not everything in the Universe is organized *for* humans.

The Doctor's perspective is wider, his understanding fuller, because the knowledge acquired by science leads to it. The Doctor's scientific outlook is thoroughly ingrained. He comes from a technocratic society with a government run to some degree like a university. He is completely tied to his technology, i.e., the TARDIS, and to his self-definition as scientist. He goes by a scientific title. His curiosity and scientific training prevent him from making the kind of prejudgments that plague and bedevil humans in the series. Tulloch and Alvarado note that "the Doctor, by means of his movements and intellectual experience, establishes a vantage point outside the historical worlds of social, racial and sexual stratification which he visits" (114). Thus, when applied ethically the scientific outlook is humbling, removing the prejudice and conceit that lead to so much of human conflict and misery.

The first step in ethical humanism is the recognition of the humanity of others and that self is not automatically superior to other. The first known philosopher to state this point clearly was Antiphon, from the fifth century B.C.E. Antiphon states that perceived differences between "foreign" and "Greek" are illusory: "For we all breathe the air through our mouths and nostrils, laugh when our minds feel pleasure or cry when we are distressed; we hear sounds with our ears; we see with our eyes thanks to daylight; we work with our hands, and walk with our feet" (qtd. Waterfield 264).[6] The principle of humanitarian equivalence is vital to any formulation of the so-called "Golden Rule," which requires that one behave toward others in the same way that one would like others to behave toward oneself. However, Antiphon's principle in its day is more revolutionary than the various formulations of the Golden Rule that came before it. These golden rules usually extended only toward members of one's own society, not toward strangers. Antiphon, however, is a true humanist in this field, regarding foreigners as worthy of equal dignity. This position allows for universal extension of the Golden Rule and is the foundation for democracy, an important concept in *Doctor Who* as we will see in Chapter 10.

So, science informs the ethical perspective in *Doctor Who* principally by widening the viewers' perceptual field. Just as Antiphon imagined that the moral universe included more than just Greeks, so the makers of *Doctor Who* perceive that the moral universe includes more than just humans. Furthermore, *Doctor Who* consistently presents shifts in the scale of thinking. What seems important as a matter of national interest or adherence to a cause loses much of its justification when viewed from the wider perspective that increasing scientific discoveries provide.

Ethical Nonaction

During the 1970s and 1980s, a strong dose of Eastern mystical philosophy, mostly Buddhist and Taoist, entered into *Doctor Who*, in accordance with the rising popularity of such thought in Western society. *Doctor Who* producer Barry Letts (1970–4) was strongly influenced by Buddhism, which is reflected in several stories he co-wrote or directed. A notable example is "Planet of the Spiders" (1974), which contrasts use of mental discipline as a means to power with mental discipline as self-examination. The story centers on a Buddhist retreat in England, where a man named Lupton has convinced some of the members that they can use the discipline of meditation to summon powers that they may use to gain mastery. Central to his plan is a special crystal that focuses and amplifies mental energy. The character contrasts to Lupton are the mentally retarded man, Tommy, and the Doctor. Tommy's primary characteristic is his innocence. When the crystal of power enhances his mind so that he becomes instantly intelligent and mature, he nevertheless maintains this essential innocence, protecting him from the evil powers. The Doctor learns that for him the goal of mental discipline is to face and eradicate the demons of his mind, in his case fear. Lupton, however, ends up destroyed by the very powers he has summoned, the evil spiders from a future world even more adept at control and manipulation than Lupton.

"Planet of the Spiders" introduces in a small way the concept of ethical nonaction. Several philosophical systems have proposed this idea, though it is best known in its Eastern forms. The fundamental idea is that the constant seeking after power and goods, the constant need to be *doing something* is both corrupting and self-destructive. Nonaction in these systems should not be confused with inaction. Nonaction does not mean doing nothing, or living a life of contemplative contentment. It really means first taking action to change oneself before taking it upon oneself to change others. It means waiting to be compelled by events into moral action instead of constantly seeking to initiate actions.

We have seen in Chapter 4 that the format of *Doctor Who* allows the program to incorporate and examine nonwestern philosophical systems, specifically Buddhism. The example of "Planet of the Spiders" shows that Buddhist ethics can fit in the *Doctor Who* format. Another Eastern philosophy that gets occasional attention in *Doctor Who* is Taoism. Whereas Buddhism best fits our discussion in a religious context, Taoism is more appropriately examined as an ethical philosophy. In particular, Taoism teaches ways to reduce both internal and external conflict and thus establish a harmonious existence.

The *Doctor Who* adventure that most overtly relies upon Taoist thinking in its structure and themes is "Warrior's Gate" (1981). In the way that both "Kinda" and "Snakedance" are partly allegorical explorations of Buddhist doctrines, so "Warrior's Gate" uses a large set of narrative devices to illustrate Taoist ideas. The main idea of concern in "Warrior's Gate" is ethical nonaction. "Warrior's Gate" demonstrates the concept of action through nonaction, at the same time highlighting the ethical problems associated with authoritarianism and rash action.

Taoism has been strongly influenced by Buddhism. This influence exists in "Warrior's Gate." The Doctor, Romana, Adric, and K-9 have found themselves in a no-place, a zone between two universes. This place is designated by "zero coordinates," so that it has neither time nor space in the conventional material sense. When two crew members from a spaceship stuck in this nowhere discuss the matter, one notes that it is a nowhere that isn't even supposed to exist, while the other states that nowhere is still somewhere. This place, then, represents what Buddhists call non–Atman. *Atman* roughly translates as "self," but Buddhism teaches that "the *atman* is nothing" (Suzuki 40). Buddhist thinking teaches that every A is also its own not–A, that both A and not–A are infinite and at the same time nothing. So non–Atman, the self's opposite, is not something, but is "absolute emptiness" that is "beyond conception," according to Zen master D.T. Suzuki (59).

Into this no-place come three sets of beings: the human space freighter crew trapped in the no-place, the time-sensitive Tharil slaves that the freighter carries, and the TARDIS crew. This no-place turns out to be a buffer zone between universes created by the time-sensitive Tharils. These creatures once ran a vast slave empire and raided human worlds to capture human slaves. The humans then built Gundan (from Japanese, a reference to a kind of warrior) robots who could travel the time winds like the Tharils and so destroyed the empire. The situation reversed and the humans took Tharils as slaves to pilot their starships. Now centuries after the fact, humans have all but forgotten this past. Thus, when the freighter crew led by the overbearing Captain Rorvik crash in the null zone, only the Tharils know where they are, and the Tharils are not telling.

All this background gradually emerges as the actual story goes along. However, to understand the Taoist concepts used in the story, one needs to know the situation. The story works by contrasting the hyperactive Rorvik and his crew, desperate to "do something" about their situation, with the peaceful Tharils, who have learned the lesson of history and gained a greater perspective. The TARDIS crew operate in the position of the viewers, uncovering the facts of the situation and learning the Tharils' Taoist perspective.

The first Taoist concept to consider involves the notion of "time sensitives." The Tharils, and to a lesser degree the Gallifreyan Doctor and Romana, are able to gain a greater perspective by being able to see beyond the moment. Their special sight gives them, Tharils especially, a kind of divinatory power. Though originally the writings attributed to Lao Tzu and commonly known as *Tao Te Ching* had nothing to do with divination, centuries later they were conjoined with the practice known as *I Ching*, which is a kind of fortune telling originally managed by tossing several sticks and "reading" the pattern created. Another common method is tossing coins. The idea is that such endeavors tap into the hidden patterns of creation and can therefore guide a person's course of action. Basically, the belief is that no event is random, only apparently so. All events connect naturally, and this connection is called "the way" (*tao*). Therefore, *deliberate* activity is not always necessary, because events will unfold in the manner of the way. In fact, deliberate action may be more harmful than good, since the way will go on no matter what one does to the contrary. Trying to go against the way that things are actually happening will bring only misery and disaster upon oneself and those one drags along. "Not being in accord with the Way/leads to an early demise" (*Tao* 74/30).

Throughout "Warrior's Gate," there are indicators of a Taoist perspective. For instance, Romana's outfit is Chinese-styled. Tossing coins repeatedly happens. The Doctor bows humbly at one point. Tharil statements, especially from the main Tharil Biroc, could come straight from the *Tao Te Ching* or the *I Ching*.

Coin tossing, however, is thematically important. The first time is early in the program when the trapped space merchants are trying to escape the no-place. Two of the crew bet on whether they will escape or not, and as the coin flies in the air, the ship attempts to cross timelines. At this moment, the spinning coin is visually superimposed over the shaking ship's interior, establishing the problems that occur when deliberate action contravenes the "random" way.

A bit later, the Doctor and Romana in the TARDIS discuss randomness and activity. Romana dismisses the idea that random events draw upon cosmic order with a viscious "astral Jung." She says the Doctor might as well toss a coin, to which the Doctor correctly responds that there is nothing random about tossing a coin.

A third important coin tossing event happens when Adric and K-9 are lost in the no-place. When the damaged K-9 admits that he is operating below minimum capacity, Adric interprets this as meaning that the perfectly logical and deliberative computer is "less than useless." Adric takes to tossing a coin to navigate through the no-place. This coin tossing shows him the way, in a sense, to the ruins where he finds the Doctor.

Along with scenes employing coins, "Warrior's Gate" contains a scene involving sticks. Two warrior robots are attacking the Doctor, who defends himself by picking up old battle axes and bits of furniture lying about. A robot smashes each of these items until the Doctor has nothing but a collection of sticks in his arm. Pinched between the two robots, he bows in apparent acceptance of his demise and the robots each smash each other on the head in trying to chop the Doctor's head. The sticks represent the *I Ching* sticks. The Doctor's inaction and acceptance of the way things appear to be going leads to his salvation.

All of the aforementioned events work primarily as reminders of the program's main Taoist theme, which is the ethical advantage of nonaction. This nonaction must be separated in concept from inaction. Both nonaction and inaction amount to "doing nothing." However, inaction results from inability to decide. Nonaction is the choice not to go against the tide of events. Inaction is passive, nonaction active. According to the *Tao Te Ching*, "Nonbeing penetrates nonspace. / Hence, / I know the advantages of nonaction" (6/43). In the nonspace in which the characters are not being, nonaction becomes the only sensible action.

The viewer can see how this theory works by contrasting the activities of the freighter crew, the TARDIS crew, and the Tharils. The freighter crew, and especially Captain Rorvik, are, as said earlier, almost hyperactive. They are determined to get something done and think that any activity, any movement at all, is better than being stuck in no-place going nowhere. This view leads some of them to be unnecessarily ruthless and others to be reckless. Rorvik, for example, believes in the strength of weapons. He tries to force the Doctor at gunpoint to take the freighter out of their microuniverse. When he learns that the Tharils travel across universes through specialized mirrors, he first has a laser aimed at the mirror, with the result that the reflected bolt nearly kills one of the crew. Then, he escalates to a bigger weapon, which nearly demolishes the room containing the mirror. Finally, he tries a backblast from his ship's warp engines, because he believes that everything has to break eventually. He is right, but unfortunately for him his ship is the thing that breaks.

This same need to do something without considering the consequences of what one does affects the crew members Aldo and Royce. However, they react with carelessness. When they are told to prepare a Tharil suspended in deep freeze for revival, they try to revive the Tharil on their own, even though neither actually knows how the equipment works. As a result, they kill the Tharil. When Rorvik attempts to force Romana to pilot the freighter, risking Romana's life, and the attempt fails, Aldo and Royce, left behind while the rest of the crew searches for a way out, decide to jolt Romana awake with electricity, without much concern for what such a jolt might actually do to her.

The source for all this destructive and dangerous activity is simply the need to do something, derived from a misunderstood notion of "positive action." The motivation comes to the fore late in the program when Rorvik, at last completely unhinged, rants, "Run Doctor! Scurry off back to your blue box. You're like all the rest. Lizards when there's a man's work to be done. I'm sick of your kind. Faint-hearted, do-nothing, lily-livered deadweights. This is the end for all of you. I'm finally getting something done!" It never occurs to Rorvik that the something he is getting done is his own demise.

The TARDIS crew operate on a fundamentally more humane and ethical principle of investigation. Rather than trying to blast their way out, or to force others to do the work for them, the TARDIS crew explore and investigate. This corresponds to the Taoist notion that right action occurs only when one has the right facts. The contrast with Rorvik and his crew is brought out when the Doctor partially activates an abandoned Gundan robot so as to gain information. Rorvik disrupts the procedure, and then when he is busy threatening the Doctor, the robot is destroyed by another robot that suddenly gets up and vanishes through the mirror. The viewer sees how threats and force make matters worse. It would have been easy enough for Rorvik to pool resources with the Doctor rather than treat him as an enemy from the beginning.

Finally, there are the Tharils. As stated above, the Tharils at one time were the slave traders. When the Doctor passes through the mirror, he passes into the Tharils' past. There, he sees the Tharils living like kings and abusing their human servants. In a symbolic gesture, the Doctor pours wine into a cup until it flows over, then spills the cup. More important thematically is Biroc's ironic statement that "the weak enslave themselves." As the example of Rorvik shows, the "strength" of force is illusory because it derives from mental weakness. Thus, the Tharils can blame only themselves for their current slave condition, which was caused by their original weakness.

What the Tharils have learned through the painful process of their history is the doctrine of nonaction. When the Doctor asks Biroc how to get out of the no-place, Biroc tells him to "do nothing," and that it will happen anyway. Later, when the Doctor and Romana are trying to prevent Rorvik from using his warp engines to smash the dimensional mirror, Biroc intervenes, again telling the Doctor to "do nothing." At this point, the Doctor gains sudden insight. Doing nothing is right, "if it is the right sort of nothing." The Taoist concept of nonaction is similar to Gandhi's idea of nonviolent resistance; eventually, a person's or oppressed group's ethical strength will prevail.

The union of *Doctor Who* with some aspects of Eastern philosophy is not so strange or forced as it may appear. The Doctor often conducts himself similarly to how the "sage" or "master" of Taoism is supposed to conduct himself. The Doctor will "act through nonaction," though contrary to Taoist philosophy he does not often "handle affairs through noninterference." He will "undertake difficult tasks/by approaching what is easy in them" and "do great deeds/by focusing on their minute aspects" (*Tao Te Ching* 26/63). One of the translators of the *Tao Te Ching* explains the concept of "nonaction" as not synonymous with inaction or absence of action. "Rather, it indicates spontaneity and noninterference; that is, letting things follow their natural course" (Mair 138).

"Warrior's Gate" demonstrates the Taoist principle that in the right circumstances, nonaction is the ethical choice. When one acts from ignorance, the results are often devastating. Resorting to force rather than cooperation has similar results. When one has all the needed facts, then one need not "act" from the motivation to be doing "something." One must consider one's own activity as part of the complex pattern that makes a situation involving moral choice. When one has the facts, the right course of action will be so obvious that it seems as though one is doing nothing at all. The weak enslave themselves; they also often destroy themselves. In many cases, the ethical choice is nonaction, because the morally weak cannot be sorted out, and they will ruin things for themselves anyway.

The idea that *deliberate* activity is not always necessary because events will unfold in the manner of the way is common in *Doctor Who,* though it is not often given a Taoist attribution. As indicated earlier, the Doctor's power as a time sensitive coupled with his knowledge as a time traveler often leads him to conclude that action meant to influence or change events is either impossible or disastrous. Either way, such arguments generally fit in with the Taoist perspective that events are part of a complex system of interactions that transpire in their own fashion apart from personal desire that they go another way. The idea that deliberate action may be more harmful than good, since the way will go on no matter what one does to the contrary, is deeply embedded in the notions of the "web of time" and the "course of history" repeatedly invoked in *Doctor Who.* Thus, in stories such as "The Aztecs" and "The Massacre" (1966), the Doctor has to insist to his companions that attempting to controvert history is at best a fool's errand and at worst highly dangerous to the person trying to do it. When one has command of all the facts, when one can see the way of events, then nonaction is the only sensible course.

The concept of nonaction previously discussed in regard to "Warrior's Gate," and its appearance outside of a Taoist context in other *Doctor Who* stories, ties into the Buddhist themes discussed in Chapter 4 of this work relating to the stories "Kinda" and "Snakedance." If one were to remove the allegorical elements from these two stories, one could see that both show non-action as among the highest of ethical standards. In "Kinda," action for its own sake is part of what starts the wheel of history, and is portrayed as either troublesome, such as when Adric tries to use the colonists' survival suit and loses control of it, nearly killing Aris in the process, or insane, such as Hindle's constant restless paranoid activity. In "Snakedance," one can defeat the Mara (a demon of both within and without) only by finding the "stillpoint" and concentrating on it.

The idea of ethical nonaction is most often seen as "Eastern" and is often mistakenly thought to be superior because it is non–Western. However, the differences between Eastern and Western philosophical systems have been exaggerated. That Eastern ideas fit comfortably within the format of the highly Western and humanistic *Doctor Who* shows that affinities between Eastern and Western thought exist. It should be no surprise that Taoism and Buddhism should be the Eastern systems used in *Doctor Who*. If one sets aside the terminology of these systems of thought, and both are laden with terminology, one can see that at their heart they are fundamentally humanist concerns. Neither Taoism nor Buddhism is particularly religious in the Western sense in that neither has any sort of god-figure that created, runs, or guides the universe; both are essentially nontheistic. Additionally, both are concerned with common sense ethical principles shared with cultures throughout the world. Both stress individual moral responsibility, the source of ethical nonaction, as the guide for social behavior. Lastly, both emphasize the use of reason and knowledge as foundations for proper understanding.

Categories of Ethical Action

Despite the references to Eastern ideas of ethical nonaction, *Doctor Who* still most often operates in a universe in which events force the Doctor into ethical action. Thus, a more constant concern of the series is what makes an action ethical. If one were to ask someone at random what qualifies as ethical behavior, one is likely to receive a list of types of behavior, that is categories of actions perceived to be "good." Paul Kurtz has taken an extended look at these categories of behavior. He has divided morality into two categories:

common moral decencies and *excellences.* Common moral decencies include avoiding vices such as lying, cheating, and stealing. Excellences are cherished values, categories or sets of behaviors that include rationality, creativity, integrity, personal freedom, and so on.

Common Moral Decencies

The Doctor is one of the most decent characters on television, yet it is very difficult to ridicule the Doctor for this decency. One of the more decent things about the Doctor is his attitude of open friendship. The Doctor views friendship itself as among the highest goods, mirroring Epicurean thought on the matter. Epicurus writes, "Of all the things that wisdom acquires for the blessedness of life, the greatest by far is the possession of friendship" (qtd. Godwin xxii).

Fundamental to the common moral decencies is the so-called Golden Rule, commonly stated as "Do unto others as you would have that they do unto you." This concept is nearly universal in human cultures, and certainly older than even its earliest biblical version (Leviticus 19:18). For example, the *Tao Te Ching,* an ancient Chinese book of wisdom sayings wholly uninfluenced by Jewish thought and tradition, states:

> Treat well those who are good,
> Also, treat well those who are not good;
> thus is goodness attained [12/49].[7]

Sigmund Freud's examination of the Golden Rule focuses on it as a pragmatic necessity, rather than as a high-minded ethical truth. Looked at strictly as a matter of what it says, one must come to the conclusion that the Golden Rule is astonishingly unnatural. If a person's love is valuable, why should he or she dispense it to any and all who happen to be around? Should not the person receiving this love be worthy of it? Furthermore, this "other" that one should love is a stranger who is not likely to return the favor of this love, and might even wish one harm. As Freud states, "Men are not gentle, friendly creatures wishing for love." Recognition of the true nature of the human animal, Freud argues is the real reason for the Golden Rule, not that it is some pristine injunction beyond logic. According to Freud, the reason for the Golden Rule is to check the aggressive tendencies of people, both one's self and one's "neighbor." In doing so, one contributes to the construction of civilization, which is impossible without such checks to people's natural violent proclivities (58–61).

A useful reformulation of the Golden Rule is Kant's. He states that each person, in every act that person does, should treat other people as ends in themselves and never as means to be used (46). Application of this principle demonstrates why Barbara in "The Aztecs" takes an unethical path, though she intends good. In trying to reform Aztec society, Barbara attempts to use the Aztec people in general, and the priest Autloc in particular, to accomplish this end. These people cannot make a fully rational consent to what Barbara wants from them because she must withhold the information she has from the future.

One can see from the examples of friendship and the Golden Rule that decencies are the foundational types of actions that help people form communities. These may have a basis in nature as survival mechanisms and are thus fundamental, but they also go beyond mere basic natural need. Decencies enhance not only personal survival, but also personal well-being, and do so by enhancing the survival and well-being of others. Thus, the Doctor is decent because at the front of his thinking is the survival and well-being of others.

Excellences

What Kurtz calls the excellences are fundamental to creating a workable system of ethical values. By an *excellence*, Kurtz means habits of behavior that when cultivated take people beyond mere existence and toward living to their full potentials. Among these excellences is the recognition of *rights*. Ruggiero goes so far as to say that "the principle that people have rights existing independently of any government or culture" is the "most reliable basis for moral judgment" (*Art* 34). Perhaps the first of these rights is the right to *respect*, what one might call the libertarian right, which is the right to be left at peace as long as one is not infringing the rights of others. Kant went so far as to say that the right to be left alone is the only true right that people have. Today's ethical theorists argue that more rights than this one in fact exist, yet they do recognize it as the foundational right upon which most others are based.

In *Doctor Who*, the Doctor repeatedly exhorts thugs, tyrants, bullies, despots, and megalomaniacs to leave someone alone. It is characteristic of the villains of the series that they have little to no respect for others. To them, other self-aware beings exist merely as means to ends. Even when the villains are on the receiving end of such treatment, they do not learn the ethical wrong of it. In "The End of Time," the Master spends part of the program trapped and used by a rich man to provide immortality for his daughter. The Master, however, does not learn to sympathize with those whom he has similarly abused. Instead, the Master works on outwitting his captor so as to invert the situation. Here one sees the contrast between the Master and the Doctor. The latter seeks to escape the abusive situation and end the abuse. The former seeks to become the abuser. The Doctor cultivates the excellence of respect.

Another right is the "pursuit of happiness," as Thomas Jefferson famously phrased it in the Declaration of Independence. Commonly misunderstood as the right to make money, which does not exist, "the pursuit of happiness" is really the right to attempt to make one's own destiny, and not to have it defined or overbearingly limited by forces such as law and precedent that reside outside the individual. Mill explains the matter this way: "Neither one person, nor any number of persons, is warranted in saying to another human creature of ripe years, that he shall not do with his life for his own benefit what he chooses to do with it" (*On* 127). Others, either individually or as a social collective, might try to exhort, persuade, cajole, or deter a person from a particular course of action, but so long as that action does not infringe on any other person's rights, society has no legitimacy in preventing a person from proceeding along what appears to be an unwise course, or to punish that person for proceeding (Mill 131–3; 164).

The most fundamental right of all is the right to *life*.[8] There are two forms of this right. One is that there is an inherent preference to preserving the lives of others over taking the lives of others. Another form of the right to life is that the living have more rights than do the dead, and that consideration should always first be given to those fully alive.

In *Doctor Who*, the first form of right to life is a repeated theme. It was particularly emphasized during the run of the tenth Doctor, who often would give an opponent a choice of standing down or of suffering lethal retaliation, often a result of the opponent's own aggressive actions. The Doctor does not focus on the retaliation, though, but instead offers the opponent some way out of a bad situation.

An example of the second form of right to life as a theme comes in "Dragonfire" (1987). Ice World is a large commercial establishment run by a ruthless former criminal named Kane. His principal concern, though, is with his memories of his beloved late partner in crime, Xana. He is obsessed with Xana, employing a sculptor to create a great statue of her, and waiting 3,000 years to exact his revenge upon the people of his home world for causing her death and his exile. The dead Xana has more importance to Kane than does any living person, an idea that leads Kane to cruel actions without giving much thought to their cruelty.

One can find other excellences in four ethical principles that Ruggiero identifies as common to most, if not all, cultural circumstances: (1) People's relationships with other people involve *obligations* that ought to be honored unless more compelling reasons exist for not doing so; (2) Specific *ideals* are common to most cultures and are recognized as enhancing freedom and happiness; (3) Considering *consequences* for actions helps determine value in terms of benefits and harms; (4) "*Circumstances* alter cases" (Ruggiero *Art* 34–5).

There are so many examples of these excellences in previous discussion of ethics in this chapter that no more will be offered here. Mainly, one should know that an "excellence" is a habit of behavior "enhancing freedom and happiness," to use Ruggiero's words.

Good Will

Another of what Kurtz calls "transformational principles" basic to morality is "a good will" ("Good" 5). Indeed, Immanuel Kant claims that a good will is the only good thing that is good without qualification. Kant calls it "incomparably higher than anything which could be brought about by it in favor of any inclination or even of the sum total of all inclinations" (*Foundations* 10). Kant, therefore, considers it an absolute quality, apart from what it may or may not effect. Kurtz agrees with Kant's valuation of good will, but argues that it must be considered also in light of its effects, in particular on human beings and their communities.

In essence, the question of a good will rests on the impetus for performing the common moral decencies and for seeking the excellences. There is a moral distinction between motivations for acting properly. One may act properly in order to avoid a punishment or to seek a reward. However, acting from a good will, from a genuine desire to do good is qualitatively superior (Kurtz "Good" 6). English novelist John Fowles states the matter this way: "*Doing good for some public reward is not doing good: it is doing something for public reward*" (81, italics in original). Acting from a good will is also much more likely to produce desirable results than is acting from the selfish desire to seek a reward or avoid a punishment. This is one reason that the Doctor is a hero and that audiences desire to watch his adventures. The Doctor seeks to do right because it is the right thing to do, and not because he may receive some reward or avoid some punishment as a direct result of *acting* good. Doing good is not an act for the Doctor, but a natural consequence of his good will.

Kurtz summarizes what acting from good will means in terms of personal outlook:

> Being of good will means that we are not mean-spirited or surly, despairing or nihilistic, vindictive or hateful. We should try to be affirmative about what life offers, not fearful or defensive; we should be hopeful, not cynical or nasty; we should exude some realistic optimism that we can influence or mitigate evil and improve human affairs ["Good" 6].

One can see that the Doctor's outlook clearly exemplifies good will as Kurtz describes it.

Among Kant's considerations of the value of a good will, he is aware that even though a good will is a supreme good, it sometimes does not accomplish what one would like.

> Even if it should happen that, by a particularly unfortunate fate, or by the niggardly provision of a step-motherly nature, this will should be wholly lacking in power to accomplish its purpose, and if even the greatest effort should not avail it to achieve anything of its end, and if there remained only the good will — not as a mere wish, but as the summoning of all the means in our power — it would sparkle like a jewel all by itself, as something that had its full worth in itself [*Foundations* 10].

There is really no better statement that could summarize the philosophic position of *Doctor Who*. The Doctor is the man of good will *par excellence*, and yet repeatedly finds thwarted his desire to spread good will and be treated with good will. Nevertheless, his example shines, and though he may fail to achieve the positive ends he seeks, he nevertheless continues to act from the position of Good Will.

It might seem as though acting with good will means ignoring reality, especially the fact that not everyone has good will and that good will does not always elicit a similar response. Let us go even further. It may seem that this good will completely ignores the fact that there are those who do evil and who wish to harm others, that good will is really blind optimism.

However, good will is not blind optimism. The person of good will tries to avoid violence, but may be forced into violence for self-defense or even self-preservation. Violence against those of evil intent may sometimes be the only way to prevent harm to others. The manifest moral difference is that the person of good will acts violently only when forced to do so, and does not use violence to gain advantage over others. For the person of good will, violence is never motivated by revenge. Never does the person of good will use violence for the enjoyment of it.

We can see that the opposite of a good will, call it a bad will, has certain fundamental characteristics of its own. Key among these is racism. There are few attitudes that exemplify a bad will quite as well as racism. It is easy enough to see why in Sartre's discussion of anti–Semitism. While some people might explain away racist attitudes as being cultural or religious or experiential responses, Sartre argues that these are not good explanations for they make anti–Semitism, and by extension racism, seem to be mere opinions. It equates a distaste for an entire class of other people with a distaste for citrus fruit or Berber rugs. Of course, it is nonsensical to equate any form of racism to mere distaste simply because one does not dislike such things as citrus or Berber rugs with the totality, the complete disgust, and the hysteria that accompanies racism. Anti-Semitism, and racism by extension, is a chosen way of life, what Sartre calls a "passion," which entirely takes over a person's reason. Sartre calls it "a global attitude" that spreads from its focus to people in general, to history, to culture. One can see that anti–Semitism or any form of racism controls the racist's perceptions and interpretations in a way that mere opinion does not. The extreme, illogical contortions of thought that pass for the racist's "reasons" are enough to show that whatever form racism takes, it is a "concept of the world," and not a mere opinion (Sartre "Portrait" 271–5).

Racism is a superb example of bad will. Just as when we strip away the actions inspired by good will and leave behind good will itself as a supreme good, so when we strip away the actions inspired by bad will, such as manifestations of the racist passion, we are left with bad will as a supreme evil.

Thus, it makes little sense to say that one who does evil may do so because of a good will, because of a genuine desire to do good. As we have seen earlier in this discussion, there are qualitative differences between the motives for doing good, and these differences will have different results. Racists may believe that they are doing good by expunging some sort of evil or error from the human strain; inquisitors and religious fanatics may be motivated by a belief that their actions genuinely benefit humanity by eradicating false ideas and the people who expound them. However, as Fowles states, such people hope for "a better world to come *for themselves* and their co-believers" (83). Though they may wish to do good, they are not acting from good will because they do not act for greater freedom. Fowles explains the consequences of such only apparently good actions: "If the intention of a good action is not finally to institute more freedom (therefore, more justice and equality) for all, it will be partly evil not only to the object of the action but to the enactor, since its evil aspects will limit its own freedom" (83).

Putting Together a Set of Fundamental Ethical Principles

Having gone through numerous ethical perspectives and theories, can we now distill all these concepts into a workable framework of fundamental principles? Does *Doctor Who* adhere to such a set of principles?

Professor Thiroux has distilled the ethical theories from multiple cultures and times into a set of clear principles.

- The Value of Life Principle
- The Principle of Goodness or Rightness
- The Principle of Justice or Fairness
- The Principle of Truth Telling or Honesty
- The Principle of Individual Freedom

The value of these five principles is that they can operate under any ethical system. Furthermore, according to Thiroux, "These principles are broad enough to take cognizance of all human beings and their moral treatment, and as such they are near or almost absolutes, in that exceptions to these principles can be made only if they can be completely justified through empirical evidence and reasoning" (177). A final value is that application of these five principles can resolve conflicts between ethical systems when situations place the systems into conflict.

Thiroux states the Value of Life Principle thus: "Human beings should revere life and accept death" (164). In practical terms, the principle places life as being the ethical priority over death. Stated another way, in a situation in which the ethical choice is to preserve life or administer death, preservation of life receives priority. That means that there is not an absolute injunction against killing, only that "no life should be ended without very strong justification" (164). The principle also means that in most cases, "an individual's right to his own life *and* death is a basic concept" (165, emphasis in original). Justifications for taking life are varied. One occurs when one person threatens another person's life and killing the threatener is the only way out of the situation. Another occurs in "quality of life" issues, such as when a person determines that life is too painful to be worth it. A third would be self-sacrifice, when losing one's own life will thereby preserve the lives of many others, and no other option for action is available.

In *Doctor Who*, the Doctor's well-known antipathy to violence is sorely tested. Again and again, he is forced into the position of killing or allowing some being to be killed. Does the Doctor violate his own standards against killing? Not, as seems to be the case, if he is operating under the Value of Life Principle. Can one reason with a Dalek? In most cases the answer is no. Daleks kill without compunction and for self-serving reasons. Daleks clearly do not adhere to the Value of Life Principle, and so when one is being attacked by a Dalek, the only logically ethical choice is to kill it before it kills. The same rule applies for many *Doctor Who* villains.

Likewise, many beings sacrifice themselves so that the Doctor may proceed saving the lives of many others. Rarely does the Doctor ask anyone to do this, perhaps even never. Always, when someone volunteers to put him or herself in danger, the Doctor questions the person to see whether he or she has made a free choice. In many other cases, the Doctor himself willingly steps in to make the sacrifice rather than have someone else take the risk, only to be pushed out or replaced. A case in point comes at the end of "The Ark in Space" (1975), when the Doctor has tricked the Wirrrn into entering a spaceship prepared to launch. In order for the plan to work, someone must stay behind to unlock the spaceship, a person who will certainly be blasted to death by the rocket exhaust. The Doctor decides to take this task himself, but Rogin knocks him out, drags him to safety, and then performs the operation himself, dying as a consequence. Similar sequences run throughout the program's history.

The Principle of Goodness or Rightness, Thiroux says, requires that people try to do three things: promote goodness over badness and do good; cause no harm or badness; and prevent badness or harm (165). To admit to the idea of morality at all is by definition to follow some idea of goodness. At a practical level, following this principle means rejecting monism, the belief that there is *a* Good, which we have seen above and will see elsewhere often leads to wrongheaded idealism in which the *idea* associated with *the* Good becomes more valued than any one life, which in turn in its extreme often leads to fascistic and totalitarian views. Instead, following the Principle of Goodness means practicing limited pluralism, the belief that there are many "goods." These goods are mostly the same as what Kurtz named as the common moral decencies and the moral excellences.

In *Doctor Who*, one can clearly see the Doctor behaving according to the Principle of Goodness. The Doctor does not actively seek to harm another or to gain personal advantage through the suffering of others. His whole career is spent in trying to prevent badness or harm. Sometimes, others are hurt or killed in the process of preventing harm. One must keep in mind that the Doctor is not an all-powerful being who can prevent anything from happening should he choose to do so. Though he has abilities beyond ordinary human capacity, he is still limited and vulnerable. Preventing all harm in any situation is simply out of the range of his powers. In "The Unquiet Dead," the Doctor believes that he is helping a race to survive by allowing them to use a young woman as a channel into this world. This race, however, is lying, and seeks to replace completely all humanity on Earth. The desire to do good can lead to harm due to misperception, misunderstanding, or deception. The situation must be set back right, limiting further harm. One cannot take back the harm that has already been done.

Additionally, as we can see in "The Unquiet Dead," the universe, even one as artificially simple on the moral level as that in *Doctor Who*, is not so arranged that harm does not happen because we do not want it to happen. Events and forces leading to harm can be greater and more powerful than anyone's ability to stop them. This is demonstrated rather well in "Doctor Who and the Silurians" (1970), when the Doctor tries to form a peace between the Silurian race and humanity. He thinks he has gained an understanding with the Silurian leader. Then that leader is killed by an ambitious upstart Silurian intractable in his hatred for humanity. This same young Silurian had let loose a virus deadly to humans without the lead Silurian's knowledge. The Doctor cannot prevent the initial spread of the virus and the deaths of many people from it, but can only work out the antidote through hard, plodding scientific means.

Despite, however, the two problems just described, a person's limited understanding of the situation causing the moral dilemma and the arrangement of events that prevents a person from stopping some harm, a person can follow the Principle of Goodness in such a way so as not willingly to add to the total amount of harm in a situation and to prevent or limit further harm. Within these constraints, ethical action based upon an idea of Goodness is both possible and logically necessary. The Doctor follows the principle admirably.

The Principle of Justice or Fairness "says that human beings should treat other human beings fairly and justly when distributing goodness and badness among them" (Thiroux 166). Another way to state this is that ethical behavior involves treating peoples as ends rather than as means, a view consonant with the various formulations of the "golden rule," and with more modern ethical theories such as those of Kant, Popper, and Kurtz. This rule does not mean that all good things must be doled out in equal proportions. Since individual humans differ, sometimes it does not make sense that everyone gets an equal share of something, especially when one person's needs are greater than another's. It does mean that all laws and rules of justice be applied equally, though. It also means that everyone should have realistic opportunities to *acquire* good things should they choose to do so.

I will discuss the specifics of Justice and its distribution later in this book. For now, it is enough to say that *Doctor Who* is often principally concerned with matters of justice and fairness. As we have seen when discussing good and evil, the "evil" characters are often given that label because they treat other beings as means to an end and not as ends in themselves. Daleks treat humans as a means of cheap labor. Cybermen treat humans as a source of supplies for creating more Cybermen. Contrary to the unjust ways of the evil characters, the Doctor places life above other considerations. A living being is an end in itself, and the goal of one's ethical existence is to preserve and enhance that life, making living beings ends in themselves.

The Principle of Truth Telling or Honesty requires that people not hide information or deliberately deceive others. If I am lying to you, then I cannot possibly be treating you as an end, as a being co-equal and thus worthy of the truth, but only as a means, as a way to get me something I desire at your expense. The rule is important "to provide meaningful communication, which is an absolute necessity in any moral system or in any moral relationship between two or more human beings" (Thiroux 168).

In *Doctor Who*, we can again see how this rule operates by contrasting the Doctor with his enemies. For the evil characters, deception is often a way of life. The Master is at the very least a master of disguise, pretending to be, among other things, a minister, a Greek scientist, an Arabic magician, a wise old leader, a navy admiral, an adjudicator, and a research psychologist. These deceptions have the same goal, to gain an advantage over others by misleading them.

The Doctor, on the other hand, lies seldom and reluctantly. In "Gridlock" (2007), he lies to Martha, then deeply regrets it when she is kidnapped, treating her abduction almost as a consequence of his lie, though it is not. A deeper consideration of the consequences of deception comes in the related stories "Human Nature" (2007) and "The Family of Blood" (2007). In order to escape a family of life-eaters, the Doctor removes his Time Lord essence, makes himself human and then hides among humans, hoping to outlast the family's life cycle. Several consequences emerge from this action. A human woman falls in love with the human "Doctor Smith," and he as human falls in love with her, not aware that this love is impossible. When he becomes a Time Lord again, he breaks her heart because it means that "John Smith" is dead. Even worse, though, is that he does not manage to evade the family entirely, and a kind of battle ensues with several lives taken. Clearly, if all this damage derives from the initial deception, then there must be a good reason for the deception. That reason, it turns out, is that the Doctor sought to allow the family to die a natural death rather than face a worse retribution at his own hands, which is finally what does happen. Of course, the Doctor is limited and could not foresee what would happen because of his deception. Yet, one can question the original decision to use deception since the results of deception are rarely good in the general sense.

The Principle of Individual Freedom Thiroux states is the principle that "people being individuals with individual differences, must have the freedom to choose their own ways and means of being moral *within the framework of the first four basic principles*" (170). This principle is contingent upon the others because without the others, it could lead to a free-for-all. Within this context, the Principle of Individual Freedom really means that there is a degree of freedom for people to choose their own ways to be moral as long as the choice does not seriously interfere with another person's life or rights. Also, one must recognize a limited amount of relativity, that the nature of the situation and the people involved figure into one's moral reckoning. People have the right to try to live in ways that best suit them. The principle includes recognizing that humans are *equal* in moral matters, not that they are equal in all things.

We can see this last principle applying across *Doctor Who*. We see it in the positive example of the Doctor, a firm believer in individual freedom and the right to self-determination. We see it in the negative example of various villains, who grasp tightly to their own rights, but recognize none for others.

Thiroux's final concern for his ethical system involves determining the priority of principles when they conflict in a given situation. Thiroux argues that as a general rule the priority is in the order given, with the Principle of Goodness being of highest priorty because it is both logically and empirically prior to all the others (172). Secondly, situation and context can determine priority of the principles (173). The particular situation helps establish the *general* rule that is to apply. By "general," Thiroux means that the rule is *generally* followed and applies to most similar circumstances. One is not *obligated* to follow the rule, which follows from the Principle of Individual Freedom, and one may violate any of the principles *with good reason* and still make a moral decision.

One of the commonplaces of fictive/dramatic scenarios is that they place characters inside *crises,* that is in a situation that requires the character to prioritize and decide the application of moral principles. One may take as an example a typical situation from "The Time Meddler" (1965). Stephen and Vicki sneak into a monastery, effectively breaking and entering, and thus violate the Principle of Goodness by doing what is ordinarily thought to be a bad act. However, a deeper understanding of the situation leads to a different conclusion regarding the morality of their action. First, they do not trust the Monk, the only person they meet related to the monastery, and have good reason to believe is not being honest with them, and may be pursuing harmful actions. Reacting to this knowledge invokes the Principle of Fairness. Second, they have good reason to believe that the Doctor is being held captive inside the monastery. Thus, the Principle of Goodness comes back in, this time as justification in releasing the Doctor from potential harm. Such action also involves the Value of Life Principle, the Principle of Fairness (unlawful imprisonment being unfair) and the Principle of Individual Freedom (there is no good reason to violate the Doctor's autonomy by holding him captive). Thus, though breaking and entering is *generally* wrong, in this circumstance it is right to a degree.

A much harsher test involves the taking of life. It must be said that the Doctor is responsible in one way or another for many deaths. The point has been exploited numerous times over the years and makes an especially common appearance in the CD audio dramas and original novels. However, too often these approaches place too much blame on the Doctor for deaths that are not really his fault. This is the guilt-by-association argument that the Valeyard takes up in "Trial of a Timelord" (1986), that the Doctor's merely being there *makes* the deaths happen, that if death occurs when the Doctor is nearby, the Doctor was responsible for the death. Such a position is logically inconsistent, and so can be ignored. Nevertheless, we can still see the Doctor as having killed or contrived the deaths of many sentient, intelligent beings. How, then, can the Doctor be a symbol of moral virtue? The Doctor chooses to use deadly means only when he has to. In "Warriors of the Deep" (1984), the Doctor knows that hexachromite gas will kill the invading reptiles, but spends quite a bit of time seeking a means of incapacitating rather than killing the invaders. However, finding no means to incapacitate, the Doctor is forced to use hexachromite, potentially to kill some so as to save many millions more. Thiroux states the prioritizing needed in these sorts of situations: "It is wrong or bad to take a person's life against his or her will, but if this person is violating the first two principles by aggressively seeking to take the lives of innocent people, one's own included, then one might have the right to attempt to stop the person from doing bad by any means one can, including killing him if no lesser means can be used" (173).

Doctor Who and Humanist Ethics

Doctor Who demonstrates the affirmative set of principles characteristic of humanism. Paul Kurtz provides a clear set of general ideas for these principles. He says, "Humanists hold that ethical values are relative to human experience and need not be derived from theological or metaphysical foundations" (*What* 35). Additionally, humanism affirms that "the good life is attainable by human beings; and the task of reason is to discover the conditions that enable us to realize happiness" (*What* 36). In sum, "Humanistic ethics ... focuses on human freedom. It encourages individual growth and development." In this scheme, people "take responsibility, individually and collectively, for their own plans and projects" (*What* 41). This is a planetary humanism that recognizes the interdependence of nearly all human activities and the need for immediate, effective environmental actions.

Calvino has stated that what counts in ethical matters "more than the weight of well-defined moralities, has been a process of ethical seeking, forever problematical and forever risky." He observes, "The most rational and all-embracing ethical construction ever attempted — that of Kant — demands that in every situation we should start again from scratch" (36). We have seen in Chapters 7 and 8 that the philosophical motifs operating in *Doctor Who* — Enlightenment rationality, humanism, existentialism, even Taoism — drives the program to the same conclusion about appropriate ethical action.

If the ultimate goal of ethical behavior is to increase the opportunities for happiness both of oneself and of one's fellows, then it is important to ask what sort of happiness we are talking about. Fromm clearly distinguishes the popular idea of happiness, which equates to having fun, and the ethical understanding similar to Spinoza's definition. This happiness is the result of "productive living" and of uniting oneself with the world through love and reason (Fromm 201–2).

What we find as an ethical system in *Doctor Who* is something close to Thiroux's. This would be a system starting from the five principles of the Value of Life, Goodness, Justice, Honesty, and Individual Freedom. There are no absolutes in such a system, only generally applicable principles. There are individual variations in moral behavior, such that reasonable people may come to somewhat different conclusions about how to act in a situation, and yet such people would be morally equal with each other. Thus, it is not as some would hold that secular humanism removes responsibility and makes anything possible, but that, as deconstructionist Paul de Man states, the death of humanism is the death of personal responsibility. A humanistic system inherently contains personal responsibility as a foundation. A principle can be violated only with good reason. Such a system of Humanitarian Ethics, as shown in *Doctor Who*, "allows for the greatest diversity and variety, while at the same time providing enough stability and order to protect all human beings while they explore their diverse ethical possibilities" (Thiroux 178).

Once one has accepted the need to act ethically, then one must also accept the burden that comes with it, which is responsibility. The story "The Fires of Pompeii" (2008) directly concerns the burden of responsibility. The Doctor is a time traveler with knowledge of future and past, and possessing an innate sense of the patterns of time in the universe. Being what he is, the Doctor is subject to the temptation to save everyone, and to set everything "right" by both his and common understanding of what "right" is. The idea, as we have seen, runs through the history of the series, from "The Aztecs" in 1964 to "School Reunion" in 2006, and further. In "The Fires of Pompeii," the Doctor and his companion, Donna, find themselves in Pompeii on the day before the famous volcanic eruption that will bury the city. Knowing what he knows of history and having the means to change it should he wish, what is the Doctor's responsibility in this circumstance?

The ethical conflict gets split between the Doctor and Donna. The Doctor's first reaction is to say that he has no responsibility at all. The destruction of Pompeii is "fixed" in history, and thus, just as with the Aztec ritual of sacrifice run amok or with the massacre of the Huguenots in Renaissance France, there is nothing to do "about" the situation. Donna, on the other hand, argues that one cannot simply allow 20,000 people to die without making some attempt to save them.

Several concerns are at issue. One is what qualifies as a "fixed" point in time. Donna points out to the Doctor that saving people is what he does, and thus not saving the citizens of Pompeii violates what is apparently an ethical rule for the Doctor. In this story, the Doctor never truly clarifies the difference between time points fixed and those in flux, but a viewer can make a shrewd guess about the difference. Roughly, it is that a "fixed" point is one the outcome of which is known. A point in flux is one about which the Doctor has little or no knowledge. Thus, he can interfere with history, for to a time traveler every point in time is history, only when he does not know what would happen or what would change as a consequence of his actions. In these circumstances, the Doctor becomes part of events rather than a manipulator of them. The idea of how a single decision affects the further course of events is actually pursued more fully in a later story, "Turn Left" (2008), in which a creature that eats energy from conflicts in time influences Donna to go back into her personal history and alter a decision. This change results in her never meeting the Doctor, with the further result that the Doctor dies, and tragedy upon tragedy befalls Earth in rapid succession as a consequence.

So, the fixed versus fluctuating time points idea conjoins with the Taoist idea of ethical nonaction, which had been explored in "Warrior's Gate." When *is* nonaction ethical? When the likely result of one's action will make matters worse instead of better, or when the consequences of one's actions cannot be determined or even guessed at, or when the pressure of circumstances pushes overwhelmingly hard against whatever action one wishes to take.

This latter maxim appears in "The Fires of Pompeii" when Donna tries to go around the Doctor and somehow save the citizens. She finds out that the Romans have no word for "volcano" and no concept to match it. Because the Romans superstitiously believe that the earthquakes and smoke plumes are signs from the gods, they do act to save themselves, but only superstitiously by performing the rituals they believe will propitiate the gods. When Donna tries to tell a young initiate of the Sybiline order about the eruption, the sisters see it as a "rival prophecy" and kidnap her so they could sacrifice her. During the actual eruption, Donna cannot even convince one of the panicked citizens to avoid the sea. So, try as she might, Donna herself cannot prevent an outcome that she already knows will occur.

There is also the problem of unknowable consequences. Let us say that the Doctor took up Donna's idea of saving all 20,000 citizens of Pompeii. To where would he take them? How would their presence affect history? Who would be born or not born as a consequence? What would result when Pompeii gets rediscovered, but there are no human remains? Plus, given that the citizens will not believe either Donna or the Doctor that a disaster is imminent, what would the Doctor have to do to save them? Would he have to abrogate their free choice because he "knows better"? However, "The Fires of Pompeii" complicates matters because it turns out that the situation is not merely a matter of history playing out as it was later recorded.

This line of thinking about how far the Doctor can defy time and history culminates in "The Waters of Mars" (2009). The Doctor arrives at the first human Mars base on the day that it will be destroyed and everyone on it killed. To complicate matters, the Doctor knows that everyone will die. Clearly, under normal *Doctor Who* circumstances the Doctor would set about rescuing people and setting things right. However, this moment is one of those "fixed points" that the Doctor had mentioned in "The Fires of Pompeii." Because of what happens at Bowie Base One, the human race will finally venture to the stars. It is, therefore, imperative for history and the advancement of the human race that events be left to run their course.

As events in "The Waters of Mars" unfold, the Doctor constantly struggles with his two impulses. The minute he realizes where and when he is, he wants to leave. Instead, he gets pulled into helping the people on the base. Nevertheless, he keeps pressing the point that he has to leave. Eventually, the Doctor has to confess to the base commander Adelaide Brooke the reason that he must leave. She tells him of a moment when she was a child during the Dalek invasion of Earth when a Dalek spotted her through a window, observed her, then left without killing her. Through these events, Adelaide realizes that she is important to history. She allows the Doctor to leave, but as he listens to crew members one by one dying, the Doctor can no longer resist his impulse to save those left.

The act of saving these people brings the ethical crisis to its climax. The Doctor decides that since he is the last of the Time Lords he is, therefore, the only person left capable of interpreting and enacting the "laws of time," and that he can, for that reason, break these laws at will. In essence, he imagines himself as the benevolent dictator over time itself. This decision puts the Doctor and Adelaide into an ethical discord. Adelaide realizes that events must pass as they should and that to do otherwise amounts to playing with people's lives and with the future of humanity, perhaps even the cosmos. Even as callous and ruthless a being as a Dalek can still see this. In a way, Adelaide realizes that each person is responsible for all of humanity, in a sense very much like Jean-Paul Sartre had in mind when he discussed the responsibility of existence. The Doctor, on the other hand, argues that he is now arbiter of what happens with time; he is now "Time Lord Victorious." As such, he can save both the "important" and the "little" people at will.

The stories of the tenth Doctor had been working up to this moment from early on. The tenth Doctor's first temptation to violate the laws of time and take charge of sorting out the cosmos as he saw fit came in "School Reunion," when the Krillitane leader offers the Doctor a way to reset time and resurrect every person who had died during his life, to bring back even his home planet. The human Sarah Jane Smith recalls the Doctor to his senses, preventing him from accepting the temptation. The event foreshadows the confrontation with Adelaide Brooke in "The Waters of Mars."

The program "Voyage of the Damned" (2007) also foreshadows the ethical conflict of "The Waters of Mars." When the Doctor tries to bring back to life a young woman who had helped him prevent a catastrophe, it is once again a human who convinces the Doctor to resist the temptation, saying that such power over life a death would make someone "a monster." The reason is that if a person could rewrite history, then for that person there are no ethical consequences, and so no ethics. Any mistake one makes can be undone, so that one never need use foresight or ethical reasoning again. The Doctor's desperation to bring back Astrid stems from his own rash promise that he would ensure that she and the other survivors of the spaceship *Titanic* disaster would all live. After all but two of the survivors with him die, the Doctor must bear the guilt of his rash promise. Would rescuing these people from death be a good act? Or, would it be just a way for the Doctor to make himself feel better and sidestep his responsibility to all self-aware life?

When in "The Fires of Pompeii" Donna convinces the Doctor to save one Roman family of no particular historical consequence from doom, it seems a compassionate and humane act. However, it sets up the idea that in some ways the Doctor can "get away with it," like the would-be thief who starts by stealing things of no consequence and then feels encouraged because he can repeat the act with impunity. Thus, the Doctor is now psychologically prepared for his big crime, leading to his sense that there are "important" and "little" people. However, the distinction of who is important and who is not important never remains as clear-cut as the Doctor seems to think at the end of "The Waters of Mars." For, not long before, the apparently wholly inconsequential Donna Noble had become at one time, to use the Doctor's own words, "The most important person in the universe." Since there is no way to know every event, every person, every thing that may be of consequence, deciding who is or is not of consequence, which event is important and which is not, is too arbitrary to risk trying.

Thus, viewers arrive at the end of "The Waters of Mars" prepared for seeing the Doctor make an ethical failure of judgment. The Doctor's arrogance at terming some people "important" and some "little" is the inevitable consequence of declaring the power over life and death. As the Doctor senses time adjusting to fit his untimely rescue, he gets his first sense that the "laws of time" exist for very good reason. Adelaide takes it upon herself to set right what the Doctor had corrupted and kills herself. This act of self-sacrifice for the good of future people unknown to her shames the Doctor. Disgraced and horrified by his own actions and attitudes, the Doctor believes that maybe he has gone too far and has now created the circumstance of his own death. In a way, he had, for he had violated the ideals for which he stood. He had become untrue to himself, and thus "killed" that person he had been for so long.

CHAPTER 10

Politics

I have to have power. The world is weak, vulnerable, a mess of unco-
ordinated and impossible ideals. It needs a strong man. A single mind.
A leader.

— Tobias Vaughan, "The Invasion"

Politics on the Ground

The very first adventure in *Doctor Who* is surprisingly a highly political
story. The tribe of Gum is in serious trouble. A pre-historic, ice age people
threatened by oncoming Winter, they are currently leaderless. In their society,
the leader is the one man who can make fire and thus symbolically protect
the tribe. However, this leader is now dead and had failed to pass on the
secret of fire to his son Za. Struggling to gain control over the tribe, Za desperately tries whatever he can think of to make fire and prove his value to his
society. However, Za has a rival, the stranger Kal, whom the tribe had taken
in after his own tribe had starved to death.

More than half of the story involves the political rivalry of the two men.
Since neither man is able to make fire, each must persuade the people of his
value as leader. To do this, each must also discount the other man's claim
while gaining support from the people of the tribe. Both men are ruthless,
cunning, and in varying degrees untrustworthy. Each man's claim is largely
based upon producing results, which determine who can better protect and
supply the tribe. Za is a visionary politician, a planner and thinker who sees
beyond immediate gratifications and understands the need for social organization and cohesion. Kal is a boastful politician, exaggerating his abilities and
status to impress. Za's negative campaign strategy is to call Kal a liar. Kal's
negative campaign strategy is to call Za a coward. Za's positive campaign
strategy is "What I say I will do, I will do," thus differentiating himself from
Kal the liar. Kal's positive campaign strategy is to insist that he is favored by
the sun-god, and so is a natural-born leader.

247

It is not hard to see the basic social analog at work. Various criticisms leveled at modern politicians can be equally leveled at Za and Kal. Certainly, their negative campaign strategies represent in basic form what modern politicians do in complex form. Just as the political campaigning is similar to modern politics, so too is the political structure of the tribe's society. Political power arises from the ability to protect and supply, in modern terms the ability to maintain police and military forces and the ability to regulate the economy. Though the perks of political power in the tribe may be significant, such power ultimately derives from the consent of the governed and rests on an unsteady balance of alliances on one side and popular support on the other.

One of Za's advantages over Kal is Za's wife, Hur, a kind of Lady Macbeth and campaign advisor in one. She keeps a watchful eye on matters, reports the people's moods to Za, and recommends various strategies. She notes, for instance, that despite whatever realistic reason Za may have for devoting his energies toward making fire, the old men, who as in many modern societies are the secret political deciders, worry about Za's obsession with fire and so favor Kal. "Old men see no further than the meat that fills their bellies," she tells him, thus noting that political campaigns are won on short-term results rather than long-term planning.

There are characters who, as in a Greek or Renaissance tragedy, represent particular perspectives on the matters in question. The Old Mother, for example, acts as a skeptic, casting doubt on claims and their motives. She notes that Za might want leadership from egotism, so that everyone in the tribe would bow to him as they had to his father. She also disdains progress (i.e., fire) and prefers the "old ways." Horg, Hur's father, acts as representative of popular sentiment, like the Choragos in a Greek Tragedy. He restates the stump speeches into easily managed and clearly stated summaries.

Unfortunately for Kal, he accidentally spies the Doctor smoking a pipe[1] and wrongly assumes that the sun-god has sent him a fire-creature to make him leader. This event leads to Kal's downfall and death, an example of the ways that one political mistake can spiral down to total defeat. Kal captures the Doctor and takes him to the tribe so that Kal can declare his political victory. Had Kal been more cautious to ensure his victory rather than rush to it, he would have won. However, by capturing the Doctor, he ends up losing the Doctor's matches. The Doctor cannot make fire for the tribe, as Kal claims, thus "proving" Za's claim that Kal is a liar. Kal gets banished, in the way that many defeated leaders and politicians go into exile. Foolishly, he tries to return to regain his prominence, resorting to an assassination of sorts by killing the Old Mother. Kal finally dies by losing a trial-by-combat with Za. These events, too, are analogous to modern politics, and one can cite several cases of exiled political leaders who foolishly try to regain their prominence from exile. Napoleon springs to mind.

The three "Tribe of Gum" episodes that make up three quarters of "An Unearthly Child" demonstrate the practical realities of politics. They do not, however, test any political theory or show favor toward any political perspective. Instead, they make it possible from the beginning for *Doctor Who* to explore politics in the abstract. Political theory and conjecture are possible in the program partly because political considerations were there from the inception. The story draws attention to two fundamental questions of political theory: (1) who should rule? and (2) what checks are there to political power?

Society

Politics is the process of social organization. As "An Unearthly Child" makes clear, it is also a deadly business. It would seem on a practical level that one would stay well clear of political ambition if one valued his or her life. To understand why politics exists at all, one must understand human nature.

The humanist psychoanalyst Erich Fromm describes humanity as being constantly in a dilemma. By whatever means, humans have evolved in such a way that humanity "transcends nature." Humans no longer live the purely passive role with regard to nature that all other animals live. Humans have reason, moral awareness, and a concept of truth. Humanity is life that has become aware of itself. However, physiologically, humans are still animals, still subject to animal drives and urges, still following many animalistic action patterns "determined by neurological structures." Thus, according to Fromm, human consciousness is always split and is always confronting a problem: the disruption of the harmony with nature that other animals continue to possess. Humanity has kicked itself out of Eden, symbolically speaking, and there is no going back. The existence of each person, then, is a problem to be solved because "it is in a state of constant and unavoidable disequilibrium." Without the original home of nature, humanity must make itself a new home, making the world into a "human" world and becoming truly human through working toward the potential known as "human." Man needs to find "*ever-new solutions for the contradictions in his existence, to find ever-higher forms of unity with nature, his fellowmen and himself*" (Fromm 22–5).

Fromm further argues that the "problem" of existence carries over from the individual to society itself. Just as each person is born in disequilibrium, so too does that birth keep society in disequilibrium. It is not just that each person psychically searches for the lost home of nature or for a new replacement home. The whole of society follows the same pattern. Because the only "secure" place is the past, and the past cannot be returned to, the human race has collectively gone through a series of stages in development roughly analogous to the development of the individual person. It has taken "hundreds of thousands of years to take the first steps into human life." Human society is a split consciousness trying to work out the definition "human." As Fromm sees it, humanity has only just begun to formulate "conscience, objectivity, brotherly love," in other words to mature. The progressive tendency is stronger than the regressive one, in general, yet each tendency is present and fighting for control (Fromm 24–7). Thus, politics is born.

A further problem exists when one is trying to understand social organization and the existence of politics. The problem is that what we call "society" has arisen mostly by accident as a result of unintended consequences, and not by intentional design (Marx *Contribution* 11–12; Popper *Open II* 93–4). Therefore, there are no clean or pure social organizations, none that are even close to perfectly engineered in reality. It is also, thereby, impossible to determine much about the future course of history.[2]

Various answers have emerged to solve the problem of social disequilibrium. Each of these answers may be seen as an ideology, a systematic view of the way society ought to operate. Each ideology has a set of assumptions, and each, when those in political power employ them, can be dangerously coercive. *Doctor Who* has looked at several of these ideologies and has promoted one political perspective above the others. We will review these ideologies, the ways *Doctor Who* portrays them, and the favored political system that emerges from these considerations.

The Ideal State

The single most influential work of political philosophy is Plato's *The Republic*. This dialogue begins when Socrates, returning home after partaking in the festival of the goddess Bendis (Artemis), gets corralled into a conversation regarding the true nature of justice. Socrates convinces the various parties to join him in building an imaginary ideal state and constructs it under the logic that bigger is better, the theory being that "justice" demonstrated at the state level will better illustrate true justice as it applies to individual persons.

Plato's ideal state is a curious sort of community. Socrates (the voice of Plato in the book) recommends censorship, especially in educational materials, so that children and young adults might not be led astray by the "lies" of fables and allegories (62–74). However, the leaders of this ideal State are allowed to lie, though poets and artists and in fact anyone else are not. As long as the lie is for "the public good," then leaders can lie both to the enemies of their State and to its citizens. All other lying is a "heinous fault," not because lying is intrinsically bad, but because if anyone other than a leader does it, then the lie is "subversive and destructive" of the state (75).

Everyone in this State is to do the job set for him or her by the State. The education system will be used to determine which children show the greatest potential to be warriors, which the greatest potential to be artisans, and so on, and the children will thus be channeled into the way of life that the State determines most suitable. Since each person will be channeled according to natural inclination, no one will be unhappy and want to perform some other kind of job to which he or she is not suited (53–6; 58–9; 83–6; 98–9; 105). Plato assigns to each rank a metal as a kind of analogy: leaders are gold, warriors silver, artisans bronze, and so on. This gives the reader a strong sense of Plato's hierarchical mentality, that though he says through Socrates that leaders are not to have extravagant luxuries nor artisans and merchants be deprived, he clearly has a concept that some kinds of people are better than others. Furthermore, Plato also makes clear that rank is not to be hereditary. Though he doubts very much that "bronze" parents will produce "gold" children, children are to be considered common property, not belonging to the parents but to the State, and thus their futures determined by their quality, not by the circumstances of their parents.

The job of the leaders of such a State is to make the whole of the State happy, not favoring any one class in it. To accomplish this job, the leaders must be philosophically enlightened, and be philosophers, yet be brought down from the heights of contemplating perfect knowledge, and with their knowledge of truth legislate properly for the good of the State. Leaders must hold "the citizens together by persuasion and necessity, making them bene-factors of the State, and therefore benefactors of each other." These philoso-pher kings will thus avoid the problems inherent in other States, namely fighting over "shadows," by which Plato means material things rather than their ideal forms, and ruling from a desire to rule, which produces the "worst" kind of State (210–1).

Plato takes the position that what is good for the State is good for every-one in it. As we shall see, *Doctor Who* has always opposed the Platonic State. For now, we should consider what faults that need opposing are in it. Plato makes a tremendous logical fallacy by arguing essentially from the "bigger is better" premise. He believes that because the State is made up of people, the State will have the same properties that people have, that what is good or bad in people is what is good or bad in the State. Further, Plato argues that because the State is bigger than a person, its virtues and faults will likewise be magnified so that the State will always be a more important consideration than the individual person.

Plato fails to realize that the whole may have different properties from those of its elements. In other words, the State may have entirely different needs and values from what its people have. In the same way that a piece of music is more than and different from a collection of notes, so too is the State more than, and different from, its citizens. Alternatively, one may say that Plato has made a false comparison. The State is significantly enough different from a person to warrant treating it as a wholly separate entity from a person.

We have taken a look at Plato's conception of the ideal state and its problems because *The Republic* is the prototype for all theories of ideal government that work from the premise that what is good for the State is good for all in it. From the humanistic standpoint, such a premise is a formula for corruption and oppression, since individual will and autonomy must be subjugated so that the leaders can enact an abstract ideal of general happiness.

One of the more famous pronouncements in *The Republic* regards the rulers of the ideal state. Socrates claims, "*Until philosophers are kings, or the kings and princes of this world have the spirit and power of philosophy, and political greatness and wisdom meet in one, and those commoner natures who pursue either to the exclusion of the other are compelled to stand aside, cities will never have rest from their evils*" (166, italics in original). Several *Doctor Who* stories test this notion of an ideal state run by benevolent wise rulers for the good of the people. In general, *Doctor Who* takes the modern view of such an idea: that human nature and empirical fact will make any such ideal state impossible to set up or maintain, that utopia really is no place at all.

Plato might agree, since all things of this real world are changeable, which to him means corruptible, and therefore incapable of the perfection of the incorruptible unchanging divine ideal realm. We have seen in previous chapters, however, that *Doctor Who* usually portrays the modern humanist perspective, which rejects either the existence of such an ideal realm or its applicability should it exist. The stories of *Doctor Who* concord with Kant's assessment of Plato's "philosopher kings" argument: "That kings should become philosophers, or philosophers kings, can scarce be expected; nor is it to be wished, since the enjoyment of power inevitably corrupts the judgment of reason, and perverts its liberty" (*Perpetual* 39).

Doctor Who takes a position on State benevolence that is much closer to John Stuart Mill's than to Plato's. Instead of allowing that the State is always in a better position to determine individual good, as Plato claims, Mill strictly limits the scope of government benevolence. First, the case is actually very rare that the government will be able to conduct business of personal interest better than those involved. Second, having the government act as parent or guardian prevents individuals from learning by experience. Third, and most important, placing the State in the position of guardian adds too much to the power of the State, which is far too likely to seize and abuse the power (Mill *On* 182–7).

Another problem of the idealized State that benevolently rules is that it presumes that humans may be arranged in the way that one can arrange machines. Each person can be assigned specific tasks and functions, and as long as everyone performs his or her function, the social machinery will run perfectly. Even in presumably democratic societies, something like this attitude is pervasive, such as when people identify themselves by their jobs, or when a person claims that some are "born to rule," and others "born to follow." According to Mill, this notion of a society of functioning human automata misses the mark through a misunderstanding of human nature. "Human nature is not a machine to be built after a model, and set to do exactly the work prescribed for it, but a tree, which requires to grow and develop itself on all sides, according to the tendency of the inward forces which make it a living thing" (*On* 100).

At least one *Doctor Who* story takes on the "philosopher kings" idea. In "The Savages" (1966), a glittering city on a distant planet houses the Elders, a scientific oligarchy dedicated to knowledge, learning, and contemplation. Such would seem an ideal situation, and even though the Elders are not exactly Plato's philosopher kings, they make a good modern equivalent. However, the Elders and the citizens of the city harbor a dark secret. They get their life energy, both their longevity and advanced mental abilities, by extracting it from other people, whom they banish outside the city limits to live a scrounging, stone-age existence. These "savages" are treated as a replaceable and reusable resource. Thus, the Elders and citizens do not see them as "people," but only as humanoid farm animals.

Plato in *The Republic* repeatedly refers to his ruling elite as "shepherds" and the governed masses as "sheep" and "dogs." Similarly, he talks of the elite as ruled by "reason," while the governed are ruled by "passion." In short, Plato thinks that only the ruling elite are human, while the governed worker/artisans are animals. In *The Republic*, the differing classes come to be considered different races, almost different species, so that, at one point, Plato states that the ruling elite must be kept "pure," and recommends infanticide, while at another, after at first having suggested that there can be some movement between social levels, he concludes that the levels should never intermix.

Plato's disciple and later rival, Aristotle, comes to similar conclusions about the ideal State in *Politics*. Like Plato, Aristotle is a believer both in the "natural law" view of society and the racial theory of human dignity. Thus, like Plato, Aristotle concludes that those endowed with the existing requisites to rule, the education, wealth, and leisure that wealth can buy, should rule (*Politics* Book III Part XIII). Aristotle talks about those who are "natural masters," whom he defines as citizens. Those who are manual laborers are not quite citizens, since they technically work for others. And, of course, slaves are not allowed citizenship. Like Plato, Aristotle believes that such categories amount to "races" of people. Aristotle insists that social positions are natural.

The sentiments that Plato and Aristotle express regarding what is best for society stem from a common desire for order and stability. A clearly structured society based upon assigned roles appears to guarantee the smooth operation of that society. Moreover, such a society appears to ensure that no one is out of place and that no talents are wasted. Thus, such a society seems ideal for accomplishing what people in general want from their social systems.

The society of "The Savages" mirrors these considerations quite closely, complete with differing social levels with differing rights and a consensus among the ruling elite that the exploited class are a different "race" more like animals than like people. The social situation portrayed in "The Savages" can be taken not just as an enactment of Plato's Republic, but also as a distorted mirror image of predominant economic theories of the nineteenth century, or indeed any theory that assumes a natural division between a social elite and a vast mass of underlings whose sole purpose is to serve the needs of the elite. Many nineteenth-century economists assumed that a smoothly running capitalist system required large numbers of poor, jobless, and mostly uneducated people to keep the capitalist system going. To maintain the fiction that this circumstance was just and right, the poor were often blamed for their circumstance, because of their ignorance or their sinful nature, or even their supposed lesser-evolved state (Fromm 335–6). Similarly, the elders in "The Savages" blame the "savages" for their exploitation, calling them less evolved and incapable of civilization.

However, historically speaking, everywhere in Western culture that such a huge division of rights between a ruling elite and a massive subclass has existed, there has been a discomforting undercurrent for the elite, a sense that they know that the way they live is ethically wrong and that their position "on top" is tenuous. Such is the case in "The Savages." On a planet where there are no rival states, what is the city doing with a large contingent of well-armed guards? These guards are always edgy. The citizens who guide the Doctor and his companions on tours of the city make sure to hide from the visitors both the existence of the "savages" and the method of life extraction. When the leader of the Elite learns that the Doctor has discovered their secret, he attempts to extract the Doctor's "essence" and so guarantee the Doctor's silence and inaction. All of these actions are those of guilty people, for only those who know that what they are doing is wrong would act this way. "The Savages" shows that a "benevolent dictatorship," or what is more properly called an aristocracy (rule by the "high ones" or "worthy ones"), cannot truly exist, since it can never extend its benevolence beyond a select few. Such a society must always rest upon an artificial division between classes of people and the exploitation of the greater part for the benefit of only the ruling few.

Another *Doctor Who* story that demonstrates the injustice that often keeps an "ideal" state running is "The Macra Terror" (1967). The society in "The Macra Terror" in many ways resembles Plato's Republic, with a ruling elite kept almost wholly separate from the governed. The rulers shepherd human cattle, who, being fed comforting lies from the elite, happily do whatever their leaders tell them, convinced of the leaders' benevolence. This ruling elite, however, is a crab-like non-human species called Macra that uses brainwashing techniques to convince the citizens of the colony that they are working for their own benefit. The Macra use the pilot, whom they have kept captive, as a puppet ruler, a benevolent face, while the true rulers, like a military junta, run operations from behind the scenes. The first rule of the brainwashing technique is to implant the idea that there are no Macra. The second rule is that a person is "happy" to serve. This strict control of information, entertainment, and access ensures that everything runs for the efficient benefit of the rulers only.

It is an interesting thought experiment, to replace a human elite with a monstrous alien one. Doing so completes the metaphor that dictatorial rulers are "inhuman monsters." It increases the viewers' distaste for the ideas associated with monsters: self-centered, absolute rule that seems always to accompany attempts at an ideal state. *Doctor Who* continually rejects this idea of government and any sense that society is "better off" with a ruling elite rather than with leaders approved by the total citizenry.

Bureaucracy

One of the many social organizations the Doctor repeatedly faces is bureaucracy. This product of industrial capitalism has become one of the main engines of modern society, supplying a large percentage of the jobs, keeping gigantic organizations running, and creating a distinct set of social relations. Bureaucrats are specialized administrators, overseeing the movements of both things and people. For the bureaucracy to function effectively, bureaucrats must indifferently treat people like things, as part of the figures and tables and charts that keep the system running, whatever system it is (Fromm 126).

The Doctor, as a *free agent*, must always have an antagonistic relationship with bureaucracy. This antagonism is brought to a crisis in "The Trials of a Timelord: The Ultimate Foe" (1986), when the Doctor enters The Fantasy Factory, the establishment of the Doctor's evil alter ego, the Valeyard. To see the "proprietor" of The Fantasy Factory, the Doctor has to pass through a series of identical clerks known as Mr. Popplewick. When the first Mr. Popplewick will not give the Doctor access because he does not have an appointment, the Doctor rushes into a room to meet another identical Mr. Popplewick. This one informs him that "the very junior Mr. Popplewick is not allowed to expect anyone." The Valeyard has organized this bureaucratic roundabout in order to humiliate the Doctor by presenting him with one of the problems he least likes. When the Doctor disdainfully refers to the system as "bureaucracy," Mr. Popplewick rebukes him: "I prefer to call it order, and the holy writ of order is procedure." When the Doctor's ally at the moment, the thief Sabalom Glitz, suggests that the junior Mr. Popplewick could have been informed, again the senior Mr. Popplewick's response is rebuke: "And upset the procedure? The junior Mr. Popplewick has his pride."

The incident momentarily allows the audience to see bureaucracy from an alternative perspective. Procedure is comforting. It provides a system of values in which all know their places and may rarely have to face the unexpected. It provides "order" and a haven from anarchy. Indeed, bureaucracy has even operated as a civilizing and modernizing force, as the Indian Civil Service (the bureaucratic arm of the British raj in India) did to the chaotic and basically medieval Indian government of the 1800s (Ibn Warraq 233–8). Even so, the absurdity of the situation, as well as its function to frustrate the Doctor, brings the audience back around to the conclusion that order alone is not enough. Too much order causes its own disorder, like the species that is so specialized to its environment that a slight shift in climate causes extinction.

Capitalism

Capitalism is the economic system of modern societies, and the strongest social influence on politics. Naturally, *Doctor Who* often has something to say about capitalism. A story openly critical of capitalism is "The Sunmakers" (1977). The story depicts, in producer Graham Williams' words, "a society that has allowed its aims to become so confused that taxation is an end in itself rather than a means of providing services for the entire community" (qtd Tulloch and Alvarado 148). More specifically, the human government has been usurped by the Usurians, who move the human population to Pluto, keep it alive through artificial suns, and then work the people to exhaustion, collecting the rewards in the form of various "taxes" on all manner of everyday activity. The government is both employer and debt collector, effectively ensuring that it never has to provide more than basic needs for those below the elite status.

The story draws attention to problems arising when ties between government and business become too close. In a lightly Marxist analysis, the story suggests that government is the weaker partner, likely to be taken over by rapacious business. What has happened in "The Sunmakers" mirrors Karl Popper's description of the dangers of a truly free market. Popper argues, "If the state does not interfere, then other semi-political organizations such as monopolies, trusts, unions, etc., may interfere, reducing the freedom of the market to a fiction." In "The Sunmakers," a monopoly has taken hold of the entire social system. In a case like this, according to Popper, the logic of a free market economy gets reversed. Rather than the producers serving the needs of consumers, the consumers become a kind of "money-supply and rubbish-remover for the producer" (*Open II* 348). This is indeed the case in "The Sunmakers," where profit and taxation meld into one.

"The Sunmakers" makes repeated references to Karl Marx's analysis of the capitalist system. In "The Sunmakers," though the highest official with whom most people have to deal is the (tax) Gatherer, the actual head of government is the Collector, a nonhuman representative of The Company. The Collector repeatedly talks in business terms, not government terms, stating clichés such as "business is business" and "a normal business operation." The Doctor invokes the Marxist perspective by misquoting Marx, telling the insurrectionists that all they have to lose is their "claims," substituting tax claims for Marx's "chains" of capitalist oppression and thereby equating the two.

The story expressly makes clear that if government and business were to unite, the result would be a wholly oppressive system. As Tulloch and Alvarado note, the story is visually "coded" with multiple references to famous stories of political oppression. The omnipresent camera eyes evoke *1984*. The government as business system evokes *Brave New World*. The renegade workers living deep underneath the main city, the design of the steam chamber used for executions, and the clock mechanism run by workers all evoke *Metropolis* (Tulloch and Alvarado 146–7).

In terms of the actual story, "The Sunmakers" focuses on capitalism as an oppressive system. In this story, the leader of the world is literally a little money-grubber, a small, hunched figure bound to a wheelchair and obsessed with profits. Additionally, the second in command is an obtuse, vain, brown-nosing sycophant. The world as corporation, then, makes the least appealing and ethical character traits the ones that are most likely to produce social success. Furthermore, the Company itself lacks any ethical values, seeing people only in terms of their ability to produce profit. The Company had moved the Earth population first to Mars, then to Pluto after the Martian resources had been totally used up. Once Pluto's resources run out, the Company plans to "close" the "branch," in other words, to commit genocide on the human race. Similarly, when the revolution against the Company seems to be winning and maintaining Pluto looks no longer economically viable, the Collector is perfectly willing to gas to death the whole population.

The world of "The Sunmakers" mimics the "pathology" of nineteenth-century capitalism as Erich Fromm characterizes it. The pathology has particular characteristics. It is based on "irrational authority," which is an antagonistic condition between superior and inferior classes of people, in which the superior class exploits the labor of the inferior class, which defends itself only to preserve a minimum of happiness (96). Fromm notes that the inferior class, always the numerical majority, is likely to have two attitudes toward the superior class: resentment and hostility because one's own interests are never met, or deep admiration and loyalty, which reduces psychic suffering because the inferior believe themselves and their superiors to be deserving of their statuses (97). In "The Sunmakers," one sees the first reaction in the would-be revolutionaries who live beneath the tower block, while one sees the second reaction in the obsequious Gatherer Hade and his extreme deference toward the Collector.

Another characteristic of the pathology of capitalism is exploitation of people by people. Labor is a commodity to be bought and used to its utmost by the capitalist employer. Since labor is in large supply, it is a cheap commodity. This is what it means to say that labor is "employed"—the person who buys labor uses (employs) it to suit the needs and ends of him or herself, the "employer." Fromm says that through this system of values, "a man, a living human being, ceases to be an end in himself, and becomes the means for the economic interests of another man" (93). Again, in "The Sumakers" the pathology becomes apparent. The capital elite enjoy tremendous luxury, such as real wood desks, while the rest are "employed" mostly just to keep the whole system going.

In capitalism, according to Fromm, *things* are held in higher regard than are people (95). What the capitalist gets from the irrational authority of a system that exploits the bodies of other people is the ability to accumulate things. "The Sunmakers" opens with a scene between a worker named Cordo and the Gatherer. Gatherer Hade sits in pompous splendor behind his large mahogany desk ready to receive the death tax Cordo must pay after the demise of his father. The Gatherer makes fun of Cordo's social position; noting that Cordo's father's legacy is very small, the Gatherer chuckles, "He must have been a very poor man." Cordo cannot set the money on Hade's table because it might scratch the wood. Noting that Cordo ordered a nice funeral for his father, Hade remarks, "Compassion is a noble thing. It is also costly." This exchange demonstrates the pathological system of values at the heart of exploitative capitalism, which places in value things such as rare wooden desks above human ethical characteristics such as compassion.

Robert Holmes, writer of "The Sunmakers," does not just attack a straw man in the form of a capitalist system no longer existing. Industrial capitalism still exists as part of the modern consumer capitalist system.[3] Additionally, the program does show awareness of modern capitalism. For instance, the society of Pluto, totally structured to the needs of the capitalist system, does not really produce anything, which makes it much more like modern capitalist enterprises. The society is marked by high degrees of quantifying and abstracting, which in turn lead to the alienation of its citizens.

Where the society of Pluto most resembles consumer capitalism is in the degree of quantifying and abstraction within the system. *Quantification* and *abstractification* are significant properties of modern capitalism (Fromm 111). Quantification is the process of turning all systems of production into numbers. Every aspect of life becomes quantifiable by some measuring system, usually symbolic of exchange value. Thus, all aspects of life may be identified by their prices. Additionally, more and more production power is used to shift money, to manipulate symbols, and to create and move raw information rather than to produce goods (Reich 429–30). Abstractification involves the removal of objects and relations from their immediate human context. Corporations become so gigantic that the numbers involved in their operations, numbers of people, clients, investors, dollars on the balance sheet, etc., become so large and their interactions so complex that no one has a firm mental grasp of what any of it amounts to. Another process of abstractification is the increasing specialization and division of labor, already notable in Marx's day but highly accelerated in modern capitalism, which separates workers from meaningful connections with what they produce (Marx *Capital* 328; Fromm 112–3).

One repeatedly sees the process of quantification in "The Sunmakers," where every aspect of life comes with a price, usually called a "tax." Even death is taxed.[4] And while the society of Pluto may be basically industrial capitalist in design, its head, the Collector, sits in a room surrounded by computers constantly running calculations and taking in data, the very symbol of a quantified system. One sees abstractification in the requirement that all workers be called "citizen," a concept rather than a name. Division of labor is acute in this society, which "grades" all its citizens by the kinds of work they do (another nod to *Brave New World*).

The result of these trends for the individual people within the society is *alienation*. Fromm provides a useful definition of alienation, which is any process by which a person is lost as the center of his or her own existence. According to Fromm, such a person "is driven by forces which are separated from his self, which work behind his back; he is a stranger to himself, just as his fellow man is a stranger to him" (124).[5] People feel as though they lose control of their own actions, for the actions seem to come from somewhere outside their own immediate existences. In "The Sunmakers," Cordo stands in for the alienated mass of workers. Members of his society disrespectfully treat him as a mere "D-grade." Near the beginning of the story, Cordo attempts suicide because he sees no way out of his tax burden. Another example is Marn, Gatherer Hade's assistant, who is clearly more intelligent than Hade and knows it, but is frustrated because the hierarchical system of the society prevents her from using her intelligence. All of the people below the elites are alienated, prevented from expressing their true selves.

In "The Sunmakers," one sees the extreme pathological condition, the "insanity," of industrial capitalism. There is an almost unbreakable wall between the exploited labor class and the ruling elite. The ruling elite willingly take without any compensating conscientious need to give back to those whom they exploit. Workers are kept repressed through drugs atomized into the ventilation system that inhibit emotional responses, making workers timid and cooperative. All that is left is the striving for ever-increasing profit, the hoarding of luxury items, the abuse of one group of humans by another, and the exercise of overt irrational authority. It is an insane society badly in need of a Doctor.

Furthermore, "The Sunmakers" demonstrates the insanity of the ethic of capitalism. The sociologist Max Weber called this ethic the "spirit of capitalism." It is a "philosophy of avarice" in which increasing one's capital is seen as a "duty" of the "honest man of recognized credit" (51). This spirit is what is behind the Gatherer's cruel jibes at Cordo. From the Gatherer's ethic, the Gatherer is an "honest" man of "worth," where amount of money equates to amount of worthiness. Cordo, a mere D-grade, is thus "worthless" and deserves no better than contempt. The true insanity of the spirit of capitalism is its inverting of ethical values. Instead of focusing on happiness, or contemplation, or contentment of the individual, or on spreading these values to other people, the capitalist in spirit sees the making of money as the transcendental value, as a pure end in itself, so that "man is dominated by the making of money, by acquisition as the ultimate purpose of his life" (Weber 53). "The Sunmakers" shows that when a society runs at all levels upon the principles of the spirit of capitalism, it becomes oppressive and dysfunctional as a society.

"The Sunmakers" demonstrates the relationship between political power and economic power as Popper explains it. In arguing against Marx's historicism, Popper declares that political power should be used to control economic power, not the other way around as Marx would have it. However, Popper warns that unchecked political power combined with economic power is a certain formula for abuse. This is where democracy comes in, as a means of directing government to use its political and economic power for the people's protection (Popper *Open II* 126–7). Pluto of "The Sunmakers" is a system of an unchecked political/economic power combination. Thus, the Doctor comes in to invert the social structure, not to implement Marx's stateless collective, but to initiate the process of democratic rule.

At the other end of capitalism is the need to consume, which helps keep the capitalist system running. According to Fromm, in the nineteenth century, consumption was a means to an end, a way to attain happiness. In modern capitalism, consumption is the end itself, and so has little relationship to the things or services being consumed. The idea is simply to *have*, with the result that what even the modest wage earner can have far outstrips what the majority of people in the industrial west of the nineteenth century would ever have dreamt of having. Another result is the *status* that having confers. In "Dalek" (2005), the billionaire Henry van Statten, who "owns" the internet, keeps a private underground museum of alien technology that he has purchased over the years, mainly because he can purchase them. In "City of Death" (1979), an alien disguising himself as the "insanely" rich Count Scarlioni can keep his human wife pleased and distracted by presenting her with a large amount of expensive art and jewelry. In both cases, having is an end in itself, and confers status through sheer amount.

It is important to understand that for the capitalist system to work, everyone within the system from lowest-paid laborer to richest capitalist must "buy into" the ethic of the system (Weber 54–7; 65). As the spirit of capitalism becomes a successful ethic, in the sense that it produces significant material comfort, it becomes an assumption of truth about how life "is." It becomes a set of rules perpetuating the ethic. For this reason, the would-be revolutionaries of "The Sunmakers" so utterly fail without the Doctor's intervention. They accept as "true" virtually all the assumptions of their social systems, and so cannot imagine different systems, merely the same system with different leaders.

We can summarize the previous discussion of capitalist economies as political systems by referring to Karl Popper's comments regarding the role of money in an open society. A significant problem is that no society has yet mastered the use of money, which leaves too much room for its greatest misuse — the ability to buy political power (*Open I* 315–6 n.67). In *Doctor Who*, there are several examples of this misuse. Henry van Statten in "Dalek" can use his money to manipulate U.S. elections. In "The Green Death," Stevens, the director of Global Chemicals, is able to pull political strings and halt Brigadier Lethbridge-Stewart's attempts to investigate its factory in Wales.

In its curious way, the story that is actually closest to a truly Marxist view of capital relations is "Vengeance on Varos" (1985). In this story, a former penal colony has become an independent world (country), while retaining much of its original prison structure. Descendents of the prisoners now work as laborers under extreme conditions for little pay. The officer elite form the government, drawing their wealth and power from governed. To maintain the system in perpetuity, the officer corps has set up a puppet governor, a randomly selected member of the officer corps who can be a ready scapegoat should problems within the economic/governmental system arise. While the governor makes policy, his policies must both accord with the wishes of the Chief Officer and please the general populace. Should these policies fail to do either, the governor's plans are put to a vote, and the governor is either rewarded with soothing light or bombarded with a cell disintegrator ray. Governors rarely last long and the system ensures that the Chief Officer remains the center of power. This man then makes deals to sell Varosian commodities and keep most of the money.

The system on Varos is a kind of analog for Marx's central ideas regarding power relations. Borrowing from Karl Popper's summary of Marx's ideas, we can start by focusing on the concept of "class interest," central to both Marx's theory of history and to "Vengeance on Varos." By "class interest," Marx means that social forces are arranged in such a way that the forces of production always benefit one segment of society at the expense of another. In *Critique of Political Economy* Marx says, "In the social production of their subsistence men enter into determined and necessary relations with each other which are independent of their wills — production-relations which correspond to a definite stage of development of their material productive forces. The sum of these production-relations forms the economic structure of society, the real basis upon which a juridical and political superstructure arises, and to which definite social forms of consciousness correspond" (Marx *Capital* 10). This is not a conscious plot on the part of the "upper" classes, but merely the result of historical forces. Marx admits that everyone wants freedom, but in reality to have freedom is to free oneself from the productive process, and the only way to do that is to make someone else do the work. This is what Marx means by saying that a political struggle is a struggle of class against class. A ruling class exists by being able to place some other class in bondage. However, because this struggle is the result of impersonal historical forces, the upper classes find themselves bound too, compelled to enslave and fight against the lower classes solely to retain the freedom that they have. Each class is thus bound to other and each defines itself by relationship to the other (Popper *Open II* 112; Marx *Capital* 8–9).

In "Vengeance on Varos," one sees the struggle and bondage of the two classes. The workers produce a small group of rebels who try to destroy the system. This in turn provides an excuse for a massive capital expenditure to wipe out rebel resistance. On Varos, this expenditure is the Punishment Dome, both a prison and the primary source of entertainment. Executions are public, which provides some of the entertainment. However, most comes from placing prisoners into a deadly obstacle course and then broadcasting their progress. The guard elite run the Punishment Dome and reap the rewards both in keeping rebellion ineffective and in providing entertainments to sell abroad. Each class becomes caught in a cultural cul-de-sac. The elites need rebels in order to "teach" the masses not to rebel. The masses need the elite for jobs and entertainments that cannot possibly satisfy their desire for freedom, thus fueling more rebellion. Each class is so tightly bound to the other that when the Doctor and Peri come along with an outside perspective, they start unraveling the bonds, resulting in the total collapse of Varos's social system. In the end, the common people are left "free," but totally bewildered by it, unable to imagine what to do with their freedom.

We can see, then, that *Doctor Who* presents a liberal critique of capitalism, not a Marxist or socialist one, though some Marxist and socialist ideas do come out. This liberal perspective seeks to moderate capitalism through *ethics*, to cut out its excesses, but not necessarily to overturn it completely.

"Planet of the Ood" (2008) provides a good, simplified example of the *Doctor Who* liberal critique. The Ood are a slave species that humans of the 42nd century use throughout three galaxies. They have first been introduced in "The Impossible Planet" (2006), but in the later story take a more central role. In "The Impossible Planet," the Ood are used primarily as domestic servants and laborers. The Doctor's companion Rose, raised on modern ethical standards, finds appalling the very concept of any species whose life is exclusively servitude. However, Rose is told that the Ood prefer servitude, and that if they do not receive orders or cannot function to serve others, they simply waste away. When Rose asks an Ood what it wants, it does not understand her question. Thus the ethical problem for the viewer becomes what to make of a thinking being that not only *wants* to be a servant, but also defines its very existence as "servant." In "The Impossible Planet" and its follow-up story, "The Satan Pit" (2006), no answer to this problem comes.

"Planet of the Ood" resets the problem in terms of the market capitalism required for the Ood to be so distributed through society. The Ood planet is not just their home world, but also the center for their breeding and distribution. It is company run and presumably owned, a family business of generations. From the beginning, viewers are reminded of the basic conceptual problem related to the Ood, that of their willingness to serve. The story opens with an advertisement for the corporation that says that the Ood have one purpose — "to serve." On this particular day, the company is giving a presentation to several wealthy and influential buyers. Thus, we view what seems to be a normal business.

However, several cues come throughout the story that remind viewers about what the company does, which is to "manufacture" and "market" bodies and labor. The story repeatedly insists upon two important points related to the problem of the Ood. The first is that whether Ood live to serve or not, they are still primarily a slave labor force, and as such degraded from ends in themselves to means to ends. The second is that such a system is not "natural," and must of necessity rest upon manipulation and lies.

That the Ood are slaves, no matter their own preferences, gets repeated through multiple cues in the story. In the first scene, a corporate executive evaluating the corporate advertisement treats his Ood personal assistant with utter disdain, calling him "you there" and yelling at him for no good reason. At the sales presentation, the executive buyers make fun of the Ood put on display, treating them with total contempt. Such contempt exists only in master-slave relationships. The company compound includes cages, guards with whips, and even an in-built system for exterminating Ood in large numbers should they present a "problem." The Doctor's new companion, Donna, brings back Rose's concerns into the consideration of the problem when she ask, "Don't the Ood get a say in this?"

All of these cues exist to rile up the audience's ethical sensibilities. Slavery is an evil social system because it is based upon using sentient, thinking beings as means to ends and not as ends in themselves. It does not matter that someone *wants* to be used in this way. That desire does not thereby become right. There is no obligation for satisfying a wrong-headed desire to be abused. Thus, something seems "unnatural" or wrong about a situation in which one person wants to be abused by the other person. Getting around one's conscience in such a situation requires both willfully ignoring the problem and convincing oneself through self-serving lies that the situation is "really" ethical when clearly it is not.

Several times someone in the show states that something is clearly wrong with the Ood and the system that exploits them. Donna and the Doctor both realize that the Ood could never have naturally developed through evolution to be perpetual servants. They simply would not have survived. The story revolves around the fact that the Ood are going "red eye," and individually developing vengeful and angry behavior, often killing their owners. The chief of security ironically refers to the red-eye condition as "red as sin." It turns out, of course, that the Ood are not naturally servile, but naturally trusting. The Ood carry in their hands a secondary brain akin to the human amygdale, which the company removes and replaces with a translation sphere. The company thereby cuts off an Ood's emotion and memory, making him or her docile and servile, incapable of self-assertion.

Why is it, therefore, that few within the human empire realize that the use of Ood clearly violates ethical principles already come to centuries earlier? One reason is willful ignorance, represented in Solana, the sales presenter for the company. The following exchange between Donna and Solana addresses this issue of willful ignorance:

> Donna: If people back on Earth knew what was going on here....
> Solana: Don't be stupid. Of course, they know.
> Donna: They know how you treat the Ood?
> Solana: They don't ask. Same thing.

But willful ignorance all by itself is not enough to keep the system running. Only comforting and self-serving lies can do that. An interesting sequence in the program relates these lies and reinforces the fact that they are lies. While Solana delivers a series of platitudes justifying to the buyers what the company does, security forces hunt down an Ood gone "red eye." By switching back and forth, the show tests the lies against reality, showing the lies to be lies. Here is a list of the lies:

1. The Ood are happy to serve.
2. We like to think of the Ood as our trusted friends.
3. We keep the Ood healthy, safe, and educated.
4. We don't just breed the Ood, we make them better.
5. What is an Ood but a reflection of us?

The ripostes to these lies are not always easy to make, but do exist.

1. To want something and to have that want met is not the same as being "happy." Furthermore, if the desire in question is delusional or formed under coercion and manipulation, then satisfying it would be unethical.
2. A servant can *never* be a friend with a master nor a master with a servant because friendships are based upon equal freedom of mind, but servitude is based upon unequal master-slave relations.
3. Providing basic living standards to servants is protection of one's investment, not a service to the servant.
4. "Better" is a relative concept, and always suspect when "better" just happens to coincide with one's convenience.
5. That the servant reflects the master is ironically true. Really, the ironical meaning of such a statement is that one cannot be a master without

having a servant, that the master needs the servant far more than the servant needs the master, and that the very existence of the servant "reflects" the unethical self of the master.

"Planet of the Ood" demonstrates quite effectively the liberal critique of capitalism that runs throughout *Doctor Who*. This critique starts from the idea that the worst forms of capitalism are always exploitative of people, possibly to the point of the most extreme form of exploitation, slavery. A business founded upon and sustained by lies to its employees and customers rests upon a weak foundation that could easily crumble, with potentially catastrophic consequences for many employees and customers. Another critique is that satisfying a falsely produced desire does not produce happiness or contentment, only mindlessness. The final critique is that all the problems just mentioned and possibly most of the problems associated with capitalism can be solved through applying the fundamental ethical principle of always treating people as ends in themselves, and never as means to ends.

Colonialism

Colonialism, empire, and especially the fall of empire are common themes in English science fiction. Therefore, they unsurprisingly show up rather frequently in *Doctor Who*. Given the program's liberal values and humanist perspective, a viewer will rightly expect that presentations of colonialism in *Doctor Who* will be highly critical of the dreams of empire.

Tulloch and Alvarado engage in an interesting discussion of the politics of *Doctor Who*. They note that as a product of the BBC, *Doctor Who* could not afford to take too strong a stance on any one political issue. The BBC position is not strict neutrality, but rather "moderation" (50–2). The story Tulloch and Alvarado use to demonstrate the moderation principle is "The Monster of Peladon" (1974), which is from the most political period of *Doctor Who* (1970–5). The story itself concerns a medieval society based principally upon mining. The government of Peladon is now a reluctant part of the Galactic Federation. As a consequence, Peladon has received the benefits of advanced technology. The situation becomes a contest between the overworked miners and those who would take advantage of Peladon's defenseless position for mercenary gain. The Doctor, who had acted as a mediating force in Peladon's acceptance into the Federation in "The Curse of Peladon" (1972), here acts as a moderating force.

The two "Peladon" stories are remarkable for a political discourse that is sophisticated relative to many other *Doctor Who* stories. That may be one reason that they remain among the more popular. In "Monster," the extremes are represented by the Earth engineer Eckersley, who stands for unprincipled capitalist exploitation; the band of rogue Martian Ice Warriors led by Azaxyr, who stand for military domination; and the rebel miner Ettis, who stands for Luddite and radical Marxist extremism. Ranged against these forces are the Federation representative Alpha Centauri, who wants to ensure Peladon's continued relations with the Federation and thus stands for internationalism; the young Peladonian Queen Thalira, who wants to maintain Peladon's peace and stability, and thus stands for managerial government; her advisor Ortron, who wants to maintain the political domination of the aristocratic elite and thus stands for aristocracy; and the lead miner Gebek, who wants to raise the miners' living standards while not damaging Peladon's traditions, and thus stands for unionism.

As Tulloch and Alvarado note, the story bears notable analogues to political situations at the time of its writing, including a miners' strike in England. It also mimics concerns about international cooperatives such as the United Nations and the European Common Market (now the European Union). Though the story demonstrates the destructiveness of extremism on both the political right (Eckersley and Azaxyr) and the political left (Ettis), it does not take an absolutely middle position.

In an interview regarding this story and the political tone of *Doctor Who*, producer Barry Letts states, "If you get a collection of intelligent ... people together, especially creative people, they will tend to be liberal/left of centre, because that is the most intelligent position to take" (qtd. Tulloch and Alvarado 54). "The Monster of Peladon" does, like many other *Doctor Who* stories, favor this slightly left-of-center political position. The Doctor, for instance, is very sympathetic to the miners' grievances and takes much more active interest in their concerns than in anyone else's. By the story's end, the Doctor has persuaded the queen to accept Gebek, a commoner, into the governing elite, thus paving the way for needed reforms to Peladon's retrograde medieval government. The representative of that government, Ortron, has to back down from his reactionary stance and make a compromise with the miners because he comes to see them as fellow Peladonians, allies in the cause against alien invasion. The Queen herself is in a tenuous political position through most of the story, since queens in Peladon are uncommon and her opinion is controlled by the traditionalist priest-advisor Ortron. The Doctor's companion, Sarah, talks to Queen Thalira, telling her that the statement about being "only a female" is wrong. "There is nothing 'only' about being a female," says Sarah, who also discusses women's liberation with the young Queen. The Doctor and Sarah, as representatives of an outside view and civilized understanding, in taking the moderate-left position reinforce the notion of its correctness.

Although Tulloch and Alvarado focus mainly on the mining dispute in the story, there is another political level operating. As script editor Terrance Dicks notes, "We are all aware now that what happens when an advanced race meets a primitive race is not always to the benefit of the primitives" (qtd Tulloch and Alvarado 53). Indeed, this problem of the consequences from contact between technologically unequal civilizations is the core political issue in the first Peladon story "The Curse of Peladon." In "Monster" the theme gets reiterated now that the contact is established. The story makes clear that though Peladon is now part of the Federation, it has little voice in Federation matters, little regard from the Federation, and virtually no protection against sophisticated capitalist predators. When the Federation representative Alpha Centauri quips that the Peladonians are "close to barbarism" and "have a great distrust of progress," Sarah smartly counters, "Maybe that's because they're not getting anything out of it." One can easily see Peladon as a substitute for African or Latin American countries in the age of the United Nations, and the Federation as an analog for the UN. In Peladon, as with many "third world" countries, contact with advanced capitalist societies threatens its traditions and social organization, causes civil war (or near to it), and sets up the weaker society as the battleground on which larger political forces operate. However benevolent the Federation may be, it is not actively enough benevolent to protect a "lesser" member such as Peladon.

The story "Kinda" (1982) treats colonialism as a kind of madness. As the story begins, a first colonial effort on the planet Deva Loka, repeatedly referred to as a "paradise," is failing. Several members of this advance guard have disappeared into the forest, leaving only three to maintain the effort. The local population is a simple nontechnological culture that lacks both language and any sort of military. Yet, the disappearance of several members of the party is placing tremendous psychological stress on the remaining three, especially the two men who represent the military detachment.

The party commander, Sanders, is overbearing, thickheaded, and unimaginative. He responds to stress by adhering absolutely to military protocol, constantly referring to "the Manual" for support. Hindle, on the other hand, plagued by self-doubt, becomes increasingly paranoid in the story. The scientist Todd, the only woman of the party, takes mostly a "what can I do?" attitude about the state of affairs. The three characters represent three typical ways that the general public of a colonial power thinks of colonialism. Sanders represents the typical duty-minded colonial, who feels honored to perform whatever service his country commands of him. He has no respect for the local Kinda people, believing them to be without culture because their culture in no way resembles his. Hindle represents the class of people required to keep the empire running. Knowing that colonials are unwanted, such people feel that the entire country is against them. They admire what they see as the "strength" of those like Sanders, and desperately try to imitate such people, usually through acts of coercive power. Todd represents the liberal portion of the public, those who dislike colonialism but reserve any action against it strictly to occasional tepid criticisms. For example, Todd calls the taking of prisoners "illogical," for which the Doctor rebukes her: "I'd call it inhuman."

The story repeatedly demonstrates that the whole colonial project is irrational, even insane. For instance, the colonials have taken several Kinda as hostages, even though the Kinda pose no threat to them at all. Sanders' reason is that it is "standard procedure." The colonials eat unappetizing standard issue rations, even though there is abundant non-poisonous food on Deva Loka. Sanders lives in a constant state of denial, unwilling to recognize that the colony is failing. In a conversation with Todd, he remarks that there are "too many opinions." He says, "Meet a few difficulties and suddenly everybody's got an opinion. That's how things fall apart." A little later in the conversation, he states that he "welcomes these difficulties." He asserts that "it was all too easy around here. I was beginning to feel at home, for the first time anywhere in forty years." In Sanders' mind, feeling at home is dangerous, probably because such a feeling will lead him to sympathize with the natives.

Those are merely the irrational actions. The story goes further by equating colonialism with madness. The most obvious example of this equation involves Hindle. When Sanders goes exploring for the lost party members, he leaves Hindle in charge. Giving even this little bit of power to Hindle pushes him over the wall of sanity. He becomes obsessed with "safety," and believes that the plants are a threat ready to destroy him and the colonizers. Feeling the need to make the survival dome "one billion trillion trillion percent" safe, Hindle wires up the whole dome with explosives because once everything is destroyed, then it will be "safe." Such is the insane logic of colonialism, which often rests on destroying the land and cultural icons of the colonized culture to "preserve" the people. Another treatment of typical colonial patterns as a form of insanity involves Hindle's construction of the new "capital city" for Deva Loka, which he and Sanders, whose mind has been made like a child's while he was on his search for the missing crew, construct out of cardboard. It is typical for colonizers to recreate the colonized land in the image of the colonizer's culture. Often, as on Deva Loka, the natives have no such concept as "capital city." Such projects are false constructions.

Another madness of colonialism shown in "Kinda" is treatment of the natives. Taking hostages because they might be hostile, even when they prove otherwise, is just one of the many mistreatments of the natives in the story. Sanders treats the natives with total disregard. To him, they are mere "primitives" and "savages," who are "not very interesting," and thus deserve whatever bad treatment they get. He rationalizes this bullying by saying, "If the Kinda are so clever, how is it they didn't build their own Interplanetary Vehicle and colonize us?"

Hindle's maltreatment of the natives is not to disregard them, but to turn them into lackeys. When he discovers that he can gain control over the two prisoners because they believe he has stolen their souls and put them into a mirror, he dresses them up in colonial uniforms and forces them to perform menial and demeaning tasks for him. This process is typical of the colonial method, by which the conquering culture forces those in the conquered culture to accept the conqueror's ways while never being fully admitted into the conqueror's culture.

In the end, "Kinda" shows that "sanity" involves "going native," as colonizers say. The Kinda wise woman Panna and her assistant, Karuna, attempt to show the colonizers how the world looks through Kinda eyes. To do this, they present the colonizers with the Box Of Jhana, a device that puts them into telepathic contact with the Kinda. This box was the cause of the disappearance of the three previous men sent to explore. Unable to see the world as others see it, they go mad. The box, however, affects Sanders and Hindle somewhat differently by destroying the imbalances in their minds. Sanders becomes childlike, losing all his bullying and militaristic manner. Hindle becomes a kind of romantic dreamer. Both decide to abandon the project and support Todd's recommendation that Deva Loka is unsuitable for colonization. It is impossible to sustain belief in the colonial plan when one escapes the limitations of cultural arrogance and sees the point of view of the colonized.

Essential to colonial empire building is the concept of nationalism. Sanders expresses a kind of nationalistic pride in asserting his culture's superiority over the Kinda. The idea that groups of people have inherent superiority keeps the colonial machine going, while the colonizers believe they bring the "gift" of civilization to "backward" and "primitive" people. In "Kinda," the Box of Jhana smashes this nationalistic colonial view, showing Sanders that a different point of view is not necessarily an inferior one.

Nationalism

Hannah Arendt, in her monumental work *The Origins of Totalitarianism*, has identified the characteristic attitudes and ideas which became *nationalism* in the nineteenth century. In the modern and widely used sense, nationalism derives from the development of the nation-state, which claims both popular representation and national sovereignty. In other words, the nation-state acknowledges that people have rights and a voice in government, but only those people who are *citizens* of the nation. Even those living within the borders of the nation-state who are not defined as citizens of the nation cannot enjoy the same rights as the legally defined citizen. The nation is determined by "common civilization," in other words by belief that *national identity* could be determined by a set of markers, such as shared history, common language, shared ancestry, and so on. The concept of *human rights* as described in Enlightenment documents and the founding documents of the American and French revolutions become renamed as *national rights*, which only those with the right ancestry or location of birth could possess (Arendt 229–31). The result of nationalistic thinking is that people within a nation come to believe that their nation is inherently better than all others, and that they are inherently better people than all others because they belong to the nation.

"Nationalism is a cheap instinct and a dangerous tool," says the English novelist John Fowles (147). Because it is based on either covetousness or jealousy, it is a cheap instinct. Those from poor countries are covetous of the well-off countries and say, "If my country had what they have, it would be the best." Those from well-off countries are jealous in the strict sense of the word, saying, "My country is best because it has what others want." Nationalism is a dangerous tool most obviously because it is an excellent tool for keeping the masses in control. One can divert attention from ugly government policies by appeal to nationalism, and one can stir up fervor against supposed enemies by the same ploy.

At this point, one needs to be aware of the distinction between nationalism and *patriotism*. Canadian political philosopher Shadia P. Drury distinguishes the two in terms of attitude towards one's country. According to Drury, patriotism "is love for one's country as it is and a willingness to defend it against foreign aggression." Nationalism takes love for one's country to extreme. It is "love of one's country as it will be once it has exterminated all its enemies, become totally unified, and achieved its grand purpose or world-historical destiny." In its most radical form, nationalism leads to *fascism*, which exaggerates the extent and power of a nation's "enemies" both internal and external, and views the nation as in a life-or-death struggle with these enemies (Drury 26–7). The fascist form of nationalism involves the belief that only the total destruction of these enemies will allow the nation to arise and take its place as the perfect model and natural leader of the world.

In *Doctor Who*, the Doctor's liberalism is played against nationalism and fascism. Many of the Doctor's foes exhibit some degree of this nationalist fervor, which may take one of several forms. It can be the radical militaristic xenophobia the Daleks demonstrate. Or, it can be the radical racism of the Cybermen, whose ethos is that all thinking lifeforms become like them and be assimilated into their society or be wiped out. It can also take the form of dangerous banality, of ordinary people who subsume their identities to the "larger cause," and so gladly commit or aid in committing atrocities because someone has told them that the nation needs them to commit atrocities.

Nationalism relies heavily upon the concept of *loyalty*. The "team player" or "party member" or "good citizen" must subsume his or her will to the needs of the abstract organization, in this case the "nation." Nietzsche states that "the true party man learns no longer — he only experiences and judges" (66). A demonstration of this idea exists in "The Sea Devils" (1972). A brief exchange between the Doctor and a government bureaucrat relates simply the contrast between the Doctor's broad perspective and the limitations of nationalism. Parliamentary Private Secretary Walker is arrogant, self-centered (concerned mostly with eating and getting others to fetch his food), unsympathetic, and cowardly. The exchange begins when the Doctor calls Walker an "idiot" and reproves him for ordering an attack:

> Walker: Our duty is to destroy the Queen's enemies. Don't you know your national anthem? "Confound their politics/frustrate their knavish tricks."
> Doctor: That, sir, is an extremely insular point of view.

Walker is a caricature and plays a *de rigueur* role representing small-minded government interference in general. Walker demonstrates in a small way what characters like Mr. Chinn from "The Claws of Axos" (1971), represent in *Doctor Who* regarding "our country first" attitudes.

The quotation from the United Kingdom national anthem with which Walker rebuts the Doctor's accusation of "idiot" is interesting itself in this regard. As Walker pronounces it, the phrase "knavish tricks" sounds to me like "navy strength." I am not sure whether there is a deliberate misquotation here because the story "The Sea Devils" highly involves the navy, or whether I just am not hearing it properly. Of more importance is that the lines quoted belong to a rarely sung verse. The entire verse is worth citing as an example of the worst extent that nationalism can go:

> O Lord our God arise,
> Scatter her enemies
> And make them fall;
> Confound their politics,
> Frustrate their knavish tricks,
> On Thee our hopes we fix,
> Oh, save us all!

The verse explicitly seeks divine aid in warfare, claiming, as nationalists do, that "God" is on the side of one set of people and favors them above all others and that these favors will go so far as to have the Almighty destroy other countries or allow their complete takeover (thus making them "fall").

The story of "The Sea Devils" does not itself take up these points as part of a debate, yet they are in there. The Doctor for the second time fails to negotiate a peace because on the one side is the "we were here first" variety of nationalism and on the other is the "we are right because we are righteous" variety of nationalism. The Sea Devils themselves take the "we were here first" side. These are prehistoric intelligent reptiles revived after millions of years who now want to take back the Earth from humanity, which is to them just a bunch of annoying apes. The argument had been expressed before in "Doctor Who and the Silurians" (1970), to which "The Sea Devils" is a kind of sequel. However, the other side, the "we are right because we are righteous" side had not been expressed or implied in the previous story. In "The Sea Devils," the sentiment is placed in the mouth of the officious and insensitive Walker, and thus is condemned by association.

Fromm identifies nationalism as a socially and psychologically immature state of existence, through which people can "experience a sense of identity after the original clan identity has disappeared and before a truly individual sense of identity has been acquired" (62). The search for identity makes one strive for identity among the herd, and the strength of the drive for identity is so intense that once many people get a label to attach to this identity, they are willing to give up their friends, families, freedoms, thoughts, and lives for the sake of preserving the identity (63).

Nationalism is a form of what Karl Popper calls "tribalism." Popper says, "Nationalism appeals to our tribal instincts, to passion and to prejudice, and to our nostalgic desire to be relieved from the strain of individual responsibility which it attempts to replace by a collective or group responsibility" (*Open II* 49). This group spirit pervades all areas of society, and to a degree is necessary for social functioning. However, tribal identity as nationalism is also a necessary component for war, and tyrants find it easy to use. Popper calls "romantic" the loss of individual identity that Fromm discusses, meaning that it involves substituting an ideal for a personality. This is the process Arthur Koestler identifies as "self-transcendent." It is the very thing that makes nationalism so "dangerous" in the opinions of Nietzsche and Fowles. Any form of tribalism, as Popper describes it, involves not just the loss of identity, but magical thinking (such as that being from X country "protects" a person) and denial of reality (such as the assumption of the "superiority" of one nation over another).

Popper examines nationalism from pragmatic perspective and finds it lacking. The supposition behind the idea of a nation is that such a thing is "natural" and that one can even find "natural" boundaries by which to draw national lines. Popper calls this a "romantic fiction" tied to racialism and tribalism that almost always leads to totalitarian thinking. The idea of geographical nations, or of linguistic or racial nations, is "entirely fictitious." A quick view of history shows that such groups that people would identify as nations routinely intermix and influence each other, and that none of the supposed common denominators of a nation (such as common language or religion) stands up to either historical or practical scrutiny. No "nation" has ever remained geographically, linguistically, or culturally permanent or unified (Popper *Open I* 288 n7; *Open II* 51).

Popper's critique of the logic of nationalism goes to the heart of what makes wrong the perspective of the Silurians and Sea Devils. The argument of "we were here first" rests on the myths of blood and soil. These myths are that location (soil) and ethnic identity (blood) are inextricably bound. As Popper's critique shows, neither is a particularly good criterion for characterizing identity. Ethnic identity is not a fixed commodity; even the Silurians and Sea Devils are not what they were. Location is the greater sticking point, though. First, as Popper argues, regional boundaries rarely have a correspondence to historical facts or ethnic identity. Borders have always been porous and indeterminate. Second, "we were here first" tries to seek historical justifications for what cannot be justified. One was "here" and then one left. History, however, does not place any value on primacy, and the general rule of history is that things change. Attempts to return to a primal scene or to claim jurisdiction by reason of historical precedence have largely failed. The "Earth" that the ancient reptiles claim as theirs no longer exists. It was what scientists call "Pangea," in a state where the continents were once all bunched together in one large land mass. That state of affairs no longer exists. And as both "The Silurians" and "The Sea Devils" show, those currently occupying a territory do not give it over without a fight. They recognize no rule of primacy.

Doctor Who repeatedly shows that an inevitable result of nationalism is war. The Silurians and Sea Devils go to war with the humans, both sides fueled by "our people first" beliefs. The nationalistic fervor imagines war as inevitable, and supports a large military as the means of preserving the society against the evil others. Military buildup spurred by nationalism becomes a projection of national identity onto the military, so that military power and national pride become almost synonymous. The race-villains of *Doctor Who*, such as the Daleks, Cybermen, and Sontarans, all follow this nationalism-military pattern.

The Doctor stands apart from these concerns. He calls himself a "wanderer" and a "traveler." Reluctant to identify his home planet (nation), he is a willing ex-patriot. He sees himself as a citizen of the universe, and the abstraction he most often fights for is "life," not "nation." As hero of the program, the Doctor symbolizes an open-minded alternative to narrow-minded nationalism.

Militarism

Nietzsche describes very well the modern condition of nation-states, which maintain armies of conquest, but claim always that such armies are for self-defense. This rationale leads to the inevitable conclusion that other nations are untrustworthy or evil; otherwise, there would be no need for "defense." "Thus all states are now ranged against each other," says Nietzsche. Additionally, according to Nietzsche, the rationale behind this state of affairs, the supposed virtue of one's nation and viciousness of the others, is "the challenge and the cause of wars." Only when the best-armed nation declares an end to armies will real peace come, because it comes from the peace of mind that freedom from fear and hatred brings (*Portable* 71–3). Though Nietzsche describes the Western world of the late nineteenth century, the description is no less valid in the early twenty-first century.

Science fiction such as *Doctor Who* is well placed to consider the world's heightened military tension through imaginative analogy. The militarism of twentieth and twenty-first century powerful nations gets indirectly addressed through surrogate races and worlds. The consequent stories raise the question of the appropriate place for a military force and the dangers of the mindset called militarism.

The term *militarism* refers to both factual and philosophical situations. The factual situations involve extensive expenditures of a society's capital on maintaining, supplying, and building a large military force. In such situations, the military can often have a significant influence in the government, even when that government is officially civilian. The philosophical situation is the nationalistic belief that one's country is the greatest, and that "great" is best demonstrated through exercise of military power.

In *Doctor Who*, the Doctor repeatedly confronts both forms of militarism. Many of the principle villains of the program are almost entirely military forces: the Daleks, Cybermen, Ice Warriors, Dominators, and Sontarans. In these races, there are no civilians to speak of. The entire social organization is military, and all social production goes into war and conquest. The Doctor also often encounters philosophical militarism. These encounters might be with military dictatorships, such as on Zanak in "The Pirate Planet" (1978). Equally as often, the encounters are with military leaders who resent civilian command and seek to usurp power and then enact factual militarism, such as in "The Savages."

However, though *Doctor Who* is consistently opposed to militarism, it is not consistently opposed to the military. The situation can appear to be a contradiction, creating an unresolved philosophical tension. In situations involving military invasion or military-style internal seizure of power, a military force or a quasi-military force of freedom fighters becomes necessary for preventing a militaristic takeover. The tension is apparent in the paired stories "The Rise of the Cybermen" (2006) and "The Age of Steel" (2006). On a parallel Earth, an industrialist inventor has created the Cybermen, humans fitted into prosthetic casings so that they become living robots. The Cybermen swiftly organize themselves into a military structure, marching in cohorts and "deleting" those who oppose them. They enact an attempted worldwide *coup d'etat*. The Doctor alone cannot defeat the Cybermen, and thus allies himself with quasi-military freedom fighters to aid in the defeat. The difference between the two sides and where the audience places its allegiance is that the freedom fighters fit the generally accepted definition of *human* as possessing independence of will and an ethical sense for preventing needless suffering. The Cybermen, however, work toward a single idea, producing more Cybermen, and could not care less about the amount of harm they inflict in achieving their goal.

The tension is even more apparent in all the stories involving U.N.I.T., the United Nations Intelligence Taskforce, later renamed Unified Intelligence Taskforce. Originally appearing in "The Invasion" (1968) and regularly appearing or referred to in *Doctor Who* afterwards, the taskforce is an international military organization set up to protect Earth against alien menace. From episodes aired between 1970 to 1975, the Doctor becomes exiled to Earth and attached to U.N.I.T. He runs into constant philosophical conflict with its leader, Brigadier Lethbridge-Stewart, generally over the value of the military. Despite his repeated characterizations of the military as "clumsy" and heavy-handed, and his ironic remarks about their "shoot first" and nationalistic mentality, the Doctor often finds that he needs U.N.I.T.

The irony of the ultimate advocate for peace and cooperation being allied to a military organization points to the fact that ideal and real often clash. The real world requires military forces. In *Doctor Who*, the problem of the military is how to rely upon it only when it is needed. There will always be some inclination toward militarism in the military. The trick is to keep both under control. This need is where independent observers and critics, such as the Doctor, have a role. The trick also relies upon civilian control of the armed forces. These two counterbalances help keep an organization like U.N.I.T. as a tool of defense, never of conquest.

There is a kind of simplification in this analogical approach that creates a good military/bad military state of mind. The prime example of this mentality is in the treatment of U.N.I.T. The story "Planet of the Dead" (2009) displays some hints of this nostalgic, gung-ho, "hurray for our side" mentality through swelling music and high-tech weaponry. So long as the military is *our* military, fighting on *our* side to protect *us*, then it appears to be safely in its place. The idea is abundantly apparent in the paired Sontaran stories "The

Sontaran Strategem" (2008) and "The Poison Sky" (2008), in which the U.N.I.T. forces are defenders of Earth against the purely militaristic Sontarans, who see no purpose other than war. The proper place for a military force as these and other *Doctor Who* stories show it is in defense, the defining difference between the *military* and *militarism.*

Doctor Who has often offered diplomacy as a potential antidote to militarism. The Doctor takes this diplomat role in "Doctor Who and the Silurians" and "The Sea Devils." The ancient humanoid lizards with advanced technology have awoken to take what they perceive to be their rightful place on the Earth. To them, humans are simply an ape infestation. The question of who has the right to the Earth is a classic *casus belli*, which pits the greatly outnumbered but technologically advantaged reptile-men against the numerically superior but technologically disadvantaged humans. The Doctor immediately sees in this situation a slaughter of disastrous proportions. In each case, he takes it upon himself to negotiate some kind of land-sharing settlement between the two sides, and in each case the diplomacy gets undermined by those of purely militaristic intent. In each case, the ancient reptile civilizations are destroyed. Where fear and aggression become the political principles, diplomacy will fail, with inevitably gruesome and deadly results.

Two later stories involving the Silurians and Sea Devils take up the principal thinking of the original stories and recast them as analogues for modern military conflicts. "Warriors of the Deep" (1984) is set in 2084, when a new Cold War is running. The action takes place on a deep sea base, the launching site of nuclear missiles. The situation of two heavily armed sides ready to destroy the Earth in the name of being "opposed" to whatever the other side believes places militarism on purely ideological and technological grounds. The military force must maintain the right attitude while being primarily caretakers of the computer-operated ballistic weaponry. The point is driven home early in the story when the TARDIS encounters an orbiting robot defender, Sentinel Six, that because of its programming has no means of assessing and evaluating a novel situation. The story, then, displays the fundamental problem of modern militarism, which places faith in the technology to do what used to require vast armies.

The Silurians and Sea Devils concoct a plan for exploiting this situation by taking over the sea base, arming and firing its missiles, precipitating a worldwide nuclear war, and then reclaiming the Earth once the war is over. The story then follows a "base under siege" scenario that once more tests the Doctor's ability to negotiate a peaceful solution. That the Doctor once again fails to do so demonstrates a persistent humanist fear, that the mentality behind militarism is so overwhelmingly strong that militaristic groups will fail to recognize peace and compromise as the options in their best interests.

The paired stories "The Hungry Earth" (2010) and "Cold Blood" (2010) bring back the Silurians and return to the same philosophical ground as prior Silurian and Sea Devil stories. However, in these two stories there are some notable differences, particularly in outcome, that express the hope of the humanist perspective to win out against militarism. In these stories, the Silurian culture itself is clearly split between a scientific/philosophical side and a military side. The military are out not merely to defend the Silurians, but to provoke a war by manipulating the situation so that they can be seen as the defenders. As in prior Silurian stories, the Doctor attempts to negotiate a truce, and seemingly again gets undermined, both by fearful humans and by military Silurians. However, the Silurian culture is much closer to a modern human society, in which the military are ostensibly controlled by a civilian government. There is, then, a power struggle spurred by the emergency, an excuse often used for a military coup. The real difference between these two stories and prior Silurian/Sea Devil stories is the outcome. The military side loses the political struggle. More importantly, in the end the Silurians go back into hiding, taking with them some willing human representatives who will help to create a future in which humans and Silurians will peacefully coexist. The outcome of the story suggests that opposing civilizations will eventually evolve out of their aggression. In other words, social maturity, already in evidence by having the military subordinate to a civilian government, will vanquish militarism.

The humanist perspective regarding the military is a delicate balance, and like all delicate balances difficult to maintain consistently. The Doctor finds the fact of military forces a regrettable necessity. Thus, while he disparages "big-booted soldiers," and "clumsy" military mentality, he can never fully extricate himself from military matters. The humanist perspective is not direct opposition to the military, but to militarism. Humanists seek to prevent the one from becoming taken over by the other. The first recourse for the humanist is to avoid impending military crisis through diplomacy, even while recognizing that diplomacy often fails. Hope, then, becomes the second means for opposing militarism, both the hope that diplomacy will *eventually* win out and is never futile, and the hope that societies will advance to the point of simply discarding militarism.

Totalitarianism

When nationalism and militarism become the dominant political thinking of a society, it is very likely to become totalitarian, the governmental form that logically results from combined nationalism and militarism. *Totalitarian* is a frequently used and misused term. In general, popular use of the term applies to almost any government action that restricts people's actions or abilities to some degree. True totalitarianism, though, is much more specific than this. It starts from two sources. The first is *nationalism*, and the second is a belief in *national destiny*. Fundamentally, it is the belief that History or Nature supply absolute rules, and that these rules single out one nation as having supreme right and sovereign authority over all others. Thus, all social laws come to conform to an idea of what History or Nature intend. For this reason, the state can act without or against the consent of the governed because those in power see themselves as merely carrying out the imperatives of a "higher power." These imperatives are described in the *ideology*, the –ism, by which the totalitarian government defines itself (Arendt 460–74).

The law in a totalitarian regime becomes not an instrument for establishing justice, but an instrument for carrying out *terror*. Totalitarian regimes define *law* as "the law of the movement of some superhuman force, Nature or History" (Arendt 465). Therefore, the totalitarian state sees the sole function of law as clearing the path for this superhuman force. The individual is irrelevant; only the "whole," which is the nation, counts. The law creates terror to eliminate individualism, clear out those not belonging to the nation, and establish the nation as a tightly bound collective, "One Man of gigantic dimension" (Arendt 466).

From a humanist and existentialist point of view, governments are always reactionary at their best. Any government's principal occupation is its own self-preservation. Thus, governments are past-oriented, not future-oriented, for to be oriented toward the future the government must create the means for its own end. This it will not do. For this reason, Fowles states, "*The state does not want to be; it wants to survive*" (176, italics in original). The mechanisms the state uses to ensure its survival are control of education, control of information, fear-mongering, and nationalism.

For these enterprises to work, the totalitarian state almost always supplies a nostalgic and historically nonexistent vision of the past as a model for the current totalitarian state. Thus, the dictators make repeated public reference to a time when everything was much better and the people were much happier. The dictators promise to make the new state a reinvigorated old state. Nazis had their Aryan ideal, an unhistorical myth of national identity and purity ruined through interbreeding with and dangerous influences of other peoples. This nostalgia runs straight back through the origins of totalitarianism in the philosophy of Plato and his followers. Plato sees in "modern" society a dangerous degeneration that must be corrected.

Fowles locates as one source of totalitarianism a cycle of state-imposed happiness. The envious equate happiness with having what the powerful have, institute revolutions to supplant the powerful with themselves, and then become just like the powerful they have supplanted. In the process, they simply replace one imposed idea of universal happiness (for instance, "tradition") with another imposed idea of universal happiness (for instance, the "state"). Such total solutions to the problem of unequal distribution of "happiness" never bring about the envisioned happiness, since not everyone agrees on the source of happiness (Fowles 66).

An example in *Doctor Who* of how the well-intentioned idea of state-controlled happiness becomes a totalitarian nightmare is "The Happiness Patrol" (1988). In this story, Helen A, the leader of space colony Terra Alpha, has determined that all citizens must be "happy." The "–ism" of this society would by happy-ism. Helen A sees the purpose of society, its social movement, as producing total happiness. The idea that a society's purpose is to create in reality a *total* ideal is what makes that society *total*itarian. Thus, the ideal for which the leaders of a totalitarian society strive need not be evil or selfish for them to produce the evil result of a totalitarian state. The nightmare of Terra Alpha is that all forms of music other than "elevator music" have been banned, that people must wear painted clown-like smiles, that everyone must greet each other with happy-sounding platitudes, that depression and sadness are capital offenses, and that millions of people are executed for the mere "crime" of not living up to the state-dictated ideal level of joy.

One can swiftly note that the "excuse" given for almost every totalitarian society is that it brings order, and with it peace. This is Davros's justification for making the Daleks ruthless killing machines seeking only survival. In "Genesis of the Daleks" (1975), Davros says, "When the Daleks are the supreme power of the universe, then we shall have peace. Wars will be eradicated. The Daleks are the power not of evil, but of good." This is the twisted logic of placing abstraction above reality. Yes, if the Daleks win, there will be peace — for the Daleks. In such a circumstance, there will be only Daleks. The promise of peace in the abstract ignores the question of whom this peace will benefit. To justify this typically totalitarian bit of "logic," Davros later tries to persuade his fellow Kaled scientists in quasi-scientific terms: "History will show that co-operation between different species is impossible. Our race must survive above all others, and to do this it must dominate ruthlessly." Here, Davros relies on misrepresented notions of natural survival and contest between species to justify political conquest and slaughter. Like all totalitarians, he invokes "history" as justification, claiming that it produces inexorable "laws" that societies always follow. In such logic, one must be on the side of "history," or be swept away.

Taking a closer look at Davros's statements will help one better understand both the philosophical origin and the philosophical poverty of totalitarian idealism. Davros repeats a form of the theory of progressive history, which Popper calls "historicism." The basic idea is that history is the struggle of nation against nation, and that this struggle in one period resolves contradictions in the previous period. Strong nations survive, weak nations perish, and thus history proceeds toward producing the ideal nation. In philosophical jargon, the theory of progressive history is *teleological* (that history heads toward a goal) and *dialectical* (that opposing ideas produce the ideal). Many such theories existed in the nineteenth century and passed into political theory by producing the two disastrous forms of twentieth-century totalitarianism. Marxist totalitarianism replaces "history" with "class." Fascist totalitarianism replaces "history" with "race" (Popper *Open II* 29–30). Davros clearly leans toward the fascist end of the spectrum.

All such historicist views are based upon a false biological analogy starting from a misconception of evolution. Darwin's theories of the evolution of species in nature are non-teleological; he clearly states that natural change does not intend to produce anything, but simply happens. Totalitarians — Marxist, fascist, and other — extract the term "evolution" and abuse it to produce a teleological twist. Thus, for them, the "goal" of evolutionary history is to produce either the Classless State (Marxism) or the Master Race (fascism), or some equally impossible ideal. According to this line of thought, the totalitarian leader's role is to hasten history's "end" by whatever means possible. Helen A of "The Happiness Patrol" intends to hasten the end of producing total happiness, which in a way is a weird version of Marx's classless state. One sees that Davros leans strongly toward the fascist side, imagining the Daleks as the Master Race. Davros, like the typical totalitarian leader, will violate almost any ethical principal, not just from "a fanatical desire to perpetuate himself in his creation" (as the Doctor says), but to bring about the intention of history, which in his mind is the dominant rule of the Dalek Master Race over all the universe. Since the goal is so grand, ethical scruples have little comparable value for Davros. Use surgery to remove free will? Not a problem. Set death traps for colleagues? Easy. Enable the genocide of one's own people? In a heartbeat.

Another connection between Davros's worldview and fascist ideology is the use, both expressed and implied, of concepts such as History, Fate, Destiny, and Soul (in the national-collective sense). Other totalitarian sympathizers in *Doctor Who* readily focus on these and related terms. Such concepts lead directly to the theories of the Great Man and the Great Nation. The theory goes like this: History and other "natural" process are constantly trying to express their ideal forms; this ideal is not apparent until it arrives; the method of producing ideal forms is dialectical conflict; conflict is, therefore, good because it is the way that the Will or Intention of History gets expressed; the

winners of such conflicts are, therefore, always *right* because their winning
proves the Will of History; those nations or individuals that *dominate* are
living embodiments of the Will of History. Davros places the matter in terms
of *survival*, but the theory is the same — survival means conflict and the strong
win, so they are right. Davros (as well as the Daleks, Cybermen, and Dominators) subscribes to the Great Nation, or Master Race, side of the theory,
with "species" substituting for "race" and "nation." The Master, Tobias
Vaughn, Professor Zaroff, Salamander, Helen A, and others subscribe to the
Great Man side of the theory, and of course nominate themselves as the great
men. They see their ascension to power as "Destiny," and their own actions
as "realistic" because they have survived the conflict of History.

In "Genesis of the Daleks," another Kaled scientist proposes the political
and philosophical alternative to Davros's dreams of power for an elite few.
Gharman offers as the alternative free choice and democratic rule. "Our race
will survive if it deserves to survive," he says, countering Davros's evolutionary
misconceptions. Though it is questionable whether there is any sort of evolutionary intention that Gharman implies by the use of "deserves," there is
the sense that evolution and history work in their own way apart from any
intention to seize control of them or to follow their path. Gharman proposes
a system of democratically chosen leaders rather than self-chosen leaders.

In the end, Gharman's vision never comes to pass because the Kaleds are
too far along in the process of becoming Daleks. Indeed, as is usually the
case, Davros's scheme seems to work, but then backfires. The Daleks refuse
to acknowledge either the Kaleds or Davros as their own race, and wipe out
the lot. It is the kind of social implosion that every totalitarian society under-
goes.

As Fowles states, and as the *Doctor Who* programs just discussed show,
the condition of envy in a society allows for easy manipulation of the many.
To the conservatives and the powerful, it justifies repression, censorship, and
tyranny. To the liberals and underprivileged, it justifies mobs, protest, and
sedition. "Angry mobs justify military dictators; and *vice versa*" (67). Fowles,
therefore, states that the true antidote to fascism is existentialism, the individual asserting his or her individuality against all systems that would suppress
that individuality (123). Thus, the existentialist who asserts his or her individuality gets labeled a bohemian, or a libertine, or an anarchist, or an enemy
of the state. Intriguingly, the Doctor as representative of a humanist/existen-
tialist individual gets variously labeled as libertine, anarchist, and enemy of
the state.

It has been well noted that the Doctor's most persistent foes are fascist
analogues. The Daleks are rabidly xenophobic, the Cybermen militarily
acquisitive, the Master purely authoritarian. The sociological reasons for this

tendency are not hard to find. Most of the cast and crew through the early eighties had fought in or grown up during World War II. The Cold War dominated international politics. A totalitarian takeover of Great Britain was their greatest political fear. Many *Doctor Who* stories almost allegorically encode this fear and a countervailing set of values.

The Daleks, being the first and most popular of the Doctor's true foes, provide an interesting case. The original Daleks story, from 1963, has multiple cues to the Nazi connection. Writer Terry Nation has worked into the story a reversal of Nazi Aryan mythology. He has the frighteningly mutated Daleks as the xenophobes. The Daleks have mutated so far away from their original humanoid form that nothing recognizably humanoid remains. Ian and the Doctor show a visible repulsion when they behold the biological Dalek separate from its mechanical casing. The other humanoid race, the Thals, is almost parodically Aryan in the Nazi sense. Tall, well-built, blond to a one, they are, as Susan describes them, "perfect." Yet, it is the Thals who are the victims of racism. The reversal shows that racism is an arbitrary distinction, that anyone can pick and choose any characteristics as "superior" or "inferior" and the result would be the same.

Nation continues his World War II allegory in his follow-up Dalek story, "The Dalek Invasion of Earth" (1964). The Daleks, with their ruthless efficiency and superior firepower, have subdued Earth. This scenario allows Nation to turn London into an analogue for war-ravaged and conquered European cities such as Paris and Warsaw. The story focuses not on the conquest[6] but on the resistance movement. The production team supported the script's narrative strategy by making everything look 1940, even though the story takes place in 2167. The only futuristic touches are all associated with the Daleks: their weaponry, spaceships, and surgically altered human drones. The story thus contrasts the comfortable familiarity of the resistance fighters with the inhuman alienness of the Daleks. Everything the Daleks do becomes not just inhuman, but anti-human. In contrast, the resistance fighters in their primitive mid-twentieth-century state are inscribed as "human," and the production crew is very careful never to make them appear beyond the viewers' expected notions of humanity. In this way, the story symbolically moves the viewer to conclude that the totalitarian values of the Daleks are "anti-human."

The conflict between those desiring an open society and those with the totalitarian urge is much older than the early twentieth century. Several of the Greek founders of Western philosophy had a strong anti-democratic belief. As shown earlier, Plato felt that democracy was a lower form of government. Before him was Heraclitus, who disliked the emerging Greek democracy because he believed that "most men are wicked" and that "the law can demand, too, that the will of One Man must be obeyed" (qtd. Popper 13). The poet

Pindar argued the notion that "natural laws" authorize conquest by the strong; as Plato quotes the lost poem in *Gorgias*, the "sovereign law" governing mortals and immortals justifies "the utmost force." Plato's student Aristotle believed that slaves deserved their slavery, the slavery itself being the proof, an example of circular reasoning. Aristotle also argues by analogy with nature, stating "ruling and being ruled are not only necessary, but also expedient; and right from birth some are suited for ruling, and are divided from those suited for being ruled" (*Selections* 456). This type of thinking is known as the naturalistic fallacy, the argument that anything occurring in nature is good, while anything not occurring in nature is bad. "Nature" is a vague concept, easily defined in whatever way one could like, and so often supplies a ready justification for brutality. The naturalistic fallacy and the consequent belief in "natural law" are central to totalitarian thinking.

The philosophers mentioned here, though renowned as founders of philosophic thinking and originators of logic, suffer from sociocentric biases in socio-political matters. They believe that the status of their own culture is the tool for determining what is politically right. They believe that the "superiority" of Greek society is "natural." Since most slaves, for example, were captured foreigners, Aristotle considered them "barbarians" and "brutes" unworthy of consideration on the same level as Greeks. Heraclitus and Plato also started from the premise that Greek society was superior to all others, an attitude that would later in history turn into nationalism.

The justification for a totalitarian system rather than a democratic one is almost always the same — too much freedom. This is the reasoning that Plato, through Socrates, gives in *The Republic*.[7] Socrates in the dialogue criticizes democracy for being just a temporarily "delightful" and "charming" object. Democracy looks pretty, but proves valueless. The reason given by Socrates in *The Republic* for denigrating democracy is that government becomes like a bazaar, where everyone chooses the governors who suit them at the moment. Such a government lacks stability. Furthermore, in competing for the favors of the voters, the governors will keep supplying the governed with enough "freedoms" to keep them satisfied. In a democracy, criminals parade like heroes, and the people disregard the "fine principles" by which a state ought to run (250). So far, the description of democracy looks very much like how politics occurs in "An Unearthly Child," with Za and Kal promising what they cannot supply and vying for greater appeal instead of for greater leadership. However, the critique of democracy in *The Republic* goes beyond these usual criticisms, a critique that belies Plato's totalitarian urge. Plato has Socrates argue that in the generous freedom of democracy, natural unequals become treated as equals, while the State has "subjects who are like rulers, and rulers who are like subjects" (255). Plato believes that democracy upsets the natural order, in which those who are naturally better than others and naturally suited to rule ought to rule.

The criticisms of democracy that Plato has Socrates express and the justifications for aristocratic or tyrannical rule by other Greek philosophers are similarly expressed by many a villain in *Doctor Who*. In "The Dæmons" (1971), the Master states that people "must be *told* what to think and what to do." He denounces "decadence" as the plague of society: "All this talk of democracy, equality, freedom. What this country needs is strong leadership." He is actually quite surprised when people do not recognize what he thinks is his inherent superiority and right to rule, and resorts to force to impose his will.

In "The Daleks' Masterplan" (1965–6), Mavic Chen, the elected Guardian of the Solar System, forms an alliance with the Daleks to place himself as Guardian of the Universe. Chen imagines that after the destruction of the Earth, "Earth will rise again, but without the shackles of infantile philosophies like democracy and equality." Chen's title, "Guardian of the Solar System," sounds very similar to the title of another tyrant, Oliver Cromwell, the "Lord Protector" of Great Britain. The title sounds like a typical office for being one step away from assuming total control of the government.

In "Tomb of the Cybermen" (1967), a small elite group calling itself the Brotherhood of Logicians has taken control of an archaeological expedition researching the history of the Cybermen. Two members of the Brotherhood, Klieg and Kaftan, seek to revive the Cybermen to use them to help conquer the Earth. In the words of Klieg, the Brotherhood seeks "logic and power." They consider themselves "the greatest man-intelligence ever assembled." Clearly, their ideal of linking mass intelligence with mass power is to arrange the world along "rational" lines as they understand it, and the only way to do that is to subvert democracy through a total takeover. Their idea of aristos (the best) in their Platonic aristocracy would be rule by the smartest, which is not far off from Plato's concept of a governing elite of philosophers.

The Brotherhood of Logicians and its intentions are not fully explored in "Tomb of the Cybermen," which is mainly a non-political story. A more fully developed version of it, though, is the Scientific Reform Society (SRS) portrayed in "Robot" (1974–5). This group is made up of scientists, engineers, and managers, most of whom work on secret government projects. Their one principal link is a research facility called Thinktank, which serves as their operational base and gives them access to top secret military equipment and information. The SRS seeks to use their connections, get hold of the nuclear missile control center, and then hold the world to ransom. In this way, the SRS can impose their idea of a rational society upon everyone else. In a reveal-ing interview with the journalist Sarah Jane Smith, one SRS member gives away the assumption behind their thinking, namely that their scientific intelligence makes them inherently superior, which gives them the right both to make judgments about how people should behave, and to impose those judgments.

One sees in these would-be dictators the unfolding of a type of dangerous historicist thinking hinted at by Aristotle, who argues that the essence of a thing or person rests as inherent potentialities that can be expressed only through change. Thus, one can see this essence only when one sees the final result of the process of change. This goal, or *final cause*, Aristotle also links to the proper place for a thing or person to be. All objects, once dissociated from their proper places, seek them. This is the reasoning that leads Aristotle to state that the human is a political animal, by which he means that the human's "natural" place is the city (Aristotle *Selections* 452–4). Really, this is a destinal argument, placing the result as a cause that impels something to that result. Therein lies the problem of easily interpreting this to mean that if a person or state dominates, then it was part of its potentiality, its essence, to do so. Aristotle himself does not reach that conclusion, and indeed expressly argues against it (*Selections* 505–7). However, many political philosophers will take up this argument in the nineteenth century, and thus provide philosophical justification for all forms of totalitarianism, both fascistic and socialistic. Certainly, the *Doctor Who* villains who argue for their "right" to rule believe in this historicist-destinal ideology.

One of the most common rationalizations for totalitarianism is the statement that what the government does is for the good of the governed. The argument is that limitations and proscriptions are needed to maximize happiness. "The Macra Terror" demonstrates that this happiness is an illusion, since the flow of rewards is one-way, toward the rulers. "The Happiness Patrol" more strictly tests this idea. The society of Terra Alpha, as created by its ruler Helen A, runs by enforced happiness. Everyone in this colony must use joyful expressions, such as "I'm glad you're happy" and "I'm happy you're glad." Expressions of displeasure, unhappiness, or depression, such as blues music, are fatally suppressed by female police, the Happiness Patrol, dressed in pink skirts and wielding large guns. Refusal to submit to this enforced happiness results in public executions of "killjoys." Private executions carried out by a sinister robot called the Kandy Man are also a regular part of the process.

The intention behind this absurd society may seem at first laudable. However, as Popper argues about totalitarianism in general, its formulation is the very cause of its oppression. If we take it as a purely utilitarian proposition to "aim at the greatest amount of happiness for the greatest number" and make of it a kind of categorical imperative to "maximize happiness," then it might seem unethical not to do everything in one's power to maximize happiness. Popper states that such a formulation produces benevolent dictatorships. He offers a more ethical formulation to "minimize suffering" (*Open I* 235 n. 6). In "The Happiness Patrol," enforced happiness does not make people happy, not even the rulers who implement the policies. Benevolent dictatorships are still dictatorships, and still operate using the methods of dictatorship. Enforced happiness or enforced equity or any other top-down enforcement does not minimize suffering, but increases it wherever the force is applied. Thus, the rationalization that oppressive measures mild or harsh are for "the good" of the people does not stand up either to logic or to experience.

The historicist thinking of totalitarian rulers is central to their ideologies. According to Popper, historicism includes the belief that history is made by Great Leaders (usually warriors and politicians) and Great Events, and that by studying these great leaders and events one may make accurate predictions of the future. Historicism involves a total disregard for the "little" people, whose lives are deemed meaningless, and whose destiny is merely to be pawns (Popper *Open I* 7–8). Additionally, the historicist view overly emphasizes change and combines it with the belief in an unchanging *law of destiny* (Popper *Open I* 13). As these characters see it, radical change *is* the unchanging law of destiny, the only thing that does not change. Great leaders are those who see the "truth" of the laws of history and destiny, and seize control of it. Heraclitus says, "One man is worth more than ten thousand if he is Great" (qtd. Popper *Open I* 17). It is easy to see that the would-be dictators of *Doctor Who* not only believe as Heraclitus does, but nominate themselves as the Great ones worth more than 10,000 of the rest of us.

Another problem inherent in any attempt to create and maintain an ideal society is that it must inevitably be formed into a dictatorship, since there is always a set of presumptions that those who engineer society know what is best for the people. Popper identifies two problematic assumptions behind such social engineering: "that there are rational methods to determine once and for all what [the ideal society] is ... and ... what the best means of its realization are" (*Open I* 161). Such social engineering is really experimentation in its worst possible sense. Since there is no experience that would provide a basis for proving either deductively or inductively what the ideal society or method of engineering should be, any theory along these lines is guesswork. Any society set up beginning from theory will succumb to the trial and error by which all theory is tested (Popper *Open I* 162–4). Errors will inevitably take place in the absence of practical experience, and the social engineers will need to adjust to accommodate. The adjustment will be either to change the plan to fit the circumstances, or change the circumstances to fit the plan. Almost always, as history has shown, the engineer will choose to change the circumstances, i.e., will resort to violence to compel people to conform to the theory.

Because the totalitarian rulers require force against those they rule, the militarism of the society gets rerouted from its original target of the evil outsiders to a new target, the evil insiders. Such is what a viewer sees in "The Happiness Patrol." If citizens were indeed happy, there would be no need for a police force and public executions. However, since most people are unlikely to be compelled to be happy and the static circumstances necessary to maintain this overall public happiness do not exist, the government turns to coercion as the primary means for keeping the State stable. The situation is experimentation in the sense of simply "giving it a go." The military-police system becomes the means of preserving the theory, the –ism driving the government and believed to be the source of social stability.

So, the urge to become a totalitarian ruler is a desire to extend the ego to encompass all known space. The would-be dictator believes him or herself to *be* the instrument of destiny that will bring about a great change and a new era. In *Doctor Who*, some would-be totalitarian rulers content themselves with dreams of ruling the world (Professor Zaroff, Salamander, BOSS). The limitation to just the world derives from reality, since the would-be dictator cannot extend his influence beyond the Earth. In *Doctor Who*, though, many would-be dictators have the chance to go beyond the earthly limit. They long to control the galaxy or the universe (the Master, Mavic Chen, Kara, the Host of the Swarm, etc.).

Furthermore, the most characteristic definition of *change* in the historicist view is *struggle*. One sees this in Heraclitus' philosophy: "War is the father and king of all things" (qtd. Popper *Open I* 16). Marx, the great figure of socialist economics, argued that history was a constant violent struggle between social classes (*Capital* 321). In the 1800s, Hegel argued that the pattern of self-assertion was the inevitable development of a *master-slave* relationship, which extends from individual relations to State relations (56). Hitler and his Nazi followers viewed history as the perpetual struggle between races. Again and again, one finds that wherever there is advocacy for authoritarian rule, there is the idea that history is driven by the engine of constant struggle.[8]

One can notice exactly the same attitudes in the *Doctor Who* villains. Davros believes that cooperation between species is impossible and that war is inevitable. More often, the attitude is implied rather than stated. The Master's belief that one must rule or serve stems from the further belief that that is the way matters have always been, a constant struggle between ruler and ruled unless the ruler is strong enough for total domination, a clear statement of the master-slave interpretation of history. In "The Dominators" (1968), the Dominators in question control ten galaxies, or at least claim to, through "rational ruthlessness" and the assumption that one takes by force and never asks if one is to dominate. The implication, again, is that struggle is the norm, and cooperation is either irrational or superfluous.

Such is the power of the urge to extend the ego that it provides the would-be dictator with an aura of strength and invulnerability. Such people have a charismatic charm that overcomes many a weaker ego. The dominant ego becomes a means by which the followers' self-transcendent identity, the habit of giving up autonomy for group identity and sometimes mob mentality, may take charge of their volitions.

In *Doctor Who*, the would-be dictators have no problem finding loyal followers, servants, and workers. In "The Enemy of the World" (1967–8), We repeatedly hear that Salamander is a revered figure, honored as a hero and savior. In "The Dæmons," the Master has no trouble recruiting local English villagers of the 1970s to follow his commands, break laws, even threaten to kill others, all without apparent need for hypnotic control over these followers. Kara in "Revelation of the Daleks" (1985) has her devoted assistant, Vogel, for her scheme of controlling the food supply of the whole galaxy. And so on. Followers are never in short supply, and are almost always willing to forgo common ethical principles not for their own glory or betterment, but for that of the charismatic would-be dictator.

The Question of Leadership

Politics has been plagued by a fundamental question: Who should rule? Considerations of this question dominate the thinking of the *Doctor Who* villains. Whether the answer is "I" or "We," the question remains central. It may be, however, that *Doctor Who* demonstrates Karl Popper's arguments regarding this question. Popper argues that the question derives from a confusion about the nature of politics, and thus produces confused responses.

Many answers have been proposed to the question of who should rule: the king, the oligarchs, the "master race," "the people." *Doctor Who* villains supply similar answers. If one is the Master or Tobias Vaughan, then the answer is, "I should rule as absolute dictator." The Daleks and Cybermen opt for the "master race" answer. Popper argues that these answers are in reality unhelpful, since they seem to solve a problem that they do not actually solve. For wherever an answer has been tried, the rulers have never proved sufficiently good, wise, noble, intelligent, masterful, and/or competent to create an absolutely reliable or stable government. This goes for rule by "the people" as much as it does for rule by tyrant. The people are no better at governing than any other sort of ruler. So, the problem of getting a good government has not been solved when the question is "who should rule?"

The theory implied in the question of who should rule is what Popper calls the "theory of (unchecked) sovereignty" (*Open I* 121). The assumption is that political power is *sovereign*, nearly absolute, and that rulers of any kind can accumulate and wield power at will. When Tobias Vaughan argues the need for a "strong" leader, he is stating part of the theory of unchecked sovereignty. When Davros states that one race must dominate above all others, he states part of the theory of unchecked sovereignty. A corollary of the theory of unchecked sovereignty unstated by Popper but stated or implied by the would-be tyrants of *Doctor Who* is that a government is *weak* when its leaders do not exercise their full sovereignty.

A look at the people who desire to be sole sovereign reveals several commonalities. One is that they all subscribe to the "great man" theory of leadership. According to this theory, those at the top are "great" for having gotten there. People such as Mavic Chen and Salamander acquire power, in part, to be admired. The source of the admiration they seek, though, is having the power. Thus, they see no reason not to be ruthless, violent, disloyal, in a word evil, when it suits them. Machiavelli notes that such rulers can be admired for their ability to survive and prosper, often rising from lowly parts of society to total control of it; however, there is no "skill" in killing one's friends, betraying trust, lying to the public, and so on, to get one's way. Therefore, says Machiavelli, their "means can lead to power, but not glory" (34). Such leaders never will receive the admiration that they seek.

While these "strong leader" or "great men" rulers seek admiration, one should not mistake this for a desire to be "loved." On this point, Machiavelli is clear. If a single ruler is to take charge of both a government and a people, then being feared is the goal, not being loved. However, being feared by itself is not enough. The leader must be feared without being hated. This means that the leader should not use power arbitrarily or for the sake of acquiring goods and property. Rather, the leader should be strict, forceful, and fair, without regard for a reputation for cruelty. Thus, though reputed to be cruel, a leader who maintains fear by threat can run a country without often needing to carry out the threat, and can acquire the loyalty of those in the military and government[9] (Machiavelli 65–7). One can see, for example, how Mavic Chen and Helen A can maintain loyal underlings willing to do their bidding, and can rule with little fear of a *coup d'état*, as long as plunder is not their aim, and as long as they use cruelty only to "make a point," so to speak.

As we have seen, however, the autocrat will more often than not hold power tenuously because the theory of unchecked sovereignty is fundamentally flawed. Primarily, it is unrealistic. "No political power has ever been unchecked," says Popper (*Open I* 121). Whoever is "in charge" must always rely upon helpers to maintain this system. Kara has Vogel, Vaughan has Packer, and Davros has Nyder. Even the master races, the Daleks and Cybermen, use spies and traitors, form alliances, and bargain deals in their quest for dominance. No power stands alone, sovereign. Reliance upon others means that the powerful must always give up some sovereignty, some authority, some control to others, and that they can never achieve the aim of total domination.

Additionally, tyrannical rulers of any sort always struggle to maintain their rule, even when it appears that they have total control. They must constantly worry about dissidents, revolts, and *coups d'état*, since violent overthrow is the only means of changing such a government. Thus, while it may seem that in the words of the Valeyard, the Doctor introduces a "corrupting" element into a seemingly stable society, and that he even foments revolution upon occasion (as in "The Sunmakers" and "The Happiness Patrol"), no other means of extricating the true tyrant exist. Since tyrants believe in their total sovereignty, never willingly relinquish power, and have the resources of the government at their command, only the force of numbers can extricate them. Once the people lose their fear of the tyrant, he or she will not remain long in power. The Doctor, therefore, in these cases works to stir the collective courage of the people. Rarely have collective uprisings gone without violence.

The theory of unchecked sovereignty does not work. The tyrant does not comfortably hold power. The question of "who shall lead" leads up a blind political alley. Therefore, Popper offers an alternative question: "How can we so organize political institutions that bad or incompetent rulers can be prevented from doing too much damage?" (*Open I* 121). More pointedly stated, the question "who shall be the rulers" needs to be replaced by the question "how shall we tame them?" (*Open II* 133). The theory that fits this question is the "theory of checks and balances" (*Open I* 122). Governmental stability is attained by institutionalized balancing of the powers of the sovereign against other powers that can check the abuses of the sovereign and provide for peaceful, regular replacement of the government.

In "Genesis of the Daleks," we see two attempts at operating just such system. In the first, scientists working in the research bunker that Davros runs with absolute authority are becoming worried by the direction of their research. They have the Doctor pass on a message to the political authority of the Kaled Council to halt research at the bunker. In the second, scientists and guards, having revolted against Davros, try to institute a democratic process for determining the course of their work. Both attempts to rein in Davros are portrayed as honorable and essentially correct. Both fail because the two groups do not understand the full extent of Davros's megalomania, and so Davros violently wipes out both the Kaled city and most of the scientists with whom he had been working. The lesson is not that checks do not work, but that they need to be strong enough to survive the worst counterattack the tyrants can create. If institutional means do not check power, other, violent, means will. Davros, for instance, is "killed"[10] by his Dalek creations, who revolt against his authority.

The Doctor and Politics

So far, we have seen *Doctor Who* work as a means to critique various political theories. However, we have yet to see what political theory emerges from the program itself. In particular, there is the question of what counters the excesses of bureaucracy, capitalism, colonialism, nationalism, militarism, and totalitarianism. To start with, one must understand that *Doctor Who* and its perspectives are products of the intellectual development of the West. Though sometimes Eastern philosophies are brought in, such as Buddhism in "Kinda," they take on very Western characteristics in becoming part of *Doctor Who*. In the development of political philosophy, an idea almost entirely peculiar to the West, and certainly most developed in Western history, is *universalism*, the idea of the unity of the human species. Even granting that sexism, racism, elitism, and other anti-universalist modes of thought and behavior run right through Western history, one must acknowledge that the West is not unique in these areas, and is not in many cases the most extreme in them. However, the West is nearly unique in having this strong counterbalancing, of universalist idealism.

This spirit of universalism runs right back to Ionian Greece (ca. 700–200 B.C.E.), where Western philosophy gets its start. Early Greek literature of the period, such as that by Homer and Hesiod, does not treat foreigners as "devils" and "savages," but rather as "different but equal," worthy of respect for their accomplishments and culture. Heraclitus in the 500s B.C.E. stated that certain properties belonged to all people, namely *Logos* (both rationality and the ability to speak) and *change*. The playwrights Aeschylus and Sophocles have characters pronounce that human similarities are much more important than transient differences such as nationality and social status. The early philosophers Hippias and Antiphon held similar views, as did the historian Thucydides, who believed in a permanent human nature apart from historical/social constructions such as "Greek" and "barbarian." Perhaps such ideas infused the anti-slavery movement in Athens in the late 300s B.C.E. Even slavery apologist Aristotle made provision to free most or all his slaves in his will. The Cynic philosophers invented the concept of *cosmopolitanism*, that the natural human state is to be citizen of many places if not the whole Earth. Stoics such as Eratosthenes likewise came to believe in human unity, an idea that greatly influenced Roman stoics such as Cicero and Marcus Aurelius.[11]

The rediscovery of classical humanism and cosmopolitanism made possible the modern worldviews, such as existentialism and modern humanism. The predominantly Enlightenment, humanist, and existentialist outlook of *Doctor Who* has its roots in many of the same observations that existentialist philosophers themselves have made. Modern life on Earth, made up of as it is of highly destructive wars, the possibility of total annihilation, extreme political crises, constant economic tension, fluid social circumstances, and traditions far removed from the social circumstances that gave rise to them, leads the thinking person towards skepticism. Irony and disbelief are not just protective psychological mechanisms, but to a large extent the only sane and rational attitudes to take toward social and political events.

The Doctor is by nature, therefore, a skeptic, and the writers of the series often privilege this skeptical attitude as essentially and necessarily correct. As was discussed in Chapter 3, the Doctor typifies the existential human, and in so doing becomes an existentialist hero. The existentialist human is aware of being estranged from society and from fellow humans, a "solitary phenomenon amidst the crowd" (Patka "Five" 45). The normal securities of identification with political causes or candidates, with nation, with local societies and clubs, can provide no solace to such a person. Indeed, such a person views these securities as basically insecure, as inherently corrupt and corrupting.

According to Patka's summation of existentialist ideas, from the existentialist political standpoint, the systems of societies such as industry, cultural institutions, economies, political bodies, religions, are adequate for taking care of people's basic needs. However, such systems cannot, in the end, provide certain, justifiable, or adequate answers to questions of existence and value. Instead, what values these systems do offer come with a requirement for the individual to subjugate his or her will to them. An individual's needs and values become subordinated to the shallow needs and values offered by the state, by politics, by the controllers of economies. Accumulations of power and wealth become the ultimate value system. Those who control power and wealth artificially restrict the range of human interests to basic material needs, manufactured false needs, social approval, and a false sense of participating in public affairs (Patka "Five" 51–3).

The Doctor's commitment to open debate and rational inquiry is not merely a scientific or scholarly concern. That Enlightenment strain that runs throughout his thinking takes a political dimension. The Enlightenment philosopher Kant states the matter clearly:

> Nature, then, has carefully cultivated the seed within the hard core–namely the urge for and the vocation of free thought. And this free thought gradually reacts back on the modes of thought of the people, and men become more and more capable of acting in freedom. At last free thought acts even on the fundamentals of government and the state finds it agreeable to treat man, who is now more than a machine, in accord with his dignity ["What Is Enlightenment?"].

So, as people begin to recognize the freedoms of the individual, especially the freedom of the intellect to roam and contemplate, and as more people demand these freedoms, this affects the State, making it more free and open.

Liberalism

In "School Reunion" (2006), Headmaster Finch, the program's villain, levels an interesting accusation at the Doctor: "You act like such a radical and yet all you want to do is preserve the old order." The dichotomy seems clear — destroy it or preserve it. However, this is a false dilemma. There is also change from within. Furthermore, there is the question of personal freedom. Too often those advocating radical change are really desiring to impose a political system upon people, presumably because those advocating change are wiser than the common people. In the end, this is to exchange one form of oppression for another, which is what Finch and others like him really want.

In *Doctor Who*, the answer at the social level to the problem of being human is liberalism. The political outlook in *Doctor Who* is, broadly speaking, liberal. Not that the program condones any specific policy, party, or platform, but that it supports a set of general principles that one usually associates with political liberalism. These include cross-cultural cooperation, environmentalism, equal rights for women and minorities, and rehabilitation of criminals rather than incarceration. Additionally, these liberal values stand in opposition to others: bureaucracy, nationalism, laissez-faire capitalism, colonialism, militarism, and authoritarian government of any kind. The program's strongest liberal message is its anti-war message.

In their book-length analysis of *Doctor Who*, John Tulloch and Manuel Alvarado characterize the political outlook of the program as consistent with the BBC's particular brand of political neutrality: skeptical, aggressive, quizzical, and amused toward all forms of political power. In *Doctor Who* the attitude gets further flavored by the Doctor's "Romantic" hero mystique. This characteristic allows him to adopt a "liberal-populist role in criticizing 'sectionalist' forces of 'Left' and 'Right,' and in rebuking the 'official' and the powerful, whether in big business, the military, government or 'militant' unions" (51–2). The political form that most resembles these critiques is liberal democracy, which places sovereignty in the hands of the people.

Democracy

Democracy of some kind is the *Doctor Who* alternative government structure to totalitarianism, whether it be nationalist totalitarianism, capitalist totalitarianism, bureaucratic totalitarianism, or despotic totalitarianism. Instead of the idea of unchecked sovereignty, which is the center of any totalitarian system, the *Doctor Who* ideal is limited sovereignty derived from the consent of the governed. The idea has its roots in ancient Athenian democracy, but gets its fullest expression in Enlightenment philosophy.

The base idea of modern democracy is the *social contract*, variously expressed by such philosophers as Thomas Hobbes, John Locke, and Jean-Jacques Rousseau. As Rousseau defines it in the 1750s, the social contract, or pact, is this: "each of us puts his person and all his power in common under the supreme direction of the general will; and we as a body receive each member as an indivisible part of the whole" (55). In 1770, Baron D'Holbach states it more succinctly, that for a government to be legitimate, it "can only be founded on the free consent of society" (92). Rousseau says, "There will always be a great difference between subjugating a multitude of men and ruling a society" (53). Rousseau shows how "sovereign" applies in virtually any system of government; whether by individual or by group, the rule for the sovereign is the same, that without the will of the people behind the sovereign, the sovereign has a troubled or failed rule. Thus, the sovereign's interest should be the well-being of the body politic, and not the well-being of the sovereign. The system works because "duty and self-interest oblige both contracting parties equally to give each other mutual assistance, and the same individuals must seek, in their double capacity, to take advantage of all the benefits which depend on it" (Rousseau 57). As good as all this sounds, Rousseau does not say that *democracy* is the form of government best suited to this social contract. That union comes later, when such American political figures as Thomas Jefferson, John Adams, and Benjamin Franklin make the express link between the two ideas in the Declaration of Independence and the Constitution of the United States of America.

The Declaration of Independence famously states that the purpose of a government bound by the social contract is the securing of the life, liberty, and pursuit of happiness of its citizens. The document distills several ideas that had been floating around in Enlightenment political thought. D'Holbach, for instance, states that government should, through its laws, ensure the liberty, property, and security of its citizenry (92). Whatever trio of terms a philosopher may use, the basic principle is the same: government is responsible for providing the circumstances by which people may freely choose to pursue their own destinies as long as doing so does not infringe upon another person's *rights*, which are those concepts that allow each person to pursue his or her own destiny. In other words, rights — such as life, liberty, pursuit of happiness, property, and security — must be equally distributed to all members of a society, so that no one, not even the sovereign, has more or different rights from any other person in society.

What makes such a society *democratic* is that under the terms of the social contract, a society may choose to replace its sovereign. As D'Holbach puts it, sovereigns are "ministers of society," not rulers of society, and "those chiefs who injure society lose the right of commanding" (92–3). He further states that "man only acquires the right of commanding men, when he renders them happy" (205). The Declaration of Independence states that when the government loses the will of the people, then the people have a right to replace their government, presumably with one that does a better job of maintaining the citizenry's basic rights. Thus, the Enlightenment idea is not that *democracy* take the form of "rule of the majority." As Rousseau points out, such a system has never truly existed, nor can it since it would require the entire populace to be constantly "in session," and thus weaken their security and rob individual members of their rights to pursue their own happiness apart from state matters (100–2). Democracy in the sense that it is used in the modern State means only that the people decide by vote who will run the government, the rules of which the people have decided upon. Government in such a system should function primarily to maintain *rights* and possess only the limited sovereignty the populace has granted it, through such means as a constitution.

According to John Fowles, the best form of government for modern life is democracy, "the right of any sane adult to vote freely for the freely-elected candidate of a freely-constituted party with a freely-evolved policy." However, the reason for this is not that democracy produces the best regimes, but because "it gives more freedom of choice to beings whose most urgent need is freedom of choice" (56).[12] The broad version of democracy as thought about in *Doctor Who* further refines Fowles' ideas by highlighting two critical components: political democracy and the right to privacy.

There is no denying the strong pro-democracy politics of *Doctor Who*. The same argument of "natural equality" that guided the Greek Sophists also guides *Doctor Who*. "The Savages" demonstrates that intelligence and sophistication provide no ethical justification for ruthless exploitation of human bodies. "Kinda" demonstrates the brutality and insanity of the "might makes right" perspective. "The Happiness Patrol" demonstrates that a society modeled upon one person's dreams only prevents everyone else from pursuing their own dreams. All demonstrate that "human nature" is the great equalizer and the only ethical foundation on which to build a just society.

Though *Doctor Who* is pro-democracy, it is much more anti-authoritarian. The program takes a position similar to Mill's: "It is not by wearing down into uniformity all that is individual in themselves, but by cultivating it, and calling it forth, within the limits imposed by the rights and interests of others, that human beings become a noble and beautiful object of contemplation" (*On* 105). In fighting against various tyrants, oligarchs, and totalitarians, the

Doctor enacts a foundational Enlightenment political idea, that "no man derives from nature the right of commanding another" (D'Holbach 205). In so far as the audience for *Doctor Who* takes anti-authoritarian ideas mostly as granted, they immediately see the views of natural superiority expressed by Tobias Vaughan, the Cybermen, the Daleks, and the Master as inherently wrong if not outright evil, and needing suppression. So, *Doctor Who* rightly shows, contrary to the beliefs of a large number of the American population and a smaller number of the English and European populations, that democracy is not the opposite and antidote to communism, but the opposite and antidote to totalitarianism.

Doctor Who never provides a model of the ideal society or any manifesto of the political philosophy that would create such a society. The creators of the program wisely realize the futility in offering any sort of specific political solution to the problems of human existence within the *Doctor Who* framework. The political perspective offered is broadly liberal, and mainly oppositional. Thus, audiences can see a little of what a better political system might be by seeing what it is not.

However, one can identify a preferred political system — democracy, a materialist political system, flexible and responsive to change. French philosopher Michel Onfray pinpoints the origin of modern democracy as Enlightenment philosophy, the same Enlightenment humanism that forms the basis of the *Doctor Who* philosophy. In the Enlightenment of the seventeenth and eighteenth centuries, philosophers and political thinkers rejected superstition, intolerance, censorship, tyranny, political absolutism, and state religion as sound bases for government. Instead, the philosophers of Enlightenment sought to extend freedom of expression, to derive law from contractual relationships, to create happiness here and now, to assign reason the highest priority in governmental affairs, and in so doing they provided the intellectual impetus for transforming modern governments into more democratic and open societies (Onfray 209–10). As Onfray describes it, democracy "lives" off of contractual arrangements, dynamics, dialogue, use of reason, diplomacy, and negotiation. It stems from "living forces" and not from imaginary ideals, golden ages, or stagnant social systems from thousands of years ago (Onfray 205).

Viewers of *Doctor Who* see the Doctor work toward rearranging oppressive societies into nascent democracies. In "The Sun Makers," he begins in the words of the Collector, "the vicious doctrine of egalitarianism." In "The Savages," the so-called "savages" are brought as equals into the elite society now robbed of its power to exploit them. In "The Happiness Patrol," the Doctor precipitates a full-out popular revolution. Interestingly, viewers almost never see the results of these transformations. The direction of the change seems to be enough, as though the idea of a new democracy makes it happen. Perhaps it comes from a recognition that the evolution of modern societies has been toward democracy.

The ideal political system is not bureaucratic, not nationalist, not fascistic, not aristocratic, not freely capitalistic, not communistic, and not conservative. Whatever it is, it probably conforms to Erich Fromm's definition of a sane society, one that allows the individuals within it to reach the peak of their human evolution by providing the social conditions by which this could happen (71). All the systems that *Doctor Who* negates are inhibitive, and thus keep individuals confined and repressed at some level lower than full maturity.

In this ideal society, the citizens possess certain properties. Kant has identified three that make a good foundation for the relationship between the citizen and the state. These are lawful freedom, civil equality, and civil independence. Lawful freedom means that the citizen is not required to obey no law to which he or she has not given consent. Civil equality means that no person is superior to any other within the state. Civil independence means that the existence and preservation of the citizen's rights come from being a member of the commonwealth, and not from any person or institution within the commonwealth (*Metaphysics* 91).

Typically, the political systems that *Doctor Who* negates work on the principle that the individual must change to fit the needs of the system, or of the abstraction that the leaders offer, such as the State or the Company. Such a state infringes one, two, or all of the rights Kant identifies as belonging to the citizen. A government that insists it has the power to grant or remove rights, such as that in "The Savages," infringes upon civil independence. A government that distributes rights and privileges unequally as a matter of custom or law, such as that in "The Sun Makers," infringes upon civil equality. A government that imposes law without consulting either the citizens or their elected representatives, such as in the alternate England of "Inferno," infringes upon lawful freedom. When the Doctor subverts or helps to subvert such a system, he does so from the knowledge that these systems inhibit human potential. The subversion is literally a "turning under," marking the beginning of a society in which the system suits the needs of the individuals in it.

Instead of top-heavy government, what *Doctor Who* offers through the Doctor's example is politics founded on a theory of *rights*. Even more particularly, the *Doctor Who* default position is that there are fundamental and universal human rights, and that evil derives from dismissing or denying these rights. These rights presuppose *freedom of thought* as the fundamental human right. Such rights are based upon the concept that "the other person is always a potential source of instruction for every other person" (C. Butler 12). This is the principle of *respect*. The respect for human rights views such rights "as a collaborative quest for objective truth" (C. Butler 12). This view of rights as discussion stems from the sense that no one be kept from the political argument, which is not to say that everyone must be included, but that anyone interested in the argument not be excluded (C. Butler 16).

To summarize, the *Doctor Who* political orientation may be seen as often in what the Doctor opposes as what he or the program expressly promotes. The *Doctor Who* position denies the idea that the State possesses more rights than do the individuals in it. It denies all forms of authoritarian rule. It denies the value of rule according to theory. The *Doctor Who* political orientation is humanist, and so is broadly liberal and somewhat libertarian. It begins with the recognition of equally distributed human rights. It upholds the idea that government's role is maintenance and protection of these rights. It upholds the idea that no government is ever perfect, and so a working government must have a mechanism ensuring its peaceful replacement; otherwise, the government will be violently overthrown.

CHAPTER 11

Justice

In all my traveling throughout the universe I have battled against evil, against power mad conspirators. I should have stayed here. The oldest civilization: decadent, degenerate, and rotten to the core. Power mad conspirators, Daleks, Sontarans ... Cybermen, they're still in the nursery compared to us. Ten million years of absolute power. That's what it takes to be really corrupt!
— The Doctor, "The Trial of a Timelord: The Ultimate Foe"

The Future

What will the future bring? The psychologist C. G. Jung begins one of his final writings with this question. It is appropriate to apply the question to issues of the current discussion as we come to a conclusion. Jung in the 1950s noted, "Historically, it is chiefly in times of physical, political, economic and spiritual distress that men's eyes turn with anxious hope to the future, and when anticipations, utopias, and apocalyptic visions multiply" (*Undiscovered* 11). Jung felt that the close of the millennium, then less than half a century away, was such a time of distress. *Doctor Who*, as a product of the turn of the millennium, participates in consideration of these physical, political, economic, and spiritual problems. *Doctor Who* points our attention to the future. The confluence of all these issues is the central concept of Justice.

Where We Are

At this point, it pays to summarize the main philosophical ideas we have so far traveled through. We have identified that the principle philosophical outlook portrayed in *Doctor Who* may be best described as *secular humanism*. According to a leading secular humanist philosopher, this outlook has six principal characteristics: "(1) it is a method of inquiry, (2) it provides a

300

naturalistic cosmic outlook, (3) it is nontheistic, (4) it is committed to humanistic ethics, (5) it offers a perspective that is democratic, and (6) it is planetary in scope" (Kurtz *What* 21–2).

Doctor Who consistently portrays this secular humanist outlook. While the program does not fully demonstrate a method of inquiry, it does uphold the value of inquiry through the Doctor's inquisitive nature, and it upholds the value of science as the best tool for conducting inquiry into nature. The program's cosmic outlook is mainly naturalistic, and individual stories follow the usual pattern in science fiction of audience estrangement leading to naturalized conclusion. In other words, the audience is presented with phenomena that could be supernatural in origin, but the plot demonstrates that these unusual phenomena are natural. Correspondingly, the program presents a mainly non-theistic outlook, one that is either deistic or weakly atheistic. The program is committed to humanist ethics both on the personal level and on the socio-political level. The Doctor's commitment to politics is anti-totalitarian and pro-democratic. Finally, the program repeatedly advocates through the character of the Doctor a big-picture, planetary outlook in the form of respect for all humans as belonging to the same "family," and in the form of environmentalist concern for the condition of the physical planet.

The principal concern of the *Doctor Who* humanist outlook is *justice*. The program works through the questions of what justice is and whether it is possible to achieve. One may view many if not most episodes as case studies in justice. The six characteristics of humanism as they develop in the stories are tools for the audience to assess the concept of justice that each episode tests.

Why Justice?

If we consider the movement of Western history, it has been a gradual process of increasing the rights, happiness, and comfort of all people within the scope of civilization. It has been an ugly, brutal struggle because those at the top of the social hierarchy, who have enjoyed the rights and comforts, have almost universally assumed that if those at the bottom of the hierarchy have these rights and comforts, it means fewer for those at the top. They cling to these rights and comforts by using the powers at their disposal, powers that their privileged position gives only to them — tradition, law, and the military/police. Of these, tradition may be, curiously, the most powerful, for it is the most effective at swaying popular mentality and in creating mobs, almost always conservative in nature. However, the gradually emerging sense has been that justice requires the spread of rights, happiness, and comfort to all, not to a few. The emergence of democracy as the ideal form of government, the elimination of slavery, the emancipation of women, the gifts of science and technology in extending our lives and improving our lives' quality, these are all matters of justice, hard-won through tedious and fatal struggle over the last four centuries. Justice has become a crucial ethical and political issue of the modern era.

Justice has been a central concern of philosophy from the earliest days. For example, in his dialogue "Euthyphro," Plato has Socrates point out that the sources of disagreement are not matters of fact, such as the result of a calculation or the weight of an object, but rather questions of whether an action is just or unjust, good or evil, honorable or dishonorable (433). Several of Plato's dialogues are specifically about the question of whether justice is possible.

Modern secular humanism is equally concerned with matters of justice. These matters focus mainly on balancing the interpersonal level (ethics) and social level (politics) of justice. The sense of justice in secular humanism derives directly from its assertions in other fields, especially the existentialist view of the person conjoined to the naturalist and materialist conclusions about the nature of the universe. Secular humanism relates to justice by stating something about its source, nature, applications, and manifestations.

The Justice of the Universe

Whether we talk about "the universe" or about "nature" or "the world," a consistent philosophical question regards whether the total environment in which living beings find themselves has any property that may be called "justice." Does justice emerge as a product of nature? Is the natural order so arranged as to produce justice?

A discussion of "Voyage of the Damned" (2007) will give access to the question of whether the universe is just. The story involves the spaceliner *Titanic,* on a cruise to orbit Earth and allow rich customers to partake of a little tourism. The ship belongs to the failing corporation owned by Max Capricorn. The captain of the ship has arranged for the *Titanic* to have an accident. He does this because he is dying and he believes that his pension and insurance payout will make his family rich.

The program approaches the question of justice this way: Is it just or fair that circumstances turn out other than as we would wish them to? Even when someone attempts to do "the right thing" as he or she understands it, if circumstances go against that person, then where is the justice? The issue comes up fairly early in the story. The captain justifies destroying the ship because he had been promised that only "old men" would be among the crew. Yet, among the crew is a brand new midshipman, hardly older than 20. This fact pricks at the captain's conscience, but he still goes through with his plan, even shooting the midshipman, though not fatally, to carry out the plan.

The program has a running theme of the rich and snooty versus the ordinary. The waitress Astrid dreams of traveling among the stars and going to exotic planets, and the closest she can come to this dream is to waitress on a cruise liner for those people who can afford such trips without giving the matter much thought. Morvin and Foon Van Hoff are an overweight couple who got their passage on the ship by winning a contest. Ordinarily, they could not afford such a trip. The rich make fun of the Van Hoffs by telling them that dinner was "fancy dress," and then laughing at their costumes. The Earth "expert" Mr. Copper had spent his life as a traveling salesman and defrauded his way into employment on the *Titanic* by pretending to have a degree in "Earthonomics." The society in which these characters live is also coming out of a segregationist period that in general still looks down upon and maltreats cyborgs. It turns out that one of the passengers, the diminutive Bannakaffalatta, is a cyborg. Against these "ordinary folk" are the rich and powerful, represented by obnoxious, self-centered, and greedy Rickston Slade. There is also Max Capricorn himself, ruthless, disdainful of any life that is not his own. Capricorn is the victim himself of prejudice against cyborgs, and is now taking revenge by tanking his own company and killing all life on Earth to do it.

The program very pointedly draws audience sympathy for the "ordinary folk" and against the rich and powerful. When the Doctor mills around the crowd before the ship gets damaged, he immediately latches on to Astrid and the Van Hoffs. The Doctor sympathizes with Astrid's ambitions, and so sneaks her into an outing to transmat to Earth for a brief look around. When he talks to the Van Hoffs and finds out how they were tricked, he uses his sonic screwdriver to pop open a champagne bottle and spray the rude rich guests. Mr. Copper's bumbling and wholly inaccurate accounts of Christmas endear him to both the Doctor and the audience. Through these introductions to the characters, the audience learns to like these characters and want to see good things happen to them.

After the asteroids strike the ship and kill most of the crew and passengers, the Doctor is left with a group consisting of Astrid, Copper, the Van Hoffs, Bannakaffalatta, and Slade. They must make their way through the damaged ship to find safety. Against them are the ship and the robot "hosts," designed to look like angels, which Capricorn had reprogrammed to kill all survivors. Through the journey, the events demonstrate the usefulness and goodness of the ordinary people, and the uselessness and contemptibility of Slade.

For example, through every difficulty, when Slade survives, he considers this a magnificent accomplishment, and wants everyone else to admire that *he* is still alive. He has no useful skill for getting through, relying entirely upon everyone else to do so. He repeatedly makes nasty remarks about the Van Hoffs' size, and recommends leaving them behind. On the other side, the Van Hoffs know robotics, Bannakaffalatta has a power unit that temporarily disables the host robots, Copper knows how to use and recharge such a power unit because he once sold them, and Astrid is constantly ready to help others.

The issue of the justice (or lack of it) in the universe arises when the Doctor rashly promises that he will save all in this group, that none will die. The audience sees the group dwindle as one by one people are killed until only two besides the Doctor remain. The first to go is Morvin Van Hoff, who falls into the ship's nuclear engine. Foon, overcome by grief, assaults the Doctor with his promise: "Bring him back. Doctor, you promised me!" After this, Foon loses interest in living, saying that her life is worthless without her husband. The Doctor tries to convince her to cross a narrow and crumbling bridge by saying that doing so is what Morvin would have wanted, but Foon throws his consolation back at him: "He don't want nothing. He's dead." A little later, Foon will take her own life by plunging after Morvin, but not without taking one of the killer robots with her. The deaths of the Van Hoffs show that justice cannot be assured even by as powerful an authority as the Doctor, that goodness of character is no guarantee against bad things happening.

However, the deaths continue. In using his power pack against the host robots, Bannakaffalatta ensures his own death. This act of self-sacrifice starkly contrasts against Slade's self-centeredness, and it foreshadows the more thematically significant self-sacrifice of Astrid later. As a thematic reminder, Copper responds to Bannakaffalatta's self-sacrifice by calling cyborgs, the underclass of this society, "good people." Astrid's death comes late in the program, when the Doctor has gotten the three remaining passengers to the main level and then goes by himself to find the cause of their troubles. Astrid convinces Midshipman Frame to transport her to where the Doctor is, saying, "He's done everything he can to save us. It's time we did something to save him." And save him she does, but in killing Max Capricorn, she ends up dying herself. The manner of these deaths demonstrates the moral superiority of the "underlings" and the failure of circumstances to turn out the way one would like no matter how "right" what one wants would be and no matter how hard one tries to accomplish it.

The Doctor, however, refuses to accept the truth that he cannot always protect people. He tries to use the teleport system to bring back Astrid, but brings back only a ghost Astrid unaware of anything but the moments before her death. Copper wisely counsels, "Doctor, let her go." Though the injustice of Astrid's death stings, it is not right to subvert what has happened, to reverse the course of events and to force matters to turn out the way one wants.

This leaves only Copper and Slade from the group that started on this trip through the ship after the crash. Slade again proves his ethical myopia when he gushingly thanks the Doctor for saving him and providing the circumstances to make him super-wealthy. Interestingly, Copper pronounces the core thematic statement of the program regarding the issue of justice in the universe: "Of all the people to survive, he's not the one you would have chosen. But if you could choose, Doctor, if you could decide who lives and who dies, that would make you a monster." The statement is important because it shows that even the most broad-minded, intelligent, caring, and ethical person in the universe still does not have perspective enough to determine with absolute surety whose life or whose death would qualify as "justice."

This is not to say that justice cannot be found. A justice of a kind comes at the end when the Doctor takes Copper to Earth to live on a credit card worth one million pounds, instead of leaving him to face the legal justice of ten years in jail for fraud. Since Copper is basically a good man whose "fraud," such as it was, provided entertainment to many and harmed no one, it does at least seem fair that he have a new life in comfortable retirement. Thus, the program opts not for the improbable justice on the cosmic scale, or what could appear to be the simple-minded justice of fairy tales, in which the good are always rewarded and the wicked always punished. Instead, the program opts for the small scale justice, at the level of people's doing what they can to make each others' lives better in a universe overwhelmingly indifferent to their fate.

Justice and the State

Some philosophers have argued that the State is the primary or a major source of justice. Plato provides some justifications for this idea in "Crito." As Plato sees it, the state is the larger entity than the individual, and therefore is the entity with more rights. G.W.F. Hegel argues that "the state is the actuality of the ethical idea." This is so, according to Hegel, because the state is "absolutely rational," being "the actuality of the substantial will," a consciousness raised to "universality." The state is the "unmoved end in itself, in which freedom comes to its supreme right." Therefore, according to Hegel, "the final end has supreme right against the individual, whose supreme duty is to be a member of the state" (155–6).

Plato makes more exact arguments than Hegel in the matter of the relationship between the state and the individual. In the dialogue "Crito," Plato has Socrates argue that the state provides the means for a person's existence, and as such the individual is not on equal terms with the state, and is dependent upon the state, and as such must abide by the state's judgment even when that judgment appears to be wrong. In the contract between the state and the individual, the individual has no right to go against the laws and rules of the state, for to do so would weaken the state and cause it to fall apart, thus depriving the good life to other citizens dependent upon the state (480–1).

In *Doctor Who*, particular episodes provide evidence to contest the idea of state-originated justice. In particular, the episodes question the idea that the state occupies a superior position than the individual, and that justice arises from this superior position. An episode from "The Keys of Marinus" (1964) demonstrates fundamental ideas of how state justice systems operate. The Doctor's companion, Ian, has wrongly been charged with murder in the city of Millenius. When talking to the investigator, Ian insists upon a guiding principal of justice in recent Western societies, that the burden is upon the state to prove that an accused person actually did the deed for which he or she is accused. However, in this society the situation is reversed, and the accused bears sole responsibility for proving his or her innocence "beyond a shadow of a doubt." Ian has already been found guilty and sentenced to death merely because he has been charged with the crime. During the trial for this crime, the Doctor manages to flush out the guilty man, who is then killed in court before he can reveal his accomplices. This evidence, instead of exonerating Ian, simply makes Ian appear guiltier in the eyes of the justices because it is possible that the perpetrator was going to name Ian as an accomplice.

The system under discussion here is meant to strike the viewer as fundamentally wrong. It appears that under these conditions, justice could not possibly be served. Why should this be so? The average viewer may not think about the matter much more than to acknowledge the feeling that this system is grossly unfair. However, it is worth thinking through why this system appears contrary to justice.

A justice system is always an arm of the state. The entire legal apparatus, from police and investigators to prosecutors and judges, belongs to and represents the state. The positions of Plato and Hegel would be that these official representatives of the state execute or ought to execute the perfect, or at least far superior, will of the state. Therefore, where corrupt officials have not tainted the system, it should successfully produce just results. However, the powers of the judicial arm may significantly vary. In Millenius, the Chief Prosecutor turns out to be corrupt, using the system for his own ends. The system itself is weak, so that none within it are able to spot the corruption.

It takes the outsiders, the Doctor's companions, to work out the truly guilty party. The system can be corrupted and the officials can be fooled because they all presume the infallibility of the system.

Another area where the state often fails to be the superior to the individual sense of justice is in the assumptions that lie behind a state's justice system. For example, the presumption of innocence or presumption of guilt as a first principle differentiates the power that the judicial side of government may have. However, the presumption of innocence, which Ian takes for granted, is in fact a relatively new concept, historically speaking. It is still accepted primarily in Western technological democracies, but is not global. Through most of history and still in most of the world, being arrested proves guilt. Since the state clearly has more *power* than most individuals, the "presumed guilty" principle certainly ensures miscarriages of justice. The presumption of guilt makes it nearly impossible for those in power to imagine the possibility of their being wrong. It is also possible that those philosophers who argue for the perfection of the state are mistaking power for perfection.

The question is about how much power the judicial arm of the state actually has. A powerful judicial arm is almost always subservient to the needs and nature of the state. The powerful judiciary has its power mainly over the people, and mostly does the work of justifying executive actions. In "The Keys of Marinus," the city of Millenius does not seem to be a grinding, totalitarian state. The judges in Ian's case are adjudicating fairly, according to the state's laws. Clearly, though, the concept of rights does not extend nearly as far in Millenius as it does in Great Britain. Millenius seems to operate with a relatively benevolent form of heavy-handed social control. Nevertheless, even in this system executing the wrongly accused becomes an all-too-easy and likely occurrence.

The example in "Keys of Marinus" helps demonstrate the flaws in Platonic and Hegelian thinking regarding the relationship between justice and the state. Perhaps theoretically the "state" as concept is a perfect expression of will and will always be ethically superior to an individual person, but no state is ideal. The humanist position taken by *Doctor Who* is that justice ought to be grounded in the natural and material experience of living people.

Furthermore, states cannot be the sole or even primary source of justice since no state has yet managed to distribute equitably powers, privileges, or properties. Contrary to what Hegel says, the state is not "mind objectified" (156), but is exactly what he claims it is not, which is "civil society." As such, the state is not universal will, but collective will. Humanists recognize that collective will is a *natural*, not metaphysical entity, and so at best exists in a conditional and shaky equilibrium. Because it is a natural entity arising from a material collective, the state is naturally flawed, easily capable of producing genuine evil.

Another factor weighing against the idea that the state is the primary source of justice is the state's role in distributing powers, privileges, and properties. According to the English novelist John Fowles, the evil of a social system is not that someone has attained happiness while someone else has not. It is "special personal privilege springing from unjust social privilege" (67), an argument that accords strongly with Martin Luther King, Jr.'s theory about what makes a law unjust. King states that an unjust law is "*difference made legal.*" He also defines an unjust law as "a code that a numerical or power majority group compels a minority group to obey but does not make binding on itself" (179). Though King does not expressly say so, he does strongly imply that where one sees a clearly unjust law operating, one has a moral obligation to defy that law. He states that "an individual who breaks a law that conscience tells him is unjust, and who willingly accepts the penalty of imprisonment in order to arouse the conscience of the community over its injustice, is in reality expressing the highest respect for law" (180). The principle source of injustice that justifies breaking the law is unequal distribution of powers and privileges.

The situation of unequal distribution is common in *Doctor Who*, and often expressly stated. One must recognize that concentrations of powers and privileges often accompany concentrations of material wealth. One of the rebels in "Vengeance on Varos" (1985) states how the ruling elite enjoy power and luxury while the rest toil for lower than living wages. A similar situation exists in "Monster of Peladon" (1974), where the miners get barely enough to eat, but the aristocrats have all the say in what happens to them. In "The Sun Makers" (1977), the head of state declares that only "grinding oppression of the masses" provides "dividends."

So, to the Valeyard's charge in "The Trial of a Timelord" that the Doctor regularly defies established authority, one can say that the Doctor acts by his conscience when faced with unjust laws. The Doctor may foment rebellion, as in "The Sun Makers," or break the power of a ruling elite, as in "The Savages" (1966), or topple governments, as in "The Happiness Patrol" (1988). In all cases, though, he does so because those in power are perpetrating gross injustices and instituting unjust laws to make what they do "legal," though not moral and therefore not just. The Doctor acts out Karl Popper's pronouncement that "no shadow of a doubt must be left that the only aim of the resistance is to save democracy" (*Open II* 152). The person who resists tyranny is not an outlaw because "a government which attempts to misuse its powers and to establish itself as a tyranny (or which tolerates the establishment of a tyranny by anybody else) outlaws itself" (*Open II* 152).

Therefore, because the state as a material collective cannot be a perfect expression of will, and because the state is susceptible to fallibility and corruption, the state cannot be the primary source for justice. At best, the state preserves, administers, and distributes justice, but its effectiveness is always conditioned on the goodness of the people running its justice system and the arrangement of that system. *Doctor Who* repeatedly demonstrates that when the state oversteps its limits and uses the justice system for some purpose other than carrying out justice, then the justice system and perhaps even the state itself need correcting.

Rights

The universe does not provide a clear system of rules for justice. The state by itself cannot provide such a system. Nevertheless, both the material universe and the state do have some input into the sense of justice and the system of justice. A third source for both the sense and system of justice is the recognition of rights. Central to a modern, Enlightenment, humanist conception of justice is the idea of rights, in particular human rights.

When someone provides a label "human rights," one usually thinks of the label as naming a thing that can be possessed or a property inherent in something. Thus, human rights are most often thought of as something people have. Sidney Hook, building on the theories of John Dewey, debunks this notion of rights as possessions or attributes. Hook writes, "Morally justifiable claims are *proposals* to treat human beings in certain ways." Given this premise, one can see that human rights are "courses of action" that governments and power holders follow. So, by this definition, the correct way to look at human rights is that a person *should be treated with dignity.* The incorrect way is to assume an "inherent dignity" that places human needs and desires above all others (Hook 28).

Hook's definition of human rights fits well with the Enlightenment, humanist, and existentialist outlooks prevalent in *Doctor Who.* The Doctor is a hero of Enlightenment values. He is a champion of rights, not of the tribe or nation, as the heroes of ancient and propagandistic literature tend to be. The Doctor's "good" derives from the notion that all sentient and intelligent persons (human or alien, which is to say quasi-human) deserve the same standard of treatment based upon the rights that existing gives them. Thus, as Hook points out, membership in the human species is not the prerequisite for being treated with the dignity that we call "human rights." Rather, the compelling reason for observing human rights is that one "is a creature capable of suffering" (Hook 28).[1] This is precisely the point of view expressed in *Doctor Who* both in words and in actions.

The fundamental difference between the *proposal theory* of human rights and the *property theory* of human rights[2] is that the latter presupposes that, like any property, human rights can be had, traded, bought, sold, denied, and reassigned. The property theory of human rights is essentially antithetical to human dignity rather than affirmative of it because the theory inherently suggests that some people have no rights if others have some rights. This rights economy, as it were, when moved to the level of government inevitably produces tyranny and totalitarianism, since those in power gather up all the rights for themselves to own. As we have repeatedly seen, in *Doctor Who* evil is the imposition of one will upon others without regard for the consequences to those others. Evil is, then, in the *Doctor Who* conception, the habit of mind that establishes a rights economy, that says, "I have more rights than you," or "My rights are more valuable than yours." Furthermore, *Doctor Who* shows how such thinking leads to disregard for the dignity of others. The egotistical person with power hoards and distributes rights as a Dark Ages king hoards and distributes treasure. The disregard the typical *Doctor Who* villain displays for the dignity and well-being of others exemplifies their "rights economy" state of mind.

The proposal theory denies the idea of rights as existing in an economy. Instead of rights being determined by who does or does not have them, rights are determined by consideration of the *consequences* of one's actions (Hook 29). Weighing consequences in the balance means that certain considerations, not principles, come first. One such is the Utilitarian consideration mentioned in Chapter 9, that one should consider which action produces the greatest good for the greatest number. Alternatively worded, this might be the consideration of which action produces the greatest amount of overall happiness (recognizing that one cannot please everyone all the time). Or, one may look at consequences in terms of Karl Popper's alternative utilitarianism, seeking that action which produces the least harm and suffering or reduces harm and suffering the most. In all cases, the question is not what will obtain a preexisting standard of equality that might never be met anyway, but what will obtain the best balance of overall good *in the given circumstances*.

It may be said that the Doctor, in deciding that one or the other agent has overstepped the bounds of behavior and so needs correction or punishment (even capital punishment), acts against the principles of the proposal theory of human rights. The argument might be that the proposal theory requires as a starting point the idea of equal treatment for all as a foundation for determining moral action or gaining justice. Hook, however, points out that the concept of equal treatment also implies the covalent opposite concept of equal *mistreatment* (29). Furthermore, a starting principle such as equal treatment for all requires a disregard for *consequences*. It presupposes that the balancing needed to achieve justice be done *before* the action one takes and regardless of the result. As long as everyone is treated equally first, so the thinking goes, all will be well. It is clear, though, that such a position denies fundamental facts, such as conflicting desires, interests, and beliefs that go into creating human society. The truth of the matter is that the same action will not produce the same result or the same level of justice regardless of the circumstances in which one applies it. Human happiness and welfare, i.e., concerns for what happens *after* one's actions, ought to come into consideration. As Hook argues, "What will produce the acceptable balance of happiness and justice sometimes may depend upon our disregarding the facts of equality" (29). We return to the idea that justice comes when a course of action produces the best overall good possible in the given circumstances. Moreover, a proposal theory of rights leads to the conclusion that justice be determined on a case by case basis.

Thus, the Doctor's uneven hand of justice is actually the morally superior position to an unthinking, predetermined level of "equality." This idea is especially true when one is dealing with those who absolutely refuse to recognize the rights of others, such as Daleks, Cybermen, the Master, and the great horde of villains that populate the *Doctor Who* universe. The dangers in the Universe come from those who would deny the rights of others in favor of their own, and these tyrants must be stopped if justice is the goal. This inevitably means that the tyrants' happiness (as measured by satisfaction from success) must be opposed when it depends upon denial of the happiness of others. If the tyrant's goal is denial of other's rights and the tyrant will not relent, then achieving justice may require that someone stop this tyrant even at the cost of the tyrant's welfare or life. The responsibility for these deaths rests with the tyrants, who could have chosen another way, not with the Doctor, who protects those whose rights are and continue to be denied and abused. *Doctor Who* enacts on a grand scale in quasi-mythical terms, which is to say the method of narrative, the conflicts of justice that happen on a small scale every day.

The Nature of Justice

One of the earliest philosophical considerations of justice is Plato's *The Republic*.[3] In this dialogue, in typical fashion, Plato's mouthpiece Socrates considers and then rejects several definitions of "justice" before settling on a definition. The main argument is that the several definitions proposed leave room for exceptions, and thus cannot be true definitions. A true definition of justice would fit all cases to which it could apply. For that reason, Socrates rejects the definition that justice is "to speak the truth and pay one's debts"

(13), "the art which gives good to friends and evil to enemies" (14), "to do good to the just and harm to the unjust" (17), and "the interest of the stronger" (21).

As one can see, in _The Republic_ Plato takes up many of the most common arguments made regarding the nature of justice, and considers each in some detail. Plato's dialogues work through the particular philosophical schools and viewpoints known in his time. Socrates takes the role of true philosophy and through him the reader sees Plato's ideas on the subject. In _The Republic_, Thrasymachus takes up the position that might makes right, arguing that justice is "the interest of the stronger." Glaucon takes the position that justice is action forced upon people in particular circumstances and not through the desire to be just or to do good. Adeimantus, Glaucon's brother, takes the stand that people act justly only because they are taught that justice is rewarded in the eternal afterlife and injustice is punished in the eternal afterlife. Thus, as Adeimantus sees it, people act justly to earn the reward and to avoid the punishment, and not through the desire to be just. Both Glaucon and Adeimantus agree that justice is a burden, not a delight, and that it is more often true that the unjust are rewarded in this life, while the just are punished or neglected. The brothers argue that it is best to contrive to appear just while doing injustice, and in this way be heaped with praise and reward.

As Plato states it through Socrates, "The injuring of another can in no case be just," because an injury, whether delivered to a friend or a foe, deteriorates "the proper virtue of man" (18–9). The statement might appear as a kind of preview of Sidney Hook's proposal theory of justice. However, Plato does not take the matter farther and does not arrive at Hook's conclusions. The statement also succinctly characterizes the reasoning for the Doctor's pacifism. One constant of _Doctor Who_ is the extent to which the Doctor will go not to injure others, even when he or his friends are being threatened. Sometimes, he must give up this position and do harm, but he reaches the point when all other options are exhausted. Therefore, _Doctor Who_ supplies a modification of Plato's rule, that injuring another cannot be just unless it be a last resort to prevent a greater injury. This modification fits the humanist case-based view of justice.

Plato defines not only "justice," but also "injustice." Through Socrates he notes that "wherever [injustice] takes up her abode, whether in a city, in an army, in a family, or in any other body, that body is, to begin with, incapable of united action by reason of sedition and distraction" (37). He further argues that injustice is "fatal" in a single person because it renders that person "incapable of action because he is not at unity with himself" (37).

Socrates argues that "injustice creates divisions and hatreds and fighting, and justice imparts harmony and friendship" (36). Looked at another way, one could say that divisions, hatreds, and fighting are evidence of injustice, while harmony and friendship are evidence of justice. This latter formulation is more in keeping with the matter as *Doctor Who* presents it. What makes the villains villainous is the amount of division, hatred, and fighting that they cause. The villains enact injustices. On the other hand, the Doctor and other good characters are good because they promote harmony and friendship.

Plato, through Socrates, argues that at least one concept of justice is "having and doing what is a man's own, and belongs to him" (124). The statement involves more than at first it seems to. By "what is a man's own," Plato means that people should be doing what they are best suited to do by birth and not some other thing. Thus, the one who is naturally inclined toward farming should be a farmer, the one naturally inclined to music should be a musician, the one naturally inclined to lead should be a leader. As Plato conceives it, the state will determine for each person what he or she is inclined to be, since the state is in theory an impartial higher consciousness than its individual citizens. Therefore, justice also involves not being a "busybody." Everyone should mind his or her own business as determined by the state. As one can infer, at the center of Plato's conception of justice is the good of the state, under the assumption that if the state operates justly, then everyone in it will be content. Plato decides that the greatest form of evil doing to one's own city is the essence of injustice (124).

Finally, after many long digressions, Socrates comes around to determining that justice involves heavenly rewards and punishments in the afterlife, agreeing in principle with Adeimantus. While in this life it appears that the unjust can reap rewards from wickedness, in the afterlife they will suffer ten times that which they inflicted in life (310). He concludes with the idea that the threat of punishment is what makes people behave (316). One can see from these conclusions why Plato prefers an authoritarian state over a democratic one, since democracy does not provide the necessary discipline to keep the body politic well behaved. Similarly, in personal matters one must be one's own authoritarian master, pursuing bodily health and banishing the falsehoods of poetry and tragedy.

In Plato's *Republic* lie the primary arguments for one of the contending definitions of justice. Plato's is a rule-based conception of justice, and his dialogues present an intellectual search for absolute rules that determine the justice of actions. Plato's concern is law and order, but principally order. Justice for him is that which produces the least amount of change in society. Since his concern is always the larger entity (the city, the society, the state), individual rights have little meaning to him. Additionally, it is clear that the logical conclusion of Plato's thinking is mainly to ignore injustices in the physical world, since in his mind they are of little consequence. Only what happens to the eternal and incorruptible soul matters to Plato.

Clearly, as we have seen in the previous chapters, the worldview presented in *Doctor Who* flatly contradicts many of Plato's ideas. As a humanist and existentialist drama, *Doctor Who* demonstrates that justice is always a matter of the here and now, a matter of concern for the material happiness and well-being of people, and not a matter to be put off into some afterlife that may or may not exist. Furthermore, justice at the state level involves that system that will best distribute the means for the well-being of the people. Democracy, imperfect as it is, is the best governmental system for attaining that end.

Plato's words in "Crito" are more direct than in *The Republic* about duty to the state, and they are chilling to anyone who holds to the liberal and individualistic philosophy of humanism. He argues that the state is "more to be valued and higher and holier far than mother or father or any ancestor, and more to be regarded in the eyes of the gods and of men of understanding." He further claims that the state "is to be soothed, and gently and reverently entreated when angry, even more than a father, and if not persuaded, obeyed" (481).

Chapter 10 of this book showed that *Doctor Who* presents a different view of the state and its ability to produce justice, a point reiterated above. From the humanist viewpoint, the state must be regarded skeptically. Only certain kinds of state arrangements can allow for a majority to have the opportunity to make a good life. In *Doctor Who*, the state is not an assured source of justice. Neither is obedience to the state inherently characteristic of justice. The state provides justice only when those in charge are monitored and their power for mischief limited.

The contending conceptions of justice provide a continuous source of tension in *Doctor Who*. Consistently, characters are presented with the alternatives of benefiting the social system or protecting the individual. We can call these "the numbers argument" and "the example argument." The numbers argument is the utilitarian one: the greatest good for the greatest number. The example argument is that each moment is unique, each action has repercussions, and each action a person takes stands as an example to humanity and a definition of humanity. It is the humanist argument that individual rights are more important than the abstract good of an abstract populace.

An example of the contest between the two beliefs comes in "The Vampires of Venice" (2010). Rosanna Calvierri is the mother to an alien piscine people who have fled a planetary catstrophe. Arriving on Earth, the Saturnyne arrange to convert young women of Venice into proper mates for the male Saturnyne survivors and to plunge the rest of Venice under water so that the Saturnyne may have a new home. As the Doctor tries to prevent the Saturnyne plan, Rosanna takes the numbers argument, stating that one city's death for an entire race's survival is a just trade-off. The Doctor takes the example argument, stating that he would sympathize with Rosanna except that she could not remember the name of a girl she executed. The Doctor's statement implies that the issue of "humanity" in the broad sense has relevance in even this situation. Rosanna's disregard for the humans she kills suggests an "ends justifies the means" perspective, implying that she did not even attempt to think of alternative and less harmful ways to get the justice she seeks.

The poet Percy Bysshe Shelley says, "This, and no other, is justice:— to consider, under all the circumstances and consequences of a particular case, how the greatest quantity and purest quality of happiness will ensue from any action" (8). We have seen in the previous chapter that a definition such as this may seem well intentioned and yet produce its opposite. "The Happiness Patrol" shows that the attempt to maximize happiness can result in patronizing and bullying on the basis that one person "knows" what is good for another.

The modern humanist conception of justice is that it must take into account the dignity, what is popularly thought of as the "humanity," of those involved in situations requiring justice. The English novelist John Fowles' argues that a fully humanist conception of justice on the broad scale starts from the realization of death's finality. Once a person becomes convinced that this life is the only house he or she will have, that person will immediately set about making the house as habitable as possible (39). This is the contemporary situation, the existential starting point of humanist thought. Justice in the existential world is the process of making life habitable to as many people as possible. The more habitable it is for others, the more habitable it is for oneself. Fowles accords with the sense of justice that *Doctor Who* usually demonstrates. In Chapter 3, we discussed how The Doctor acts from the assumption of death's finality. The Doctor constantly works from the assumption that "getting along" is almost always the best option not just for dealing with contending rights claims, but for sometimes preventing the contention as well. The central idea behind these actions is that making life habitable for all benefits all, which is where Utilitarianism fits in. However, the utilitarian position does not have primacy; it may simply happen that in a particular case, the utilitarian rule is the best for making a just choice. The humanist position is that in situations when life is at stake, the determination of justice must come from intelligent reflection upon the particulars of the case, so as to produce the best possible outcome.

Distributing Justice

One way to think of justice is as a system of delivering rewards and punishments. These rewards and punishments are distributed based upon whether and how a person exceeds, meets, or violates a social rule regarding treatment of others. Justice is concerned with what people *have done*, not what they will do or might do. Additionally, modern ideas of justice focus on the actions of individuals; *mass punishment* violates commonly held standards of justice by being unfair, punishing those who do right to pressure those who do wrong. *Mass reward* would also be regarded as unfair on similar grounds, rewarding those who do not excel for the actions of those who do; however, most people regard mass reward as a tolerable violation of justice. The concept of justice rests upon clear principles for determining right and wrong (Thiroux and Krasemann 124–5). One can divide the theories of how to distribute justice as Retribution (distribution of rewards and punishments based upon what people deserve), Utility (distribution of rewards and punishments based upon results), Fairness (distribution of rewards and punishments based upon equal personhood), and Restoration (distribution of rewards and punishments to compensate for victims).

Perhaps the best modern theory of justice regarding how it should be administered is that formulated by the American twentieth-century philosopher John Rawls. His is certainly the best for enlightenment on how justice gets distributed in *Doctor Who*. Rawls calls his theory of distributive justice "justice as fairness." This requires as a starting point for justice a "veil of ignorance" (Thiroux and Krasemann 133), or what Rawls calls the "original position." In other words, the principles of justice should be derived without any regard for any person's particular social status or individual talents. Such an original position would ensure justice for all by regarding neutrally both individuals and society.

In *Doctor Who*, the veil of ignorance certainly operates as a principle. The Doctor does most often work from the position that social status and particular ability are not matters of concern for distributing justice. As the Doctor practices it, the "original position" gets used most often when he makes a new encounter. Although in its pure sense, the original position should apply equally to all, when the Doctor encounters long-standing enemies, such as the Daleks, he naturally finds it hard to operate under a veil of ignorance since such a veil would be pure pretense. Even in these cases, though, the Doctor will still be open to a chance for change. "Evolution of the Daleks" (2007) shows the Doctor setting up to deal with a deadly group of Daleks, but asking for them to change their plans and offering them mercy and help, then setting his plan into action only after the Daleks refuse the offer. This is but one of several similar scenes in *Doctor Who*. The pause before delivering the restorative, often deadly, act demonstrates recourse to Rawls's original position. The Doctor allows for the possibility that a Dalek is not always "Dalek" as he defines it, that even the most evil of minds is capable of thinking outside the defining parameter of "evil."

Rawls identifies two "moral powers": people's "capacity for a sense of justice and their capacity for a conception of the good" (xii). Rawls argues that a just society provides the conditions for people to develop adequately their two moral powers. Such a society allows people to apply their sense of justice and their "powers of practical reason" (xii). Such a society offers what Rawls calls "equal political liberties," which include "freedom of thought, liberty of conscience, and freedom of association" (xii).

Several chapters of this book have discussed the matters of people's moral powers and the possibility for a just society. These earlier chapters explained that in *Doctor Who*, the application of practical reason, what is more commonly called "critical thinking," is necessary for determining proper action in most areas of life. Only through the capacity for practical reason, the application of critical thinking skills, can one approach an understanding of what the "good" might be. Similarly, the *Doctor Who* position on what makes a good society lands in favor of an open, democratic society that allows for just those freedoms and liberties that Rawls values.

According to Rawls, "Justice is the first virtue of social institutions" (3). Rawls' concept of justice runs counter to basic utilitarianism, which argues that justice is the result of actions that produce the greatest good for the greatest number. Rawls argues, instead, that justice "does not allow that the sacrifices imposed on a few are outweighed by the larger sum of advantages enjoyed by many" (3). Rawls' idea of social justice, instead, is like his "original position," a zero point applied to all within the society. Rawls calls this idea the "Equality Principle," that everyone in a society gets the maximum amount of possible liberty and that there is no imbalance in liberty, at least as a starting point. For Rawls, the only occasion for tolerating an injustice is when "it is necessary to avoid an even greater injustice" (4). Similarly, an inequality in society should exist only when the inequality is to everyone's benefit (Thiroux and Krasemann 133). The example Thiroux and Krasemann give is of doctors. These professionals receive higher pay than average workers because they make greater sacrifices to achieve their specialized knowledge and ability, plus what they do with that knowledge benefits society as a whole. The inequality is just, though, only if everyone has an equal opportunity to the necessary education. The principle of permissible, limited inequality Rawls calls the "Difference Principle."

Earlier discussions of ethical and political matters in *Doctor Who* arrived at similar conclusions to Rawls'. Normally in *Doctor Who*, the example is by way of the negative. One sees the equality principle and difference principle in action through seeing their contraries. An unjust society in *Doctor Who* is one that makes *difference* a principle of law. Imbalance in such a society means that those with "more" do not give back to the society that lets them have more. Instead, imbalance in these societies is a vicious circle in which the imbalance delivers power, which is then used to maintain or increase the imbalance at the expense of those who have "less."

As one cans see, for Rawls justice is a matter of society, "the way in which the major social institutions distribute fundamental rights and duties and determine the division of advantages from social institutions" (6). Rawls contends that "the justice of a social scheme depends essentially on how fundamental rights and duties are assigned and on the economic opportunities and social conditions in the various sectors of society" (7). Justice pertains to the political arrangement or type of society. Some arrangements cannot produce justice because they are inherently unbalanced. If Rawls' theories are true, dictatorships can never be just societies nor can they ever be benevolent, because the society itself is founded upon imbalance and runs to preserve the imbalance. Democracies afford the best opportunity for providing the political apparatus that would make social justice possible.

Again, one can see Rawls' principles in *Doctor Who* through the many negative examples. The society of "The Savages" is unjust because the Elders enjoy nearly all the rights and duties a society can possibly give, while the exploited Savages have no rights, and their sole duty is to sacrifice against their wills their bodily energy to the Elders. The society of "The Sun Makers" is unjust because all wealth and political power are concentrated and distributed to a very few at the "top" of society, and everyone else must work to maintain the imbalance, mostly to the detriment of everyone else.

An important component of the kind of justice that Rawls and others with similar views imagine is that justice is tied to *fairness*. The focus on balanced distribution of rights, privileges, and opportunities derives from the principle of fairness. This principle derives from an inherent sense of justice that most people have. According to Rawls, the determination of justice comes in part from matching the sense of justice with systematic, clearly expressed principles of justice (41). By *sense* of justice, Rawls means intuition about what justice is, plus the idea that justice "makes sense" in the common use of the phrase. Principles of justice, on the other hand, derive from applied conscientious and intelligent application of a person's beliefs and knowledge of a situation calling for justice. The political system is the framework in which individuals can apply their sense of justice through using their intelligent reasoning. The more just a society is, the more it allows individual people to use their own reasoning to determine justice and the less it tells them or mandates what justice is.

Justice as it works in *Doctor Who* most often corresponds to the idea that the primary component of justice is fairness. Why does the Doctor immediately side with the Van Hoffs in "Voyage of the Damned"? Their humiliation derives from the unfair distribution of power that money creates; the rich can scoff at them and feel no remorse for treating others as though they have no dignity. Additionally, the Doctor repeatedly stands against those who use power to take from others without permission. When the Doctor sets about toppling a government, it is because that government has lost its sense of justice and has institutionalized unfairness as a norm.

Justice as fairness involves not just the duties a government owes its society, but also the duties that people owe to their society and to each other. Rawls states, "No moral requirements follow from the existence of institutions alone" (306). He argues that within a well-ordered society there are certain "natural duties." In other words, Rawls proposes a modified version of Kant's deontological ethics. These duties include the duties of helping another in need, of not harming or injuring others, of not causing unnecessary suffering (98). These are *natural* duties because they apply regardless of "voluntary acts" and without requiring connections to social institutions and practices, and thus "they obtain between all as equal moral persons" (98–9). The natural duties fit within an ordered (hence largely just) society as a tacit contract. In this sense, Rawls ties justice to the "social contract" derived in Enlightenment philosophy and explained in Chapter 10 of this book.[4] Furthermore, the triad of helping another in need, of not harming or injuring others, and of not causing unnecessary suffering succinctly summarizes the sense of justice that the Doctor displays.

To summarize, *Doctor Who* regularly displays the sense of justice which philosopher John Rawls has called "justice as fairness." This sense of justice operates at both the social-political level and the personal-ethical level. Rawls states that justice "shows itself" in two ways. One is the willing participation in just institutions that both apply to and benefit a person and his or her associates. The willingness indicates the justice of the institution (415). A contrary implication is that the willingness of many people to throw off what would seem to be their obligations within an institution indicates the existence of injustice within the institution. In other words, in a story such as "The Sun Makers" or "State of Decay," the existence of resistance to the institution, especially of those desiring complete overthrow of the institution, indicates the level of injustice in the system. If injustice did not exist, there would be no reason to rebel because no one's sense of justice had been compromised. The second way that justice shows itself is in the willingness of the members of a society to work for, or at least not against, a just institution (415). The institutions provide the opportunity for justice to happen by operating as though blind to such matters as social position and innate ability; everyone in a just society is presumed to start with the same properties — personal dignity, an innate sense of justice, and a basic set of human rights. Justice is administered fairly when the administration of justice does not take away or detract from personal dignity, the sense of justice, and basic human rights.

Crime

There is no doubt of the intimate relationship between the concept "justice" and the concept "crime." Modern culture is caught between two extreme ideas about the nature of crime, as the muddled legal codes demonstrate. Fowles describes the dichotomy: "One is that all criminals have complete free will; the other is that they have none" (160). The law generally operates on the first view, while advocates of social justice generally argue for the second view. Therefore, Fowles is among those who believe that law is separate from justice. The law dictates specific punishments meted under the notion that the criminal should have known better. The law rarely takes into account the factors that led the perpetrator to commit the crime, such as poor education, poverty, heredity, and upbringing. Thus the law acts as a kind of deterrent, and a not very effective one. The law is therefore inhumane by applying punishment rather than cure (Fowles 160–1). According to Fowles, "In a truly just world, culpability would clearly be a scientific, not a moral, calculation" (161). The scientific execution of justice would focus on curing criminals of those factors that pushed them into crime. "No society is innocent of the crimes committed in it" (161).

However, Fowles argues, modern society does not attempt the scientific cure because of its members' emotional attachments to the outmoded ideas of "sin" and "crime." These two terms, originally deriving from different sources, the first from Christianity and the second from Greco-Roman law, have become synonymous and derive from the flawed idea that "an evil deed can be paid for" (161–2). Yet, it is clear that this never amounts to justice, not even in the limited sense of equity. Here, Fowles agrees with Shelley, who says, "The emptiness and folly of retaliation are apparent from every example which can be brought forward" (12).

The humanist sense of justice as it relates to crime, then, is not retaliatory. Neither is it automatically restorative. Instead, it starts from the recognition that crime often has more than one cause. There is the character of the criminal, but also the character of the society. Distributing justice, then, depends upon determining and managing both the personal and social factors that led to the crime.

Doctor Who generally takes the multiple cause point of view regarding crime. An example in "The Trial of a Timelord: The Mysterious Planet" (1986) can set the terms of the issue in this conversation. The Valeyard states that the Doctor's crime was "being there," referring to the Doctor's violation of the Timelords' "cardinal rule" of noninterference in the affairs of other worlds. The Valeyard as prosecutor takes a legalistic position here; the law says it is wrong and, therefore, it is wrong. The legalistic position is that any transgression of the law is a crime by definition, and there are no mitigating circumstances such as the nature of the person committing the crime, the nature of the society, or the nature of the law itself.

Unfortunately, the confused writing of the trial portion of "The Trial of a Timelord" insufficiently portrays the issues, positing two weak defenses for the Doctor's crime of interference. One, stated twice (in "The Mysterious Planet" and "Terror of the Vervoids") is that the Doctor's interference was requested, and the other is that the trial itself was corrupt and thereby invalid. Crimes are matters of specific instances, and justice systems usually take each instance as a "count." Thus, a person is tried and punished for a single crime or for multiple instances of the same kind of crime. This fact of trial proceedings is why the Doctor's defense of being requested to help is invalid. While in some instances he is requested, and therefore not guilty of interference, in other instances his presence is not requested, and so legally he is guilty in those instances. That the trial is corrupt invalidates only that specific trial proceeding. It does not invalidate the charges nor the arguments presented against the defendant.

The trial portion of "The Trial of a Timelord" fails to tackle the legalistic position that the Valeyard states and that both he and the Inquisitor represent. The legalistic position is a definitional argument. The law defines particular kinds of acts as crimes. By this reasoning, any violation of the law is criminal and any violator of the law is subject to punishment. The weakness of the legalistic position is that it never questions the validity of a law. For the legalist, the existence of the law is its own justification. As discussed earlier in this chapter and in other chapters in this book, however, laws are not always ethical, nor do they always accord with the sense of justice. There are unjust laws, and from a humanist perspective, it is not a crime to break an unjust law. The obvious question, then, is whether the Timelord law of noninterference is an unjust law. To answer this question, the considerations are these: (a) the rationale for the law, (b) the soundness of that rationale, and (c) the influence of other relevant factors.

The rationale of noninterference law is a fear of the misuse of power. Its origin, according to the Doctor in "Underworld" (1978), is in the Timelord involvement in the affairs of the planet Minyos. When the Timelords arrived, the Minyans thought of them as gods. The Timelords then gave the Minyans technological aid, i.e., some of their "godly" powers, which led the Minyans to force the Timelords off Minyos. The Minyans then used their new technology to start a world war that destroyed the planet. It is further implied in various *Doctor Who* stories that the noninterference law exists to prevent Timelords from abusing the power that technological superiority gives them.

The noninterference rule, therefore, appears justified on the basis of its rationale. It exists to prevent abuses and protect others. Its soundness, though, is weak when it is applied as an absolute rule binding upon all Timelords in all circumstances. If a Timelord can *never* interfere, then this means that the Timelord must stand aside and allow any and all cruelties and injustices to proceed. The absolute application of the law prevents a Timelord from using his or her personal sense of justice. The law if applied absolutely sets the state in the position of moral superiority; it implies that the state knows better than the individual what is right. As discussed in Chapter 10, the argument of the state's moral superiority is absurd. The state is never morally better than the people who are running it. Law is simply a tool, and so can be misused as easily as it can be used. The corrupted trial of "The Trial of a Timelord" shows this fact. The trial itself turned out to be a tool of the state, a way of silencing the Doctor who had accidentally discovered a crime the Timelord government itself had committed. Even so, if the motivation for the trial were true and merely to see that justice was served, the trial would still not achieve justice. A law that allows for no exception or admits to no mitigation cannot be just because it denies the free will and rational judgment of the individual and ignores causative and mitigating factors.

The free will and rational judgment of the individual are among the relevant factors that ought to be taken into account beyond the mere definition of the law. If law is to achieve justice, then its application must involve all the relevant facts of the case. The most important factor is whether the injustice of violating the law prevents an even greater injustice. The noninterference law requires a Timelord to stand by and watch injustice happen, or to leave and let it happen. In either case, if the Timelord has the chance and ability to prevent the injustice, correct the imbalance causing the injustice, or reduce the effects of the injustice, which is the greater crime, to walk away from an ongoing injustice or to violate the noninterference law?

In the case of the Doctor and his adventures, the answer is that where one can make a difference for the good, one ought to. The noninterference law is good as a general rule, preventing abuses and avoiding harmful interference where none is needed. The humanist perspective on law that follows along the lines of Rawls' theory of justice as fairness thinks of all laws in a similar fashion: good as general rules, usually correct to obey, but not binding when violating the law prevents or reduces a greater injustice. The *Doctor Who* position is that "crime" is not simply a matter of definition.

Retribution

Though Plato in general does not adhere to humanist principles of justice, in at least one instance he does. In the dialogue "Crito," a day or two before his execution Socrates states that the notion of rendering evil for evil is never right (479–80). If punishment is merely a matter of doing harm because another has done harm, then it is useless. Furthermore, it places the punisher in the position of the criminal, visiting degradation upon another. Nevertheless, crimes cannot be allowed to go without some kind of punishment. The problem is that punishment is really not simply a matter of plain retribution, of delivering pain for pain.

Existentialists argue differently, stating that one must realize that while one has the freedom to make one's life and even one's own morality, that freedom is still contingent. One of the conditions is that a person is always connected to other equally free people. Another is that a person cannot truly be separated from a society. When one person abuses another, i.e., commits a crime, that person degrades the other's dignity and degrades the bonds linking free individuals. There must be some recompense for such degradation.

There are at least two ways that humanists generally see as proper forms of punishment. One is making the criminal understand the degradation he or she has caused. The other is to identify the sources that caused the criminal behavior and rehabilitate the criminal when it is possible to do so. The naturalist philosopher and historian Richard Carrier puts the point succinctly: "We ought to care more about reforming bad people than punishing them, and a lot more about fixing the social causes of evil than locking up their products" (116). These ideas of what to do with criminals fit the humanist philosophy because both allow for the free will of the criminal and both acknowledge the ability of people to change for the better, primarily through education.

One should not mistake punishment or even retribution for vengeance. Vengeance is a self-consuming evil. What use is a life devoted to vengeance? Such a situation simply piles injustice upon injustice. It does not allow the criminal to understand the degradation he or she has put others through.

We can take as an example Miss Mercy Hartigan in "The Next Doctor" (2008). She seems to have been a victim of abuse, overlooked by the "good men" of Victorian London. This abuse has caused in her a desire for revenge against not just them, but also the whole society that allowed the abuse to take place. As a result, she has allied herself with the Cybermen to take control of London. This alliance includes using abandoned and orphaned children as slave labor. The vengeance has so taken hold of

Miss Hartigan that while she can appreciate the irony of a merciless person called Mercy, she cannot feel even remote sympathy for those who are also abused. Vengeance has so twisted her reasoning that when the Doctor offers her a chance to change course or face the consequences, she rejects the offer. Only when she realizes that she has doomed herself does she regret what she has done.

The example of Mercy Hartigan demonstrates a key element in the humanist sense of justice shown in *Doctor Who*: *choice*. In "The Poison Sky" (2008), the Doctor, rather than taking the advantage and blasting the Sontarans out of the sky, transmats onto their ship with a device that will burn up the air inside the ship and destroy the ship, taking Sontarans and the Doctor as well. He does this because his sense of justice compels him: "I have to give them a choice." So important is this principle of choice that the Doctor would sacrifice himself, since he knows that the Sontarans would rather accept defeat than retreat. Similar sorts of choices run throughout the program. Choice brings together the concepts of proper punishment. First, it recognizes that a criminal has chosen a criminal act, and even though there may have been compelling social and personal reasons for the choice, that choice was not inevitable. The purpose of punishment in this way of thinking is education, to get the criminal to see the consequences of his or her action through understanding the degradation it caused, and education for learning how to identify and control the forces that make criminality tempting. Rehabilitation necessitates allowing a criminal a second chance after this education process is done. The released person now again has the choice to commit crime or to avoid it, but an *informed choice*. This is the function of education in punishment. Should the released criminal persist in committing crimes even after rehabilitation, then stricter measures become justified.

Planetary Humanism

Media professors Tulloch and Alvarado identify the primary ethical position of *Doctor Who* as a "liberal discourse of 'tolerance' and 'balance'" (42). These are but the starting points, however, for a more complete concept of justice centered on what American philosopher Paul Kurtz has called planetary humanistic ethics. According to Kurtz in *Forbidden Fruit: The Ethics of Humanism,* the parameters of planetary humanist ethics include believing and acting upon the following principles: accepting the Promethean ideal; morality separate from religious dogma; the right to privacy, pursuit of happiness and exuberance; freedom and autonomy of the individual; behavior according to the common moral decencies; responsibility for self and others; striving for ethical excellence; and an open political system based upon recognition of human rights.

Planetary humanistic ethics are separate from religious dogma and stricture. Morality is a matter of existential necessity and personal conscience, and not a matter of supposed preexisting prohibitive rules with eternal punishments attached. The reason for this is abundantly clear in *Doctor Who*. As one can see in the Promethean myth, gods often seek to keep humanity down and preserve the good for themselves. Kurtz provides an effective summary of this position, noting that religion has a negative effect on truth, blocks ethical progress, leads to repressive views, fosters intolerance, prevents social progress, is often aesthetically ugly, and generates profound apprehension of the unknown (*Living* 91–3). I have shown earlier in this book that *Doctor Who* generally takes a skeptical position with regard to religion. Multiple programs characterize religion as dogmatic, intellectually backward, and hostile to personal freedom. Even those stories portraying a more relaxed view of religious matters portray religion's only good in its function as social glue, binding people by reminding them of archetypes or by giving them rituals of social cohesion.

Along with individual rights, one also has specific responsibilities. High among these responsibilities is the requirement to live according to common moral decencies. High among these decencies are integrity, trustworthiness, benevolence, and fairness (*Forbidden* 80–96). Accepting the common moral decencies is the first step in the larger process of taking responsibility for oneself and others. All of the preceding attributes of the Promethean ideal combine in the process of striving for ethical excellence. Kurtz's list of excellences is a good basis for understanding the way to ethical personal fulfillment. These excellences include: autonomy, intelligence, self-discipline, self-respect, creativity, motivation, affirmation, health, *joie de vivre*, and aesthetic appreciation (*Forbidden* 111–25).

Finally, the personal achievement of a Promethean posture must be put into larger practice in the creation and maintenance of an open society, the only sort of political and social system under which the Promethean ideal may be available to everyone. Thus, Plato was right when in *The Republic* he has Socrates argue that justice must exist on both the personal and political levels, and that these levels must work in accord to achieve justice. However, Plato was wrong in his ideas about many of the personal and especially political traits that would achieve justice. In *Doctor Who*, the viewer repeatedly sees that closed, aristocratic, functionalist societies do not create the conditions for justice. Neither are closed-minded, arrogant, and rigid personalities likely to produce justice in their actions.

A contrasting set of values more in keeping with the *Doctor Who* ethos is Karl Popper's formulation of humanitarian justice:

(a) an equal distribution of the burden of citizenship, i.e., of those limitations of freedom which are necessary in social life; (b) equal treatment of the citizens before the law, provided, of course, that (c) the laws show neither favor nor disfavor towards individual citizens or groups or classes; (d) impartiality of the courts of justice; and (e) an equal share in the advantages (and not only in the burden) which membership of the state may offer to its citizens [*Open I* 89].

Popper makes a further contrast between the humanitarian view of justice and the totalitarian view of justice. There are three demands or proposals of humanitarian justice: the elimination of "natural" privileges; the principle of individualism; and the proposal that the task and purpose of the state is "to protect the freedom of its citizens." These three proposals are the exact opposites of the totalitarian proposals for justice, expressed by Plato and followed by numerous governments: the insistence upon "natural" privilege; the principle of collectivism; and the proposal that the task and purpose of the individual to maintain the stability of the state (*Open I* 94).

In *Doctor Who*, one can see the Doctor's favoring the humanitarian trio through his thorough opposition to the totalitarian one. The Doctor's enemies all favor at least one of the totalitarian propositions for justice. Megalomaniacs such as the Master, the Rani, Tobias Vaughan, Mavic Chen, and Salamander regularly insist upon the doctrine of natural privileges, always nominating themselves as the privileged. Many of the Doctor's opponents are collectivized races, such as the Daleks and the Cybermen, who take collective identity to the extreme. Submission to state will is given in stories such as "The Sun Makers" and "The Happiness Patrol."

The Ethical Society

We can now bring together the strands of the discussion about justice. On the basis that justice is a social matter, a concern of how a society treats the people within it, we can see the humanist concept is that a just society is an ethical society, and that the society replicates the properties of the ethical individual, which have been explained in Chapter 9. *Doctor Who* provides a glimpse of what an ethical society might look like. It does so through the statements and actions of its characters, primarily the Doctor. Since so many diverse minds have worked on the *Doctor Who* project, no singular, clear plan or model of an ethical society is put forward. Because of the type of program that it is, none was ever likely to be put forward. Yet, certain assumptions and ideas discussed in the previous chapters have run throughout the series, and these assumptions and ideas give those watching the program a view through the cracks.

A society may be defined as a group of people who assent to a set of rules and consent to abide by them. The explicit rules of society are called *laws*. The implicit rules of society are called *morals*. People within the society are generally expected to abide by these rules because members of the society assume that only if most or all of them abide by the rules will the society be able to function and maintain itself. The society creates punishments for those who deviate from either the laws or morals of that society.

History demonstrates that the members of a society on the whole tend to believe that their laws and morals are not merely *for them*, but are universally applicable, inherently better than any other society's laws and morals, and unfailingly correct. That is to say that a society's members are educated and encouraged to be sociocentric. Thus, they come to *believe* that their laws and morals *will always be right*. So strong is the sociocentric mental apparatus that a society's members tend to feel that their very being is at stake should someone question or challenge these beliefs. Many will actually feel physical distress when presented with any argument or idea contrary to their own society's laws and morals. What they usually call *justice*, therefore, is whatever social mechanism exists for removing what challenges their laws and morals.

This is not to say that it is inherently wrong to remove any and all challenges to a society's laws and morals. Murder, for example, is a challenge to most societies' laws and morals. Thus, murder in most cases is prohibited and murderers removed from society by imprisonment or execution. However, many challenges to a society's laws and morals are not like murder, not *destructive* of life, liberty, or property. Nevertheless, these challenges are often punished, and the challengers removed just as if the challenge were physically destructive.

An example of the kind of society described above, which is in fact more normal than not, is in "Inferno" (1970), in the fascistic England of an alternate timeline. There, one who questions the political decisions of the leadership has his or her rights removed, becomes a non-citizen at the very least, and dead at the most. Such a person is forced to be a kind of slave worker. The label for such a person is "anti-social" where "social" means in most of the society's members' minds "against *my* society as embodied in our laws and morals." To question even some aspect of society is to challenge the *whole* of it in most people's minds, and so to remove the anti-social element would be the only "rational" choice. The oil engineer Sutton, for example, escapes "the chop" because his skills are useful to the State. He can be enslaved and made to work under constant threat of death. He is just one, though, among many since this project is a "Scientific Labor Camp." Such would constitute *justice* in most people's minds because their anxiety from the challenge gets reduced or eliminated as a result.

We can see, however, that such a society is in fact not based upon justice, and its operations are unjust. For example, the society rests upon a power disparity, in which different laws and morals apply at different levels. Also, to maintain the power disparity, the social elites ensure that the general populace remains uneducated and ignorant. In the alternate Britain of "Inferno," the massive drilling project that is the story's setting is a government secret, heavily monitored by the military. When the drill cracks open the Earth's crust and unleashes forces that will destroy Britain and maybe the world, the social powers continue to lie to the public via their media about the cause of the new earthquakes and related phenomena. Such a society is not healthy because those with less power can never trust those with more. Eventually, somewhere, the evidence will show they are being lied to. Thus, in this alternate Britain, when the disaster happens, the workforce, from repairmen to scientists, almost all abandon the project despite the heavy military presence.

Furthermore, such a society instills in its members a heavy and rigid mental structure, or framework of thinking. Because the way people think affects their behavior, the heavy framework causes most of them to be inflexible, unimaginative, and intolerant. We can see this process in Brigade Leader Lethbridge-Stewart (an alternate version of the regular character Brigadier Lethbridge-Stewart). When the Doctor accidentally arrives in this drilling project, dubbed the Inferno, the Brigade Leader assumes the Doctor to be a spy. Only late in the sequence of events, after the main disaster, does he give up this belief, despite all prior evidence of its falsity. The Doctor, for instance, does not behave like an enemy agent, is not on any list of known agents, has no identity that the military intelligence can trace, states his intention clearly and repeatedly to stop the project, and so on. The more mentally flexible Section Leader Shaw (the alternate version of regular character Liz Shaw) also believes for some time that the Doctor is a spy. Unable to accept, early in the story, that something falls outside the framework her society has fashioned, the only alternative she can see is that he belongs to a "crackpot free speech group."

One can see the effect that a disaster has on the individuals within this unjust and unhealthy society. When the drill unleashes the Earth's destructive forces, Brigade Leader Lethbridge-Stewart falls back on the social rules that have allowed him to survive. He cannot for a long time believe that his beloved government would abandon him and everyone else on the project. When he gradually realizes that he has been abandoned, he becomes angry and frightened, unable to cope with the situation because he cannot fathom any way by which his society would collapse.

And yet, the entire situation is the fault of the inflexible society that relies upon rigid social organization, compartmentalization, and specialization. Professor Stahlman, who runs the Inferno, can never be challenged, questioned, nor removed, no matter how clearly dangerous the project is. He is in charge, the government placed its trust in him, so therefore he cannot be wrong. Public safety is an irrelevant consideration. The country needs a new source of energy no matter the cost. Thus, at all levels, personal, governmental, legal, and moral, this society has doomed itself. It has created all the right conditions for a total disaster. Under these circumstances, justice is impossible to achieve.

One can see that the "negative image" of this fascist Britain in "Inferno" is always implied in the "real" Britain of the *Doctor Who* world. The Doctor says of Brigadier Lethbridge-Stewart, "There are times when you strongly remind me of your other self." The same could be said of the "real" Britain, which still has disparities in social power, rigidity of social structure, an over-reliance upon authority, and so on.

The Just Society in the ideal, in contrast, would begin with a recognition of the value of the principles and practices of critical thinking applied to the laws and morals of the society. Thus, *all* laws and *all* morals would be constantly up for review by the populace. No law or moral would be held as "sacred." Tradition would never be accepted as a reason for adhering to a law or moral. Such a society would have an *educated* populace. Education itself would be a system fostering the tools for reflective judgment, and encouraging open-mindedness in public debate. In short, the *just* society is an *ethical* society in which all persons are treated as ends in themselves, and not as means to ends. The just society is a group of ethical individuals.

The Ethical Person

Ultimately, we may think of the ethical society and the ethical person as sharing the same basic qualities. Among these qualities is an orientation toward justice. We can call this orientation ethical because it is based on judging what constitutes *right behavior*. The just and ethical person, as we have seen in the analysis of *Doctor Who*, is *sane*, just as the just and ethical society is *sane*. Humanist and psychoanalyst Erich Fromm characterizes this sanity by observing the particular kinds of attitudes bundled in it: *"Mental health is characterized by the ability to love and create, by the emergence from incestuous ties to clan and soil, by a sense of identity based on one's experience of self as the subject and agent of one's powers, by the grasp of reality inside and outside ourselves, that is, by the development of objectivity and reason"* (69, italics in original).

One watches *Doctor Who* not because the Doctor brings chaos and disorder, and not because everywhere he goes death follows. This is a false interpretation that many characters in the series make, and that the producers and writers of the *Doctor Who* novels and audio dramas repeatedly make.[5] It mistakes coincidence (the Doctor is there, so is trouble) for causality (the Doctor must be the cause of the trouble). One watches *Doctor Who* because the Doctor is the most *sane* character in the program, because he brings some small amount of sanity into situations in which insanity is the rule, and because dispelling dangerous insanity is a valuable kind of *justice*.

Perhaps no better description of the ethical seeker of justice exists than Bertrand Russell's:

> Those whose lives are fruitful to themselves, to their friends, or to the world are inspired by hope and sustained by joy: they see in imagination the things that might be and the way in which they are to be brought into existence. In their private relations they are not pre-occupied with anxiety lest they should lose such affection and respect as they receive: they are engaged in giving affection and respect freely, and the reward comes of itself without their seeking. In their work they are not haunted by jealousy of competitors, but are concerned with the actual matter that has to be done. In politics, they do not spend time and passion defending unjust privileges of their class or nation, but they aim at making the world as a whole happier, less cruel, less full of conflict between rival greeds, and more full of human beings whose growth has not bee dwarfed and stunted by oppression [186–7].

It is the individual character of this unique creation, the Doctor, whose life is oriented toward producing *justice*.

Return to the Future

A century or more from now, in an age of world-spanning instant media, climate crises, and working space colonies, will people still be watching *Doctor Who*? Will someone somewhere still be making *Doctor Who*? I think *Doctor Who* will still have a sizeable niche. I think its format is flexible and open enough that it can survive continuous production into the future. Though the look of today's programs may become outdated, its thematic and narrative elements will not be. *Doctor Who* will still teach audiences that "other" is not the same as "evil," that societies survive or fall based upon how well they treat their citizens, that the human species can move on to the next phase of wisdom. *Doctor Who* will still be breaking down ideologies, still unveiling surprises, and still opening the eyes of wonder on the vast, unknown universe.

Chapter Notes

Chapter 1

1. Readers interested in a more detailed pursuit of these generic matters should read David Butler's "How to pilot a TARDIS: audiences, science fiction, and the fantastic in *Doctor Who*" in *Time and Relative Dissertations in Space: Critical Perspectives on* Doctor Who, pp. 19–42. Butler and I agree on the applications of Todorov's theories to *Doctor Who*. I disagree with Butler on a key point of his discussion. Butler argues that because *Doctor Who* often crosses genre boundaries, its status as "science fiction" is unstable and the program should not be seen as "science fiction," but rather as "adventure." However, even though Butler refers to Darko Suvin's writings about science fiction, and I too use Suvin's work, Butler relies upon a weak definition of science fiction, one that Suvin himself would not really agree to. Butler uses the popular conception of media science fiction, that it must contain big-budget special effects worked out on a grand scale of storytelling. As my comments later in this chapter reveal, science fiction, even television and film science fiction, is a fluid genre unlike other literary genres. While most other literary genres have highly distinct characteristics and clear demarcations about narrative elements, such as character, setting, and plot, science fiction has none of these characteristics. It can be defined more by orientation toward certain aspects of the material world than by mechanistic characteristics. Thus, almost any other genre can be science-fictionalized. The result is a science fiction story with characteristics of the other genre; rarely does the relationship go the other way. Thus, I assert that *Doctor Who* really *is* science fiction, just not that kind of science fiction. I do agree with Butler that *Doctor Who* is all the better for not being *that* kind of science fiction.

2. A notable exception to this rule occurred when Graham Williams took over as producer of the program (1977–80). Williams, inexperienced at producing, took a more "hands off" approach than previous producers, and was the only one to view it primarily as a children's show rather than a family show. Thus, production values lagged, scripts were allowed to fill with irrelevant humor, and actors, especially Tom Baker, were allowed to insert silly humor into the program. All this led many fans to see this period as the "send up" era, in which the program made fun of itself to the detriment of its best qualities.

3. Probably the most "Enlightenment" science fiction author in temperament, style, and thought is Stanislaw Lem. His stories contain an intellectual rigor that few others match.

4. Literary critic Mark Rose has described the contradiction at the center of the science-fictional representation of the world. Rose notes that there is an "unresolvable incompatibility between science fiction's materialistic ideology and its status as a romance form concerned with essentially religious material and committed to a vision of the world as a conflict between good and bad magic" (44). I will demonstrate in this book that the two views are neither incompatible nor is their conflict irresolvable.

5. This statement marks part of the nineteenth century philosophical shift that will create existentialism, which is discussed in chapter 3 of this book.

6. In surveys taken during the 1970s, Bainbridge found that between 31 and 48 percent of the science fiction readership in America identified themselves as nonreligious. These numbers are drastically higher than the 4 to 8 percent of the general population who so identified themselves. There is little reason to suppose much change in these numbers today. The percentage of Americans currently identifying themselves as nonreligious has gone slightly up, some polls reporting as high as 14 percent (Flynn 16). The percentage of irreligious scientists has remained roughly the same for the last century, about 65 percent. Given these numbers, there is little likelihood of shift in religious attitudes among science fiction readers and viewers.

7. Tulloch and Alvarado provide a more thorough account of all the various cues in "An Unearthly Child" that draw a viewer's attention to the contrasts that center around the mysterious

absent identity of the Doctor. From the signature tune and opening titles to the closing shot of a shadow looming over the TARDIS, the viewer sees the familiar/unfamiliar, normal/mysterious, earthly/unearthly, home/expatriate dichotomies that create the narrative tension and focus of the program and have driven it to this day. See *Doctor Who: The Unfolding Text*, 16–35.

8. *Star Trek*, in contrast, consistently undermines the value of such intelligence by having its most intelligent character, Mr. Spock, shown as constantly "lacking" an even higher element of humanity — emotion. The revised *Star Trek* series of the 1990s, *Star Trek: The Next Generation* recapitulated this intelligence/emotion duality elevating the latter and denigrating the former in the character of the android officer Data. The elevation of emotion over intelligence stems from a rather facile and simple-minded definition of "humanity." *Doctor Who*'s approach to the question of what defines "human" is deeper, more intellectually honest, and more philosophically sound.

9. Not all critics are satisfied with *Doctor Who*'s liberal humanism. In particular, post-structuralist, post–Saussurean, post–Lacanian, post-historical, post-modern, post-post critics such as Tat Wood truly dislike liberal humanism in general. In "The empire of the senses: narrative form and point-of-view in *Doctor Who*," Wood makes a case for *Doctor Who*'s complicity in a post-imperial power structure nostalgic for the good old days of English world domination, further claiming that this is really what liberal humanism is all about anyway. Wood argues that in delimiting what is "known" and "unknown," and by privileging certain points of view, namely those of our comfortably English Doctors and companions, the program uses its monsters as simulacra women and indigenous peoples first characterized as out of control and then brought back into control. I find this line of thinking shallow and unconvincing. The problem is that the typical method of postmodernist criticism of this kind is to throw terminology at a subject purportedly under study so that the critic can gain mastery over it. By tossing out chic terminology such as "mirror stage," "panopticon" (Foucault's, not Gallifrey's), "spectacle" and so on, and presuming either that the reader has facility with these terms or that the reader will simply accept his use of the terms, Wood can proceed without ever defining the terms or addressing the soundness of the presumptions behind them. In this way, a critic can turn anything into anything else. An alien who "lacks" some human characteristic, such as emotions, can be suddenly made into a symbolic woman with a mere twist of a couple of terms and enough verbiage so that no one notices a bait and switch is in action. That the alien "lacks" something and the woman "lacks" a phallus is enough connection for this ethereal and false analogy to be turned into an equation. If one

works backwards, from the conclusions to the premises, one finds that the whole logical structure is a series of non sequiturs, and that the only real evidence used to support this charge of imperialist apologetics is that those who made the show are English. The essay is an elaborate guilt-by-association argument that presumes that no one who is not in possession of postmodernist theory has a mind of his or her own and is thoroughly a pawn in the historical forces of which the possessor of theory is magically free.

Chapter 2

1. Though we are repeatedly told that the Doctor is not a doctor of medicine (c.f. "An Unearthly Child" with Doctor 1 and "The Seeds of Death" with Doctor 4), we do find out in "The Moonbase" with Doctor 2 that he studied medicine with Joseph Lister.

2. The one-off television movie, *Doctor Who*, opens with Doctor 7 reading H.G. Wells's *The Time Machine* and ends with Doctor 8 reading the same book. In "Dragonfire," Doctor 7 is reading Bernard Shaw's *The Doctor's Dilemma*. In "City of Death," Doctor 4 says that he handwrote the original draft of Shakespeare's *Hamlet* because Shakespeare had injured his writing hand. In "The Twin Dilemma," Doctor 6 strides up a hill while reciting Longfellow's poem "Excelsior." In "The Mind Robber," Doctor 2 is able to tell that he is talking to Lemuel Gulliver simply by listening to the character talk, and can even speak some of Gulliver's narrative. These all together show a broad knowledge of literature in English.

3. In "Time-Flight," Doctor 5 makes a joke at the expense of Bishop Berkeley.

4. In "The Abominable Snowmen," Doctor 2 reveals knowledge of Tibetan Buddhism. In "Planet of the Spiders," Doctor 3 reveals that he had a mentor, a kind of personal guru. In "Terror of the Zygons," Doctor 4 uses a special hypnotic ability on Sarah and a shallow breathing technique, both of which he learned from a Tibetan monk.

5. This brief is quoted in many places, notably on the many websites devoted to *Doctor Who*, on various documentary TV programs about *Doctor Who*, and in some of the official *Doctor Who* spin-off novels.

6. Another answer to my question is "In Psychology," but since that is not my concern in this book, I leave my reader to fill in the rest.

Chapter 3

1. See, for instance, Nietzsche's *Twilight of the Idols*, in which he identifies four "theses" regarding philosophy: 1) "The reasons for which 'this' world has been characterized as 'apparent' are the very

reasons which indicate its reality; any other kind of reality is absolutely indemonstrable"; 2) "the 'true world' has been constructed out of contradiction to the actual world: indeed an apparent world, insofar as it is merely a moral-optical illusion"; 3) "To invent fables about a world 'other' than this one has no meaning at all ... we avenge ourselves against life with a phantasmagoria of 'another,' a 'better' life"; 4) "Any distinction between a 'true' and an 'apparent' world ... is only a suggestion of decadence, a symptom of the *decline of life*" (qtd. *The Portable Nietzsche* 484). Indeed, Nietzsche goes on at some length in characterizing and disproving what he calls an "error" — the notion that an ideal, unreal world is the true world and the real world is but a shadow or inferior copy of that ideal world.

2. The main set of philosophers grouped under the term *existentialist* include: Søren Kierkegaard, Friedrich Nietzsche, Karl Jaspers, Martin Heidegger, Gabriel Marcel (who reputedly coined the term "existentialism," but later rejected association with it), Jean-Paul Sartre, and Albert Camus. An existentialist outlook may also be found in the literary works of Fyodor Dostoevsky, Rainer Maria Rilke, and Franz Kafka. There is quite a diversity of opinion amongst these thinkers. However, they may roughly be divided into the Christian existentialists, the agnostic existentialists, and the atheist existentialists. Christian existentialists, such as Kierkegaard and Marcel, view human existence as the struggle toward true communion with God, which rejects popular "crowd" notions of religion and morality and instead focuses on how the individual meets that goal. It will become clear in this and later chapters that *Doctor Who* has little in common with Christian existentialism. The agnostic existentialists, such as Jaspers and Heidegger, believe in some transcendent realm, perhaps even a kind of divinity, yet do not associate themselves or their theories with any one religion or spiritual system. The atheist existentialists, such as Nietzsche, Sartre, and Camus, on the other hand argue that the individual is apart from crowd notions precisely because there is no deity to lend any legitimate authority to those notions. There is only life as it is lived and must be lived in order for the human race to survive its own vices. Sartre is particularly influential on the later *deconstructionist* movement in French aesthetic and linguistic philosophy, most notably Jacques Derrida, Roland Barthes, and Jean Baudrillard. Among atheist iconoclasts, Nietzsche holds sway, particularly in the U.S., England, and Germany. Although there is no explicit rejection of the concept of God or of any particular religious orthodoxy in *Doctor Who*, nevertheless the outlook expressed fits those of the agnostic and atheist existentialists quite well.

3. The Doctor slightly misquotes three lines, saying:

"That's why this tree
Doth continue to be,
Since observed by yours faithfully, God."

The part that the Doctor is quoting comes from a response to a satirical limerick. The two limericks together read thus:

"There once was a man who said "God
Must think it exceedingly odd
If he finds that this tree
Continues to be,
When there's no one about in the Quad."

Dear Sir, Your astonishment's odd:
I am always about in the Quad.
And that's why the tree
Will continue to be,
Since observed by Yours faithfully, God."

The first limerick was written by Ronald Arbuthnot Knox, a Catholic priest, scholar, and writer of doggerel whose best-known work was a parody of ponderous scholarship that used Sherlock Holmes as its ostensible topic. Knox wrote it in parody of Berkeley's theory of perception. The second limerick some have also attributed to Knox, but most believe it is an anonymous response to him. The two limericks together cleverly work through Berkeley's basic theory. If the tree has no one to perceive it, then it must cease to be. Yet, common sense says that it does not cease to be; therefore, something must be perceiving it, and the only likely candidate is God. Therefore, God exists. So goes Berkeley's argument. However, this is clearly circular reasoning, presuming the point that most needs proving ("to be is to be perceived") and then proceeding as though it were proved. Further, it leads inevitably to the conclusion that matter does not exist, since it is all a "matter" of perception. There is no thing there, just a perception of it, which is the reason it would disappear if it were not perceived. Berkeley, therefore, curiously conflates Plato's two realms of existence, the real and the ideal, into one. There is only ideal. The famous intellectual Samuel Johnson, according to his biographer Boswell, said, "I refute it *thus*," while kicking a stone.

4. Heidegger's work is notoriously complex, virtually impenetrable at times, even in its original German. It is made worse for the non-German speaker because Heidegger relies quite heavily on German etymology and special linguistic tricks peculiar to German to exemplify many of his key points. For this reason, one must often rely on authoritative secondary sources to help make sense of Heidegger's philosophy.

5. Sartre uses the word "passion" in a similar fashion during his analysis of anti-Semitism. To Sartre, anti-Semitism is a passion because it removes or destroys a person's rationality, and limits one's choices to those dictated by the logic of the

passion. See chapter 9 of this book for further analysis.

6. "The Pyramids of Mars" (1976).

7. "The Invasion of Time" (1978), in which the Doctor claims his right to the presidency as a ploy to protect Gallifrey from an invading force, is the first of these. The right stemmed from a gambit the Doctor used in "The Deadly Assassin" (1976) of offering himself as a presidential candidate in order to obtain immunity from imprisonment. These two programs offer the most sustained portrayals of Gallifreyan life in the series. In "The Five Doctors" (1983), a disorganized High Council of Timelords offers the Doctor the presidency, which he accepts only as a means to escape back to his vagabond life. And in "The Trial of a Timelord: The Ultimate Foe" (1986), the Doctor is again offered the presidency, which this time he rejects outright.

8. "Revelation of the Daleks" (1988) and "The Silver Nemesis" (1988) both give strong suggestions of some special position the Doctor once occupied.

9. "The End of the World" (2005).

10. "The End of Time" (2009).

11. "Planet of the Daleks" (1973), "Genesis of the Daleks" (1975), "The Brain of Morbius" (1976), "The Deadly Assassin" (1976), "The Invasion of Time" (1978), "Arc Of Infinity" (1983), "The Five Doctors" (1983), and "The Trial of a Timelord" (1986).

12. The famous existentialist novel *The Stranger,* by Albert Camus, focuses almost wholly on this tension between social forces and self-determination.

13. While in this book I do not give much consideration to peripheral *Doctor Who* productions, I think it is important to note that a major exception to the existentialist attitude toward death in *Doctor Who* exists in the radio production, subsequently novelized, "The Ghosts of N-Space" (1996), featuring Doctor 3 and written by ex-*Doctor Who* producer/director/writer Barry Letts. In this story, an afterlife is taken completely as granted, yet this afterlife is not treated as a supernatural passing on into a permanent spirit world. Rather, Letts uses the usual *Doctor Who* tactic of giving quasi-scientific explanations to normally "supernatural" phenomena, and thereby naturalizing them. Thus, though the story is out of character in that it does not treat death as finality, it is in character in treating a supernatural afterlife as a part of the natural order.

14. The program, perhaps because it was considered family viewing in the 1960s, pulls its punch a bit here by serving up a new companion, Dodo Chaplet from London in the 1960s, who could possibly be a descendant of the serving woman Anne Chaplet from 16th century Paris. However, since surnames are passed down from the male line, that would be so only if Anne Chaplet had had an illegitimate son or married

another Chaplet, events that the program's producers probably had not thought about.

15. The series of *Doctor Who* CD audio dramas has pursued this problem when the Doctor plucks a new companion, Charlotte Pollard, out of the R101 disaster, thus setting up a string of historical paradoxes since she had "in reality" died in the crash.

Chapter 4

1. There are some different definitions of *metaphysical* that are primarily materialistic, such as that of Immanuel Kant. He takes *metaphysics* to mean the contemplation of laws both physical and moral using what he calls *pure reason,* that is to say without reference to physical contingencies. By *laws,* Kant means universally applicable rules. Since such rules are independent of any one circumstance to which they can apply, they are "beside the physical," yet they do not carry a separate and independent existence from the world of facts, since their existence depends entirely on the existence of the totality of facts to which they would apply, and because they come into existence only through the human act of the *will,* by which Kant means "choice" and "intention" and "desire" rolled together into one concept.

2. The specific context of Berengar's claim involved an ongoing controversy about the Eucharist. Berengar, a central figure in this controversy, argued that reason dictated the impossibility of transubstantiation, that wine and bread cannot materially (substantially) become something else, since it was contrary to nature for them to do so. He put forward other more theological arguments, but the central concern of interest here is Berengar's surprising insistence upon *reason* as God's gift separating humans from the rest of creation, and upon *dialectic* (i.e., logic) as the method by which reason works.

3. The full statement comes from John's defense of eloquence (rhetoric): "If man is superior to other living beings in dignity because of his powers of speech and reason, what is more universally efficacious and more likely to win distinction, than to surpass one's fellows, who possess the same human nature, and are members of the same human race, in those sole respects wherein man surpasses other beings?" While the part I quoted is extracted from an if-clause, which could be taken as conditional and not declarative, the clause itself forms the essence of a rhetorical question, and thus is declarative by implication.

4. During this exchange, Ian remarks that he wonders how the Doctor would have time to have read Pyrrho's work, to which the Doctor responds that he met the man. If Ian were referring to what exists of Pyrrho's writings in Ian's time of 1963, then the Doctor would find very hard to read Pyrrho's

works, since none exist. The Doctor had more rightly referred to reading about the teachings of Pyrrho. The philosopher himself apparently wrote only one poem, which does not survive. The rest of his ideas are recorded second-hand or even more indirectly from writings about Pyrrho or about the thoughts of his followers. Most of these sources come from a century or so after Pyrrho's death.

5. Sadly, Donna's growth as a character throughout the 2008 season is thwarted at the end. The producers opted for an ending that has her memory of the entire time she spent with the Doctor erased, so that she returns to being the more obtuse Donna of "The Runaway Bride." Even though the Doctor and Donna's mother and grandfather know that she was once, briefly, "the most important person in the universe," this hardly compensates for the total erasure of the character's development. The loss of memory could be seen as the "tragedy" of Donna. This erasure and reset of the character, which had been done similarly before in 1969 with Jamie and Zoe, is analogous to the "it was only a dream" ending. Both endings lead to the same "what was the point of that trip" dissatisfaction. Characters with whom the audience sympathize need to develop and mature. The audience needs the reward of their successfully becoming better.

6. Revealed in "Time and the Rani" (1987).

Chapter 5

1. Frazer describes the Cailleach as a remnant of the Corn-Mother goddess. Cailleach means "old woman" or "old wife" is Scots Gaelic, and into the twentieth century at various locations in Scotland the last cut stalk of corn would be fashioned into a doll called "Cailleach" that received various treatments in order to prevent famine the following year (403).

2. In Ezekiel in the Bible, Gog is a prince from the land of Magog (Ezek. 38:2), while in Revelation Gog and Magog are nations that will join Satan's army one thousand years after the first resurrection (Rev. 20:8). *Ogros* is the Spanish plural form of *ogro*, or *ogre* in English.

3. This ending is rather complicated. In "Journey's End," the Doctor had been keeping his severed, regenerated hand preserved in a jar, and had directed his regenerative energies into this hand so as to prevent his own regeneration. When the TARDIS is later threatened with destruction and only Donna is on board, the energies are released, causing the hand to regenerate in the body of the Doctor, but also causing two amalgamations between the Doctor and Donna, thus consummating the Doctor-Donna verbal pairing that had been running through the season. The new Doctor looks like Doctor 10, but has a human body. Donna receives Timelord mental abilities. Eventually, this new human Doctor goes into the par-

allel universe in which Rose now belongs and the two are presumed to live together. In this way, Rose can get her Doctor, and the audience can get its Doctor.

4. Gaining a female companion while traveling with a male companion only may also have the effect of diffusing speculations about homosexual relations if there is just the older man/younger man pairing.

5. For further discussion of rebirth rituals involving caves and solar deities, see Jung's discussion of a portion of the eighteenth Sura of the Koran (*Four Archetypes*, 69–81).

6. Thompson more blatantly uses a rhetorical trick that Campbell and Frye are a bit slyer about, and that is using religious and mythical metaphors to describe academic activities outside of the subject of myths, and then proceeding as if the metaphors were facts. Thompson talks about biological science as a process of priestly education, as though biology classes were part of a seminary school producing scientist priests (39). This is clearly, however, a false comparison. Science training is very little like a seminary and the very purpose is different. Training for priesthood is a process of indoctrination. The students must accept a preconceived set of "truths," never questioning these supposed truths and never adding anything substantially new to them. Science training is precisely the opposite, requiring skeptical inquiry that often leads to throwing out old "truths" when newly found facts point to a different conclusion. Thompson's procedure is logically fallacious and leads to the false generalizations that everything is in one way or another "myth." Thompson also makes great sweeping generalizations about scientists, social scientists, artists, politicians and so on, so he can dismiss what they do and thus make what he does appear that much grander. These generalizations almost never stand up to even mild scrutiny on a factual basis. He treats what scientists write as a *discourse*, especially biological science, as though a scientific publication were a piece of creative writing. Like another popular syncretist, the physicist Fritjof Capra, Thompson takes sentences from scientific writing, removes them from their context, and then compares them to apparently similar statements by mystics and in mythology. He then concludes, wrongly, that the scientists are only discovering what the mystics and ancient peoples knew all along. However, one can very easily take almost any sentence and rifle through a sample of random works and come up with another sentence that appears very similar. That does not mean that the sentences describe the same phenomenon or are even about the same subject. Additionally, this technique means that Thompson is attacking what scientists, almost always biologists or social scientists, are not saying rather than what they are saying. Campbell and Frye do this

sort of presto-changeo only occasionally, but mostly stick to the fields of literature and religion. The myth critics tend to be very wrong when they try to apply their method to areas outside of mythology and literature. However, to give them their due, Thompson, Campbell, and Frye are very perceptive and informative when discussing myths and mythic patterning.

7. *On the Nightmare* (rev. 1950) by American psychoanalyst Ernest Jones is a thorough psychoanalytical account of the relationships between dream and myth contents. Though most modern psychological investigations now discount the psychoanalytic interpretation of this content, which characterizes it as displaced anxieties resulting from unresolved childhood complexes, the connection itself is still revealing, and demonstrates the foolishness of taking myths and folktales as genuine historical occurrences.

Chapter 6

1. For a discussion of science vs. religion and the example set by "Meglos," see Chapter 7.

2. Readers should not confuse this use of "fish people," meaning simply people who identify themselves with the perceived sacred powers of the fish in abstract form, with the "fish people" in the story, who are captured humans turned into piscine-homo hybrids through the technical skills of the mad Professor Zaroff.

3. Flame has been a regular source of punishment in religions. In Christianity, it was used to execute "heretics" and "witches," various "unbelievers." The fire was supposedly a foretaste of the eternal fire of Hell from which these "sinners" would soon be suffering. The Doctor in the scene from "Planet of Fire" is to be sacrificed to flame because he challenges the religious system on Sarn.

4. Lonergan gets around the problem of the mythic components of religion by distinguishing between "mythic consciousness" and "belief." While mythic consciousness is the unreflective acceptance of mythic content as "true," belief is the virtually unconditioned grasp of a concept that gives rise to a rational necessity to prove or disprove the concept (707). Existentialists and secular humanists would argue against such a distinction, calling it both special pleading and equivocation.

5. Two regular writers of *Doctor Who* were definitely atheists, Malcolm Hulke and Douglas Adams. However, neither of these writers wrote expressly about religion in their *Doctor Who* scripts. Russell T. Davies, producer and head writer for four years (2005–9), in interviews has not denied an atheistic tone and theme to his scripts both for *Doctor Who* and the two spinoff series he created, *The Sarah Jane Adventures* and especially *Torchwood*.

6. For instance, some fundamentalist Christians believe that dinosaur bones were placed on the Earth by the Devil, thus turning fact (real bones that prove that real dinosaurs lived really long ago) into fiction (a lie propagated by the great enemy).

7. One can note the crude example of *Dianetics*, the "bible" of Scientology, which is advertised by listing a problem, such as depression, then citing a page on which the problem will be supposedly fixed.

8. Karl Ernst von Baer (1792–1876) discovered the mammalian egg cell, the membranes that surround an embryo, and the functionings of those membranes, and through embryology laid some of the groundwork for a general theory of evolution. Although late in his life he was a leading critic of Darwin's theories, von Baer's criticism was on what he thought were scientific, not religious, grounds.

9. Confusingly, this interpretation of the events, namely that whatever the Doctor has encountered at the bottom of the Satan Pit is not really "the Devil," gets contradicted in the later story "Planet of the Ood" (2008), when the Doctor says to his companion Donna that he actually did meet the Devil.

10. Most of the concepts and characterizations that most people in the Christian world believe about the Devil do not, in fact, come from the Bible, which actually has very little to say on the matter. These concepts usually come from the typical habit of early Christians to label pagan gods as "evil," and reassign the associated characterizations and religious practices as belonging to their own symbol of evil.

11. The statement in "The Impossible Planet" is "The Beast and his armies shall rise from the pit to make war against God." This statement certainly sounds like something from "Revelation," but the closest statement to it in "Revelation" is as follows in the King James version: "And when they shall have finished their testimony, the beast that ascendeth out of the bottomless pit shall make war against them, and shall overcome them, and kill them" (Rev. 11:7). It is tempting to try to work out the who, what, and why of this most perplexing book called "Revelation." For example, many commonly assume a singular beast called the Beast, yet there are at least two, one rising from the sea (Rev. 13:1) and one rising from the land (Rev. 13:11), neither of which is directly linked to the beast from the bottomless pit mentioned two chapters previously, and seemingly alluded to again in chapter 17, when the beast is said to make war against "the Lamb." This beast from the pit in chapter 11 does not make war against God directly, but against his two prophets ("they" who give testimony). The bottomless pit itself had been earlier mentioned in chapter 9, when a "fallen star" is given the key to open the

abyss, from which emerge poisonous locusts that look like battle horses, attack people but not grass, and have an angel for a king, named "Destruction." It seems that Matt Jones, author of the "The Impossible Planet" and "The Satan Pit" is paraphrasing and condensing parts of "Revelation" to make the story smoother and more coherent. Those curious for an explanation of "Revelation" in its historical and literary context should consult *A History of the End of the World,* by Jonathan Kirsch.

12. Zed, the last letter in the English alphabet corresponds to Omega, the last letter of the Greek alphabet, often imbued with religious significance since the New Testament was written in Greek.

13. The Ood's telepathic ability is measured on a scaled visible readout, thus making what appears as a supernatural ability into just another part of the natural order.

14. Someone at this point may have already thought that there are religious "seekers" who do not claim to have total knowledge, yet do adhere to religious ideas. However, the word "seeker" is something of a giveaway, since if a person is seeking an answer, that means that he or she does not possess it or does not think that he or she possesses it. Seekers do not *believe,* for if they had an answer to believe in, they would stop seeking. Furthermore, seekers usually exist within a creed and not often apart from one. Most religious seekers, therefore, seek only confirmation of an answer they already have.

Chapter 7

1. For the curious, the answer is that the Captain has fixed massive gravitational engines to the planet, which has been gutted of all its minerals. The engines "flip" the planet to a new location, hence the change in constellations, where it surrounds a smaller planet and mines that one dry of its minerals, hence the sudden mineral wealth.

2. The other great contribution to the philosophy of science is *The Structure of Scientific Revolutions* (1962, rev. 1971), by Thomas S. Kuhn. The particular concerns of Kuhn's book are not part of our concerns regarding science in *Doctor Who.* However, they are worth repeating. In brief, Kuhn discusses the history of science, and notes that in every scientific field there are alternating periods of "normal" science and "revolutionary" science. During normal phases, scientists principally work from the assumption of the fundamental truth of an existing scientific model, or "paradigm" as Kuhn calls it. Scientists in general do not actively seek to refute the theory, but rather to confirm it, and work primarily on filling in the gaps or correcting minor errors in the existing theory. However, gradually the gaps and errors be-

come more numerous and pronounced, or simply will not go away. Eventually, there comes a point when a theory must stand or fall. Along comes a brief revolutionary period, during which someone creates an entirely new theoretical apparatus by subverting or eliminating the troublesome assumptions of the previous dominant theory. Vigorous debate and experimental activity ensue, and if the new theory withstands these initial tests it quickly becomes the new paradigm and activity settles back into its normal state. Like Popper's contribution to the philosophy of science, Kuhn's focuses on science as a community endeavor.

Chapter 8

1. The notion fits into Plato's theory of reality as a shadow stage filled with copies of eternal ideal forms, and his theology, which settles on the idea of permanent and unchanging gods. These theories have had far-reaching consequences in philosophy, most especially in Christian theology, which often relies heavily on modified versions of Plato's idealism. Fitting Plato's theory to Genesis, for instance, theologians have posited that Adam and Eve were likewise permanent and unchanging, and that banishment from the Garden of Eden brought change, i.e., corruption, to humanity. Theologians have also discussed God in terms of the eternal and unchanging, the "first mover" that is not itself moved. One finds the Platonic strain running through Augustine, Boethius, Aquinas, up to modern Thomist philosophers. Always, there is the duality: perfect unchanging Heaven, imperfect corrupted Earth.

Chapter 9

1. Kant goes much farther with these considerations. He argues that moral principles exist apart from experience as "pure rational concepts" understandable only by proper philosophical contemplation, which he calls *metaphysics.* Kant differs from Plato in his description of these ideals, however, because Kant does not say that moral principles *exist* in an ideal world of which the material world is a mere shadow. Kant, instead, argues that moral principles as pure ideas come into existence only when one acts upon them from duty (the desire to do what is good or right purely for its own sake) (48). Kant says, "Since moral laws should hold for every rational being as such, the principles must be derived from the universal concept of a rational being in general" (28). *Doctor Who,* as an action-adventure family program, does not really delve into questions of origin and type regarding morals, but merely of ethical application, so our conversation in this chapter will focus on ethics.

2. Carl Sagan works out this argument in some detail in *The Dragons of Eden: Speculations on the Evolution of Human Intelligence* (1977), focusing on genetic variance, number of possible brain states, and similar large number statistics. Arthur Koestler argues a slightly different version based upon Ludwig von Bertalanffy's General Systems Theory, saying that *free will* is a product of the *degrees of freedom* inherent in a recognizably hierarchical and probabilistic system. Koestler compares the situations to games. Noughts and crosses (tic-tac-toe in America) has little hierarchical complexity and a highly fixed set of rules, so that there are few degrees of freedom and thus fewer choices to make freely. Chess, on the other hand, is hierarchically complex with a significantly high number of degrees of freedom, thus allowing more choices to be freely made. Ethical considerations run similarly, according to Koestler, from cases of few to no degrees of freedom (determinism) to multiple degrees of freedom (free will) (236–41).

3. In *The Ghost in the Machine* (1967), Koestler argues that true consciousness and limited free will are "emergent properties" of the nested hierarchical systems which make up the human organism, and thus transcend their physical origins. Computer scientist and artificial intelligence expert Douglas Hofstadter offers a similar line of reasoning, but in computer terms in *Gödel, Escher, Bach: An Eternal Golden Braid* (1980). If one considers neurons as on/off switches allowing bits of information to pass through, and brain biology as the "program," then complex mental phenomena are an emergent property of the hierarchy of programming functions, and act somewhat independently from the binary programming at the "bottom" of the system. The process is comparable to a typical computer program operating at the user level. The interface, what people call a "program," is a top-level product of lower-level systems that runs somewhat autonomously from the binary code upon which it is built.

4. For the curious, I will explain Boethius' idea of "the Good." Boethius imagines the Good as coextensive and coexistent with God, and to some extent coequal to God (61–5). From Plato, Boethius uses the idea that "the Good" is an ideal form that exists in Heaven rather than on Earth. Like Plato, Boethius assumes the material world to be only a corrupted copy of the "true" eternal world of Heaven (61). As Boethius sees it, the various things that people seek to make themselves happy are or once were good, but human "error" (of judgment) and "depravity" have ruined them, which is consistent with both Plato's and Christianity's belief in a world degenerating from its original ideal state. Thus, the things that appear good on Earth are merely corrupted copies of the "true," heavenly Good. According to Boethius, "The good is defined as that which, once it is at-

tained, relieves man of all further desires" (43). Since only perfection will satisfy that definition, and only God is perfect, then the Good must be God. Boethius and *Doctor Who* are greatly apart, not only because *Doctor Who* is essentially agnostic (a supernatural being may or may not exist, but even if it does it clearly does not involve itself in the running of the universe in any detectable way), but also because Boethius takes the Platonic assumption that "perfect" is the same as "unchanging." Boethius assumes along with Plato that all change is degenerative and demonstrates "corruption." In *Doctor Who*, however, change is seen in evolutionary terms as both necessary and teleological (tending toward a goal, which sharply contrasts with modern Darwinian biology, which assumes that evolution just happens and is not going anywhere). "Death is the price we pay for progress," says the Doctor in "Brain of Morbius" (1976), and there is not a more succinct statement that runs so counter to the Christian idea that death is the punishment for disobedience and the mark of humanity's "fallen" and degenerate state.

5. Bentham determines "good" in a similar way as Epicurean philosophers, by relating it to *pain* and *pleasure*. A thing or action is *good* when it reduces pain and/or increases pleasure. Bentham attempts to quantify *good* by the amount of pleasure produced. Mill modifies Bentham's formulation, recognizing that some things and actions are inherently good and qualitatively better than others. Mill, intriguingly, extends the principle to "the whole sentient creation," thus arguing that animals, too, have the right not to have pain deliberately inflicted on them.

6. Antiphon, a prominent figure among the philosophers known as "Sophists," like virtually all Greek philosophers prior to Plato, is known exclusively through fragments and paraphrases lodged in other writers' works.

7. The translation I use here comes from a set of manuscripts older than the standard manuscripts used in most English translations of the *Tao Te Ching*. These manuscripts do not use the standard verse order. The verse quoted is in most translations verse 49, but in this translation is verse 12. For further explanation, see the introduction and afterword by Victor H. Mair of his translation, Bantam books, 1990.

8. "Right to life" as I am using the term should not in any way be confused with the misuse of the terminology by those opposed to legalized abortion, nor in any way as an agreement with this misguided idea.

Chapter 10

1. This is the only time the Doctor smokes in the history of the program.

2. The impossibility of social prediction is a

conclusion that Popper comes to, but Marx does not. Marx, of course, famously argued that the study of class relations can lead to an understanding of the macroevolutionary changes in social development. That virtually none of his predictions came true is evidence in favor of Popper's position of the impossibility of social prediction.

3. One may see the development of capitalism as going through three stages so far. The first is *industrial* capitalism of the eighteenth and nineteenth centuries, so accurately described by Marx, Engels, Weber, and Veblen. The second phase is *consumer* capitalism, the principal economic system of the twentieth century that Fromm discusses in *The Sane Society*. The third, now just emerging, is *information* capitalism. The processes of quantification and abstractification have taken over the system, so that economic power is no longer in the hands of those who control production of goods (industrial capitalism) or who buy and sell the most stuff (consumer capitalism), but instead is in the hands of those who control raw data and its systems of storage and delivery. The bureaucrat is giving up a great amount of authority to the new "essential" character in the drama — the information manipulator. Companies exist whose sole purpose is the storage of data, while many of the biggest corporations now provide the "service" of transmitting data. A host of analysts and efficiency experts are now taking control of the workers' lives, and are even further removed from the humanity of the workers and themselves than were the bureaucrats. This is not to say that either industrial or consumer capitalism will entirely disappear. The process is evolutionary, and as in biological evolution vestiges of older forms exist in the newer. Just as the human body contains an appendix, a remnant from the time that our ancestors ate raw leaves, and a limbic brain, the "new" brain being built on top of and using the older system, so too do economic systems build on and use older forms. Even feudalism is not entirely dead. Additionally, the evolution of corporations seems to follow the evolution of capitalism itself. Contemporary capitalist society necessarily includes industrial manufacturing and distribution increasingly removed off-site from the principal scene of capitalist activity, consumer shops and delivery services, on top of which is the information network connecting manufacturers to suppliers to consumers. A company begins in the industrial phase of single or limited ownership and development of a "product" to market. If the company is successful enough, the owners will "sell out," or go public, making the company into a stockholder corporation and placing it into the consumer market. Finally, the company will abandon its traditional delivery method for goods and services by using fast information systems

(the internet, for instance), thus turning even the physical products into abstract data to be matched to physical objects. *Doctor Who* may become an interesting document in the history of this transformation.

4. This point should not be confused with the misleading label of "death tax" that American conservatives often use to describe the estate tax, a levy on large, and only on large, legacies so as to prevent concentrated accumulation of wealth.

5. Fromm makes a very interesting and compelling analysis of both the sources and results of this process of alienation, but it is too detailed to go into in this book much beyond what I have already used. One of the more interesting factors is that Fromm's book is now over 50 years old, but if one were to take out the cold war references the analysis still accords very well with the situation that exists now.

6. Such a story would probably have been far too expensive for *Doctor Who* at that time.

7. Plato has Socrates assume that the historical order in the transformation of governments in Athens is natural and universal. Furthermore, this transformation is always degenerative. Thus, aristocracy (rule by social elites, though Plato calls it "rule by the best") degenerates into timocracy (rule by those who love honor), which degenerates into oligarchy (rule by the rich), which degenerates into democracy (rule by the common people), which degenerates into tyranny (rule by a strong individual) (235).

8. It must be noted that Marx and those who follow his lead do not advocate authoritarian rule as such. Marx argued that the labor class would inevitably initiate a violent revolution that would overthrow the ownership class, which begins the process leading to true communist socialism. The intervening step would be a centralized state that would seize control of the means of production and distribute them by equitable procedures. This intervening step is a temporary period of oligarchic authoritarian rule in which the communist party elite would determine the dispensation of property. According to Marx, once that process was complete, the state would dissolve, leaving pure equitable communism after it. In practice, matters have never worked out that way. Again and again, revolutionaries claiming to establish Marxist socialist systems have halted at the level of state control, establishing instead long-running authoritarian rule either by party (the post-Stalin Soviet Union, post-Mao China, post-Minh Vietnam) or by dictator (Stalinist Soviet Union, Maoist China, Cuba).

9. One must note that Machiavelli is *not* advocating that all governments follow this "strong leader" model of government. In *The Prince*, Machiavelli distinguishes between what he calls "principalities," what we would call autocracies,

and "republics." Machiavelli makes clear that what he says about the qualities of "princes" applies only to autocrats, and not to elected governors. In Chapter 34, Book I of *The Discourses*, in which Machiavelli discusses at length the politics and history of ancient Rome, he argues that states are better off with elected leaders rather than with leaders who have seized power. He also argues that in times of trouble, a state can legitimately elect a temporary dictator while retaining ultimate power in the elective body, but that the dictator must be only a temporary leader. While Machiavelli is not, and could not have been, an advocate for the modern democratic state, he is no apologist for totalitarian rule.

10. I place "killed" inside quotation marks because Davros is eventually brought back several times, though the original intention for the character was clearly to have him die. Intriguingly, in each case that Davros returns, he must face a similar result, when some or all of the Daleks revolt against any idea that he has authority over them.

11. For a more thorough accounting of the history of universalism in the Greco-Roman world, see Ibn Warraq's *Defending the West* (85–121).

12. Fowles' political analysis is much more complicated than what I have provided here. He is concerned principally with the irony that while democracy is the best form of government through its offer of free choice, it also ensures the nearly complete powerlessness of the individual voter (56–9). Since *Doctor Who* is rarely concerned about the mechanisms of power, but only with governmental systems and philosophies in the most abstract, a summary of Fowles' political theories is not appropriate in this book.

Chapter 11

1. Looking at this last statement, one could clearly see that there is an argument against use of animals, wild or domestic, as resources. In other words, killing animals for food, clothing, medicine, or other purely human needs, is an act against their rights as creatures of dignity, if as Hook says "dignity" involves the ability to suffer. Hook himself does not make the animal rights argument, and *Doctor Who* sometimes touches on it only to pull away. However, this idea of dignity is central to many animal rights activists, principal among them the philosopher Peter Singer.

2. The designations of *property theory* and *proposal theory* of human rights are mine, not Hook's, but derive directly from his characterization of the two outlooks.

3. Plato is justly famous for his representations of the famous "Socratic method" of philosophy, which is to proceed by taking a claim and then questioning it through using various hypothetical circumstances under which the claim may fail or contradict itself. *The Republic* is Plato's most famous work, though not perhaps for everything it has to say. Rather, its fame rests principally in the "allegory of the cave," which comes late in the work and lays out the foundation for his belief that "reality" is a collection of shadows cast from the ideal forms located in Heaven, and that only philosophers are able to see this truth. Maybe most people are right to ignore the rest, for it is not a particularly good example of effective use of Socratic method. The logical procedure in *The Republic* goes like this: Socrates asks a rhetorical question — is it not true that.... One of the other persons in the dialogue says something like, "Yes, that is very true." This process goes on for several questions, and then Socrates pops out a conclusion.

4. Rawls distinguishes natural duties from obligations. A natural duty applies to persons generally, and thus is similar to a natural ability. Natural duties apply irrespective of social position or institutional rules. Obligations, however, derive from specific circumstances and agreements of people "cooperating together in a particular social arrangement" (99). We acquire obligations from "doing things voluntarily" when the institution is as just as one can reasonably expect (302). The distinction is important for Rawls' theory of justice, but is too fine for *Doctor Who*. Therefore, I am sticking to the *Doctor Who* broad spectrum approach to considerations of justice, which often conflates justice, duty, obligation, and rights as variations on a theme.

5. The number of *Doctor Who* novels and audio dramas that rest on the "it's the Doctor's fault" premise are too numerous to go into here. The idea of having the Doctor as cause of trouble first appeared in the TV series in "The Face of Evil" (1977), in which the Doctor arrives to witness the consequences of a mistake he had no idea that he had made. An alternative version of this is that the mere presence of the Doctor and his companions causes trouble. This theme first appeared in "The Ark" (1966), in which Dodo brings a cold virus on board a ship of the far future. The people on the ship have no immunity to such diseases, which had been wiped out centuries before. Both stories just mentioned maintain the standard of Doctor as figure of justice, though, by devoting much of the plot to having the Doctor fix the problem he inadvertently caused. In the novels and audio dramas under question, however, most of the narrative energy goes to demonstrating that "it's all the Doctor's fault," often *ending* with this "revelation." As such, they miss the point and undercut the very reason for the program's success — the Doctor's status as a unique form of hero.

Works Cited

Aldiss, Brian. *Trillion Year Spree: The History of Science Fiction.* New York: Avon, 1983.

Arendt, Hannah. *The Origins of Totalitarianism.* 1968. San Diego: Harcourt, 1985.

Aristotle. *Nicomachean Ethics.* Trans. Roger Crisp. Cambridge: Cambridge University Press, 2000.

_____. *Selections.* Trans. Terence Irwin and Gail Fine. Indianapolis: Hackett, 1995.

Asimov, Isaac. "Those Crazy Ideas." 1960. Rpt. *Inquiry: Questioning, Reading, Writing,* 2d ed. Ed. Lynn Z. Bloom, Edward M. White, and Shane Borrowman. Upper Saddle River: Prentice Hall, 2004: 142–51.

Bacon, Francis. *The New Organon.* Ed. Lisa Jardin and Michael Silverthorne. Cambridge: Cambridge University Press, 2000.

Bainbridge, William Sims. *Dimensions of Science Fiction.* Cambridge: Harvard University Press, 1986.

Baron D'Holbach, Paul Henri Thierry. *The System of Nature,* Vol. 1. Trans. Samuel Wilkinson. Teddington: The Echo Library, 2006.

Barthes, Roland. *Mythologies.* Trans. Annette Lavers. London: Jonathan Cape, 1972.

Bateson, Gregory. *Mind and Nature: A Necessary Unity.* 1979. Rpt. New York: Bantam, 1980.

Bentham, Jeremy. *An Introduction to the Principles of Morals and Legislation.* Oxford: Clarendon Press, 1996.

Bignell, Jonathan. "The Child as Addressee, Viewer and Consumer in Mid–1960s *Doctor Who.*" In Butler, *Time and Relative Dissertations in Space,* 43–55.

Bloom, Allan. *The Closing of the American Mind: How Higher Education Has Failed Democracy and Impoverished the Souls of Today's Students.* New York: Simon & Schuster, 1987.

Boethius. *The Consolation of Philosophy.* Trans. Richard Green. 1962. New York: Macmillan, 1988.

Bova, Ben. "The Role of Science Fiction." *Science Fiction Today and Tomorrow.* Ed. Reginald Bretnor. New York: Harper & Row, 1974: 3–14.

Burke, Kenneth. *The Philosophy of Literary Form: Studies in Symbolic Action,* rev. ed. New York: Vintage, 1957.

Butler, Clark. "Human Rights: The Ethics Behind the International Legality." *Philo* 5.1 (2002): 5–22.

Butler, David. "How to Pilot a TARDIS: Audiences, Science Fiction and the Fantastic in *Doctor Who.*" Butler 19–42.

_____. Introduction. *Time and Relative Dissertations in Space,* 1–15.

_____, ed. *Time and Relative Dissertations in Space.* Manchester: Manchester University Press, 2007.

Calvino, Italo. *The Uses of Literature.* Trans. Patrick Creagh. 1982. San Diego: Harcourt Brace Jovanovich, 1986.

Campbell, Joseph. *The Hero with a Thousand Faces.* Princeton: Princeton University Press, 1949.

_____. *Historical Atlas of World Mythology Vol. I: The Way of the Animal Powers, Part 1: Mythologies of the Primitive Hunters and Gatherers.* New York: Harper & Row, 1988.

Capra, Fritjof. *The Tao of Physics.* New York: Bantam, 1976.

Carrier, Richard. *Sense and Goodness Without God: A Defense of Metaphysical Naturalism.* Bloomington: Author House, 2005.

Clifford, W.K. *Lectures and Essays.* Ed. Leslie Stephen and Frederick Pollock. London: Macmillan, 1886.

Descartes, René. *Discourse on Method and Other Writings.* Trans. Arthur Wollaston. Harmondsworth: Penguin, 1960.

_____. *Philosophical Essays and Correspondence.* Ed. Roger Ariew. Indianapolis: Hackett, 2000.

Dewey, John. *How We Think.* Amherst: Prometheus, 1991.

Drury, Shadia P. "Fascism American Style." *Free Inquiry,* April/May 2009: 26–7.

Ehrman, Bart D. *God's Problem: How the Bible Fails to Answer Our Most Important Question—Why We Suffer.* New York: HarperOne, 2008.

Ellis, David. "The Language-Game of God." *American Atheist,* February 2007: 16–21.

Ferry, Luc. *Man Made God: The Meaning of Life.* Trans. David Pellauer. Chicago: University of Chicago Press, 2002.

Flynn, Tom. "Secularism's Breakthrough Moment." *Free Inquiry,* April/May 2006: 16–7.

Fowles, John. *The Aristos,* rev. ed. London: Pan, 1968.

Frazer, James George. *The Golden Bough: A Study in Magic and Religion.* New York: Macmillan, 1927.

Freud, Sigmund. *Civilization and Its Discontents.* 1930. Trans. Joan Riviere. Garden City: Doubleday, 1958.

Fromm, Erich. *The Sane Society.* New York: Holt, Rinehart and Winston, 1955.

Frye, Northrop. *Anatomy of Criticism: Four Essays.* Princeton: Princeton University Press, 1957.

Gallagher, Donald A. "Karl Jaspers: Existenz and Transcendence." Patka, 111–25.

Godwin, John. Introduction. Lucretius, ix–xxxii.

Gregg, Peter B. "England Looks to the Future: The Cultural Forum Model and *Doctor Who.*" *The Journal of Popular Culture* 37.4 (2004): 648–61.

Griffin, David Ray. Introduction. *The Reenchantment of Science: Postmodern Proposals.* Ed. David Ray Griffin. Albany: SUNY Press, 1988: 1–46.

Haining, Peter. *Doctor Who—The Key To Time.* London: W.H. Allen, 1984.

Hart, Joseph K. *Inside Experience: A Naturalistic Philosophy of Life and the Modern World.* New York: Longmans, Green and Company, 1927.

Hecht, Jennifer Michael. *Doubt: A History.* New York: Harper San Francisco, 2003.

Hegel, Georg Wilhem Friedrich. *Hegel's Philosophy of Mind.* Trans. William Wallace. Oxford: Clarendon Press, 1894.

_____. *Philosophy of Right.* Trans. T.M. Knox. Oxford: Clarendon Press, 1942.

Heidegger, Martin. *Being and Time.* Trans. John Macquarrie and Edward Robinson. New York: Harper & Row, 1962.

Hofstadter, Douglas. *Gödel, Escher, Bach: An Eternal Golden Braid.* New York: Vintage, 1980.

Hook, Sidney. "Reflections on Human Rights." 1970. Rpt. *Free Inquiry,* Aug./Sept. 2007: 28–31.

Hume, David. *An Enquiry Concerning Human Understanding,* 2d ed. Ed. Eric Steinberg. Indianapolis: Hackett, 1993.

Jarrat, Susan C. *Rereading the Sophists: Classical Rhetoric Refigured.* Carbondale: Southern Illinois University Press, 1991.

Jaspers, Karl. "*Existenzphilosophie.*" Trans. Felix Kaufmann and William Earle. Kaufmann, 131–205.

John of Salisbury. *Metalogicon.* Trans. Daniel D. McGarry. Berkeley: University of California Press, 1955.

Jones, Adam Leroy. *Logic, Inductive and Deductive: An Introduction to Scientific Method.* New York: Henry Holt, 1909.

Jung, C.G. *Aion: Researches Into the Phenomenology of the Self.* Trans. R.F.C. Hull. New York: Pantheon, 1959.

_____. *Four Archetypes: Mother/Rebirth/Spirit/Trickster.* Trans. R.F.C. Hull. Princeton: Princeton University Press, 1969.

_____. *The Undiscovered Self.* Trans. R.F.C. Hull. New York: Mentor, 1958.

Kant, Immanuel. *Foundations of the Metaphysics of Morals,* 2d ed. Trans. Lewis White Beck. Upper Saddle River: Prentice-Hall, 1995.

_____. *The Metaphysics of Morals.* Ed. and

trans. Mary Gregor. Cambridge: Cambridge University Press, 1996.

_____. *Perpetual Peace.* New York: Columbia University Press, 1939.

_____. "What Is Enlightenment?" Trans. Mary C. Smith. Columbia University Library. <http://www.columbia.edu/acis/ets/CCREAD/etscc/kant.html#note1>.

Kaufmann, Walter. "Existentialism from Dostoevsky to Sartre." Kaufmann, 11–51.

_____, ed. *Existentialism from Dostoevsky to Sartre.* New York: Meridian, 1956.

King, Martin Luther, Jr. "Letter from Birmingham Jail." 1963. Rpt. *A World of Ideas,* 7th ed. Ed. Lee A. Jacobus. Boston: Bedford/St. Martin's, 2006: 173–89.

Koestler, Arthur. *The Ghost in the Machine.* 1967. Rpt. London: Arkana, 1989.

_____. *Janus: A Summing Up.* New York: Vintage, 1978.

Koller, John M. *Oriental Philosophies,* 2d ed. Englewood Cliffs: Prentice Hall, 1985.

Kurtz, Paul. *Forbidden Fruit: The Ethics of Humanism.* Amherst: Prometheus, 1988.

_____. "A Good Will." *Free Inquiry,* April/May 2005: 5–7.

_____. *In Defense of Secular Humanism.* Buffalo: Prometheus, 1983.

_____. *Living Without Religion: Eupraxsophy.* Amherst: Prometheus, 1989.

_____. *The Transcendental Temptation: A Critique of Religion and the Paranormal.* Amherst: Prometheus, 1991.

_____. *What Is Secular Humanism?* Amherst: Prometheus, 2007.

Lamont, Corliss. *The Philosophy Of Humanism,* 7th ed. New York: Continuum/Ungar, 1990.

Langer, Susanne K. *Philosophy in a New Key: A Study in the Symbolism of Reason, Rite, and Art,* 2d ed. New York: Mentor, 1952.

_____. "Signs and Symbols." 1944. Rpt. *Inquiry: Questioning, Reading, Writing,* 2nd ed. Ed. Lynn Z. Bloom, Edward M. White, and Shane Borrowman. Upper Saddle River: Prentice Hall, 2004: 131–7.

Lao Tzu. *Tao Te Ching.* Trans. Victor H. Mair. New York: Bantam, 1990.

Lastrucci, Carlo L. *The Scientific Approach: Basic Principles of the Scientific Method.* Cambridge: Schenkman, 1963.

Lerner, Laurence. *The Truest Poetry: An Essay on the Question What Is Literature?* London: Hamish Hamilton, 1960.

Locke, John. *An Essay Concerning Human Understanding.* London: Routledge, 1894.

_____. *Of the Conduct of the Understanding.* Ed. F.W. Garforth. *Classics in Education Series.* Institute for Learning Technologies, ILTweb. 15 Aug 2009. <http://www.ilt.columbia.edu/publications/CESdigital/locke/conduct/toc.html>.

Lonergan, Bernard J.F. *Insight: A Study of Human Understanding.* New York: Longmans, 1958.

Lucretius. *On the Nature of the Universe.* Trans. R.E. Latham. Intro. Rev. John Godwin. 1951. London: Penguin, 1994.

Machiavelli, Niccoló. *The Essential Writings of Machiavelli.* Trans. and ed. Peter Constantine. New York: Modern Library, 2007.

Mair, Victor H. "Afterword." Lao Tzu, 119–53.

Marx, Karl. *Capital, The Communist Manifesto, and Other Writings.* Ed. Max Eastman. New York: Modern Library, 1959.

_____. *A Contribution to the Critique of Political Economy.* Trans. N.I. Stone. Chicago: Kerr, 1904.

Mele, Alfred. *Self-Deception Unmasked.* Princeton: Princeton University Press, 2001.

Mihalich, Joseph. "Jean-Paul Sartre." Patka, 126–37.

Mill, John Stuart. *John Stuart Mill's Philosophy of Scientific Method.* Ed. Ernest Nagel. New York: Hafner, 1950.

_____. *On Liberty.* New York: John B. Alden, 1885.

_____. *Utilitarianism.* London: Longman, Green, and Co., 1901.

Moenkemeyer, Heinz. "Martin Heidegger." Patka, 93–110.

Morris, Charles. *Varieties of Human Value.* Chicago: University of Chicago Press, 1956.

Morris, Desmond. *The Naked Ape.* New York: McGraw-Hill, 1967.

Nielsen, Kai. *Ethics Without God,* rev. ed. Amherst: Prometheus, 1990.

_____. *Naturalism Without Foundations.* Amherst: Prometheus, 1996.

Nietzsche, Friedrich. "Live Dangerously." Trans. and ed. Walter Kaufmann. Kaufmann, 101–12.

_____. *The Portable Nietzsche*. Ed. and trans. Walter Kaufmann. New York: Viking, 1954.

Onfray, Michel. *Atheist Manifesto: The Case Against Christianity, Judaism, and Islam.* 2005. Trans. Jeremy Leggatt. New York: Arcade, 2007.

Palmer-Fernandez, Gabriel. "Contemporary Religious Terrorism." *Free Inquiry*, Aug./ Sept. 2006: 27–31.

Patka, Frederick."Five Existentialist Themes." Patka, 13–72.

_____. Introduction. Patka, 5–9.

_____, ed. *Existentialist Thinkers and Thought*. New York: Citadel Press, 1962.

Paul, Richard, and Linda Elder. *Critical Thinking: Tools for Taking Charge of Your Professional and Personal Life*. Upper Saddle River: Prentice Hall, 2002.

Pico della Mirandola, Giovanni. "Oration on the Dignity of Man." Trans. Richard Hooker. <http://www.fordham.edu/halsall/med/oration.html>.

Pigliucci, Massimo. "The Sin Of Scientism." *Skeptical Inquirer,* November/December 2003: 21–2.

Plato. *The Republic and Other Works*. Trans. B. Jowett. New York: Anchor, 1973.

Popper, Karl. *The Open Society and Its Enemies I: The Spell of Plato*, 5th ed. Princeton: Princeton University Press, 1966.

_____. *The Open Society and Its Enemies: II. The High Tide of Prophecy: Hegel, Marx, and the Aftermath*, 5th ed. Princeton: Princeton University Press, 1966.

Poundstone, William. *Labyrinths of Reason: Paradox, Puzzles and the Frailty of Knowledge*. New York: Doubleday, 1988.

Rafer, David. "Mythic Identity in *Doctor Who*." Butler, *Time and Relative Dissertations in Space*, 123–37.

Rawls, John. *A Theory of Justice*, rev. ed. Cambridge: Harvard University Press, 1999.

Reich, Robert B. "Why the Rich Are Getting Richer and the Poor, Poorer." 1991. Rpt. *A World of Ideas: Essential Readings For College Writers*, 7th ed. Ed.

Lee A. Jacobus. Boston: Bedford/St. Martin's, 2006: 420–33.

Rifkin, Lawrence. "Humanism, Meaning, and Wonder." *Free Inquiry,* Oct./Nov. 2008: 49–50.

Rose, Mark. *Alien Encounters: Anatomy of Science Fiction*. Cambridge: Harvard University Press, 1981.

Rousseau, Jean-Jacques. *Discourse On Political Economy and the Social Contract*. Trans. Christopher Betts. Oxford: Oxford University Press, 1994.

Ruggiero, Vincent Ryan. *The Art of Thinking: A Guide to Critical and Creative Thought*, 7th ed. New York: Pearson Longman, 2004.

_____. *Thinking Critically About Ethical Issues*, 6th ed. Boston: McGraw Hill, 2004.

Russell, Bertrand. *Proposed Roads to Freedom—Anarchy, Socialism and Syndicalism*. New York: Henry Holt, 1919.

Sagan, Carl. *The Dragons of Eden: Speculations on the Evolution of Human Intelligence*. Rpt. 1977. New York: Ballantine, 1978.

_____. *Pale Blue Dot: A Vision of the Human Future in Space*. 1994. Rpt. New York: Ballantine, 1997.

Sartre, Jean-Paul. *Existentialism and Human Emotions*. 1957. Trans. Bernard Frechtman and Hazel E. Barnes. Secaucus: Citadel Press: 1999.

_____. "Portrait of the Antisemite." Trans. Mary Guggenheim. Kaufmann, 270–287.

Schick, Theodore, Jr., and Lewis Vaughn. *How to Think About Weird Things: Critical Thinking for a New Age*, 4th ed. Boston: McGraw-Hill, 2005.

Schopenhauer, Arthur. *Essay on the Freedom of the Will*. Trans. Konstantin Kolenda. 1839. New York: The Liberal Arts Press, 1960.

Searle, John. *Minds, Brains and Science*. Cambridge: Harvard University Press, 1984.

Shelley, Percy Bysshe. *The Necessity of Atheism and Other Essays*. Buffalo: Prometheus, 1993.

Shermer, Michael. *How We Believe: Science, Skepticism, and the Search for God*, 2d ed. New York: Henry Holt, 2000.

Snow, C.P. *The Two Cultures and a Second Look*. New York: Mentor, 1963.

Soros, George. *The Bubble of American Supremacy: Correcting the Misuse of American Power*. London: Weidenfeld & Nicolson, 2004.

Stumpf, Samuel Enoch, and James Fieser. *Philosophy: History and Problems*, 7th ed. Boston: McGraw-Hill, 2008.

Suvin, Darko. *Metamorphoses of Science Fiction: On the Poetics and History of a Literary Genre*. New Haven: Yale University Press, 1979.

_____. "On the Poetics of the Science Fiction Genre." *Science Fiction: A Collection of Critical Essays*. Ed. Mark Rose. Englewood Cliffs: Prentice-Hall, 1976: 57–71.

Suzuki, D.T. *The Field of Zen*. New York: Harper & Row, 1969.

Thiroux, Jacques P., and Keith W. Krasemann. *Ethics: Theory and Practice*, 9th ed. Upper Saddle River: Pearson Prentice Hall, 2007.

Thompson, William Irwin. *The Time Falling Bodies Take to Light: Mythology, Sexuality and the Origins of Culture*. New York: St. Martin's, 1981.

Thrower, James. *Western Atheism: A Short History*. Amherst: Prometheus, 2000.

Todorov, Tzvetan. *The Fantastic: A Structural Approach to a Literary Genre*. Trans. Richard Howard. 1970. Ithaca: Cornell University Press, 1973.

Tolkein, J.R.R. "On Fairy-Stories." *The Tolkein Reader*. New York: Ballantine, 1966.

Tulloch, John, and Manuel Alvarado. *Doctor Who: The Unfolding Text*. New York: St. Martin's, 1983.

Warraq, Ibn. *Defending The West: A Critique of Edward Said's Orientalism*. Amherst: Prometheus, 2007.

Waterfield, Robin. *The First Philosophers: The Presocratics and Sophists*. Oxford: Oxford University Press, 2000.

Weber, Max. *The Protestant Ethic and the Spirit of Capitalism*. Trans. Talcott Parsons. Los Angeles: Roxbury, 1998.

Williston, Byron. "Self-Deception and the Ethics of Belief." *Philo* 5.1 (2002): 62–83.

Wittgenstein, Ludwig. *Wittgenstein's Tractatus*. Trans. Daniel Kolak. Mountain View, CA: Mayfield. 1998.

Wood, Tat. "The Empire of the Senses: Narrative Form and Point-of-View in *Doctor Who*." Butler, *Time and Relative Dissertations in Space*, 89–107.

Index

347